Lecture Notes in Computer Science 3597

Commenced Publication in 1973
Founding and Former Series Editors:
Gerhard Goos, Juris Hartmanis, and Jan van Leeuwen

Shinji Shimojo   Shingo Ichii
Tok Wang Ling   Kwan-Ho Song (Eds.)

Web and Communication Technologies and Internet-Related Social Issues – HSI 2005

3rd International Conference on Human.Society@Internet
Tokyo, Japan, July 27-29, 2005
Proceedings

 Springer

Volume Editors

Shinji Shimojo
Osaka University, Cybermedia Center
5-1 Mihogaoka, Ibaraki, Osaka 567-0047, Japan
E-mail: shimojo@cmc.osaka-u.ac.jp

Shingo Ichii
University of Tokyo, Graduate School of Mathematical Sciences
3-8-1 Komaba, Meguro-ku, Tokyo 153-8914, Japan
E-mail: ichii@ms.u-tokyo.ac.jp

Tok Wang Ling
National University of Singapore, Department of Computer Science
3 Science Drive 2, Singapore 117543
E-mail: lingtw@comp.nus.edu.sg

Kwan-Ho Song
National Internet Development Agency, Korea
E-mail: khsong@nic.or.kr

Library of Congress Control Number: 2005928958

CR Subject Classification (1998): K.4-6, K.8, C.2, H.5, H.4, H.3, J.1, J.3

ISSN   0302-9743
ISBN-10   3-540-27830-3 Springer Berlin Heidelberg New York
ISBN-13   978-3-540-27830-6 Springer Berlin Heidelberg New York

Springer is a part of Springer Science+Business Media

springeronline.com

© Springer-Verlag Berlin Heidelberg 2005
Printed in Germany

Typesetting: Camera-ready by author, data conversion by Scientific Publishing Services, Chennai, India
Printed on acid-free paper   SPIN: 11527725   06/3142   5 4 3 2 1 0

Preface

The Internet has now become an integral part of everyday life for hundreds of millions of people around the world. The uses of the Internet have augmented commerce, communication, education, governance, entertainment, health care, etc. E-mail has become an indispensable part of life; the Web has become an indispensable source of information on just about everything; people now use government Web sites to receive instructions and information, and file paperwork with the government; many major online businesses have been created, such as Amazon, eBay, Google, Travelocity, eTrade, etc.

However, the uses of the Internet have also had serious negative effects, including spam, the spreading of viruses and worms, spyware, phishing, hacking, online fraud, invasions of privacy, etc. Viruses and worms often bring down tens of millions of computers around the world; many people get duped into furnishing their personal identifications, and bank and insurance account information, etc.; hackers break into government and corporation computers to steal critical data; unsubstantiated rumors about individuals or organizations spread like wildfire on the Internet, etc. Further, the uses of the Internet are creating new paradigms in areas such as copyright, governance, etc. The widespread use of peer-to-peer file sharing systems, started by Napster, is forcing a reassestment of the value of holding copyright on digital media. Internet postings by vocal citizens to the Web sites of the news media, government offices, and elected government officials are impacting government policies and swaying the opinions of other citizens.

The aim of the International Conference on Human.Society@Internet is to promote an orderly advancement of the uses and technology of the Internet based on a deeper understanding of the effects of the Internet, both positive and negative, on humans and on society. As the uses of the Internet have become so ubiquitous, the need for a deeper understanding of the effects of the Internet is now becoming stronger and, as a consequence, the relevance and importance of the International Conference on Human.Society@Internet. have grown stronger too.

The Steering Committee for the International Conference on Human. Society@Internet would like to express its gratitude to the principal organizers of this year's conference, Prof. Shingo Ichii and Prof. Shinji Shimojo, for their hard work in organizing the conference, along with all members of the organizing committees of the host country, Japan, and the other countries/regions. We hope that the papers selected for inclusion in this proceedings will help enhance the understanding of the effects of the uses of the Internet, of the solutions to some of the problems that have been exposed, and of some of the emerging new applications of the Internet.

May 2005

Won Kim
Kwan-Ho Song
Tok Wang Ling

Out of 118 submissions of research papers from 15 countries/regions, the Program Committee accepted 32 papers for oral presentation in regular sessions, and 9 papers as short contributions for a poster session. Each submitted paper was evaluated by three reviewers. In addition to the accepted papers, the technical program of the conference included 2 keynote addresses, 1 panel session and 2 tutorials.

We would like to thank all the authors who submitted papers for their interest and cooperation with the paper submission and revision processes, and the members of the program committees in 11 different regions of the globe.

May 2005   Shinji Shimojo

Organization

Global Organizing Committee

Global General Chair	Won Kim, Samsung Electronics, Korea
Global Co-general Chair	Kwan-Ho Song, National Internet Development Agency of Korea, Korea
Global Co-general Chair	Tok Wang Ling, National University of Singapore, Singapore
Host Country General Chair	Shingo Ichii, University of Tokyo, Japan
Global PC Chair	Shinji Shimojo, Osaka University, Japan
Global Panel Chair	Katsuyuki Yamazaki, KDDI R&D Laboratories, Japan
Global Tutorial Chair	Kenichi Yoshida, Tsukuba University, Japan

Host Country Function Chairs

Host Country Co-chair	Yuji Oie, Kyushu Institute of Technology
Host Country Co-chair	Hiroshi Tanaka, Tokyo Medical and Dental University
Host Country Co-chair	Yoshifumi Masunaga, Ochanomizu University
Registrations Chair	Masaya Nakayama, University of Tokyo
Local Arrangements Chair	Takashi Sakamoto, VeriSign Japan K.K.
Finance Chair	Chang Kyu Kim, Trian Consulting, Ltd.
Proceedings Chair	Mikio Ishihara, Allied Telesis, K.K.
Treasurer	Hiromitsu Anamizu, Japan Medical Information Network Association
Webmaster	Jin Miura, Nihon Unisys, Ltd.

Country/Region General Chairs and Publicity Chairs

North America

Osmar Zaiane, University of Alberta, Canada

Europe

Lenoid A. Kalinichenko, Russian Academy of Sciences, Russia

China

Xiaofeng Meng, Renmin University of China, China
  (Publicity Chair)
Nan Yang, Renmin University of China, China

Hong Kong

Qing Li, City University of Hong Kong, China
(Publicity Chair)
Elvis Leung, Hong Kong Hospital Authority, China

India

Mukesh Mohania, IBM India Research Lab, India
(Publicity Chair)
Vineet Kansal, Ideal Institute of Technology, India

Indonesia

Ismail Khalil Ibrahim, Johannes Kepler University of Linz, Austria
(Publicity Chair)
Syopiansyah Jaya Putra, Syarif Hidayatullah State Islamic University, Indonesia

Korea

Kyung-Chang Kim, Hong-Ik University University, Korea

Malaysia

CheeSing Yap, Iverson Associate Sdn. Bhd., Malaysia
(Publicity Chair)
Chik Heok Tan, Universiti Tunku Abdul Rahman (UTAR), Malaysia

Oceania

Xiaofang Zhou, University of Queensland, Australia
(Publicity Chair)
Markus Kirchberg, Massey University, New Zealand

Singapore

Tok Wang Ling, National University of Singapore, Singapore
(Publicity Chair)
Sourav Saha Bhowmick, Nanyang Technological University, Singapore

Taiwan

Chin-Chen Chang, National Chung Cheng University, Taiwan
(Publicity Chair)
Timothy Shih, Tamkang University, Taiwan

Country/Region Program Committee Chairs

North America

(PC Chair)
Won Kim, Samsung Electronics, Korea

Europe

(PC Co-chair: Web technologies, uses and ill effects of the Internet)
Sergei Kuznetsov, Russian Academy of Sciences, Russia
(PC Co-chair: communication technologies)
George Samaras, University of Cyprus, Cyprus

China

(PC Co-chair: Web technologies, uses and ill effects of the Internet)
Ge Yu, Northeastern University, China
(PC Co-chair: communication technologies)
Hai Jin, Huazhong University of Science and Technology, China

Hong Kong

(PC Co-chair: Web technologies, uses and ill effects of the Internet)
Hong Va Leong, Hong Kong Polytechnic University, China
(PC Co-chair: communication technologies)
Liu Wenyin, City University of Hong Kong, China

India

(PC Co-chair: Web technologies, uses and ill effects of the Internet)
S.K. Gupta, IIT Delhi, India
(PC Co-chair: communication technologies)
Atul Kumar, IIT Kanpur, India

Indonesia

(PC Co-chair: Web technologies, uses and ill effects of the Internet)
Arif Djunaidy, Institute of Technology Sepuluh Nopember, Indonesia
(PC Co-chair: communication technologies)
Hendrawan, Bandung Institute of Technology, Indonesia

Japan

(PC Chair)
Shingo Ichii, University of Tokyo, Japan

Korea

(PC Co-chair: Web technologies, uses and ill effects of the Internet)
Myoung Ho Kim, KAIST, Korea
(PC Co-chair: communication technologies)
Sang Lyul Min, Seoul National University, Korea

Malaysia

(PC Co-chair: Web technologies, uses and ill effects of the Internet)
Hong Tat Ewe, Multimedia University, Malaysia
(PC Co-chair: communication technologies)
Sze Wei Lee, Multimedia University, Malaysia

Oceania

(PC Co-chair: Web technologies, uses and ill effects of the Internet)
Arkady Zaslavsky, Monash University, Australia
(PC Co-chair: communication technologies)
Wanlei Zhou, Deakin University, Australia

Singapore

(PC Chair)
Kian-Lee Tan, National University of Singapore, Singapore

Taiwan

(PC Chair)
Sing-Ling Lee, National Chung-Cheng University, Taiwan

Program Committee

Hideki Sunahara, Nara Institute of Science and Technology
Toshio Kosuge, University of Electro-communications, Tokyo
Kazushi Yamanouchi, Iwate Prefectural University
Takao Terano, Tsukuba University
Keiko Okawa, Keio University
Mikio Ishihara, Allied Telesis K.K.
Jin Miura, Nihon Unisys, Ltd.
Takashi Sakamoto, VeriSign Japan K.K.
Masaki Minami, Keio University
Hiroki Nogawa, Tokyo Medical and Dental University
Jun Nakaya, Tokyo Medical and Dental University
Masahiro Nishibori, Tokyo Medical and Dental University
Kazutoshi Sumiya, University of Hyogo
Sachio Hirokawa, Kyushu University
Kyoji Kawagoe, Ritsumeikan University
Takashi Honishi, NTT Cyber Space Laboratories
Yoshihide Hosokawa, Nagoya Institute of Technology
Yoshihiko Ichikawa, Yamaguchi University

Korea

Doheon Lee, KAIST
Eui Kyong Hong, University of Seoul
Hyunchul Kang, Chung-Ang University
Jae Soo Yoo, Chungbuk National University
Jin Hyun Son, Hanyang University
Kyu-Chul Lee, Chungnam National University
Yon Dohn Chung, Dongguk University
Jin-Soo Kim, KAIST
Hwansoo Han, KAIST
Sang Ho Lee, Soongsil University
Yunmook Nah, Dankook University
Myung Kim, Ewha Womans University
Hong Sung Chang, Samsung Electronics
Jongwon Choe, Sookmyung Women's University
Eun Yong Ha, Anyang University
Hoyoung Hwang, Anyang University
Wha Sook Jeon, Seoul National University
Byoung Wan Kim, Seoul National University
Sue Moon, KAIST
Jongmoo Choi, Dankook University
Chang-Gun Lee, Ohio State University, USA
Donghee Lee, University of Seoul
Sam H. Noh, Hong-Ik University

Malaysia

Chee Sing Yap, Iverson Associate Sdn. Bhd.
Chik Heok Tan, Faculty of Information and Communication Technology,
   Universiti Tunku Abdul Rahman (UTAR)

Oceania

Boualem Benatallah, University of NSW
Damien Bright, University of South Australia
Frada Burstein, Monash University
Gill Dobbie, University of Auckland
Vadim Doubrovski, IBM Australia
Julie Fisher, Monash University
Graeme Johanson, Monash University
Shonali Krishnaswamy, Monash University
Seng Wai Loke, Monash University
Rahim Mahbubur, Monash University
Zoran Milosevic, DSTC, University of Queensland
Mark Nolan, IBM Australia
Debbie Richards, Macquarie University
Nigel Watson, Microsoft Australia
Gerald Weber, University of Auckland
Yanchun Zhang, Victoria University
Ai Cheo Yeo, Monash University
Geoff Beckworth, Telstra
Young Ju Choi, University of Tasmania
Xiangjian (Sean) He, University of Technology, Sydney
Craig Linn, University of Western Sydney
Paul Nicholson, Deakin University
Dharmendra Sharma, University of Canberra
Arthur Tatnall, Victoria University
Yun Yang, Swinburne University of Technology
Matthew Warren, Deakin University

Singapore

Pin-Kwang Eng, Institute of InfoComm Research, Singapore
Chi-Chi Hung, National University of Singapore
Bin Cui, National University of Singapore

Organization and Sponsorship

Organized by
Human.Society@Internet Steering Committee

Hosted by
JSPS 163rd Committee on Internet Technology, Japan

Co-hosted by
Japan Medical Information Network Association, Japan

Government Agencies
Japan Society for the Promotion of Science, Japan
National Internet Development Agency of Korea, Korea

Government Co-sponsors
Ministry of Internal Affairs and Communications, Japan
Ministry of Education, Culture, Sports, Science and Technology, Japan
Ministry of Health, Labour and Welfare, Japan
Ministry of Economy, Trade and Industry, Japan

Academic Societies
The Database Society of Japan
Japanese Association of Medical Informatics
Information Processing Society of Japan
The Institute of Electronics, Information and Communication Engineers,
    Information and Systems Society, Japan
The Institute of Electronics, Information and Communication Engineers,
    Communications Society, Japan

Non-profit Agencies
The Medical Information System Development Center, Japan
Japanese Association of Healthcare Information Systems Industry, Japan

Table of Contents

Internet Applications II

Information Retrieval

Medical Applications

Multimedia

Web Retrieval and Applications

E-Learning

Security II

Wireless II

Short Contributions

Implementation and Usability Evaluation of AAC System for Handicapped Persons

Myoung-soo Park[1], Jonk-ki Kim[2], and Tai-sung Hur[3],
Nag-hwan Kim[4], Eun-sil Lee[1], Yo-seop Woo[1], and Hong-ki Min[1]

[1] Dept. of Inf. & Telecomm. Eng., Univ. of Incheon, Korea
[2] Dept. of Information Security, Konyang University, Nonsan, Chung-Nam, Korea
[3] Dept. of Computing & Information Systems, Inha Technical College, Incheon, Korea
[4] Dept. of Computer Application Control , Kyonggi Institute of Technology, Korea
pooohaha@incheon.ac.kr

Abstract. This study generally is purposed to implementation and usability evaluation of augmentative and alternative communication system (hereinafter referred to as an "AAC system"). Also the device is aimed as an AAC system using symbols for HCI, allowing a handicapped person to make a general communication with others in a free and convenient manner. This study specifically presents a method of predicting predictions, which contributes to reducing the size of the AAC system. This method includes selecting vocabulary and classifying it by domains so as to meet the characteristics of the AAC communication, using a noun thesaurus for semantic analysis, and building a sub-category dictionary. Accordingly, this study has verified the system by applying it to linguistically handicapped persons with different kinds of handicaps two times.

1 Introduction

Recently people are increasingly interested in AAC systems for persons suffering from speech disorders. As such persons successfully participate in education, social activities, religion, leisure, occupation, etc., necessity is required for changing the way of their communication. One of the most influential elements that affect on the necessity for changing is the development of technology. Development of such technology affects on successful communication of the people who have serious communication disorders, and remarkably on the AAC field for the people whose communication cannot be satisfied using spoken language.

Therefore, selection of the first vocabulary is considered very important when developing such an AAC system [1]. This is because poor vocabularies or improper selection of vocabularies from the AAC system may cause increased frustration of the AAC system users [2]. Various prediction methods are sometimes applied for allowing the AAC system users to use the system more easily. Accordingly, in this study, we constructed a database by collecting and analyzing actual utterances, selecting vocabularies of higher frequencies and using a lexical thesaurus and a sub-categorization dictionary on the basis of the selection, and it was intended to develop a system to predict and recover the grammatical morphemes such as auxiliary words

S. Shimojo et al. (Eds.): HSI 2005, LNCS 3597, pp. 1–8, 2005.

or endings of words, complements, annexed words and conjunctions to present a relevant sentence by assuming that they will be omitted at the time entry [4].

Also this study has verified the AAC System for the evaluation of its usability by applying it to real situations.

2 Vocabulary Selection

It is to divide a relevant area into different sub-areas depending on situations such as features of user's age or disorder level, places, topics, etc., to collect and analyze vocabularies in order to allow the users to use them easily in a specific place or situation that frequently occurs because icons are used in this research to define the relevant area. It is necessary to collect and analyze vocabularies used by the persons suffering from speech disorders from a different point from the existing Korean processing research, in that the persons suffering from speech disorders are chief users.

In order to construct a vocabulary database which is the first step of developing the AAC system, we collected spontaneous utterances during break times in schools and in daily living in order to collect vocabularies used frequently by ordinary people. The domain of place is divided into regions such as home, restaurant, transportation, school, hospital and shopping. In this research, total 9,559 vocabularies were analyzed from the situational utterances by 24 schoolchildren and 20 adults at schools, etc. by recording their utterances. The ratio of the vocabularies of higher frequencies to the entire vocabularies was then measured. The block diagram for database process of colleted sentences is shown in the following Fig. 1.

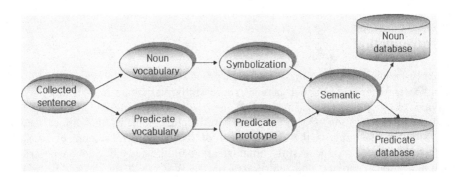

Fig. 1. Database process of collected sentences

3 Symbols Corresponding to the Vocabularies

It is necessary to define semantic symbols for each relevant area through consideration of ambiguity and multiplicity of meaning of vocabularies of natural language, and through analysis of the user interface of efficient symbol arrangement. This study is carried out the research by using the system of this study, analyzing the relationship between vocabularies and symbols, designing proper symbols corresponding to the vocabularies database and efficiently arranging them in each area. An example of symbols corresponding to the vocabularies database is shown in the Table 1. We dealt also in actual sentence taking the mother change of the predicate part into account to the prototype, and an example to become a sentence generation in the symbol user interface is as follows.

Table 1. Corresponding of symbol for noun vocabulary

Sentence	Corresponding of symbol
When is the exam?	+ 언제이다(predicate prototype) + ?
Do you have the red bag?	+ + 있다(predicate prototype) + ?
Borrow the writing note-book!	+ +빌리다(predicate prototype) +!

4   Creating a Sentence Through Prediction of Predicates

It is impossible to enter all elements of a sentence through semantic symbols. In general, grammatical morphemes such as auxiliary words or endings of words and the components such as conjunctions or predicates are omitted at the time of entry. The study of predicting and recovering such vocabularies is the key part of this research. To this end, it is necessary to apply the syntax theory by sentence units for the study of morphemes that are primary units of omission and the recovery of omitted parts in a sentence. It is also necessary to use the result of word sense disambiguation study in the meaning of vocabularies for settling multiplicity or ambiguity of meaning on a vocabulary basis.

In this study, we intended to develop a sub-categorization dictionary that is a Korean argument structure and a thesaurus that is a hierarchical structure between concepts, to develop an algorithm for settling ambiguity of meaning of vocabularies using the dictionaries and to apply it to this study.

Therefore, for a given sentence, the system was made by constructing a database through interpretation of lexical meanings for respective vocabularies to allow predicates to be selected through a popup menu when a user presses a noun semantic symbol as an entry, the meaning of the predicate being matched to the noun.

In order to predict predicates, required is a step of deriving what is desired to be expressed by matching the meanings of the vocabulary, as represented in a noun thesaurus, and the situations expressed by predicates, as contained in a pattern dictionary, with the semantic dependency. This is referred to as a "limited selection, " and predicates are predicted by the limited selection. Field for predicate application enables making various sentences and changing basic predicate forms to desired application forms.

A sub-categorization dictionary is build up based on the thesaurus, sentence pattern and predicate application forms. The sub-categorization dictionary includes basic forms of predicates, application form, and nouns related to predicates, and postpositional words, together with the meanings thereof. The sub-categorization dictionary is based on the reference numbers of sentences, application forms of predicates, and postpositional words to be added to nouns that are inputted. Thesaurus dictionary of nouns and sub-categorization dictionary are build-up and predicates for an inputted semantic symbol are presented by the limited selection.

5   A Method of the Evaluation of the AAC System's Usability

This study has verified the AAC System for the evaluation of its usability by applying it to real situations after educating members of the Federation of the Deaf, and handicapped persons from special schools. For an easy analysis of the results, we also have added a monitoring program which records the contents of semantic symbols touched by the users of the system, to grasp conditions of the handicapped persons' use of the system.

In the period of program use training, some of the researchers have trained the handicapped persons individually, and the evaluation of usability has been carried out two times. Furthermore, we have let the users select the associated semantic symbols appropriate to given situations beyond sentence-given training. In the period of program use training, we have recorded the degree of preciseness and the time taken to combine semantic symbols and generate sentences fitting to each given situation. The goals and subjects of the evaluation, the noteworthiness with regard to each user's handicap, and the environments of the verification are shown in Table 2.

Table 2. Method of the Evaluation

	The 1st evaluation	The 2nd evaluation
Goals	To record the indoor/outdoor efficiency of the system and the time taken to generate sentences, and to measure the degree of preciseness	To investigate the degree of preciseness in sentence generation, the time for it, and usability of the system
Subjects	Woman A (Age 23), Woman B (Age 48), Man A (Age 56) ,(Deaf & Able to use sign language)	Woman A (Age 16), Woman B (Age 17), Woman C (Age 20), (The 1st degree physical handicap in cerebral palsy)
Noteworthiness	-Man A and Woman B, unacquainted with computers -Able to use sign language in most communications	-Difficulty in the system users' operation of the program -Difficulty in mutual communication
Environments of The verification	- 1 Mini laptop (Touch Screen available) - 1 Tablet PC - 1 Small-sized laptop -The AAC system	- 3 Tablet PCs - The AAC system

6 Results

6.1 Results of System Implementation

We have analyzed 9559 total vocabularies consisting of 4000 vocabularies from ordinary children's utterances, 1787 from deaf children's, 3772 from situational utterances. *"Yeogi* here, *igeo* this, *meokda* eat, *hada* do, *gada* go, *mueot* what, *eopda* not exist, *doyda* become, *itda* exist" appear to be words with high-frequency as well as core words in all the utterances of ordinary children, deaf children, youths and adults. Thus, these words can be regarded as words used frequently in common regardless of situation and age. As a result of the implementation of the AAC system after the construction of database by selecting core words and words with high frequency, we get the following output process.

For example, in order to send the sentence "When is the exam?" using the AAC system, one selects a domain in a certain area as in Fig. 2, chooses a semantic symbol corresponding to "exam" to have related predicates predicted as in Fig. 3, and then select a predicated and a sentence-ending as in Fig. 4. Consequently, the sentence is generated and outputted as in Fig. 5.

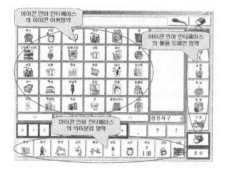

Fig. 2. Example of construction of semantic symbols in an area

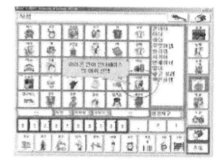

Fig. 3. Selection of a semantic symbol and prediction of related predicates

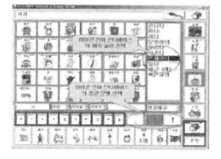

Fig. 4. Selection of a predicate and a sentence ending

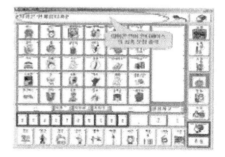

Fig. 5. Generation and output of the final sentence

6.2 Evaluation of Usability of the AAC System

6.2.1 Analysis of the Mean Time in the Combination of Semantic Symbols

Next, we have verified the system by on-the-spot investigation. The verification has been carried out in the 1st and 2nd evaluations. Because the 1st evaluation was for the deaf, we did not give a sentence directly to them, but made a sign-language translator explain a given situation to the linguistically handicapped persons in the sign language in order to lead them to combine semantic symbols by themselves. Sentences presented in given situations are those like "I'd like to book an air ticket for Jeju-do in Busan," and "Which symbol can I touch?"

The result in Fig.6 is the mean time in three auditory handicapped persons' combination of semantic symbols into a sentence for evaluation. This result has been yield in the way that the subjects were led to deal with the system after a sign-language translator gave them a situation. Y-axis is the time by minute, and X-axis the period of the program training. As a result, it took the mean time of 6 minutes on the first training day to combine semantic symbols for a situation, because they were not acquainted with the tools yet.

However, the subjects got more acquainted with the positions of icons and the methods of tool using as it got along with the passage of training time. Thus, we can realize that they reached the degree in which they combined a sentence in a short time finding out relevant semantic symbols simultaneously. In the result in Fig.7, where physically handicapped persons participated in the evaluation, there were few differences in the mean time for execution. In the preceding verification, the mean time for the combination in the training period was much long partly for the reason that older AAC system users were not able to deal with computers adeptly. Contrastively, the handicapped persons who participated in the 2nd evaluation were educated for computer using, which resulted in the differences in the mean time for execution.

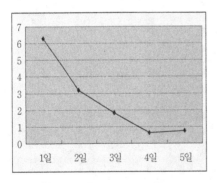

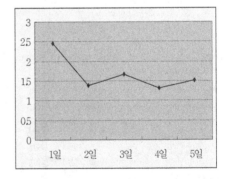

Fig. 6. 1st evaluation by the auditory handicapped persons

Fig. 7. 2nd evaluation by persons with cerebral palsy <Mean time for the combination of semantic symbols>

6.2.2 Evaluation of the Degree of Preciseness of the Sample Sentences

The next result has been yield from the discrimination of the sentences combined and produced by linguistically handicapped persons for the 50 sample situations. It consists of the mean data of three linguistically handicapped persons. In Fig.8, y-axis is the number of produced sentences, and x-axis the period of the program training. Different from the case of the combination of semantic symbols, it took much long time for the linguistically handicapped persons to make a precise sentence in the case of the production of sentences, but the meanings of the sentences are almost precise. In the 2nd evaluation by physically handicapped persons, they had much difficulty exactly selecting semantic symbols put in the portable computers because the movement of their body parts was inaccurate.

Thus, we can find out that the degree of preciseness of the generation of Korean was much lower in this case than in the preceding cases. The tablet PC's used as mobile tools were designed for electric pen control. Thus, the physically handicapped persons had deficiency in concentration for the selection of semantic symbols because of their serious tremor of the hands. This tremor of hands caused the degree of preciseness of the generation of Korean to be lowered strikingly because a single symbol could be touched multiply on a single occasion.

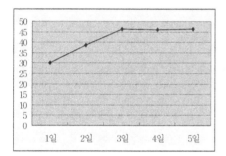
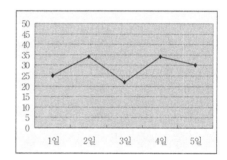

Fig. 8. 1st evaluation by auditory handicapped persons

Fig. 9. 2nd evaluation by persons with cerebral palsy <Degree of preciseness of sample sentences>

Photo1 shows the AAC system is used by auditory handicapped persons, who can use their hands freely. Photo 2 shows the AAC system is used by persons with cerebral palsy, who can't freely use their hands.

Photo 1. Scene of the AAC system using (Case of auditory handicapped persons)

Photo 2. Scene of the AAC system using (Case of persons with cerebral palsy)

7 Conclusions

This study has collected and analyzed linguistically handicapped persons' words, and hence has characterized the properties and trends of their usage. Based on this, we have constructed a machine-readable lexical database and various electric dictionaries like a sub-categorization dictionary.

In order to evaluate whether the implantation of an efficient system readily available to linguistically handicapped persons in real life is fulfilled, this study has verified the system by applying it to linguistically handicapped persons with different kinds of handicaps two times. The most important thing in the application of the system to actual situations is to generate precise expressions in a given time as soon as possible.

However, the 1st evaluation shows it took much time to generate a sentence combining semantic symbols in the training period. This is because the users of the AAC system were not acquainted with computers. On the other hand, students educated for computers participated in the 2nd evaluation, and hence were readily acquainted with the AAC system. But, even in this case, the physically handicapped persons showed lower degrees of preciseness of sentence generation because of their tremor of the hands. This means that the AAC system should be varied along with types of handicaps, cognitive abilities, ages, and degrees of handicaps.

This study is expected to further conditions in which people who are alienated from the development of information-communication may develop their potentials and lead ordinary social life easily, and to help those patients with temporary handicaps caused by an accident. Besides, this study can also contribute to technological development in the area of icon systems with a touch-screen interface like guidance systems and reservation systems, both of which are utilized prevalently at present.

Acknowledgements

This study was supported by research fund from University of Incheon and Multimedia Research Center of the Korea Science and Engineering Foundation.

References

1. Sharon L. Glennen, DeCote, Ed.D, *"The Handbook of Augmentative and Alternative Communication."* Singular Publishing Group, Inc. 1996
2. Gittins, D. Icon-based Human-Computer Interaction, International Journal of Man-Machine Studies, 24, 519, 543, 1986
3. Kathleen F. McCoy and Patrick Demasco, "Some Applications of Natural Language Processing to the Field of Augmentative and Alternative Communication" In Proceedings of the IJCAI-95 Workshop on Developing AI Applications for People with Disabilities, Montreal, Canada, August, 1995.

Tracking Data Management of Spatial DBMS Using Topology for Location-Based Services[*]

Soon-Young Park[1], Yong-Il Jang[1], Warnil Chung[2],
Chung-Ho Lee[2], and Hae-Young Bae[1]

[1] Dept. of Computer Science and Information Engineering, Inha University,
Yonghyun-dong 253, Nam-gu, Incheon, 402-751, Korea
{sunny, himalia}@dblab.inha.ac.kr, hybae@inha.ac.kr
[2] Internet Server Technology Group, Electronics and Telecommunications Research
Institute, Gajeong-dong 161, Yuseong-gu, Daejeon, 305-350, Korea
{wnchung, leech}@etri.re.kr

Abstract. With the rapid advances of wireless and positioning technologies, an interest in LBS (Location-Based Services) is gradually rising. To provide LBS, tracking data should have been stored in database with the proper policies and managed efficiently. In this paper, tracking data management technique using topology is proposed. Tracking data is corresponded to the moving path of an object. In proposed technique, database is updated when moving object arrived at a street intersection or a curved road which is represented as the node in topology and we can predict the location at past and future with attribute of topology and linear function. In this technique, location data that are correspond to the node in topology are stored, thus reduce the number of updates of data. Also as using topology as well as existing location information, accuracy for prediction of location is increased than applying only linear function or spline function.

1 Introduction

With the advances of wireless and positioning technologies and spread of wireless devices, an interest in LBS (Location Based Services) is gradually rising. LBS can be defined differently in origin, commonly is defined as "system that measures correctly the location of person or object based on communication network, then exploit that" [1]. To provide LBS efficiently, a database management system (DBMS) which stores and manages the tracking data efficiently is required. Also it is important to analyze the location information exactly using the stored historical information [15]. However, it is impossible to store the whole tracking data of the moving object which is continuously changing. So it has been proposed that tracking data are acquired by sampling its location at regular time intervals. It would impose a serious performance problem and network overhead [3, 5, 6]. In order to solve these problems, methods

---

[*] This research was supported by the MIC (Ministry of Information and Communication), Korea, under the ITRC (Information Technology Research Center) support program supervised by the IITA (Institute of Information Technology Assessment).

S. Shimojo et al. (Eds.): HSI 2005, LNCS 3597, pp. 9–18, 2005.
© Springer-Verlag Berlin Heidelberg 2005

using dynamic attribute such as current positions, speeds and directions of the moving object has been proposed. In these techniques, when calculated value with dynamic attribute exceeded the fixed threshold, database is updated [2, 3, 5]. But these methods are not able to reduce cost effectively because it should acquire historical information continuously in order to measure the dynamic attributes of moving object.

The uncertainty is represented in database because the tracking data are acquired at regular time intervals [5, 6]. So if user requests the location of the object, though exact location information is not stored in database, it is answered. Thus we should predict the location information in any way. Existing approaches perform the prediction of the location at future and past by linear function or spline function. But to apply only linear function or spline functions are less accurate as it does not consider moving path of object.

Therefore, we suggest the tracking data management using topology of moving object for constrained trajectory. As a result, using proposed technique, we predict the arrival time, when it is going to arrive at a location and where does it correspond to the node of topology. And we decide when to update the time, to insert the location in database. Also when queries for uncertain location information are requested, firstly we predict the location using stored historical data, topology and apply the linear function and then provide the location information. It contributes to reduce the number of update operations of data that we store the location corresponding to the topology of object movement as nodes, provide the location prediction using the minimum historical data. Also unlike the case which represents the route between two points as polyline function, we represent the route between two points as linear function. Therefore to predict the location using topology, historical information, attribute information of moving object is more accurate than to predict the location using only linear function or spline function.

The remainder of this paper is organized as follows. Section 2 briefly reviews related work. Section 3 presents proposed tracking data management technique using topology for LBS efficiently. Section 4 presents the experimental results to compare proposed technique using topology with other approaches. Finally, conclusion and future work are discussed in section 5.

2 Related Work

There are three commonly used representations of collections of spatial objects, respectively called spaghetti, network, and topological models. They mainly differ in the expression of topological relationships among the component objects. Topological relationships include adjacency, overlapping, disjoint, and inclusion [9].

The tracking data should be stored in DBMS using efficient location acquisition policies. The uncertainty of location information is unavoidable because of the delay for data transmission or the lack of the location information. But by selecting appropriate location acquisition policies, we are able to improve the accuracy for location data, also reduce network cost and database update cost [10]. In order to resolve these problems, DOMINO project [8] proposed two policies. First policy is to decide update time considering increment/decrement of speed and moving direction. To represent their method, they create the current query relation that is responsible for the current query processing. It includes speed, direction as attribute. When new location information is transferred from moving object, transferred value is compared with the information that had been stored in database. If compared value reaches threshold, data are inserted to database. Thus, it is able to reduce I/O accesses. But to set the threshold is ambiguous and to predict for uncertain location information is less accurate because they don't exactly consider moving route. Second policy is to insert the location information by fixing the threshold to decide update time. The threshold is computed synthesizing degree of deviation, degree of uncertainty, update cost from update time to next update time. But it can't decrease transmission cost because location information is transferred continuously. To store all of the locations of a moving object which moves continuously is impossible. Therefore, the data which are stored in database is inherently imprecise. We call this property uncertainty [11]. To answer to the whole queries that are associated with time, DBMS enables to predict the location information that is not stored in it. In many projects, they predict the location of moving object based on the dynamic attribute i.e. location, speed, direction. DOMINO project handles prediction for the future location of moving object only [7, 8]. CHOROCHRONOS project proposed the prediction method for location information using the linear interpolation. CHOROCHRONOS project also supposed the representation of uncertainty [4, 5].

When someone asks for the location at time tx, the uncertainty for an answer is represented as in Fig. 1. In this case, radius $r1$, $r2$ is represented as in the equation below (vm is the speed of moving object, tn is a time at point n). The intersection area that is shown by the shaded portion in Fig. 1 is predictable area. Since we do not have any further information, we assume a uniform distribution for the location within the shaded area.

$$r_1 = v_m(t_1 + t_x)$$

$$r_2 = v_m(t_2 - t_x)$$

(1)

There are equations that are computed using linear interpolation.

$$x_x = \frac{x_{i+1} - x_i}{t_{i+1} - t_i}(t_x - t_{i+1}) + x_{i+1}$$

$$y_x = \frac{y_{i+1} - y_i}{t_{i+1} - t_i}(t_x - t_{i+1}) + y_{i+1}$$

(2)

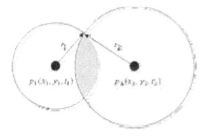

Fig. 1. Uncertainty between Samples

However, there are limitations for accuracy to apply linear interpolation only. So prediction techniques using the polynomial interpolation is proposed to lower the error rate. For the prediction of the location information that uses the polynomial interpolation, we need to guess the location using four points in time by contrast with the linear interpolation using two points in time. However both linear interpolation and polynomial spline interpolation have low accuracy because they do not exactly consider moving route of moving object.

3 Tracking Data Management Using Topology

In this section, we describe the attribute of topology in order to explain proposed technique. We introduce location acquisition policies using topology and prediction technique for uncertain location. The topology in this paper represent route of moving object in order to decide the update time and predict uncertain location information. Specially, we use the topology for road in here. The topology for road includes a link

Table 1. Attributes of Link Table

Name	Description
LinkID	ID for Link
StartNodeID	ID for Start node
EndNodeID	ID for End node
Length	Length of Link
LinkCode	Kind of Link
	ex. IC, JC, etc.
RoadCode	Kind of Road
	ex. highway, national road, etc.
LinkFacility	Kind of Facility
	ex. tunnel, overpass, etc.
RoadNum	Number of Road
Width	Width of Road
Lane	Number of Road Lane
RoadName	Name of Road

Table 2. Attributes of Node Table

Name	Description
NodeID	ID for Node
NodeAttr	Attribute of Node
NodeRange	Range of Node
NodeName	Name of Intersection
NumLink	Number of Link
LinkID#	ID for Connected Link
AdjNodeID	ID for Adjacent Node
X	X Coordinate of Node
Y	Y Coordinate of Node

table and a node table. A link table stores the set of links and a node table stores the set of nodes. Node is a point that represents an intersection between 2 lines. Link is a segment of a line between two nodes.

Table 1 shows the attributes of the link table. And Table 2 illustrates the attributes of the node table. By using attributes of the node table and link table, we decide the update time when we apply the location acquisition policies.

The topology should have been stored in database in advance to provide the location-based services. Our object is to calculate the time when moving object reaches a curved road or an intersection. Then, it should store location information at that time in database. For our object, we should compute the expected time that will reach moving object to most nearest node from current location to acquire the next location information. To calculate the expected time, we should yield average speed according to the historical information that has been stored in database. Consider a moving object is *MObj*, if a *MObj* lies on the point (Xn, Yn) at time Tn, average speed is computed by equation (3) below. Since to yield the average speed by using all historical data cause poor performance, we use the constant value, k, to restrict the historical data.

$$v = \frac{\sum_{k=1}^{n-1} \sqrt{(X_{k+1} - X_k)^2 + (Y_{k+1} - Y_k)^2}}{\sum_{k=1}^{n-1} (T_{k+1} - T_k)} \tag{3}$$

Time taken by *MObj* to move from a node to the next node is computed by equation (4) below. L represents the distance between two points.

$$t = \frac{L}{v} \tag{4}$$

After computing average speed v and time t according to above equations, finally we can decide the update time. In the equation below, UpdateTime is expected time when location information is acquired, and CurrentTime is current time of the moving object.

$$\text{UpdateTime} = \text{CurrentTime} + t \tag{5}$$

If a node is connected with several nodes in contrast to above case, we use existing way that acquires the location information at regular time intervals and update in database. Next algorithm shows the location acquisition policy using topology.

Algorithm 1. The Location Acquisition Policy using Topology

```
Input  : Current location of moving object, CurX, CurY
Output: Update time
Procedure DecideUpdateTime(CurX, CurY)
Begin
  bOnNode := IsOnNode(CurX, CurY);
  If(bOnNode)
    LinkNum := FindLinkNum(CurX, CurY);
    If(LinkNum = 1)
      LinkID := FindLink(CurX, CurY);
      NodeID := FindNode(LinkID);
```

```
        Return DecideUpdatTime(CurX, CurY, LinkID,
                NodeID)
      Else
        Return LimitTime;
      Endif
   Else
      LinkID := FindLinkID(CurX, CurY);
      NodeID := FindNode(LinkID);
      Return DecideUpdateTime(CurX, CurY, LinkID, NodeID)
   Endif
End
```

The uncertain location means that location data does not exist in DBMS. Although the queries for uncertain location are requested by user, the answer should be possible with all existing data. First, we store the location information applying to the location acquisition policy. At that time, the location information between two adjacent times is two points that lie on same link or both ends of nodes that are connected by a link. That means route that the moving object limited to linear path like a straight line. Thus, it is enough to apply to the linear interpolation for accuracy. However, if the location data that exist in DBMS include some error, to apply the linear interpolation only may cause the incorrect result. So, first of all we confirm whether the location information exist between two adjacent time or not. If location information exists, apply to the linear interpolation. The uncertain location prediction algorithm using topology is represented as next algorithm 2.

Algorithm 2. The Uncertain Location Prediction Algorithm using Topology
```
Input : PastTime, ID for moving object, MObj
Output: location of moving object at PastTime, PastX,
        PastY
Procedure FindPastPosition(PastTime, MObj)
Begin
   bTimeExist = FindTime(PastTime, MObj);
   IF(bExist)
     Return Select(PastTime, MObj);
   Else
     FindAdjTime(PastTime, BeforeTime, NextTime, MObj);
     bNode = ExistNode(BeforeTime, NextTime, MObj);
     If(bNode)
       NodePosition = FindNode(BeforeTime, NextTime,
       MObj);
       Return FindPos(BeforeTime, NextTime, PastTime,
                NodePosition, MObj);
     Else
       Return FindPos(BeforeTime, NextTime, PastTime,
                MObj);
     Endif
   Endif
End
```

The prediction of the future location is conducted by using an attribute in topology. In existing studies, the future location is predicted by reflecting the speed and direction of moving object. But since it only considers the moving route, it represents less accuracy, any place that are not road are predicted. To solve this problem, then to improve the accuracy, we use the topology. The prediction for the future location is to get location of moving object at few minutes or seconds later. For this, we should use the topology information as well as the current location information of moving object. As you see Table 1 and Table 2, both a link table and a node table store the variety of attributes, and we can add few attributes as occasion demands.

Table 3. Additional Attributes of Node Table for Prediction of the Future Location

Name	Description
LinkID#	ID# for Connected Link
TLinkID#	Passed Link for LinkID#

TLinkID# is added to a node table to support the future prediction. It is movable link among the link connected with LinkID#. Algorithm 3 represents the prediction algorithm for the future location.

Algorithm 3. The Prediction Algorithm for the Future Location
```
Input : Current location of moving object, CurX, CurY
Output: predicted Future location, FutureX, FutureY
Procedure FindFuturePosition(CurX, CurY, FutureTime)
Begin
   Vel = CalVelocity(MOID);
   LinkID = FindLinkID(CurX, CurY);
   NodeID = FindNode(LinkID, CurX, CurY);
   If(CalTime(CurX, CurY, NodeID, Vel) <= T)
     Return FindPosition(CurX, CurY, LinkID, Vel);
   Else
     ConLinkID = FindConLink(LinkID, NodeID);
     Return FindPosition(CurX, CurY, LinkID, ConLinkID,
            Vel);
   Endif
End
```

When we predict uncertain location, the uncertainty of predicted result was presented as in Figure 1. The shaded area is expectable location of the object. Thus, if the shaded area becomes smaller, the uncertainty also decreases and accuracy improves.

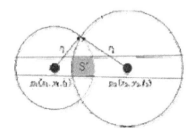

Fig. 2. Accuracy of Location Prediction

Since the topology includes the length information and width information of road, the accuracy of prediction using topology is able to be represented as in Fig. 2. The accuracy probability about the location prediction is 1/S', which is higher than that of Fig. 1.

4 Performance Evaluation

In this section, we compare and estimate the performance for proposed techniques. In first experiment, we estimate the performance of the system that is applied to the location acquisition policy using topology by comparing with sampling its position at regular time intervals. Then we evaluate the accuracy of proposed prediction techniques of uncertain location by comparing with existing method.

In order to perform a comparison for the tracking data management, we created the sample data. To acquire a sample data, we used a map and a topology of the road of Incheon metropolitan city in Korea. For the simulation, the speed of moving object limited 60 Km/h and 30 Km/h, the route of moving object limited around of Inha University. A node table has 9176 records and its size is 251Kbyte, and a link table has 14111 records and its size is 1.32Mbyte.

In Fig. 3, we measure the update number for limited distance. This experiment evaluates the update number when we update using topology by comparing with sampling its position at regular time intervals. Fig. 3 represents the update number according to distance. The sample data for location is acquired every 5 seconds. As you see in Fig. 3, the acquisition count acquired by sampling increases proportionately. However, the update number for tracking data using topology is almost constant regardless of speed.

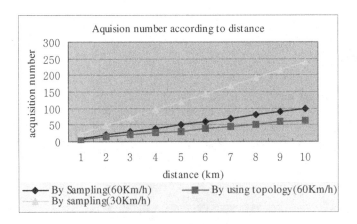

Fig. 3. Acquisition Number according to Distance

In Fig. 4, we perform a comparison for accuracy about prediction of uncertain location. Suppose that we receive a search query for specification visual point, we answer the query using existing linear interpolation and the linear interpolation using topology, then compare the incidental and value. Fig. 4 expresses accuracy about uncertain location information by time. This experiment sends the query every 10 seconds using stored historical data. In the result of Fig. 4, the prediction using topology shows constant accuracy. But, prediction that uses linear interpolation shows variable accuracy.

This displays that if the object passes the intersection or the broken path, the value of transferring object cannot be predicted, and hence cannot replace the result. So this remains an exceptional case.

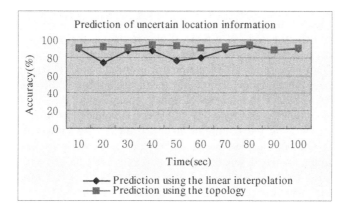

Fig. 4. Prediction of Uncertain Location Information

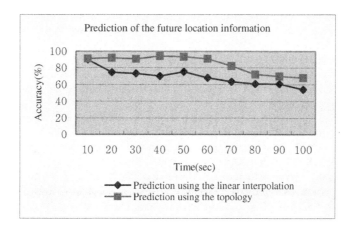

Fig. 5. Prediction of the Future Location Information

Fig. 5 expresses the accuracy about prediction of the future location. In this experiment, we suppose that users send query at every 10 seconds like the experiment given by Fig. 4. When we predict the future location commonly, prediction of the far future represents lower accuracy than relative future. But, the prediction of the future using the topology represented relatively similar accuracy between far future and relative future.

5 Conclusion

Many systems that have managed on tracking data management have stored the location information by sampling it at regular time intervals or by considering the direction and speed of the moving object. But it is not able to offer the exact location information and amount of the data increase by geometrical progression because they didn't consider the moving route of moving object.

In this paper, the tracking data management using topology of moving object has been proposed for moving object constrained trajectory. As a result using proposed technique, we predict the arrival time, when it is going to arrive at location where it is corresponding to the topology of a node. Then we decide that time as update time, insert the location in database. Also when queries for uncertain location information are requested, firstly we predict the location using stored historical data, topology and apply to the linear function and then provide the location information.

It contributes to reduce the number of update operations of data that we store the location corresponding to the topology of object movement as nodes, provide the location prediction using the minimum historical data. Also unlike the case which represents the route between two points as polyline function, we represent the route between two points as linear function. Therefore to predict the location using topology, historical information, attribute information of moving object is more accurate than to predict the location using only linear function or spline function.

References

1. 3rd Generation Partnership Project: Technical Specification Group Services and System Aspect; Location Services (LCS); Service description, Stage1 (Release4), 3GPP TS 22.071.
2. The CHOROCHRONOS Participants, CHOROCHRONOS: A Research network for Spatiotemporal Database systems, SIGMOD Record, Vol.28, No.3, 1999.
3. P. Rigaux, A. Voisard, and M. O. Scholl, Spatial Database: With Application to GIS, Morgan Kaufmann Publishers, 2001.
4. D. Pfoser and C.S. Jensen, Capturing the Uncertainty of Moving Object Representation s, CHOROCHRONOS, Technical Report CC-99-2, 1999.
5. D. Pfoser and N.Tryfona, Fuzziness and uncertainty in Spatiotemporal Applications, CHOROCHRONOS, Technical Report CH-00-04, 2000.
6. D. Pfoser and N. Tryfona, Requirement, Definitions and Notations for Spatiotemporal Application Environments, CHOROCHRONOS, Technical Report CH-98-09, 1998.
7. A. Prasad Sistla, O. Wolfson, S. Chamberlain, and S. Dao, Modeling and Querying Moving Objects, Proceedings of ICDE, 1997.
8. A. Prasad Sistla, O. Wolfson, S. Chamberlain, and S. Dao, Querying the Uncertain Position of Moving Objects, Proceedings of Temporal Databases, 1997.
9. O. Wolfson, A. Prasad Sistla, B. Xu, J. Zhou, and S. Chamberlain, DOMINO: Database fOr MonINg Objects tracking, Proceedings of SIGMOD, 1999.
10. O. Wolfson, B. Xu, S. Chamberlain, and L. Jiang, Moving Objects Databases: Issues and Solutions, Proceedings of SSDBM, 1998.
11. S.-Y. Wu, and K.-T. Wu, Dynamic Data Management for Location Based Services in Mobile Environments, Proceedings of IDEAS, 2003.

Optimized Initiation Phases for Anonymous Auction Protocols

Eun-Jun Yoon, Eun-Kyung Ryu, and Kee-Young Yoo*

Department of Computer Engineering, Kyungpook National University,
Daegu 702-701, South Korea
{ejyoon, ekryu}@infosec.knu.ac.kr, yook@knu.ac.kr
Tel.: +82-53-950-5553; Fax: +82-53-957-4846

Abstract. Electronic Commerce (EC) has made rapid progress in recent years. Internet auctions have become especially popular in EC. Recently, Jiang-Pan-Li (JPL) proposed an improvement on Chang et al.'s efficient anonymous auction protocols in order to overcome the security weakness in the initiation phase of Chang et al.'s protocol. The current paper, however, points out that JPL's initiation protocol is inefficiently designed and then, two optimized initiation protocols are presented to resolve such problems.

Keywords: Security, Auction protocol, Anonymity, Efficiency, Initiation protocol.

1 Introduction

The Internet has been providing an electronic commercial environment, where efficient and secure auctions are in demand [1][2]. It usually has three transactional types: Traditional English auction [3], Dutch auction and sealed-bid auction [4][5]. The traditional English auction is also known as a public bid auction, wherein each bidder casts his/her own bid, and the bid must be higher than the bottom price. The bottom price is adjusted upwards after a round. The auction goes on until there is only one bidder left who is willing to offer the price. The Dutch auction is similar to the traditional English auction, but it begins with the top price, and then the price goes down round after round until the first bidder decides to offer the price. In a sealed-bid auction, unlike the previous two kinds of auctions, all the customers who are willing to name their bids are gathered. All bidders submit their own bids to the auctioneer. After the opening phase, the auctioneer makes all bids public and determines the winner.

In 2003, Chang and Chang [6] presented simple and efficient anonymous auction protocols, which follow the original principals of the different kinds of auctions such as the traditional English auction, Dutch auction and sealed-bid auction. They claimed that their approach can ensure the anonymity of the

---

* Corresponding author.

S. Shimojo et al. (Eds.): HSI 2005, LNCS 3597, pp. 19–27, 2005.

bidders in the simple and efficient way. Also, they claimed that the bidders have their confidentiality maintained, and the scheme is practical. Recently, Jiang-Pan-Li (JPL) [7], however, formally analyzed the initiation phase of Chang et al.'s protocol on the basis of authentication tests [8][9][10] in order to disclose the security problems of the initiation phase. Then they proved that the replay attack on the initiation phase of Chang et al.'s protocols, which can inhibit the following auction phase. Furthermore, JPL proposed an improvement on the initiation protocol. Also, they [7] formally analyzed the improved protocol with authentication tests, and proved the security of their protocol system.

However, we will show that JPL's initiation protocol is inefficiently designed. That is, in order to ensure the secure authentication and recency for the bidder and to avoid a replay attack, the protocol requires a great deal of verification time, public key computations and system resources between the bidders and auctioneer. Accordingly, the current paper points out that JPL's initiation protocol is inefficiently designed and then presents two new initiation protocols to resolve such problems. First, we propose an optimized method by using a collision-resistance one-way hash function that can reduce public key computations. Second, we propose an optimized method by using a timestamp that needs only one public key computation. As a result, the proposed two protocols can resist the replay attack and they are more efficiently designed than JPL's protocol.

The remainder of the paper is organized as follows: Section 2 briefly reviews JPL's initiation protocol and Chang et al.'s anonymous auction protocols. In Section 3, we point out that JPL's initiation protocol is inefficiently designed. The proposed two optimized protocols are presented in Section 4, while Section 5 discusses the security and efficiency of the proposed protocol. Conclusions are provided in Section 6.

2   Related Works

This section briefly reviews JPL's improved initiation protocol for anonymous auction protocols [7] and Chang et al.'s anonymous auction protocols [6]. Chang et al.'s anonymous auction protocols contain two phases, the initiation phase and the anonymous auction phase. In the initiation phase, an auctioneer and bidders communicate with each other and share the common secret session key. In the anonymous auction phase, the anonymous traditional English auction, anonymous Dutch auction and the anonymous Sealed-bid auction will run on the basis of the initiation phase. For more information, please refer to Chang et al.'s protocols in [6].

2.1   Notations

Some of the notations used in this paper are defined as follows:

- R: just auctioneer.
- U_i: m bidders, where $1 \leq i \leq m$.

- ID_i: the identity of U_i.
- CA: certification authority.
- B: the bid of U_i.
- n, g: large prime n and generator g in cyclic group Z_n^*, in which the Diffie-Hellman problem is considered hard.
- a_i, b: session-independent random exponents chosen by U_i and R, respectively.
- K_i: shared common secret session key computed by U_i and R.
- T: the timestamp.
- $H(\cdot)$: a collision-resistance one-way hash function.
- E: public key cryptography.
- $||$: the concatenation of data.

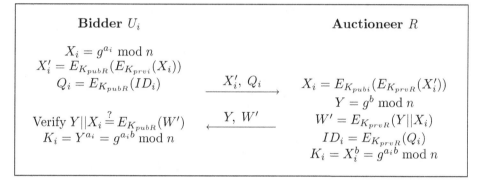

Fig. 1. JPL's improved initiation protocol

2.2 JPL's Improved Initiation Protocol

The JPL's improved initiation protocol [7], such that R and U_i share a secret session key K_i, is illustrated in Figure 1. For simplicity, we omit mod n from the expressions.

1. U_i chooses a random exponent a_i and computes $X_i = g^{a_i}$, $Q_i = E_{K_{pubR}}(ID_i)$, and $X_i' = E_{K_{pubR}}(E_{K_{prvi}}(X_i))$. Then, U_i sends messages X_i' and Q_i to R.
2. After receiving X_i' and Q_i, R computes $X_i = E_{K_{pubi}}(E_{K_{prvR}}(X_i'))$, chooses a random exponent b, computes Y and W', where $Y = g^b$, $W' = E_{K_{prvR}}(Y||X_i)$, and broadcasts messages Y and W'.
3. R computes $ID_i = E_{K_{prvR}}(Q_i)$ and $K_i = X_i^b = g^{a_i b}$.
4. U_i checks to see whether $Y||X_i = E_{K_{pubR}}(W')$ holds. If the equation holds, U_i authenticates R and computes $K_i = Y^{a_i} = g^{a_i b}$. Otherwise, U_i has to wait for the next broadcast of the messages Y and W'.

Shared information: Common secret key $K_i = g^{a_i b} \bmod n$.

Bidder U_i		**Auctioneer R**

Select B, T
$S = E_{K_{prvi}}(B\|T)$
$D = E_{K_{pubR}}(S)$
$C = H(B, T, K_i)$

$\xrightarrow{\quad B,\ T,\ D,\ C \quad}$

$C'_i = H(B, T, K_i)$
$S' = E_{K_{prvR}}(D)$
Verify $C'_i \overset{?}{=} C$
Verify $B\|T \overset{?}{=} E_{K_{pubi}}(S')$

Fig. 2. Anonymous traditional English auction and Dutch auction

---

Shared information: Common secret key $K_i = g^{a_i b} \bmod n$.

Bidder U_i		**Auctioneer R**

Select B, T
$F = E_{K_{pubR}}(B\|T)$
$S = E_{K_{prvi}}(B\|T)$
$D = E_{K_{pubR}}(S)$
$C = H(B, T, K_i)$

$\xrightarrow{\quad F,\ D,\ C \quad}$

$B'\|T' = E_{K_{prvR}}(F)$
$S' = E_{K_{prvR}}(D)$
$C'_i = H(B', T', K_i)$
Verify $C'_i \overset{?}{=} C$
Verify $B'\|T' \overset{?}{=} E_{K_{pubi}}(S')$

Fig. 3. Anonymous sealed-bid auction

2.3 Anonymous Auction Phase

The anonymous auction phase has three transactional types: The anonymous traditional English auction, anonymous Dutch auction and anonymous sealed-bid auction.

The Anonymous Traditional English Auction and Dutch Auction: After the four steps that were mentioned in the 'Initiation phase', each bidder U_i and the auctioneer R share the common secret key K_i. The transaction of the anonymous traditional English auction and Dutch auction are illustrated in Figure 2 and the protocol is as follows:

1. U_i selects B and T, and calculates $S = E_{K_{prvi}}(B||T)$, $D = E_{K_{pubR}}(S)$ and $C = H(B, T, K_i)$. Finally, U_i sends B, T, D and C to the auctioneer R.
2. After receiving B, T, D and C, the R will check whether $C_i' = C$ and $B||T = E_{K_{pubi}}(S')$ hold, where $C_i' = H(B, T, K_i)$ and $S' = E_{K_{prvR}}(D)$. If the two equations hold, the bid is valid; otherwise, the bid is invalid.

Anonymous Sealed-Bid Auction: After following the initiation protocol described in the 'Initiation phase', each bidder U_i and the auctioneer R share the common secret key K_i. The transaction of the anonymous sealed-bid auction is illustrated in Figure 3 and the protocol is as follows:

1. U_i selects B and T, and calculates $F = E_{K_{pubR}}(B||T)$, $S = E_{K_{prvi}}(B||T)$, $D = E_{K_{pubR}}(S)$ and $C = H(B, T, K_i)$. Finally, U_i sends F, D and C to the auctioneer R.
2. After receiving F, D and C, the R will check whether $C_i' = C$ and $B'||T' = E_{K_{pubi}}(S')$ hold, where $C_i' = H(B', T', K_i)$, $B'||T' = E_{K_{prvR}}(F)$ and $S' = E_{K_{prvR}}(D)$. If the two equations hold, the bid is valid; otherwise, the bid is invalid.

3   An Analysis Regarding the Efficiency of JPL's Initiation Protocol

In this section, we point out that JPL's initiation protocol is inefficiently designed. In order to analyze the communication costs of the protocol, we assume that the mod n length is 1024 bits in order to make the discrete logarithm problem infeasible, the public key length is 1024 bits (for RSA), the hash function digest is 160 bits (for MD5 and SHA-1). JPL's protocol is based on the intractability of the discrete logarithm problem and public key computations. The total size of the communication messages in JPL's protocol is $(3m+1) \times 1024$ bits, where m is the number of bidders. The symmetric key computations and hash functions are faster than the public key computations. On a typical workstation, the public key computations can be performed 2 times per second, symmetric key computations can be performed 2,000 times per second and hash function can be performed 20,000 times per second [11].

In Step 2 of JPL's protocol, R computes Y and W', where $Y = g^b$, $W' = E_{K_{prvR}}(Y||X_i)$, and broadcasts messages Y and W' to all U_i. Yet, in order to ensure the secure authentication and recency for the bidder and to avoid a replay attack, the protocol requires a long many verification period and many public key computations between U_i and R. In order that all U_i verify W' with $Y||X_i$, R must broadcast W' of the m bidder numbers because all X_i values are different and secure values of each bidder. In other words, after R gets the X_i of every U_i through public key computations from the received X_i' and computes W' of the m bidder numbers, R must send W' to each U_i. Thus, it requires many public key computations unlike Chang et al.'s initiation protocol, whereby R broadcasts only two values; Y and W', to every U_i. Accordingly, the improved protocol does not preserve the merits of Chang et al.'s protocol.

Also, upon receiving Y and W' from R, each U_i computes $Y||X_i$, and it must verify $Y||X_i$ with W', including its X_i. Also, it requires a long verification period and many public key computations so that they can determine whether W' includes its own X_i. Furthermore, if an attacker sends a modified W' which requires an extended verification period, many public key computations and system resources, U_i must verify every W_i of the m bidder numbers in order to find out if W' includes its own X_i. Thus, U_i can be faced with a Denial of Service (DoS) attack because of the extended verification period, many public key computations and significant system resource consumption. From our analysis it can be determined that JPL's improved initiation protocol is inefficiently designed.

4   Proposed Optimized Initiation Protocols

This section proposes two optimized initiation protocols in order to overcome the above mentioned problems with JPL's protocol.

4.1   First Optimized Method

First, we propose an optimized method by using a collision-resistance one-way hash function that can reduce public key computations by the auctioneer by sending W' in Step 2. The first proposed optimized initiation protocol is illustrated in Figure 4 and the protocol is as follows:

1. U_i chooses a random exponent a_i in the cyclic group Z_n^* and computes $X_i = g^{a_i}$ and $X_i' = E_{K_{pubR}}(E_{K_{prvi}}(ID_i||X_i))$. Then, U_i sends messages X_i' to R.
2. R computes $ID_i||X_i = E_{K_{pubi}}(E_{K_{prvR}}(X_i'))$, chooses a random exponent b, computes Y, K_i and W', where $Y = g^b$, $K_i = X_i^b = g^{a_i b}$, $W' = H(ID_i||X_i||K_i)$, and broadcasts message Y and W'.
3. U_i computes $K_i = Y^{a_i} = g^{a_i b}$ and checks whether $H(ID_i||X_i||K_i) = W'$ holds. If the equation holds, U_i authenticates R. Otherwise, U_i has to wait for the next broadcast of the message Y and W'.

4.2   Second Optimized Method

Second, we propose an optimized method by using a timestamp that needs only one public key computation by the auctioneer that sending W' in Step 2. The second proposed optimized initiation protocol is illustrated in Figure 5 and the protocol is as follows:

1. U_i chooses a random exponent a_i in the cyclic group Z_n^* and computes $X_i = g^{a_i}$ and $X_i' = E_{K_{pubR}}(E_{K_{prvi}}(ID_i||X_i))$. Then, U_i sends messages X_i' to R.
2. R chooses a random exponent b, computes Y and W', where $Y = g^b$, $W' = E_{K_{prvR}}(Y||T)$, and broadcasts message Y, T and W'.
3. R computes $ID_i||X_i = E_{K_{pubi}}(E_{K_{prvR}}(X_i'))$ and $K_i = X_i^b = g^{a_i b}$.
4. U_i checks the validity of the timestamp T. If it has been used before, U_i rejects this message. Otherwise, U_i checks whether $Y||T = E_{K_{pubR}}(W')$ holds. If the equation holds, U_i authenticates R and computes $K_i = Y^{a_i} = g^{a_i b}$. Otherwise, U_i has to wait for the next broadcast of the messages Y and W'.

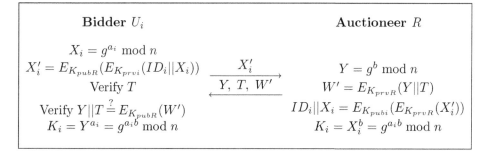

Fig. 4. The first proposed optimized initiation protocol

$$
\begin{array}{cc}
\textbf{Bidder } U_i & \textbf{Auctioneer } R \\[4pt]
X_i = g^{a_i} \bmod n & \\
X_i' = E_{K_{pubR}}(E_{K_{prvi}}(ID_i\|X_i)) \xrightarrow{\quad X_i' \quad} & Y = g^b \bmod n \\
\text{Verify } T \xleftarrow{\quad Y,\ T,\ W' \quad} & W' = E_{K_{prvR}}(Y\|T) \\
\text{Verify } Y\|T \overset{?}{=} E_{K_{pubR}}(W') & ID_i\|X_i = E_{K_{pubi}}(E_{K_{prvR}}(X_i')) \\
K_i = Y^{a_i} = g^{a_i b} \bmod n & K_i = X_i^b = g^{a_i b} \bmod n
\end{array}
$$

Fig. 5. The second proposed optimized initiation protocol

5 Security and Efficiency Analysis

This section discusses the security and efficiency of the proposed two optimized protocols in initiation phase. The computational costs of JPL's protocol and the proposed two optimized protocols in initiation phase are summarized in Table 1.

Theorem 1. *The first proposed optimized initiation protocol can resist the replay attack and is more efficient than JPL's protocol.*

Proof. Upon receiving Y and W' from R, each U_i computes K_i by using Y and checks whether $H(ID_i\|X_i\|K_i) = W'$ holds. The protocol, however, does not need to perform public key computations in order to find out if W' includes its own X_i unlike JPL's protocol. It only needs one hash function computation in each U_i. The total size of the communication messages in the first proposed optimized protocol is $(m+1) \times 1024 + m \times 128$ bits, where m is the number of bidders. Therefore, the first proposed protocol is much more efficient than JPL's protocol in terms of communication costs. If, however, a malicious attacker sends a modified W' that requires an extended verification period and many system resources, U_i can be susceptible to a DoS attack because of the aforementioned reasons.

Theorem 2. *The second proposed optimized initiation protocol can resist the replay and DoS attacks, also it is more efficient than JPL's protocol and our first proposed optimized protocol.*

Table 1. Comparisons of computational costs

	The total size of communication messages
JPL's protocol	$(3m + 1) \times 1024$ bits
First optimized protocol	$(m + 1) \times 1024 + m \times 128$ bits
Second optimized protocol	$(m + 2) \times 1024 + 64$ bits

m : the number of bidders

Proof. Upon receiving Y and W' from R, each U_i checks the validity of the timestamp T. If any attacker replayed message Y, T and W', the message can be easily detected since the timestamp has been used before. As a result, U_i will reject this modified message. Furthermore, U_i computes the transmitted data Y concatenated with timestamp T and checks whether $Y||T = E_{K_{pubR}}(W')$ holds. Obviously, the second proposed optimized initiation protocol can resist the replay attack. Even if, a malicious attacker sends a modified W', the attacker cannot succeed in its DoS attack because the protocol uses a shortened verification time and one public key computation in order to check whether $Y||T = E_{K_{pubR}}(W')$ holds. Also, the protocol does not need to perform public key and hash function computations in order to find out whether W' includes its own X_i unlike JPL's protocol and our previously proposed protocol. We assume that the timestamp length is 64 bits. The total size of the communication messages in the second proposed optimized protocol is $(m + 2) \times 1024 + 64$ bits, where m is the number of bidders. Therefore, the proposed protocol is much more efficient than JPL's protocol in terms of communication costs. As a result, the second proposed optimized initiation protocol can resist the DoS attack and it is more efficient than JPL's and our first proposed optimized protocol.

6   Conclusion

The current paper pointed out that JPL's initiation protocol is inefficiently designed and then two new initiation protocols were presented to resolve such problems. First, we proposed the optimized method by using a collision-resistant one-way hash function that can reduce the number of public key computations. Second, we proposed the optimized method using a timestamp that needs only one public key computation. As a result, the second proposed optimized initiation protocol can resist the replay attack and is more efficiently designed than JPL's protocol.

Acknowledgements

This research was supported by the MIC (Ministry of Information and Communication), Korea, under the ITRC (Information Technology Research Center) support program supervised by the IITA (Institute of Information Technology Assessment).

References

1. H. Kikuchi, M. Hakavy, and D. Tygar. Multi-round Anonymous Auction Protocols, IEICE Transactions on Information and System, Vol.E82-D No.4 (1999) 769-777.
2. K. Omote and A. Miyaji. An Anonymous Sealed-bid Auction with a Feature of Entertainment, Transactions on Information Processing Society of Japan, (2001) 2049-2056.
3. M.K. Franklin and M.K. Reiter. The Design and Implementation of a Secure Auction Service, IEEE Transactions on Software Engineering, (1996) 302-312.
4. M. Kudo. Secure Electronic Sealed-bid Auction Protocol with Public Key Cryptography, IEICE Transactions on Fundamentals, Vol.E81-A No.1 (1998) 20-27.
5. K. Omote and A. Miyaji. A Practical English Auction with One-time Registration, Lecture Notes in Computer Science of Information Security and Privacy-Proceedings on ACISP 2001, Springer-Verlag, (2001) 221-234.
6. C.C. Chang and Y.F. Chang. Efficient Anonymous Auction Protocols with Free-wheeling Bids, Computers & Security, Vol.22 No.8 (2003) 728-734.
7. R. Jiang, L. Pan, and J.H. Li. An Improvement on Efficient Anonymous Auction Protocols, Computers & Security, (2005) Articles in Press.
8. J.D. Guttman. Security Protocol Design via Authentication Tests, Proceedings of the 15th IEEE computer security foundations workshop, IEEE CS Press, (2002).
9. J.D. Guttman and F.J. Thayer. Authentication Tests and the Structure of Bundles, Theoretical Computer Science, Vol.283 No.2 (2002) 333-380.
10. F.J. Thayer, J.C. Herzog, and J.D. Guttman. Strand Spaces: Proving Security Protocols Correct, Journal of Computer Security, Vol.7 No(2/3) (1999) 191-230.
11. M.S. Hwang, I.C. Lin, and L.H. Li. A Simple Micro-payment Scheme, The Journal of Systems and Software, Vol.55 (2001) 221-229.

mSCTP for Vertical Handover
Between Heterogeneous Networks

Seok Joo Koh and Sang Wook Kim

Department of Computer Science,
Kyungpook National University, Daegoo, Korea
{sjkoh, swkim}@cs.knu.ac.kr

Abstract. Stream Control Transmission Protocol (SCTP) is a new end-to-end transport protocol that is featured 'multi-homing.' The mSCTP (mobile SCTP) is defined as SCTP with the capability of dynamic address reconfiguration. This paper describes a framework of mSCTP handover for supporting vertical handover between heterogeneous IP networks such as WLAN and 3G Cellular systems. We show some experimental results of the mSCTP vertical handover on Linux platforms. From the experimental results, we see that the handover latency of mSCTP depends on Round Trip Time (RTT) between two SCTP endpoints, possibly with the handover latency of 1 second below.

1 Introduction

In the next-generation wireless mobile networks, the vertical handover between heterogeneous IP networks is one of the challenging issues, as shown in the example of the handover between WLAN and 3G Cellular systems. Mobile IP (MIP) has so far been considered as an IP mobility scheme [1, 2]. MIP is a network-layer mobility protocol and requires the support of the special agents such as Home Agents and Foreign Agents in the network.

Stream Control Transmission Protocol (SCTP) [3] is a new end-to-end transport layer protocol next to TCP and UDP. In particular, the SCTP multi-homing feature enables SCTP endpoints to support multiple IP addresses. Each SCTP endpoint can send and receive messages from any of the several IP addresses. One of the several IP addresses is designated as the primary address during the initiation.

The recent works on SCTP include the capability of dynamic IP address reconfiguration during an association, which is called ADDIP extension [4]. While an SCTP association goes on, the ADDIP extension enables the SCTP to add a new IP address, to delete an unnecessary IP address and to change the primary IP address used for the association. In this paper we define mSCTP (or mobile SCTP) as the SCTP with the ADDIP extension.

In this paper, we describe a framework of the mSCTP handover. The mSCTP can be used to provide the vertical handover for Mobile Terminals that are moving between heterogeneous IP networks. The mSCTP could also be used along with MIP for mobile sessions that require the location management. Some related studies on mSCTP [5, 6] include the experimentations of mSCTP using Network Simulator (ns-

S. Shimojo et al. (Eds.): HSI 2005, LNCS 3597, pp. 28–36, 2005.

2) [7, 8], where the mSCTP performance is compared to the MIP. On the other hand, in this paper, the mSCTP handover is experimented over a real testbed based on Linux Platform using the recently released Linux Kernel SCTP codes [9, 10, 11].

This paper is organized as follows. Section 2 describes an overview of mSCTP handover. In Section 3, we describe some experimental results of mSCTP vertical handover that have been performed on the Linux testbed, in which the performance of mSCTP will be analyzed in terms of handover latency. Section 4 concludes this paper.

2 mSCTP Handover

The mSCTP is defined as SCTP with the capability of dynamic address reconfiguration that has recently been made in IETF [4]. The mSCTP can be used to support the vertical handover of mobile terminals, as illustrated in Figure 1.

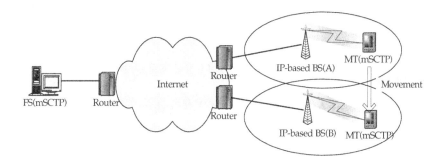

Fig. 1. mSCTP Handover

In this figure, it is assumed that a Mobile Terminal (MT) initiates an SCTP session with a Fixed Server (FS). After initiation of an SCTP association, the MT moves from Base Station (BS) A to BS B, as shown in the figure.

In the figure, it is assumed that a Mobile Terminal (MT) initiates an SCTP session with a Fixed Server (FS). After initiation of an SCTP association, the MT moves from Base Station (BS) A to BS B, as shown in the figure.

Then, the overall mSCTP handover procedures could be done as follows:

(1) Session is initiation by MT

In the initial stage, we assume that FS has 'IP address 1', whereas MT uses 'IP address 2'. Note in this phase that the MT is in the single-homing state, and it uses IP address 2 as its primary IP address in the SCTP association.

(2) Obtaining a new IP address

Now, the MT is moving from A to B and it is now in the overlapping region. In this phase, the MT will obtain a new address 'IP address 3' from the BS B by using any scheme for address configuration such as Dynamic Host Configuration Protocol (DHCP).

(3) Adding the new IP address to SCTP association

After obtaining a new IP address, the MT informs FS that it will use a new IP address. This will be done by sending SCTP Address Reconfiguration (ASCONF) chunk [4] to FS. The MT may receive the responding ASCONF-ACK chunk from the FS. The MT is now in the dual homing state. The old IP address (IP address 2) is still used as the primary address, until the new IP address 3 will be set to be "Primary Address" for MT.

(4) Changing the primary IP address

While the MT further continues to move toward BS B, it will set the primary address as the new IP address according to an appropriately configured rule. Once the primary address is changed, the FS will send the outgoing data to the new primary IP address of MT, whereas the old IP address may be used as a backup address to recover the lost data chunks.

(5) Deleting the old IP address from the SCTP association

As the MT progresses to move toward BS B, if the old IP address gets inactive, the MT will delete it from the association.

The procedural steps for handover described above will be repeated each time the MT moves to a new BS, until the SCTP association will be terminated.

3   Experimental Analysis of mSCTP Handover

In this section, we describe some experimental results of the mSCTP vertical handover that have been performed over Linux platform.

3.1 Test Environment

We consider the handover of MT that is moving between two heterogeneous IP networks. The mobility pattern tested in this paper is shown in Figure 2. In this figure, an MT is moving to a new area via the overlapping region where the MT is temporarily in the dual-homing state.

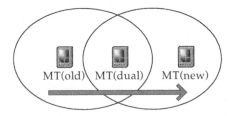

Fig. 2. Mobility Pattern for mSCTP Handover

To simulate the vertical handover of mSCTP over Linux testbed, we construct a small test network as shown in Figure 3. The test network consists of two terminals (FS and MT) and a router. Those two terminals are equipped with the mSCTP implementations given in the Linux Kernel 2.6.8 [9, 10]. The MT has the two network interfaces (i.e., two NICs), and thus it can be attached to the router in the dual-homing state.

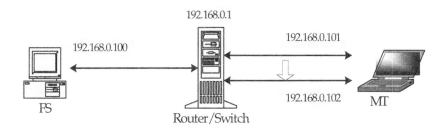

Fig. 3. Mobility Pattern for mSCTP Handover

Over the testbed, the mSCTP handover of MT proceeds as follows:

(1) Session Initiation

The MT initiates an SCTP session with FS. Initially, the MT uses IP address 192.168.0.101, and the FS binds to 192.168.0.100. After initiation, two endpoints exchange data packets.

(2) Add-IP

When the MT is going to a new network area (i.e., overlapping region), it enables the second network interface and obtains a new IP address (192.168.0.102), and then adds the new IP address to the SCTP association. This Add-IP functionality is triggered when the MT calls the socket API of "sctp_bindx()" function [11].

(3) Primary-Change

In the meantime, the MT informs the FS about the change of the primary IP address. Now, the FS will send the data to the new primary address. Note that this Primary-Change is triggered when the MT calls the appropriate "setsockopt()" function [11].

(4) Delete-IP

After a pre-specified time period, the MT deletes the old IP address from the SCTP association. Note that this Delete-IP functionality is also triggered by calling the socket API of "sctp_bindx()" function.

In the test experiments, FS transmits data packets of 1,000 bytes to the MT periodically, and the MT also sends a few data to the FS. By using the 'ethereal' [12], we captured the trace of the packets that have been exchanged between FS and MT.

From such the packet trace, we measured the 'handover latency' as a performance metric of mSCTP [5, 6]. More specifically, in this paper, the handover latency is defined as the gap of 'the time when the MT received the last data packet over the old IP address' and 'the time when the MT received the first data packet over the new IP address'.

3.2   Results and Discussion

It is noted that the handover performance may be affected by the time when the link-down of the old network link occurs. So, we measured the performance of the mSCTP handover for the two scenarios, as shown in Figure 4.

Figure 4 illustrates those two scenarios. Fig. 4(a) shows the case in which the MT performs Add-IP before the Link-Down event, whereas in Fig. 4(b) the Link-Down occurs almost the same time with the Add-IP.

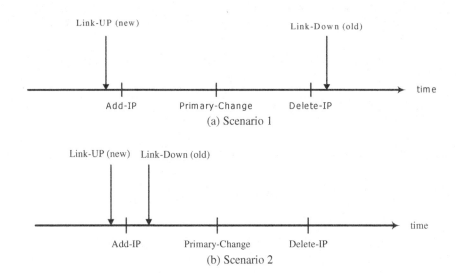

Fig. 4. mSCTP Handover Scenarios

① Scenario 1(Fig. 4(a)):
   When Link-Down of the old link occurs after the Delete IP. This scenario simulates the case in which the MT moves relatively in a slower speed.

② Scenario 2 (Fig. 4(b):
   When Link-Down of the old link occurs just after Add-IP. This scenario simulates the case in which the MT moves relatively in a faster speed.

A. Results for Scenario 1

Figure 5 shows the experimental result of Scenario 1, in which all the SCTP control and data packets for the association are captured using Ethereal.

In the figure we see that FS (192.168.0.100) and MT (192.168.0.101) establish an SCTP association through the packets 1 to 4. Then those two endpoints begin the data transport.

Packet 6 contains the ASCONF chunk of MT, which is used to ass the new IP address '192.168.0.102' to the association. FS responds with the ASCONF-ACK chunk at Packet 8. Packet 17 is used for MT to request the change of Primary Address to the FS. It is in the packet 18 noted that FS responds with ASCONF-ACK chunk over the new IP address (192.168.0.102). After that the FS sends DATA packets to MT over the new IP address, as shown in Packet 23. As per Scenario 1, MT performs the Delete-IP operation at Packet 27 before the Link-Down of the old network link occurs.

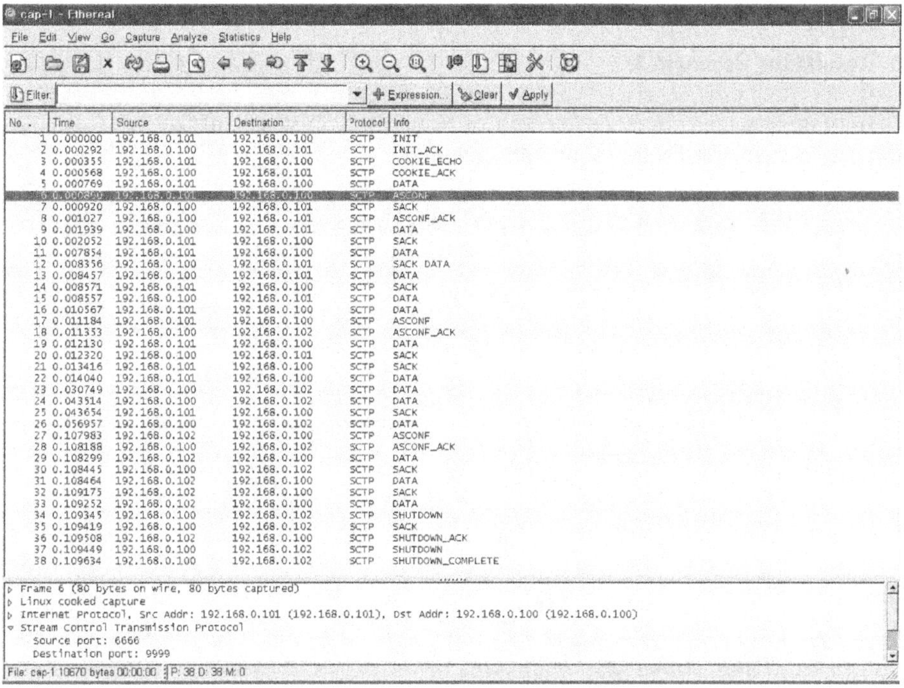

Fig. 5. Result of mSCTP Handover for Scenario 1

From the result, we also note that even after the Primary-Change, the MT still uses its old IP address as the source IP address of the DATA packets (see Packets 19 and 22). This is because the Primary-Change operation is applied to the FS, rather than MT. That is, the source IP address of DATA packets transmitted by MT is not affected by the Primary-Change operation. Only after the Delete-IP operation, MT uses the new IP address as its source IP address (see Packets 29 and 31).

In Figure 5, the handover latency of mSCTP is measured as "0.030 – 0.008 = 0.022 (sec.) = 22 (ms) ", which corresponds to the gap of the times recorded at Packet 15 (last data packet of old IP address) and 23 (first data packet of the new IP address). Seeing the packets between Packet 15 and 23, we can divide the overall handover latency into the following components:

– Time duration required for exchanging ASCONF and ASCONF-ACK for the Primary-Change operation (see Packets 17 and 18), which is roughly equal to the Round Trip Time (RTT).
– Kernel processing time at FS for changing the primary address and setting the address as the primary destination address (see Packets 20 ~ 23).

We note that the kernel processing time (the second component) is usually a constant value, independently of the RTT and the network condition. In particular, the processing time may be relatively a small value compared to the RTT in the legacy large networks, Accordingly, we may state that the overall mSCTP handover latency is proportional to the RTT between two SCTP endpoints in the network.

B. Results for Scenario 2

Figure 6 shows the experimental result of Scenario 2, in which all the SCTP control and data packets for the association are captured.

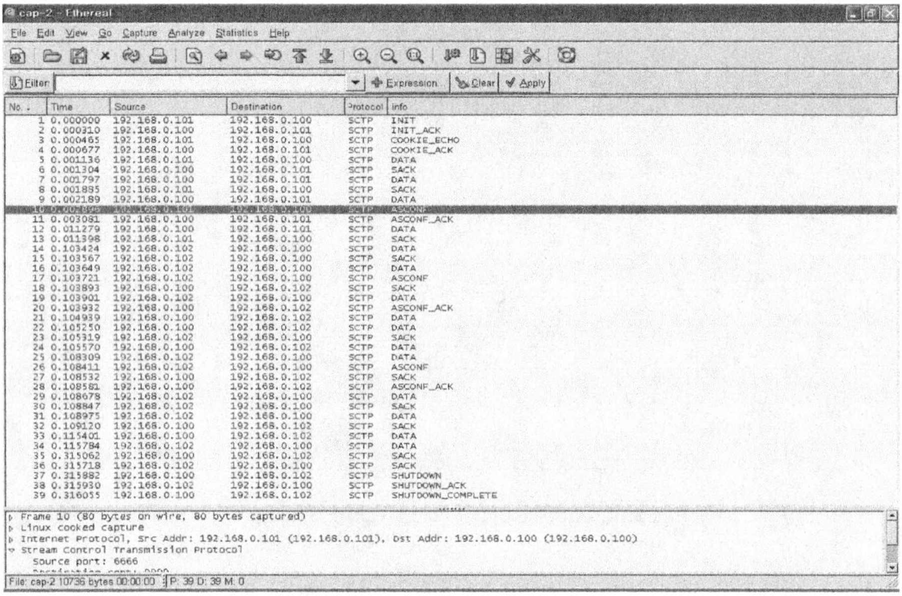

Fig. 6. Result of mSCTP Handover for Scenario 2

Figure 6 shows the same result as Figure 5, other than the following differences:

- Differently from Figure 6, the MT uses the new IP address as its source IP address of the DATA packets (see Packet 14). This is because the Link-Down of the old link occurs just after the Add-IP operation (see Packet 10 and 11).
- After Packet 17 for Primary-Change, all the packets for MT use only the new IP address (192.168.0.102).

From the figure, the mSCTP handover latency is measured as "0.104 – 0.011 = 0.093 (sec.) = 93 (ms)", which corresponds to the gap of the times recorded at Packet 12 (last data packet of old IP address) and 21 (first data packet of the new IP address). Scenario 2 requires the handover latency greater than Scenario 1 by 70 (ms), which is approximately equal to the time taken for processing the Link-Down event at MT (see Packets 13 and 14). If this processing time is relatively a small constant value, we can see that the mSCTP handover latency depends on the RTT between two SCTP end-points, as done in Scenario 1.

Another interesting point of Figure 6 is that FS cannot send any DATA packet to MT until the Primary-Change is performed (Packet 17), since the old IP address has already been deleted by the Link-Down event at the time of the Add-IP operation (see Packet 11 and 12). Accordingly, we can recommend in this case that the fast-moving MT should perform the Primary-Change operation as soon as possible (hopefully at the same time of the Add-IP operation). This will be helpful to further reduce the handover latency of mSCTP.

4 Conclusions

In this paper, we described a new handover scheme based on SCTP, which is called mSCTP. The mSCTP can be used for vertical handover between heterogeneous IP networks such as WLAN and 3G systems. The mSCTP can also be used together with Mobile IP for the sessions that require the location management.

We have described some experimental analysis of the mSCTP handover, which is performed over a Linux testbed network. In the testebd, we experimented the mSCTP handover for the Mobile Terminal that is dual-homed to two different network interfaces. From the experimental results, it is shown that the SCTP handover performance mainly depends on the RTT (round trip time) between two SCTP terminals, possibly with the handover latency of 1 second below.

For further study, the mSCTP handover experimentations need to be performed on the real large-scale networks, so as to analyze the handover performance in a more realistic manner.

Acknowledgement

This research was supported by the MIC, Korea, under the ITRC support program supervised by the IITA

References

1. Perkins, C., et al., "IP Mobility Support for IPv4", IETF RFC 3344, August 2002
2. Johnson, D., et al., "Mobility Support in IPv6", IETF RFC 3775, June 2004
3. Stewart R., et al., "Stream Control Transmission Protocol", IETF RFC 2960, October 2000
4. Stewart, R., et al., "Stream Control Transmission Protocol (SCTP) Dynamic Address Re-configuration", IETF Internet Draft, draft-ietf-tsvwg-addip-sctp-08.txt, June 2004
5. Chang M., et al., "A Transport Layer Mobility Support Mechanism", LNCS 3090, pp. 287 - 296, May 2004.
6. Chang M., et al., "Transport Layer Mobility Support Utilizing Link Signal Strength Information", IEICE Transactions on Communications, Vol. E87-B, No. 9, pp. 2548-2556, September 2004.
7. Network Simulator 2, Available from http://www.isi.edu/nsnam/ns/
8. ns-2 modules for SCTP, Available from http://www.cis.udel.edu/~iyengar/research/

9. Linux Kernel Archives, Available from http://www.kernel.org/
10. Linux Kernel SCTP Project, Available from http://lksctp.sourceforge.net/
11. Stewart, R., et al., "Sockets API Extensions for Stream Control Transmission Protocol", IETF Internet Draft, draft-ietf-tsvwg-sctpsocket-09.txt, September 2004
12. Ethereal, Available from http://www.ethereal.com/

Increasing TCP Capacity in Wireless Multihop Networks

Changhee Joo and Saewoong Bahk*

School of Electrical Engineering and Computer Science,
Seoul National University, Seoul, Korea

Abstract. It is reported in the literature that a TCP connection with small window size achieves high throughput in wireless multihop networks. In this paper, we claim that TCP can benefit more from delaying ACK rather than limiting the window size. Since the induced delay may result in lengthy transfer time for short connections, we propose an adaptive delayed ACK algorithm at the receiver to enhance TCP performance.

1 Introduction

As wireless networks become prevalent, there is an increasing demand of network connectivity in infrastructureless environments such as emergency situation. TCP is a natural choice as transport layer protocol because of its widespread use in the Internet. However, it is not clear that TCP works well in wireless multihop environments [1].

TCP provides a reliable service by using acknowledgement (ACK), which is returned by the receiver for each data packet. This two-way feature does not cause a serious problem in wired networks because most of links are full-duplex. In wireless networks, most nodes support half-duplex. The shared medium forces only a single transmission to be available at a time so that TCP ACKs consume network bandwidth and may cause collisions with data packets.

There are many efforts to improve TCP performance in wireless multihop networks. Since the shared feature of medium makes wireless environments unique, protocols used in wired networks may not adequate. Recently, it is pointed out that TCP fails to achieve its best performance even without mobility [1].

The delayed ACK option [2] can make performance improvement in wireless multihop networks [3,4,5]. While normal TCP receiver sends out an ACK for every packet, the option halves the amount of ACKs by sending out an ACK for every other packet, thus allowing less collision with data packets in wireless links and reducing the instability in TCP algorithms. For short connection, a large initial window option [6] is recommended to be used along together.

---

* This research was supported partially by the University IT Research Center Project and the ubiquitous Autonomic Computing and Network Project, Ministry of Information and Communication (MIC), in Korea.

S. Shimojo et al. (Eds.): HSI 2005, LNCS 3597, pp. 37–44, 2005.

Ack thinning is a generalized term of the delayed ACK option. It is used to boost TCP performance in asymmetric networks [7]. The receiver sends out an ACK for number of data packets, which is adjusted in a manner of AIMD based on information conveyed in additional TCP options. Altman *et al* also proposed dynamic delayed ACK, which changes the frequency of ACKs according to sequence number [5].

The remainder of the paper is organized as follows. We provide a generalized delayed ACK option model in section 2. In order to achieve high performance for both short and long file transfer, we propose an adaptive scheme delaying ACK in section 3. Evaluating our proposal through simulations in section 4, we conclude our paper in 5.

2   Generalized Delayed ACK Option

It is observed that TCP performance can be improved by the delayed ACK option where the receiver sends an ACK for every other received packet. In this paper, we generalize the delayed ACK by making the receiver delay the ACK according to the window size (simply *dack_wnd*), which is given by the number of packets that the receiver waits for before sending the ACK.

The receiver with *dack_wnd* = 1 works as the normal ACK, where the receiver sends an ACK for every incoming packet, and the receiver with *dack_wnd* = 2 as the conventional delayed ACK. The generalized delayed ACK is also equipped with a timer as the conventional delayed ACK and sends an ACK when the timer expires even if the number of received packets is less than *dack_wnd*. We compare the long-term TCP throughputs of the algorithm when *dack_wnd* and maximum window size (*max_wnd*) vary, which limit the congestion window at the sender.

From the TCP connections with varing *dack_wnd* over a single-hop topology, we obtain the long-term throughput as shown in Fig. 1. The results present that the longer the receiver delays the ACK, the more TCP throughput the sender obtains if it has *max_wnd* larger than *dack_wnd*. In case of *max_wnd* < *dack_wnd*, the receiver should wait for a lengthy timeout (set to 100 ms), which degrades TCP performance very much.

Fig. 2 shows the transfer time ratios of delayed ACK for various *dack_wnd*s to normal ACK according to file transfer size where *max_wnd* is fixed at 64. Through extensive simulations of transferring various sizes of files, we will observe that connections with smaller *dack_wnd* finish up earlier for the case of the file size of smaller than 320 packets, and connections with larger *dack_wnd* take advantage of the reduced number of ACKs for transferring large sized files.

The long-term TCP throughput in a single-hop connection can be simply obtained. Considering RTS-CTS-DATA-ACK exchange, we can obtain the long-term throughput as

$$Throughput = \frac{dack\_wnd \cdot S}{dack\_wnd \cdot T_{DATA} + T_{ACK}}$$

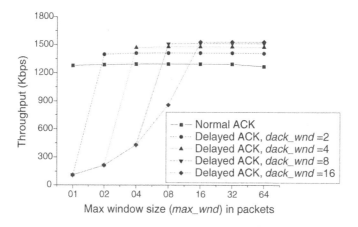

Fig. 1. Long-term TCP throughput with various *dack_wnd* and *max_wnd*

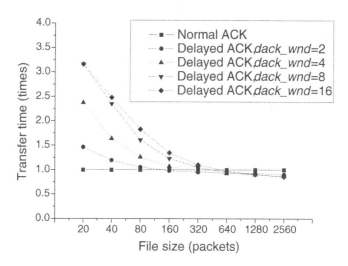

Fig. 2. Transfer time ratios of delayed ACK of various *dack_wnd* to normal ACK ($max\_wnd = 64$)

where S is the data packet size, T_{DATA} and T_{ACK} are the transmission times of TCP data packet and ACK including the contending period, DIFS, SIFS, and transmission of RTS, CTS, TCP data packet (or TCP ACK), and MAC ACK. Assuming 2 Mbps bandwidth and 1460 bytes of packet size, the long-term throughputs is 1.26 Mbps for normal ACK ($dack\_wnd=1$), and 1.39 Mbps for delayed ACK with $dack\_wnd=2$. This analysis results match well with the simulation results shown in Fig. 1. We can also obtain the maximum throughout in a single-hop connection. TCP can achieve up to 1.52 Mbps with $dack\_wnd$ of 13 since at most 13 transmissions are possible before the timeout of 100 ms occurs. More increase of *dack_wnd* does not bring forth further performance improvement.

3   Receiver-Oriented Adaptive Delaying

The delayed ACK option at the receiver can be accompanied by large initial window (LIW) option at the sender in [4]. The LIW option enables the sender to set the initial window larger than 1. It cures the problem of lengthy transfer time for small files by sending out more packets than *dack_wnd* at the start-up period. However, it requires synchronization between sender and receiver because the TCP with larger initial window often results in lower performance if the delayed ACK option is not used at the receiver [1].

We propose an alternative algorithm named adaptive delayed ACK (ADA). It changes *dack_wnd* in a manner of additive increase and multiplicative decrease (AIMD). It is receiver-oriented and does not require any modification at the sender.

The receiver delays the ACK until it receives *dack_wnd* packets from the sender. On receiving the *dack_wnd*-th packet, it increases *dack_wnd* by 1 and sends the ACK. Initially the receiver sets *dack_wnd* to 1, so it sends out the first ACK immediately.

Fig. 3 illustrates the packet exchanges between TCP sender and receiver at its start-up. The sender and the receiver are presented as solid vertical lines. A transmission of a data packet is presented by a solid arrow from left to right, and

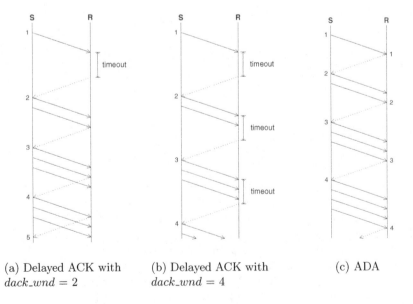

(a) Delayed ACK with *dack_wnd* = 2

(b) Delayed ACK with *dack_wnd* = 4

(c) ADA

Fig. 3. Packet exchanges at initial start-up

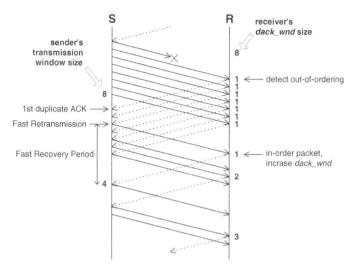

Fig. 4. Packet exchange of ADA after a packet retransmission

transmission of an ACK is presented by a dotted arrow in the reverse direction. The number at the beginning of solid arrow indicates the sender's transmission window size, and the number at the beginning of dotted arrow in (c) indicates $dack\_wnd$.

In case of $dack\_wnd = 2$, the receiver gets a packet and waits another before generating an ACK. However, the sender does not release more packets to network (before it gets an ACK) because the sender's window is only one. This deadlock state is resolved by the receiver's timer but the timeout period T inevitably makes a performance degradation. The timeout period presented in Fig. 3 is shortened to save space. For larger $dack\_wnd$, the performance is degraded seriously because there are multiple timeouts before the sender's window size grows more than $dack\_wnd$ as shown in Fig. 3 (b).

ADA avoids such timeouts by adjusting $dack\_wnd$. It removes the first timeout by initializing $dack\_wnd$ to 1. Afterward, it infers the sender's window size and sets $dack\_wnd$ accordingly. Fig. 3 (c) ensures its exact inference and successful packet exchanges without timeout.

Our algorithm uses a timer like in the delayed ACK option [2]. The timer expires when the receiver does not receive a packet for some time because it delays ACK too long due to the sender's congestion window or packet drops in the network. The timer starts when the receiver receives the first packet arrived after the receiver sent out an ACK. If the timeout period of T sec elapses, the receiver shrinks $dack\_wnd$ by a half and sends out the delayed ACK. The timer also prevents $dack\_wnd$ from being increased over the network capacity because it expires when the number of packets transmitted during T sec exceeds the capacity.

Upon unexpected events such as receiving a packet with PSH flag [8] or receiving an out-of-order packet, the receiver sets $dack\_wnd$ to 1 and sends an

ACK (or a duplicate ACK) immediately conforming to RFC 1122 [2]. Fig. 4 illustrates a typical scenario of packet exchange after a packet loss. When the receiver detects a packet out-of-ordering, it sends out an ACK with the highest sequence number that it has received in order, and set $dack\_wnd$ to 1. This speeds up the recovery of congestion window at the sender after a packet retransmission. The receiver can not increase $dack\_wnd$ until the missing packet is received. Finishing recovering the lost packet, the sender has a halved window size while the receiver opens $dack\_wnd$ from 1.

Since the ADA algorithm reduces the number of ACKs, the loss of an ACK may cause performance degradation. We reduce the impact of ACK loss by using another timer. This timer starts after ACK transmission and expires if the receiver does not receive any packet during T sec. Upon a timeout, the receiver retransmits the latest ACK. Since three duplicate ACKs create false Fast Recovery at the sender, the receiver should not generate more than two retransmissions for the same ACK. So, on the third timeout, the receiver sets $dack\_wnd$ to 1 and waits for the sender's retransmission.

4 Simulation

We evaluate ADA by measuring transfer time for single-hop and multihop TCP (Reno) connections. We use NS-2 [9] with IEEE 802.11 MAC in ad hoc mode. The transmission rate is 2 Mbps and RTS-CTS handshake is used. We compare the performances of normal ACK, delayed ACK and our ADA. Each result is an average of 10 simulation runs.

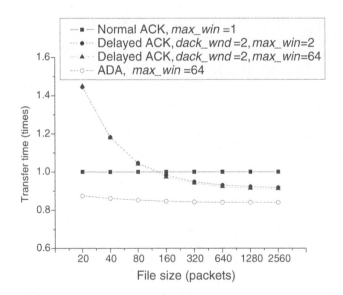

Fig. 5. Transfer time ratios of delayed ACK and ADA schemes to normal ACK

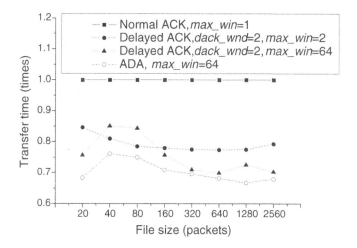

Fig. 6. Transfer time ratios of delayed ACK and ADA schemes to normal ACK in the 8-hop topology

Fig. 5 shows the transfer time ratios of various ACK schemes to the normal ACK scheme with $max\_wnd = 1$ according to the file size. When $dack\_wnd$ is fixed at 2, TCP achieves better throughput for large file transfers, but requires relatively long time for small file transfers. This is because the sender waits for an ACK after sending the first packet at the start-up. The ACK is sent out after a lengthy timeout at the receiver ($T = 100$ ms). When we increased max_wnd to 64 and $dack\_wnd$ to 16 for the delayed ACK, there was no performance improvement. ADA shows the best performance in all the cases. Its adaptive feature reduces the number of ACKs and avoids unnecessary timeout.

In multi-hop environments with the chain topology of 9 nodes, where nodes are separated by a distance of 200 ms, connections with larger max_wnd achieves higher throughput because they benefit from spatial bandwidth reuse. ADA outperforms the delayed ACK with $max\_wnd = 64$, but the improvement is not so remarkable as in the single-hop case.

5   Conclusion

TCP protocol achieves high long-term throughput by reducing the number of ACKs in wireless multi-hop networks but it suffers from a lengthy timeout for small file transfers. It was observed that the sender should have max_wnd larger than $dack\_wnd$ to reduce the transfer time. To avoid a lengthy timeout in transferring small files, we proposed the ADA algorithm that controls $dack\_wnd$ in a manner of AIMD. ADA is receiver-oriented and does not require any synchronization or modification at the sender. Through simulations, we showed its performance gain over the conventional delayed ACK scheme.

References

1. Z. Fu, P. Zerfos, H. Luo, S. Lu, L. Zhang, M. Gerla, *The Impact of Multihop Wireless Channel on TCP Throughput and Loss* Infocom, 2003.
2. R. Braden, *Requirements for Internet Hosts - Communication Layers*, RFC 1122, October 1989.
3. A. Kherani, R. Shorey, *Performance Improvement of TCP with Delayed ACKs in IEEE 802.11 Wireless LANs* WCNC, 2004.
4. S. Xu, T. Saadawi, *Performance of evaluation of TCP algorithms in multi-hop wireless networks*, Wireless communication and mobile computing 2 (1), 2002.
5. E. Altman, T. Jimenez, *Novel delayed ACK techniques for improving TCP perfomance in multihop wireless networks*, PWC, 2003.
6. M. Allman, S. Floyd, C. Partridge, *Increasing TCP's Initial Window*, RFC 2414, September 1998.
7. H. Balakrishnan, V. Padmanabhan, R. Katz, *The Effects of Asymmetry on TCP Performance*, ACM Mobicom, 1997.
8. W. Stevens, *TCP/IP Illustrated, Volume 1*, Addison Wesley, 1994.
9. The UCB/LBNL/VINT Network Simulator (NS), Available at "http://www.isi.edu/nsnam/ns/".

A Study on Scalable Bluetooth Piconet for Secure Ubiquitous

Dae-Hee Seo, Deok-Gyu Lee, and Im-Yeong Lee

Division of Information Technology Engineering, SoonChunHyang University,
#646, Eupnae-ri, Shinchang-myun, Asan-si, Coogchungnam-Do, 336-745,
Republic of Korea
{patima, hbrhcdbr, imylee}@sch.ac.kr

Abstract. Due to the changes in the wireless information environment, there has been an increased demand for various types of information. Accordingly, many wireless communication technologies have been studied and developed. In particular, studies on ubiquitous close distance communications are well underway. Lately, the focus has been on the Bluetooth technology due to its applicability in various environments. Applying Bluetooth connectivity to new environments such as ubiquitous or sensor networks requires finding new ways of using it. Thus, this research analyzed the vulnerability on the limited number of slaves in a piconet configuration through the current Bluetooth communication and proposed an expanded Bluetooth piconet formation method, regardless of the number of slaves inside the piconet even if it is not configured in a scatternet. In the proposed method, a security service was applied and the vulnerabilities of the current piconet configured as an expanded form of the current tree-shaped structure.

Keywords: Mobile systems, Bluetooth piconet, Group Management.

1 Introduction

Currently, mobile devices are widely used, and there are various studies regarding the communication channels between the layers of each device. These studies expect to overcome the constraints that the mobile devices should be located in a specified location or not. As a result, research on the interface in a wireless environment to enable the devices to communicate with each other led to the Bluetooth technology.

Bluetooth research started with the research of the communication group in Ericsson, which developed a wireless interface at low price and low power consumption.[1]

These studies were done in earnest with the inauguration of the Special Interest Group (SIG) in 1998 composed of Ericsson, Nokia, IBM, TOSHIBA, and Intel. Bluetooth is a wireless communication protocol for transmitting information to fixed or mobile devices, forming the piconet with two or more devices sharing a channel with a master in the center to be extended to a scatter net[2].

S. Shimojo et al. (Eds.): HSI 2005, LNCS 3597, pp. 45–56, 2005.
© Springer-Verlag Berlin Heidelberg 2005

Accordingly, Chapter 2 shows the basics of Bluetooth, and the security services presents the security requirements for forming an expanded type of piconet. Chapter 3 analyzes the possible weakness due to the limit of the number of slaves. Chapter 4 suggests the method for forming an expanded piconet in making Bluetooth communication, overcoming the weakness shown in the previous chapter. Chapter 5 presents the analysis and comparison between the existing method and the suggested method based on the security requirements suggested in Chapter 2. Chapter 6 presents the conclusion[1].

2 Mobile Network Technology Bluetooth

2.1 Overview of Bluetooth

Bluetooth is a compound word of 'blue' and 'tooth'. Its origin can be traced to the Viking Herald who unified the Scandinavian countries of Denmark and Norway. As the project name of Swedish company Ericsson, Bluetooth involved developing the technology that enables a wireless interface at low price and low power consumption.

The name remained unchanged to this day. Nevertheless, there were some attempts to change the project name. Some companies interested in Bluetooth formed an organization in May 1998 to pursue further research on wireless, near field communication. The organization tried to investigate the multiplex communication connected to the cellular net using cellular phones, which are connected to the existing cables. This organization is the first group regarding the subject and is known as the Special Interest Group (SIG)[3].

Various kinds of wireless, near field communication methods such as IrDA, IEEE802.11, and SWAP appeared before the advent of Bluetooth. Nonetheless, Bluetooth got more recognition than the other methods due to several reasons. For one, companies believe that worldwide sales are possible with mass production. Likewise, mass production gives the advantage of a low price, which induces synergistic effects resulting in lower cost of parts and consequently increased shipment. In a user's point of view, Bluetooth has the advantage due its easiness and effectiveness since it enables the wireless interface to a cellular phone or other devices at low power consumption [3-6].

2.2 Security Requirements in forming an Expanded Type of Piconet

Bluetooth is convenient because it can be applied to various types of environment. In particular, the availability of forming a small network as described in the previous paragraphs is one of the many advantages of Bluetooth.

Nevertheless, there are still problems and constraints in the application method to the new environment such as the Ubiquitous and sensor networks and the increasing

[1] This research was supported by the MIC(Ministry of Information and Communication), Korea, under the ITRC(Information Technology Research Center) support program supervised by the IITA(Institute of Information Technology Assessment).

number of mobile devices per person with the generalization of those devices. Accordingly, if the individual oriented piconet is formed, the restriction of the existing piconet is unavoidable. And a new method to complement this restriction is the forming the expanded type of piconet. The expanded piconet enables the formation of a piconet regardless of the number of slaves. Accordingly, it is a method of overcoming the restriction in the number of slaves in case of expanding the piconet to the scatter net. Hence, the following security requirements should be satisfied to form a safe and effective piconet that overcomes the restriction regardless of the number of slaves:

- Mutual authentication: In addition to the mutual authentication in the process of setting Bluetooth's initial security key lock, a safe mutual authentication process on the expanded piconet is required.

  ✓ Mutual authentication between masters: Mutual authentication between masters is divided into two, i.e., authentication in the same level and authentication in the lower level. It should be executed separately from the authentication in the process of setting the key in the existing Bluetooth communication.

  ✓ Mutual authentication between the master and slave: A new mobile device in the expanded piconet should engage the piconet in a safe process of mutual authentication in the expanded piconet.

- Confidentiality and integrity: To guarantee the confidentiality and integrity of the security requirements in the group communication process, various cryptograph algorithm and hash functions should be used.

- Key updating range: Considering the characteristics of mobile devices with frequent withdrawal and use of a group key with its updates, the key updating range should be restricted to the mobile device that is to withdraw from the current group

- Security of participants against seceders: Even if seceders occur during group communication, the security of the group participants should not be breached by the security weakness induced by the seceders.

- Effectiveness: Considering the restricted space of the wireless environment and the computing capacity, the effectiveness of the computation and communication volumes should be maintained.

3   Analysis of the Existing Method

a. Analysis of the Weakness in the Network of Bluetooth Communication

Bluetooth network is created for a special objective, and all the devices are connected to each other wirelessly. For individual devices, the distance between devices becomes an issue for receiving direct messages from other devices during the broadcasting of messages.

It has characteristics of movement when mobile devices move into and out of the communication area of other devices. It is a network for very special purposes regarding the characteristics of forming a network using Bluetooth technology and its structure is susceptible to attacks. Likewise, it requires a very complex security system [5-8].

These kinds of security issues for the Bluetooth network can be divided into the independence of systems, authorization and key management, and confidentiality and integrity.

b. Independence of Systems

Every device in the network formed by Bluetooth depends mutually on the messages broadcasted. At the same time, the methods are very weak against the Denial of Service (DoS). For example, any individual can attempt to intercept or tap the information broadcasted. Moreover, this individual can identify the sender transmitting messages in the network by transmitting incorrect information into the network. Hackers can track the sender who transmits messages in two networks by attacking the routing protocol. Likewise, the change in routing protocol can induce the change in topology. The Bluetooth devices change the power mode frequently when the devices are not active to reduce power consumption. A hacker can attack the power status of the devices to make them active, thereby requiring more power consumption which leads to power off eventually.

c. Authorization and Key Management

Authorization and key management is important in keeping the Bluetooth network safe. Strict authentication is required in an ad-hoc network to all possible types of attack, based on the technology of authentication and key management of a trusted third party.

d. Confidentiality and Integrity

Confidentiality and integrity are weak in the Bluetooth network. Confidentiality can be maintained using authentication and encryption. In wireless communication, hackers can acquire transmitted messages without encryption very easily. Confidentiality and integrity can be considered simultaneously.

4   The Proposed Scalable Bluetooth Piconet for Secure Ubiquitous

The method suggested here is a safe and effective communication method for complementing the weakness of the piconet formed by Bluetooth. It restricts the number of slaves in its Bluetooth application in wireless, near field communication to a new network environment. The suggested system consists of the objects of Bluetooth masters and Bluetooth slaves.

4.1   System Parameters

The following describes the system parameters of the key management method enabling free subscription and withdrawal of mobile devices in the Bluetooth environment.

$*$: (Bluetooth Master(M), Bluetooth Slave(S), Bluetooth slave which is to withdraw from the piconet (DEL))

P_j , Q_j : The arbitary public key generated by the piconet master; private key pair (one of the j number of public key pairs arbitrarily generated in piconet).

e , β , k , α , r : Pseudo random number

$H()$: Secure Hash Function

$E()$: Block cipher algorithm

n : System coefficient that center server exhibits

T_* : Time Stamp

BD_ADDR : 48bit Bluetooth address

$Connection\,\mathrm{Re}\,uqest$: Connection Request Message

MD_{state} : Mobile Device State

M_w, M_{res} : Mutual authentication message in piconet slave; the response message to the mutual authentication message

ID_* : Identifier with Master and Salve ($i = 1,2,....,n$)

AID_* : Middle value of Slave's

4.2 Protocol of the Suggested Method

a. Group Initialization

The Bluetooth piconet master performs the initialization step for piconet group communication by computing the unique ID list of each slave using the slaves in the current piconet and the public BD_ADDR of the established combination key and slaves.

$$(Combinationkey_{S_1} \oplus BD\_ADDR_{S_1}) = AID_{S_1}$$

$$H(AID_{S_1}) = ID_{S_1}$$

The total Slave ID list I is as follows:

$$I = (ID_{S_1}, ID_{S_2}, ID_{S_3},...., ID_{S_7})$$

b. Steps for the New Slave Device When Subscribing to a Group

When a new mobile device wants to subscribe to the existing piconet as a new entity, the corresponding slave updates I of the piconet master should be added after the authentication process and the generation of the initial security key to approve the mobile device as a new piconet entity.

c. Piconet Communication Steps

① Bluetooth master computes ID_{S_1} by generating I' excluding slave device ID in the whole ID list I for communication with mobile devices corresponding to ID_{S_1} in each slave in the same piconet

$$I' = (ID_2, ID_3,...., ID_7)$$
$$ID_{S_1}' = (H(I) - H(I'))$$

② Bluetooth master generates the pseudo-random number α_M and computes w_M as follows:

$$w_M = \alpha_M^{ID_{S_1}^{-1}} \bmod n$$

Based on these contents, the Bluetooth master of piconet transmits w_M and α_M to the slave (ID_{S_1}).

③ The Bluetooth slave (ID_{S_1}) receives w_M and α_M from the Bluetooth master in the piconet, computes w_{S_1}, and sends B_{S_1} and T_{S_1} to the Bluetooth master accordingly.

$$w_{S_1} = \alpha_M^{ID_{S_1}^{-1}} \bmod n$$

$$y_1 = ID_{S_1} * r_{S_1}$$

$$B_{S_1} = w_{S_1}^{y_1} \bmod n$$

④ Upon receiving B_{S_1} and T_{S_1} the master generates the arbitrary j number of the arbitrary group key pairs, selects the arbitrary group key pair (P_{S_1}, Q_{S_1}), and sends it to the corresponding slave after encryption with session key C_1.

$$C_1 = \alpha_M^{(r_{S_1} * AID_{S_1})} \bmod n$$

(Verification $B_{S_1} \bmod n = w_{S_1}^{y_1} \bmod n = (\alpha_M^{ID_{S_1}^{-1}})^{(ID_{S_1} * r_{S_1})} \bmod n = \alpha_M^{r_{S_1}} \bmod n$)

Following this process, the Bluetooth master executes the subscription steps by adding a Bluetooth slave to the corresponding piconet.

d. Piconet Withdrawal Steps
A mobile device that withdraws from a piconet sends messages, requiring withdrawal from the piconet to the corresponding piconet master device.

① A device intending to withdraw executes the withdrawal steps by computing V_{DEL} and sending V_{DEL} and T_{DEL} to the corresponding master.

$$V_{DEL} = E_{C_1}(H(AID_{DEL} \oplus Combinationkey_{DEL}))$$

②Upon receiving V_{DEL} and T_{DEL}, the Bluetooth master does the XOR operation and verifies the identity with the BD_ADDR_{DEL} conforming to the corresponding ID.

$$(CombinationKey_{DEL} \oplus AID_{DEL}) = BD\_ADDR_{DEL}$$

$$H(CombinationKey_{DEL} \oplus AID_{DEL}) \equiv H(BD\_ADDR_{DEL})$$

Piconet withdrawal service is accomplished by deleting the corresponding ID of the Bluetooth slave corresponding to the generated BD_ADDR from the whole ID list I.

e. Initial Setting Steps for the Expanded Piconet
It is an initial step for expanding the piconet to accept the 8th valid mobile device for a piconet when the maximum number of slaves for the piconet is set to 7, and the 8th valid mobile device requests for connection to the piconet.

① The 8th valid mobile device sends the connection request message and its P_{S_8} to the corresponding master.

② Upon receiving the connection request, the piconet master checks the P_{S_8} and the connection request message of the 8th valid mobile device. It then sends the broadcasted message requesting for the status of its piconet slave (power status, computing performance, memory).

③ Upon receiving the broadcasted message, the corresponding piconet slaves send the required messages of the power status and computing performance and memory as P_*, V_* to the piconet master.

$$V_* = E_{C_*}(MD_{state} \| T_*)$$

④ Upon receiving the information from the piconet slaves, the piconet master compares each information and selects a mobile device with the highest power and computing performance and memory. At the same time, it requests for communication with the 8th mobile device of the selected one in forming a lower piconet.

$$I' = (ID_{S_1} \| ID_{S_2} \| ID_{S_4} \|,...., \| ID_{S_7})$$
$$ID_3' = (H(I) - H(I'))$$
$$V_M = E_{C_{S_3}}(ID_{S_3} \oplus \alpha_M)$$

f. Steps for Establishing the Subordinate Piconet

The upper piconet slave that received the communication request in forming the lower piconet from the upper piconet master executes the initial setting up steps for the piconet and establishes communication with the 8th mobile device.

① The slave assigned to the master device of the piconet executes the authentication process by following the initial security key generation process with the 8th mobile device. It generates I_1 as the master of the expanded piconet master and adds it to accept the new mobile device as its own piconet entity.

$$I_1 = (ID_{S_3} \| ID_{S_8})$$

② The communication inside the piconet in forming the lower piconet repeats steps b to d.

g. Communication Between the Upper Master and Lower Master-1

If the communication between the highest master A and the lower master B (= slave 3) in the expanded piconet is requested, the following steps are required for the initialization of the security communication service:

① The lower master B selects a random number k_{S_3} and transmits it to the highest master A.

② The highest master A receives the random number k_{S_3}, computes X, and sends the following to the lower master. ($\beta_3 \in \{0,1,2\}$)

$$b = H(ID_{S_3} \oplus \beta_{S_3})$$
$$X = k_{S_3}^{\beta_{S_3}} g^b \bmod n$$

- X can have values of $g^b, k_{S_3} g^b, k_{S_3}^2 g^b$ according to the value of β.

③ The highest master sends b to the lower master to check the confidential information. The lower master computes $g^b \bmod n$, and β_3 becomes 0 if the computed value is X. Otherwise, it should be checked whether the value $g^b \bmod n$ multiplied by k_{S_3} is X or the value $g^b \bmod n$ multiplied by $k_{S_3}^2$ is X to identify the value of b.

The Bluetooth security service will be selected according to each s value.

- Security service 1($k_{S_3}{}^0$): Requests for authorization and authentication. Automatic access is allowed only from reliable devices. For unreliable devices, manual authorization is required.
- Security service 2($k_{S_3}{}^1$): Requests for authentication only. Access to the application is allowed after following the authentication process. Authorization is not required.
- Security service 3($k_{S_3}{}^2$): Open to all devices. No authentication is required and access is automatically allowed. (For the initial connection, security service 3 applies. If there are continuous connection requests, however, the supplementary service of the automatic conversion into security service 1 can be supplied).

The communication initialization process between the upper master and the lower master is executed through these steps.

h. Authentication for Communication Between Lower Masters in the Same Level

For the communication between lower masters in the same level, they should follow the verification process of the upper master. The lower master of the sender requesting for communication is designated as A, and the lower master of the receiver as B (= slave 3 of the highest master piconet).

① The lower master A computes v_{S_3} using the α_M transmitted confidentially during the communication process with the highest master in step e.

$$v_{S_3} = \alpha_M^2 \bmod n$$

A lower master calculates the following and sends X_{S_3} to the highest master.

$$X_{S_3} = r_{S_3}^2 \bmod n$$

② The highest master generates the k-bit arbitrary number $e_i (e_i = (0,1), i = (1,\ldots,k))$ and sends it to the lower master A.

③ The lower master A computes Y_{S_3} and sends it to the lower master B.

$$Y_{S_3} = r_{S_3} \sum_{i=1}^{k} \alpha_{S_3}^{e_i} \bmod n$$

④ The lower master B transmits Y to the highest master with its own ID^{-1}.

⑤ In executing the verification process, the highest master computes the following:

$$Y_{S_3}^2 = X_{S_3} \sum_{i=1}^{k} v_{S_3}^{e_i} \bmod n$$

If the execution process is correct, the result is transmitted to the lower master.

The lower master should repeat this process. The mutual authentication process through the highest master is executed upon completion of the protocol execution.

i. Communication Between the Mobile Devices in the Expanded Piconet in the Same Level (slave-slave)

[Detailed step 1] Mutual authentication process

① The mobile slave 1 in the same level sends the V_{S1} required for the secure communication with the slave 2, mutual authentication message M_{S_1} and Time stamp T_1 to the slave 2 device.

$$V_{S_1} = E_{c_1}(g^{r_{I_1}})$$
$$X_1 = H(M_W \parallel g^{r_{s_1}}) \bmod n$$

② The slave device 2 performs the decryption for the received V_{S1} with its own individual key and computes the following for verifying the integrity and confidentiality followed by the mutual authentication initialization process with the slave 1.

$$X_1' = H(M_W \parallel g^{r_{s_1}}) \bmod n$$

If $X_w = X_w'$, the response message M_{res} in the authentication message M_W of the slave 1 is generated and computed by sending V_{S2}, X_2, T_2 to the slave 1.

$$V_{S_2} = E_{C_1}((M_{res} \parallel g^{r_{s_2}})$$
$$X_2 = H(M_{res} \parallel g^{r_{s_2}}) \bmod n$$

③ The slave 1 performs the decryption for the encrypted V_{S2} transmitted by slave 2 using its own individual key to verify its confidentiality and verifies the integrity and authentication data after generating X_2' and comparing it with the transmitted X_2.

[Detailed step 2] Session key setting phase

The following are the steps for the slave 1 and slave 2 to generate the session key after executing the initial steps for mutual authentication:

① The slave 1 sends Z_{S1}, information for the session key generation for the encrypted communication with the slave 2, $Cert_1$ as the public key certification, and time stamp T_1 to the slave 2.

$$Z_{S_1} = H(r_{S_1} \oplus T_1)$$

② The slave 2 checks the certification of the public key transmitted from slave 1 and saves Z_{S1} and T_1 temporarily. The slave 2 then sends Z_{S2}, information for session key generation, $Cert_2$ as the public key certification of the slave 2, and time stamp T_2 to the slave 1.

$$Z_{S_2} = H(r_{S_2} \oplus T_2)$$

③ The slave 1 checks the $Cert_S$ of the slave 2 from the transmitted value. If it is found to be valid, then the slave 1 and slave 2 will generate the session key K as follows:

$$K = H(Z_{S_1} \oplus g^{r_{S_1}} \parallel Z_{S_2} \oplus g^{r_{S_2}})$$

5 Analysis of the Suggested Method

The suggested method has the following security characteristics:

- Mutual Authentication: In the suggested method, key size inside the piconet is $k|n|$. Accordingly, safety can be maintained as long as the key size is not increased too much. Hence, an encryption algorithm such as the Elliptic Curve Crypto System with an effective key size is expected to be applied. Likewise, the issue that factorization in prime factors is difficult is tantamount to saying that the (P,V) is safe for mutual authentication of the suggested method.

- Confidentiality and integrity: The mutual confidentiality in the session key generation in forming the piconet can be maintained through the verification process ($B_{S_1} \bmod n = w_{S_1}^{y_i} \bmod n = (\alpha_M^{ID_{S_1}^{-1}})^{(ID_{S_1}*r_{S_1})} \bmod n = \alpha_M^{r_{S_1}} \bmod n$). In other words, the confidentiality based on the problem of discrete algebra using the inverse power of its own ID and the data transmission integrity for the messages excluding the broadcasted ones is supplied by the hash function.

- Key updating range: Considering the characteristics of mobile devices with frequent withdrawal and use of a group key with its updates, the key updating range should be restricted to the mobile device that is to withdraw from the current group. In this suggested method, if the update of the group key occurs in the group environment, continuous communication with other devices is enabled by deleting the ID of the corresponding devices from the registered ID list of the piconet master. The updating range is minimized by introducing the updating method after deleting the corresponding mobile devices, which withdraw the key updating range using the combination key using ($Combination key_{DEL} \oplus AID_{DEL}) = BD\_ADDR_{DEL}$ from the ID list.

- Security of participants against seceders: Since seceders from the piconet communication cannot compute ID^{-1} in generation of the session key C for every session, it cannot compute the corresponding session key. Hence, even if seceders occur, security weakness is not revealed when communicating with the current participants.

- System independence for guaranteeing safety against any attack on power consumption: The suggested method can guarantee safety against any attack on power consumption, which is anticipated in the Bluetooth network. Specifically, even if the hacker's device requests for a connection using continuous power consumption, it can be protected by registering the BD_ADDR of the unauthenticated mobile devices in the process of security service setting with Bit Comment method and shutting it out early.

- Effectiveness: For the wireless method, the suggested method keeps the exponential computation to the minimum and tries to increase the effectiveness based on the hash function and XOR computation.

Table 1 compares the existing method and the proposed method, and shows the analysis results.

Table 1. Analysis of the proposed scheme

Security Requirements		Bluetooth spec v1.1	Proposed scher
Mutual Authentication	*Master and Mater*	Δ	O
	Master and Slave	Δ	O
Confidentiality and integrity	*Transfer Data*	Δ	O
	Store Data	Δ	O
Key updating range		×	O
Security of participants against seceder		×	O
System independence for guaranteeing safety against any attack on power consumption		×	O
Effectiveness		Δ	Δ

[× : Danger, Δ : Vulnerabilities, O : Secure]

6 Conclusion

For the Ubiquitous as the next generation IT technology, Bluetooth as a wireless near field communication technology is applied as a new technology element and studied extensively. To enable Bluetooth to complement the weakness in the beginning and encourage a new way of adoption, studies on the method of complementing the weakness of the Bluetooth technology is essential.

Accordingly, this paper suggested a new type of method after analyzing the weakness of the existing Bluetooth technology. It defines a piconet as a new group if a new network is formed and extended in the piconet even though it is not expanded to the scatter net. In addition, in case a safe configuration is required, an effective and safe method is described by showing the new contents of the subscription, withdrawal, and update. It is expected that various types of studies on safety issues should be continued particularly on the implementation and application of the methods suggested in this paper and the different types of group safety requirements in the future.

References

[1] http://www.bluetooth.com (Bluetooth White Paper)
[2] http://www.bluetooth.or.kr (Bluetooth Sepcification v1.1)
[3] http://www.niksula.cs.hut.fi/~jiitv/bluesec.html (Juha T.Vainio, "Bluetooth Security", jssmd 2000)

[4] jakobsson, Markus and Wetzel, Sussane. "Security Weaknesses in Bluetooth". http://www.bell-labs.com/user/markusj/bluetooth.pdf
[5] "Bluetooth Wireless Technology bridging the gap between computing and communication" http://www.intel.com/mobile/bluetooth/index.htm (February 18, 2001)
[6] Sutherland, Ed. "Despite the Hype, Bluetooth has Security Issues that cannot be ignored". November 28, 2000. http://www.mcommercetimes.com/Technology/41 (February 19 2001)
[7] Nechvatal. J, Elaine. B, Donna. D, Morris. D, James. F, Edward. R, "Status report on the first round of the development of the advanced encryption standard." Computer Security Division Information Technology Laboratory, National Institute of Standards and Technology, Aug., 1999.
[8] Dae-Hee Seo, Im-Yeong Lee, Dong-Ik Oh and Doo-Soon Park, "Bluetooth piconet using non-anonymous group key", Euraisa-ICT 2002, 2002.

A Mobile Phone Malicious Software Detection Model with Behavior Checker

Teck Sung Yap and Hong Tat Ewe

Faculty of Information Technology,
Multimedia University, Malaysia

Abstract. There have been cases reported for the new threats from mobile phone technologies and it has raised the awareness among the technology and antivirus vendors. Malicious programs such as Viruses, Trojan, and Worms have been created and targeted at mobile phone. This paper discusses the possible attacking model on mobile phone adapted from malicious attack on computer. It also presents the types of attack and appropriate solution model for mobile phone. A prototype of the simulation of malicious software and detection software on mobile devices is developed and the results of applying this approach to simulated malicious software and detection software on mobile device are also presented.

1 Introduction

Computer viruses are well-known and dangerous risks to today's corporate computer environment. Related threats include other forms of destructive programs such as network worm, Trojan horse, Bacteria, Logic Bomb, Password Catcher, Trapdoors and war. Collectively, they are sometimes referred to as malicious program. Loss of data and crashed email servers are the main elements left in the wake of any virus attack [1], [2].

Another field, which could be affected by malicious program, is mobile phones. Incredibly fast development of wireless technology will soon turn them from an ordinary tool of voice transaction into a universal mobile communications portal with the rest of the world. Mobile phones will be powered with all features of modern PCs connected to the Internet. They will be equipped with operating system, text editors, spreadsheet editors and database processors similar to modern ones. Finally, users will have the ability to exchange with executable files. As exactly as it is with PCs, some of them may contain malicious programs [3], [4]. From previous research carried out by Gupta, V., & Gupta, S. [5], new wireless technology has opened up new exciting opportunities in the mobile e-commerce market such as financial transactions and online purchasing, with sensitive data transfer using mobile phones, thus security is one of the most important issues to be considered on this new service.

Viruses have been created to exploit vulnerabilities on mobile devices. The first mobile phone virus, a worm named Cabir, running on Symbian OS mobile phones, was discovered on 14th June 2004. Although this virus have not spread wildly, and are only a minor threat, they clearly demonstrate that mobile devices have become a

S. Shimojo et al. (Eds.): HSI 2005, LNCS 3597, pp. 57–65, 2005.

target for virus writers [6]. Subsequently, the finding of security flaws in Bluetooth enabled devices has explored the growing concern over the vulnerability of mobile phones. Bluejacking and bluesnarfing are the two forms of new intrusion. Bluejacking is a technique of sending anonymous messages to Bluetooth enabled device and bluesnarfing allows attackers to hack in and download data stored in mobile phones such as contact details and diary entries without leaving any trace [7].

The experts have warned that when mobile phones become more intelligent and powerful, the risk of mobile virus infecting mobile phones increases [3], [4], [8]. The development of standard technologies in mobile networks and the ability to constantly connect to the Internet, offer many Internet-based functionalities and services. It is anticipated that by 2005, mobile networks will be hit by a malicious program costing approximately $471 million for every five million users affected [9].

This paper discusses the potential threats of mobile phone and proposes an appropriate solution against malicious attack. It discusses the existing mobile phone threats including potential malicious attacks and suggests a solution model against the attacks. It also demonstrates the ease that certain types of malware (malicious software) can be implemented on a mobile phone and a proof-of-concept solution program is presented.

2 Present Mobile Phone Threats

The security challenges in the mobile environment are similar to the problems we have encountered in the PC world. Open platforms are becoming popular in smartphones, for example the Symbian operating system is used in more than 20 million mobile phones at the moment. Mobile phones are vulnerable to new forms of attack as they become more powerful in their capabilities.

Virus creators also exploit the vulnerabilities of Bluetooth enabled devices that could lead to explore others' personal data. Hacker can steal confidential data and retrieve the complete memory contents of the mobile phone including pictures and text messages. Bluetooth enabled mobile phones are easier to target because the system are designed to accept external connections from simple electronic devices. Bluejacking and Bluesnarfing are just 2 types of attacks on Bluetooth wireless technology.

Bluejacking is a technique of sending anonymous messages to other Bluetooth enabled device and receiving authentication response. The system becomes vulnerable as soon as the information exchange succeeds and all the data on the target device become available to the originator. On the other hand, bluesnarfing is an act of stealing and downloading data such as telephone number by hacker without alerting the owner of the target device. The undetected attack is affecting a number of popular models of mobile phones manufactured by Ericsson and Nokia.

In June 2004, the world's first mobile worm called "cabir" has been discovered. The worm was developed by an international group of hackers and was anonymously sent to experts in various countries. It replicates on the Symbian operating system used in several models of mobile phones made by Nokia, Siemens and Ericsson. It shortens the device's battery life by constantly scanning for other Bluetooth enabled devices. Although the worm will not damage a phone or its software, it is anticipated that more similar or worse threats are just waiting to emerge.

3   Potential Mobile Phone Threats

To discover new threats to mobile phones, we should mirror the development of malware (malicious software) on computer, which can duplicate attacking model for mobile phones technologies. It is likely that we will also see new kinds of attacks: malicious program in games, screensavers and other applications, resulting in false billing, unwanted disclosure of stored information, and deleted or stolen user data.

3.1   Trojan

The primary concern of malicious attack is from Trojan applications. Nowadays, it is very common to find a computer Trojan that transmits spam emails to Internet user [10]. This will interrupt network performance and create lots of inconvenient issues to user, but generally involves no direct cost to the user. However, a similar Trojan on a phone could impose a heavy financial penalty on the consumer. In next section, it shows a Trojan application that sends SMS messages without any notification. These messages could be used to spam other users at random, or could be targeted at users stored in the phonebook. Such Trojans could be further developed, again requiring little programming effort, to send their messages to reverse billed numbers, generating revenue for the developers. For example, an application that sends messages at a rate of $1/sms, if the infected application runs for an average of 100 SMS/day, it would cost user $100/day. Consumers will only receive mobile billing after 30 days before the mobile owner realizes that his phone has been infected by malicious program.

3.2   Worm

The second area of attack is to develop a self-replicating mobile application. This type of malicious program can be developed from a Trojan by attaching a copy of itself to the MMS messages. For such viruses to work, interaction with the message recipient is required. But one thing for sure is that MMS message service does not allow any application file to attach with it for this moment [10].

3.3   Virus

Virus is the most destructive program designed to damage files or otherwise interfere with the mobile phone's operation. Similar attacks can be developed for other nefarious reasons, such as copying the contents of the phone's address book and sending them elsewhere, corrupting or deleting the numbers in the address book, blocking incoming call, and a whole host of other denial of service attacks [10].

4   Developing a Simple Mobile Phone Attack

For this section, we are not going to elaborate how to develop all of the malware application described in the previous section, but will outline the development of a simple Trojan implemented for the Symbian operating system, as an example of the ease with which such a form of malware can be developed. This application consists of a simple graphic user interface with a Trojan embedded within the code that sends an SMS to the first contact number in the phonebook when the function has been executed.

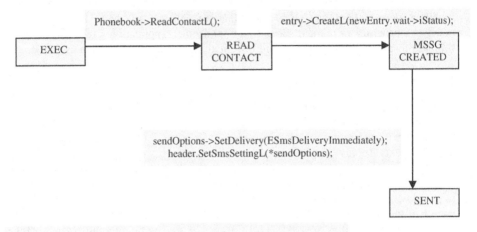

Diagram 1. Malware attack model

Diagram 1 is a pictorial representation of malware's behavior and attack model on Symbian operating system. When the Trojan application has been executed, "EXEC", it will retrieve the first contact from phonebook, "READ CONTACT", and create a SMS message entry for it, "MSSG CREATED". This message will be scheduled to send out for the contact owner.

Fig. 1. Malware interface

Fig. 2. SMS message

Figure 1 and 2 illustrate the Trojan application interface and the sent message as it appears in the Sent Message folder after it has been scheduled to send out.

This application can hide behind any program or software, when it has been triggered, similar malicious activity will happen. As discussed in previous section, a more malicious attack is the one that continually sends messages without user acknowledgment; which will bring high financial cost to the user.

5   Proposed Solution Against Mobile Phone Attack

The security issue about mobile phones' threats has awakened the awareness of security software provider and also the mobile phone manufacturer. At present, at least three software companies have released personal security software for emerging smartphones, which are exposed to the attack of a new wave of phone viruses. F-Secure is one such firm, selling antivirus and encryption software for smartphone operating systems made by Palm, Microsoft and the Symbian platform common in Europe.

5.1   Antivirus Techniques

In order to propose a good solution for mobile phone attack, we should examine how the current computer antivirus software works. We'll start with some common antivirus techniques and find an appropriate solution for this case. Three different antivirus techniques that are used to locate and eliminate viruses will be discussed. These include scanning, behavior checking and integrity checking. Basically, the scanner searches for specific code, which is believed to indicate the presence of a virus, behavior checkers look for programs that do things that viruses normally do and integrity checkers monitor for changes in files [10].

Scanning. Scanning for viruses is the oldest and most popular method for locating viruses. Back in the late 80's, when there were only a few viruses floating around, writing a scanner was fairly easy. Today, with thousands of viruses and many new ones being written every year, keeping scanner up to date is a major task. For this reason, many professional computer security scanners are obsolete and not useful. However, scanners have important advantages over other type of virus protections as they allow one to catch a virus before it ever executes in your computer [10].

Behavior Checker. Behavior checkers watch your computer for virus-like activity, and alert you when it takes place. Typically, a behavior checker is a memory resident program that a user loads in the AUTOEXEC.BAT file and then resides in the background looking for unusual behavior [10].

Integrity Checker. Typically, an integrity checker will build a log that contains the names of all the files on a computer and some type of characterization of those files. That characterization may consist of basic data like the file size and date/time stamp, as well as a checksum. Each time the user runs the integrity checker; it examines each file on the system and compares it with the characterization it made earlier [10].

5.2   Proposed Solution

In this paper, behavior checker will be the proposed technique to apply in the mobile phone platform where it can detect malicious activities appeared in the system. Over the years, this technique has evolved when antivirus vendors moved their direction into behavior checker technique to overcome the limitation of current antivirus software [11]. Behavior checker does not require virus pattern for detection but it monitors activities or behavior of application running in the system. Misuse detection method will be used for the above-mentioned solution where it detects attacks as instances of attack behavior [12], [13]. This approach can detect known attacks accurately and generate low false alarm rate. So, misuse detection needs to package with a list of known attack behaviors in a particular system. This method is efficient because mobile phone features are quite limited and it is easy to compile a potential attack behavior list for detection purpose.

We will present a proof-of concept solution program based on the malware behavior created in previous section. Both the program will be tested in Nokia Mobile Phone running Symbian operating system. Symbian OS uses message type modules (MTM) to define message types. Each MTM is composed of four classes that are used as base classes for specific message handling implementation. Whenever any application wants to use any of the messaging functionality it needs to create a session with the message server. A detector application can observe all the sessions that have been created with the message server and then monitor all the message events that take place in a session.

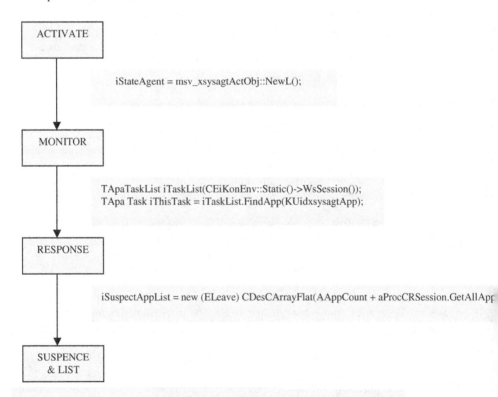

Diagram 2. Simplified Malware Detection Model

Diagram 2 is a pictorial representation of detection model for proposed solution for mobile phone. When detector application has been activated, "ACTIVATE", the detector engine will be started and sits behind the system to monitor activities within the message server, "MONITOR". The detector application is notified of every event that takes place within the session. The message event of interest is "EmsvEntryCreated", which is used to create new entry in any of the folders such as the Inbox, Outbox and Sent Items. Whenever "EmsvEntryCreated" events are inherited by unauthorized program and detected by the detector, "RESPONSE", the activity session will be suspended and the user will be alerted with a list of suspected malware, "SUSPEND & LIST". It shows that when the event is misused by any application, the solution should be able to provide fast response on it.

In Figures 3 and 4, it shows the application interface of detector engine and a list of suspected malicious programs for user further actions.

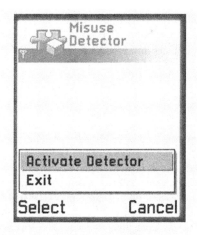

Fig. 3. Misuse Detector   **Fig. 4.** Suspected Application List

Detection Specification. This proof-of-concept program has shown the detection concept based on specific attack behaviors to monitor all malicious activities within the message server. Thus, we can detect all the malicious activities occurred. The attack behaviors for this program are:

− monitor any application using message server service without user authorization
− monitor "EmsvEntryCreated" event within message server sessions

Any program with this attack behavior will be suspended for further action. This solution has proven to provide an accurate detection to any malicious program, which tends to send SMS without notification. This solution model can be extended to monitor a sequence of events within a session and it can provide a more comprehensive detection engine for mobile phone system.

6 Conclusion

Security impact is an important issue to mobile phone technology in the near future. As mobile devices continue to become more prevalent and packed with greater processing power and wireless capabilities, they will become a more enticing target of choice for virus creators.

This paper has demonstrated the ease with which malware application can be developed and discussed potential threats on mobile phone. The Trojan application implemented for Symbian operating system shows its destructive action by sending anonymous SMS. From the experiment, the SMS is successfully sent and no security protection exists for such malicious activities.

This paper has proposed an appropriate security solution model on mobile phone for future security development. Misuse detection method based on behavior checker technique has been applied to a solution program to detect above-mentioned Trojan application. This solution has proven to provide an accurate detection to any malicious program, which tends to send SMS without notification. Based on a very similar solution model, we can add more modules, which help in tracking other malicious activity related to the file-system, the contacts database and even the phone module.

References

1. Davis, R. "Exploring computer viruses", Aerospace Computer Security Applications Conference, Fourth, Pages: 7/11, 12-16 Dec. 1988
2. Slade, R. (1996). Guide to computer viruses (2nd ed.). New York: Springer-Verlag.
3. Jamaluddin, J.; Zotou, N.; Coulton, P., "Mobile phone vulnerabilities: a new generation of malware," Consumer Electronics, 2004 IEEE International Symposium Pages:199 - 202, Sept. 1-3, 2004
4. Dagon, D.; Martin, T.; Starner, T., "Mobile Phones as Computing Devices: The Viruses are Coming!", Pervasive Computing, IEEE , Volume: 3 , Issue: 4, Pages:11 - 15, Oct-Dec 2004
5. Gupta, V., & Gupta, S., "Securing the wireless internet", IEEE Communication Magazine, Vol 39, No.12, 2001, pp 68-74
6. eFinland (1 Nov 2004). Preparing for Mobile Phone Viruses [Online] Available: http://www.e.finland.fi/netcomm/news/showarticle.asp?intNWSAID=29431 [2004, November 1]
7. BluejackQ (No Date). What is Bluejacking [Online]. Available: http://www.bluejackq.com/what-is-bluejacking.shtml
8. BBC News World Edition. "Mobile Virus Threat Looms Large" [Online] Available: http://news.bbc.co.uk/2/hi/technology/2690253.stm
9. Belson, Ken. "A Brand New Worry: Mobile Phone Viruses", International Herald Tribune: The IHT Online Available: http://www.iht.com/cgibin/generic.cgi?template=articleprint.tmplh&ArticleID=119373
10. Mark A. Ludwig (1995). Black Book of Computer Viruses. American Eagle Publication, Inc.
11. Ellen, M.(2002, February 1). Behavior blocking repels new viruses [Online] Available: http://www.nwfusion.com/news/2002/0128antivirus.html

12. D. Denning, "An Intrusion-Detection Model," IEEE Transactions on Software Engineering 13(2), pp. 222-232 (Feb. 1987)
13. H. Teng, K. Chen, and S. Lu, "Adaptive Real-Time Anomaly Detection Using Inductively Generated Sequential Patterns," Proceedings of the 1990 IEEE Symposium on Research in Security and Privacy, pp. 278-284 (May 1990)

Mobile Password System for Enhancing Usability-Guaranteed Security in Mobile Phone Banking

SangJun Lee[1] and SeungBae Park[2]

[1] Department of Internet Information Communication, Shingyeong University,
1485 Namyang-dong, Hwaseong-si, Gyeonggi-do, Korea
aura88@empal.com
[2] Department of Computer Science, Chodang University, 419 SungnamLi, MuanEup,
MuanGun, JeonlanamDo, Korea
sbpark@chodang.ac.kr

Abstract. To use mobile phone banking, we have to input personal identification number, account password and security card number. When it comes to the time of using wireless public key infrastructure practically, it will be equipped with the four-stage password input system by adding the certificate password. In this paper, we introduce DAS4M(Dynamic Authentication System for Mobile phone user) password system where the password could prevent from being exposed to other people during inputting. To discuss and simulate the validity of the proposed system, we develop a mobile application which is operable on the WIPI mobile platforms. The proposed system enhances the exposure rate of the password compared to the incumbent mobile phone banking password input system up to more than 84 times. Moreover, through the experiment with the usability which has the tradeoff relationship with the password security in terms of input time, error rate and user response, we can observe that it does not make a big difference as a result.

1 Introduction

Today with mobile phones, we can make a call, surf the Internet, take the photo and listen to the music. In addition, we can bring the bank in it online. The mobile banking, which offers all services in a bank, makes it possible anytime anywhere to deal with all services such as banking service, credit card, transportation card and so on. Especially as a result, we can expect that the relationship between bank industry and telecommunications industry will become mutual cooperative rather than competitive; the matching infrastructure of mobile phone banking through the e-commerce and the popularized mobile device will be implemented; moreover, as developmental condition of the new business model has enhanced more and more, the popularization of mobile phone banking is expected [1].

Even for using the PC banking which can be used most conveniently so far, we have to equip the Internet-connected PC and also store the authentication in the PC or the external memory. After installing the authentication into the PC, only if we can correctly input the authentication password, account password, transfer password and security card password, we can eventually use the PC banking. Even if we prepare

S. Shimojo et al. (Eds.): HSI 2005, LNCS 3597, pp. 66–74, 2005.

and finish the long works for personal security, there are still many problems relating to the security, and due to the authentication, using the dedicated PC makes it more inconvenient.

Unlike the incumbent PC banking which requires the knowledge of the PC and the Internet, the mobile banking where all of the banking serviced can be provided by making a call with the hot keys. In order to use the mobile phone banking, most of all we have to purchase the mobile phone. On its back side, we have to insert a banking IC chip, a hardware lock equipment. The banking IC chip is a smart card which stores all of the customer's personal information and account information and can not be duplicated. To use the mobile phone banking, we must input the three sorts of password that are the PIN(Personal Identification Number), banking account password and security card password of the banking IC chip. In the near future, if the WPKI(Wireless PKI) becomes available, the four stages of password will be employed. Despite the drastic forty-year-long development of IT technology, the password input system has not been changed that much.

By the customer survey of mobile banking users, their most urgent need is the enhancement of personal information protection(63.1%)[2]. It is the password for protecting the personal information that is regarded as the most important personal information. In this paper, we define a new scheme for the authentication systems called DAS4M(Dynamic Authentication System for Mobile phone user) password system. DAS4M is a password system which can block the leakage of the personal information or password to the other people during inputting. We propose a system which has been developed on the WIPI platform with the mobile JAVA application and analyze its security and usability.

This paper is organized as follows. In Section 2, we define the kinds of the authentication system including the password method and the kinds of security attacks. The DAS4M is defined in Section 3. We demonstrate implementation of DAS4M on WIPI platform and analyze them in Section 4. Finally, in Section 5, we make a conclusion.

2 Authentication System

The password in mobile phone banking is a media for authenticating the user. In this paper, we estimate the value of password-based authentication system in terms of authentication system and the value of the research about it. In addition, we present the patterns of the security attacks and introduce the enhancing way of the password system.

2.1 Kinds of Authentication System

The authentication or identification process is a process to assure the identity of the user before login the designated system[3] and the user authentication is a procedure that makes sure that the user approaching to the system is the right user. The user authentication is applicable to the practical areas such as the Intranet system, access control system, Internet solution, system, access control to resources, and so forth.

There are three ways for the user to prove the identity to the server. Like a smart card or an authentication token, the user just gets and uses them. Second, there are ways which use the biometrics like finger prints or voices. Last there is the mixing ways which use both. For the first way can be classified into three systems: password-based system, symmetric key cryptography-using challenge-response system and private/public key-using digital signature or zero-knowledge system. For its convenience, the password-based system is the most popular among them so far because it just requires for the user to input only the name of the user and the password by the user[3].

2.2 Patterns of Attacks on Authentication Systems

The well-known attacks which must be guarded in the authentication system include[4,5]:

1) Replay attack: The attacker replicates messages sent in past and resends them at a later time to verifier.
2) Pre-play attack: The attacker determines a message from the recorded messages in past communications for current communication.
3) Off-line dictionary attack: The attacker replicates past communications, and then examines a dictionary in search of a password that is consistent with the recorded communication. If such a password is found, the attacker concludes that this password is applicable in an attack.
4) On-line dictionary attack: The attacker repeatedly chooses a password from a dictionary and tries to use it in order to impersonate as the user. We do not consider this attack, because there are practical ways of preventing the attack [6,7];.
5) Server compromise attack: The attacker acquires sensitive data stored at the verifier to impersonate as a user [6].

2.3 Research Scheme of Password-Based Authentication System

The password system is the most widely spread entity authentication system because of its advantage for the performance including implementation, usability on the Web, price, and so on. The attacks which must be guarded in the password system include password disclosure at the system which allows on-line dictionary and shoulder surfing attacks.

In an on-line dictionary attack, an attacker repeatedly picks a password from the dictionary and tries to use it in order to impersonate as a user. One way of preventing such the on-line dictionary attack is limit the number of failed runs [6,8].

In a shoulder surfing attack, an attacker uses a user's password, obtained by looking over a user's shoulder when the user is typing the password, in order to impersonate as the user [9,10].

According to our investigation, three password systems have been presented for enhancing the security against the shoulder surfing attack. The first password system is that requires a password over the fixed length [11]. The second password system displays the alphabets on the interface in randomly selected order repeatedly, and a user selects his alphabet in the displayed alphabets [12]. The last system displays an image on the interface, and a user selects his/her portion on the image repeatedly [13]. In these password systems, the attacker learns a user's alphabet exactly if only the attacker looks over the user's shoulder when the user inputs the alphabet.

The password input system in mobile phone banking should be guaranteed the safety against the shoulder surfing attack and designed for the convenient use.

3   Dynamic Authentication System for Mobile Phone User

3.1   The Present Password Usage in Mobile Phone Banking

For mobile phone banking, three kinds of password must be tap in like the Fig.1. While tapping in the password code in the keypad of the mobile phone, the shoulder surfing attack happens. Moreover, in the current technology, the system is easily exposed to the shoulder surfing attack due to the same tap-in characters to the real input character while tapping in the right codes in the keypad.

Fig. 1. Password Input Screen in Mobile Phone Banking(three processes)

3.2   Dynamic Authentication System

The Dynamic Authentication System(DAS) is a scheme proposed in the our previous work for the authentication systems considering the securities against both on-line dictionary and shoulder surfing attacks, and also the performance[14]. DAS has been defined in Definition 1.

Definition 1. A authentication system is DAS if it satisfies: (1) The security against the on-line dictionary attack is the same as that of the password system; (2) The interface consists of the cells, and each cell contains its own alphabet in randomly selected order without replacement; (3) An attacker of a shoulder surfing attack can learn user's alphabet only if the attacker has remembered all alphabets, contained in the cells, in the order; (4) The performance is to be as near as possible to that of the password system.

3.3 DAS 4M

Dynamic Authentication System for Mobile phone user(DAS4M) is a extended version of DAS for the mobile phone users. The definition of the DAS4M can be described as follows.

Definition 2. DAS4M satisfies the following four factors : (1) The entered password is determined by position of keypad corresponding to keypad arrangement on the mobile phone display; (2) The arrangement of the keypad on the display get changed randomly; (3) The display which shows the arrangement of keypad disappears before inputting password; (4) The designated arrangement of keypad can be shown to confirm at any time and use the # button as the function key; (5) The rearrangement of the keypad is possible anytime by pushing the "*" button.

We develop the demonstration application in order to estimate the real applicability as well as to keep safe against the shoulder surfing attack.

4 Demonstration Application

4.1 Environment

Mobile platform implies a software system which has a right API(Application Programming Interface) applicable to mobile applications, or other developing environments. The mobile platform consists of two platforms at large: for downloading the application and for developing the device. The former is called wireless Internet platform and its popularized kinds are Sun Java, Qualcomm BREW and WIPI. The latter platform is known as Microsoft Windows Mobile for Smartphone, Symbian OS, PalmOS, Ericsson Mobile Platform, etc.

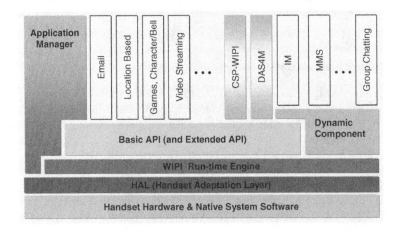

Fig. 2. WIPI Platform Architecture

WIPI(Wireless Internet Platform for Interoperability) is made by KWISF(Korea Wireless Internet Standardization Forum). WIPI is a mobile standard platform specification providing the environment for application program loaded on the wireless devices[15]. WIPI platform has the conceptual structure like Fig. 2. By exploiting the WIPI API, the applications such as email, game, CSP-WIPI can be developed[16].

4.2 Application of DAS4M Based on WIPI Platform

In this paper, DAS4M is implemented on specification of WIPI version 2.0. DAS4M is simulated on KTF WIPI Emulator[17] as a mobile application using WIPI Basic API. Since DAS4M is abiding by the standard, a mobile phone banking user can use it regardless of telecommunication companies in Korea.

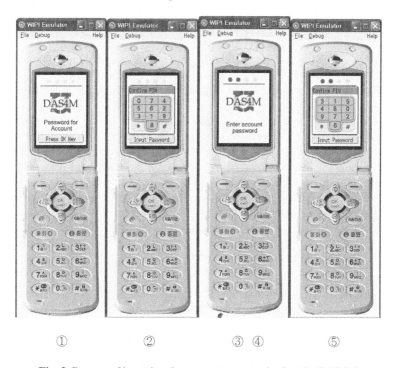

①   ②   ③ ④   ⑤

Fig. 3. Process of inputting the account password using the DAS4M

For instance, the process of inputting the account password "6742" into the application of DAS4M is depicted in Fig.3, ① The message asking the account password appears. ② After pushing the "#" button, the random arrangement of the keypad is shown on the display. The user after seeing the display has to remember the position of the series of the number "6742". While pushing the "#" button, the arrangement of the keypad can be checked; whereas, it will disappear after releasing the "#"button. The user must push the button "5" for "6", "2" for "7", "3" for "4" and "6" for "2". Just in case of forgetting the arrangement of the keypad, push the "#"

button. During the completion of one account password input, the arrangement of the keypad should observe the same arrangement. Pushing the "*" button makes the rearrangement of the keypad randomly. ③ Push "5236" button after disappearing the display. ④ After inputting "52" for "67", in case the user could not remember the position of "42" on the keypad, while pushing "#" button, double-check the arrangement of keypad like the past procedure. ⑤ After entering "52" for "67", in case the user could not just forgot the position of the keypad and want to the new keypad arrangement, push "*" button. Based on the new arrangement, to input "42", push "49" button.

4.3 Security and Usability of DAS4M

To show the validity of the proposed DAS4M, we test and compare the security and the usability of mobile phone banking between using DAS4M based mobile phone banking and the traditional password system based mobile phone banking. We experimented following sequence. First, we offered different twenty kinds of four-digit numbers of passwords to twenty college students and evaluated the test result. Then we thought them how to use the proposed system. Finally, we also gave them another different twenty kinds of four-digit numbers of passwords and evaluated test result.

We mainly focused on the on-line dictionary attack and the shoulder surfing attack as presented in section 2.3. Therefore, we tested the security when inputting the three passwords (PIN password, security card password, bank account password). In Table 1, "same" means that there is no difference between the traditional password system and the DAS4M in terms of the exposure to the on-line dictionary attack. When entering the password where nothing blocks the view of person peeping at the display, in traditional password system, the password exposure rate is 92.4%; on the other hand, DAS4M is only 1.3%. When user does not input the password right after the disappearing of keypad arrangement or user does change the keypad arrangement frequently, the exposure rate converges to 0 %.

Table 1. Password Security Exposure Rate(Mean±Standard Deviation, Min, Max)

Password security items	Traditional Password	DAS4M
On-line dictionary attacks	Same	Same
Shoulder surfing attacks	92.4±1.8, 89, 96	1.3±2.5, 0, 10

As the usability items, we consider the input time, error rate and the user response. Like in Table 2, for the user who is used to using the DAS4M, it takes 4.9 seconds to input, the probability of wrong input is around 15.1% and we observe that the user get attracted to the DAS4M as the usage time goes by. Compared to the traditional password method, DAS4M has the big standard deviation due to the individual variations.

Table 2. Password Usability Items(Mean±Standard Deviation, Min, Max)

Password usability items		Traditional Password	DAS4M
Input times (second)	Before learning	2.4±0.4, 1.7, 3.2	7.3±1.7, 5.1, 12.3
	After learning	1.6±0.3, 0.9, 2.3	4.9±1.5, 3.8, 10.6
Error rates (%)	Before learning	9.4±1.2, 7, 12	58.9±14, 31, 78
	After learning	5.2±1.7, 2, 8	15.1±3.6, 11, 24
User Response	Before learning	Cumbersome	Interesting but difficult
	After learning	Cumbersome	Relieved

5 Conclusions

We introduce the DAS4M password system in mobile phone banking by enhancing the incumbent password system which is fragile against the shoulder surfing attack. From the experiment, we present that the password exposure rate can be dramatically reduced. Compared to the traditional password system, it is a little inconvenient in terms of the usability but it has favorable comments from many users. In addition, there is a problem that the user who does not get accustomed to the new DAS4M password system was prohibited from using the mobile phone banking service on that day and had no choice to go to visit the bank. However, this can be resolved by widespread use of DAS4M.

References

1. DaeHo K. (ed.): Digital Convergence, Communication Books, Seoul (2004)
2. JiBum J., HanJu K, : Survey and analysis of mobile commerce, Weekly Technique Review, Vol. 1139. ETRI, (2004)
3. MahnYong L, et al. Cryptography and Application, Saengrung Publisher, Seoul (2002)
4. SeungBae, P., MoonSeol K., SangJun L.: Authenticated Key Exchange Protocol Secure against Off-Line Dictionary Attack and Server Compromise, Lecture Notes in Computer Science, Vol. 3032. Springer-Verlag, Berlin Heidelberg New York (2004) 924-931
5. SeungBae, P., MoonSeol K., SangJun L.: User Authentication Protocol Based on Human Memorable Password and Using ECC, Lecture Notes in Computer Science, Vol. 3032. Springer-Verlag, Berlin Heidelberg New York (2004) 1091-1094
6. Halevi, S., Krawczyk, H.: Public-key cryptography and password protocols. ACM Security (CCS' 98) (1998) 122-131
7. Jablon, D.: Strong password-only authenticated key exchange. ACM Computer Communication Review, ACM SIGCOMM, Vol. 26, No. 5 (1996) 5-20

8. Bellovin, S. M., Merrit, M.: Augmented encrypted key exchange: Password-based protocol secure against dictionary attack and password file compromise. In ACM Security (CCS'93) (1993) 244-250

9. Boyko, V., MacKenzie, Patal, P. S.: Provably secure password authenticated key exchange using Diffie-Hellman. Advances in Cryptology Eurocrypt'00, LNCS Vol. 1807. Springer-Verlag (2000) 156-171

10. Gong, L.: Optimal authentication protocols resistant to password guessing attacks. In 8th IEEE Computer Security Foundations Workshop (1995) 24-29

11. Bellare, M., Pointcheaval, D., Rogaway, P.: Authenticated key exchange secure against dictionary attacks. Advances in Cryptology Eurocrypt'00, LNCS Vol. 1807. Springer-Verlag (2000) 139-155

12. http://www.realuser.com/cgi-bin/ru.exe/_/homepages/index.htm

13. http://www.domainmart.com/news/NYT_symbols-as-passwods.htm

14. SeungBae, P., MoonSeol K., SangJun L.: New Authentication System, Lecture Notes in Computer Science, Vol. 3032. Springer-Verlag, Berlin Heidelberg New York (2004) 1095-1098

15. WIPI Specification, http://www.kwisforum.org

16. SangJun L.: A Mobile Application of Client-Side Personalization Based on WIPI Platform, Lecture Notes in Computer Science, Vol. 3314. Springer-Verlag, Berlin Heidelberg New York (2004) 903-909

17. Ktf WIPI Emulator, http://wipidev.magicn.com/

Development of the Efficient OWL Document Management System for the Embedded Applications*

Hak Soo Kim, Hyun Seok Cha, Jungsun Kim, and Jin Hyun Son

Dept. of Computer Science and Engineering, Hanyang University in Ansan, Korea
{hagsoo, hscha, jskim, jhson}@cse.hanyang.ac.kr

Abstract. To provide ontology-based context understanding services in the embedded application areas, efficient ontology document management schemes are required. Even though some related systems have been developed, they are not appropriate for the embedded system environment with some limitations on memory, disk space and computing power, such as home networking, telematics and intelligent robotics. In this regard, we have developed the embedded system-oriented OWL semantic document management system using the relational databases. We first design a relational data schema appropriate for the OWL documents and then develop a transformation mechanism to store OWL documents. Additionally, the RDQL semantic query processor is additionally implemented for the experiments.

1   Introduction

Nowadays, many researchers may take high interests in the context understanding services, and in reality their concepts have been applied to various embedded application areas, especially such as home networking, telematics, and intelligent robotics. Because the concept of context-awareness is basically considered to be enabled by the semantic web technologies [1, 2], most applications which want to provide context-understanding services may use or adopt semantic web-related international standards: OWL [3] as a web ontology language and Web Services for interaction between software modules. For the purpose of context understanding services, the way to efficiently store and manage ontology documents should be discussed first of all. In this paper, we propose a new data schema refined for embedded applications and develop a transformation mechanism to store OWL ontology documents to the relational schema.

The XML-based [4] semantic web specification in W3C is composed of five stack layers [5]: resource description framework, ontology vocabulary, logic, proof,

---

* This work was supported by grant No.R08-2003-000-10464-0 from the Basic Research Program of the Korea Science & Engineering Foundation. This work was supported by the Ministry of Information & Communications, Korea, under the Information Technology Research Center(ITRC) Support Program.

S. Shimojo et al. (Eds.): HSI 2005, LNCS 3597, pp. 75–84, 2005.

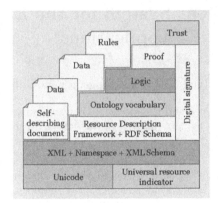

Fig. 1. Semantic Web Stack

and trust layer as in Figure 1. Here, only resource description framework and ontology vocabulary layers are officially standardized as RDF(RDFS) [6, 7] and OWL, respectively. With RDF and RDFS, we can describe web resources with simple statements, and also define classes and properties that may be used to describe other classes and properties as well as web resources. On the other hand, OWL, a revision of the previous DAML+OIL [8, 9], provides more facilities for expressing meaning and semantics by extending RDF and RDFS. Within these semantic languages, a web resource is represented by a simple statement with a triple data structure (subject, predicate, object). There are several semantic query languages proposed, for example, such as RQL and RDQL for querying RDF and RDFS documents, DQL for DAML+OIL documents, and OWL-QL for OWL documents. Now, RDQL and OWL-QL are considered as de-facto standards.

The rest of this paper is organized as follows: In Section 2, we describe the existing semantic web ontology storage systems as related work. We propose our relational data schema in Section3, and explain the developed ontology management system in Section 4. Section 5 shows the efficiency of our system by analyzing the experimental results. Finally, we summary our paper by addressing the further work in Section 6.

2   Related Work

The semantic storage systems developed so far are Jena [10, 11], Sesame [12], Parka [13] and TAP [14]. Especially, Jena and Sesame are noticeable as ontology management systems comparable with our proposed system. Jena, developed by HP, is a Java-based semantic web framework in which users can easily build semantic web-enabled applications. Using Jena, we can store XML-based semantic web documents including RDF, RDFS, DAML+OIL and OWL, and query the stored documents with RDQL query language. On the other hand, Sesame released by Aduna (in cooperation with NLnet Foundation and OntoText) is basically a storage system for RDF(S) documents, which supports RQL and RDQL as semantic query languages. Being extended by BOR, Sesame+BOR can support DAML+OIL documents as well as RDF(S) documents.

Jena stores semantic documents to the supported databases (e.g., MySQL, PostgreSQL and Oracle 9i) using its own memory-based semantic model. In case of Sesame, we can also use MySQL, PostgreSQL and Oracle 9i as a document storage source, and documents can be easily uploaded and deleted by the web interface. Since Sesame can store only RDF(S) documents, Sesame+BOR by the help of a reasoner for DAML+OIL and OWL, BOR [15], is used for storing DAML+OIL or OWL documents. Parka is a RDBMS-based semantic management system for managing web ontology documents and processing semantic queries. However, it is not appropriate for managing large-scale documents because it can't store more than about 250 million triples. TAP is similar with Parka and accessed by Web through Apache module. However, it does not provide a graph matching mechanism for RDQL semantic queries. It just provides simple triple matching mechanism using the GetData function.

Notice that Sesame and Jena use directly reflects the main properties of RDF when building their storage system. In the semantic web, a resource is represented by a simple statement with a triple data struct (subject, predicate, object) depicted as a RDF graph. In other words, Sesame and Jena store and manage RDF documents upon the data schema designed according to the triple structure. The data model proposed in [16] is also similar to those of Sesame and Jena. Similarly, [17] makes use of the basis constructs of a RDF document, i.e., class and property, for building its storage model. Even though it is very efficient in a small-scale document management system, its efficiency will be dramatically reduced for a large-scale one. While the above mentioned systems have been all designed using existing RDBMS, [18], however, has developed its own storage system for RDF documents. Because of that, this system is efficient as well as light when managing resources represented by RDF triples. However, it can't be easily extended for managing the DAML+OIL or OWL-based documents.

3   Proposed Relational Data Schema

In this section, we would analyze Jena and Sesame+BOR and then propose our efficient data schema which is comparable with Jena and Sesame. Table 1 shows the performance comparison between Jena and Sesame. In this Table, Sesame+BOR is used for the comparison since Sesame is able to store just RDF and RDFS.

As Table 1 says, Jena just needs 7 number of tables for storing RDF, RDFS, DMAL+OIL and OWL documents. However, it is certain that Jena is not appropriate for large-scale semantic document storage systems. The reason would be described in the below.

Jena does not allow users to pose a query to all tables in a database, different from Sesame+BOR. In the case of Jena, when a document called 'A' is stored,

Table 1. Performance Comparison between Sesame and Jena

	Jena 2.1	Sesame 1.1 + BOR
number of tables	7	20
number of statements being able to handle	small	more than 3,000,000

Jena keeps the document in a database by assigning it a graph ID. And then, Jena processes user queries through the graph ID by building the memory-based Jena model corresponding to the document retrieved from the database using the graph ID. Because Jena performs query processing for each document, it is difficult to support a semantic query for all documents stored in a database. On the other hand, we in Sesame+BOR can perform semantic queries for the all documents stored in a database. As shown in Table 1, Sesame+BOR can manage a large volume of documents. The basic intention of Sesame+BOR when managing RDF, RDFS, DAML+OIL and OWL documents is to generate and store additional information by inference from the original documents. Hence, Sesame+BOR may store and manage much more information than Jena. Basically, both of Jena and Sesame+BOR use RDF triple information when storing semantic documents. Because all OWL constructs used to construct an OWL document are inherited from the RDF(S) constructs, resources described by OWL constructs can also be represented by a simple statement with a RDF triple structure (subject, predicate, object) without loss of information. As a result, Jena and Sesame+BOR can be considered as good storage system for managing OWL-formated documents.

Because our goal is to propose a data schema in which OWL semantic documents can be effectively stored and then efficiently retrieved when querying the stored documents with RDQL. Because DAML+OIL and OWL are almost identical semantic document format, Jena and Sesame+BOR systems which all support DAML+OIL document format and RDQL semantic query language can be compared with our proposed storage system.

In principle, Jena is designed as single document-based storage system. In other words, whenever we insert a semantic document to Jena, two tables, jena_gnt$n$_reif and jena_gnt$n$_stmt (Here, n is a graph ID dependent on each document) are newly generated while other basic common tables are shared as in Figure 2. In the case of the query processing in Jena, we can query only for each document while Jena may load it into the memory model. On the other hand, Sesame+BOR provides the common relational schema which would be shared for all inserted documents as in Figure 3. Hence, the query can be targeted to the all data stored in Sesame+BOR system. Here, note that Sesame+BOR's table will generally contain too much data because it may generate much more additional information by inferring from the original inserted document. In this regard, we think that our proposed storage system would be the same as Sesame+BOR, but contain as less data as possible without information loss compared to the original documents. Because of that, we assure that our proposed system be appropri-

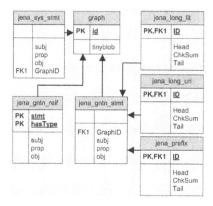

Fig. 2. Jena's Data Schema

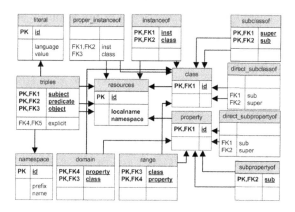

Fig. 3. Sesame+BOR's Data Schema

ate for embedded systems with the limited resources such as home networking, telematics, and intelligent robotics.

Because OWL [2] is extended upon RDF and RDFS, its constructs to construct OWL documents are inherited from the RDF(S)'s six core constructs [7]: rdfs:Class, rdfs:subClassOf, rdf:Property, rdf:domain, rdf:subPropertyOf, and rdf:range. We design and implement, therefore, our storage system with the relational data schema based on these six core constructs as in Figure 4. Basically, our proposed schema is based on the following three policies: First, information loss does not occur during storing OWL documents. Second, the efficiency in the process of inserting and retrieving OWL information should be importantly considered. The efficiency of the ontology management system may be mainly estimated by the cost of semantic query processing. In our consideration, the efficiency is related to two different factors which are inverse proportional with each other: the data processing cost in a DBMS itself and the query processing cost in an inference engine as in Figure 5. To minimize the data processing cost

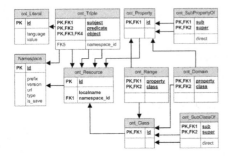

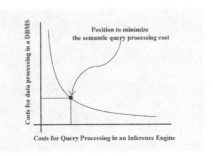

Fig. 4. Our Proposed Data Schema   **Fig. 5.** Cost Efficiency Graph

in a DBMS itself, the amount of data stored and the number of tables should be smaller. On the other hand, much more additional information by the inference processing had better be generated and stored when inserting ontology documents into a DBMS to minimize the query processing cost in an inference engine.

As shown in Figure 5, the origin of the coordinate axes may be an ideal point to be the minimum cost of semantic query processing. Hence, the nearest point on the graph from the origin is one that we want to find out during designing and implementing the ontology management system. It is very difficult to theoretically justify the proposed system may meet the requirements of the point. We do, therefore, heuristically design our system that can possibly meet the requirements with the data schema as in Figure 4. Finally, the proposed ontology management system should be scalable, which means that the system should be able to cover new ontology constructs to be specified in the future. Because our schema supports the triple-based graph model with the six generic ontology constructs mentioned in the above, it can manage ontology documents built with the newly specified ontology constructs.

According to the above mentioned three design policies, the data schema in our proposed system is composed of ten number of tables as in Figure 4. Initially, the contents information represented with the triple data structure in an ontology document would be stored to the following four basic tables: ont_Triple, ont_Resource, ont_Literal, and Namespace. The other six tables would keep additional information which may be utilized during semantic query processing by an inference engine. Because semantic languages such as RDF(S), DAML+OIL, and OWL considered in this paper are all based on the RDF triple-based graph model, our four basic tables can cover OWL-based ontology documents. Because the other six tables are originated from RDF's six core constructs, it is utilized to infer semantic queries. The key table of the schema is ont_Resource. Since a semantic web document is constructed from describing web resources with a triple data structure, ont_Resource is to be the core table for storing semantic documents. The RDF triples (subject, predicate, object) from ont_Resource table are stored in ont_Triple and all namespaces are stored in Namespace table. And, the inferred information from the triple information of resources is stored to the six tables stemmed from the RDF's six core constructs.

4 Development of the Ontology Management System

Based on the data schema designed in the above section, we design and implement the ontology document management system. Figure 6 shows the overall architecture of the system which is composed of four components: Database Generator, Semantic Query Supporter, Inference Engine, and Database. First of all, the database contains ontology documents according to the data schema designed in the above throughout the database generator which inserts ontology documents into the database. The database generator gets an ontology document and then inserts it into the database after validating. We can do simple and semantic queries using the semantic query supporter. For simple queries meaning simple information retrieval, the semantic query supporter can process them by directly accessing the database. For semantic queries meaning information retrieval by the inference process, the semantic query supporter can process them by the help of the inference engine. We support RDQL being currently in the process of the international standard as a semantic query language by W3C.

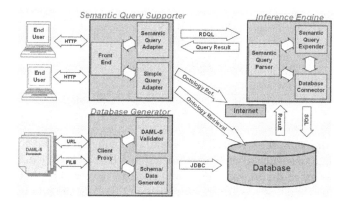

Fig. 6. Ontology Management System Architecture

5 Experiments

In this section, we compare our system with Sesame+BOR by the several experiments. To show our system's validity, we evaluate the two systems in the aspects of the number of stored records and the average query processing time.

Figure 7 shows an ontology document example which defines a class "USState" and its corresponding RDF graph. When we insert the document of Figure 2 into Sesame+BOR and the proposed system in this paper, Table 2 compares two tables containing triple records generated by Sesame+BOR and our system, respectively. While the Sesame+BOR system extracts all possible RDF triple information by inferring the original document, our system generates only necessary triples based on the RDF graph model as in Figure 7. As a result, Sesame+BOR may keep much more amount of triple data than our system.

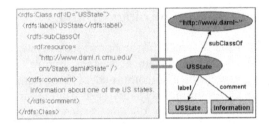

Fig. 7. Example of an OWL document and its RDF Graph

Table 2. Comparison of the stored triple information

subject	predicate	object	subject	predicate	object
USState	type	resource			
USState	type	class	USState	type	class
USState	subClassOf	resource			
USState	subClassOf	USState			
USState	subClassOf	State	USState	subClassOf	State
USState	label	USState	USState	label	USState
USState	comment	Info.	USState	comment	Info.
State	type	resource			
State	type	class			
State	subClassOf	resource			
State	subClassOf	State			

Sesame+BOR   Our System

By extracting only the essential triples and removing tables not to keep duplicated data, high efficiency of query processing in a DBMS itself can be achieved. In case of deleting and updating the stored records, it is certain that our system is more efficient than Sesame+BOR. As shown in Figure 8, the number of records generated by Sesame+BOR is almost twice than our proposed system. If we experiment it with much more big and complex semantic documents, we would be able to find out that our system is more useful for the embedded applications.

On the other hand, to compare the two systems in the aspect of the efficiency in RDQL semantic query processing, we have measured the average query processing time for the five different queries as in Figure 8. The five semantic RDQL queries are:

- Query 1: Retrieve all subjects satisfying the predicate and object requirements
- Query 2: Query for the immediate descendant relationship
- Query 3: Query for the descendant relationship
- Query 4: Query on the Range and Domain properties
- Query 5: Retrieve all instances for a certain class

We notice that our system can support the query efficiency similar to existing Sesame+BOR. As a result, our proposed storage system can provide reasonable query efficiency while keeping as small amount of data as possible.

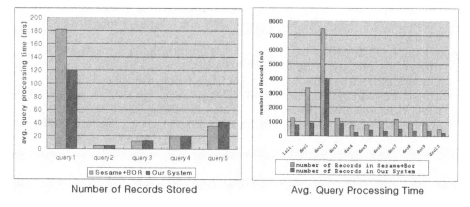

Number of Records Stored   Avg. Query Processing Time

Fig. 8. Number of Records Stored and Avg. Query Processing Time

6 Summary and Further Work

Even though several ontology management systems have been developed, they
are not appropriate for the embedded system environment with limitations on
memory, disk space, and computing power. In this regard, we propose a relational
data schema that is appropriate for managing OWL documents in the embedded
environment such as home networking, telematics and intelligent robotics. And
then, the ontology document management system is designed and implemented,
based on the data schema. In addition, several experiments are provided to justify
our proposed system. As further work, we plan to study the way to efficiently
process semantic queries using new inference and indexing mechanisms which
can properly utilize the properties of semantic queries.

References

1. T. Berners-Lee, J. Hendler, and O. Lassila: The Semantic Web. Scientific American,
   vol.284, no.5, pp.34-43, 2001.
2. A. Maedche, S. Staab: Ontology learning for the semantic web. IEEE Intelligent
   Systems, vol.16, no.2, pp. 72-79, 2001.
3. Deborah L. McGuinness, Frank van Harmelen: OWL Web Ontology Language
   Overview W3C Recommendation. Feb 2004. See http://www.w3.org/TR/owl-
   features/.
4. Francois Yergeau, Tim Bray, Jean Paoli, C. M. Sperberg-McQueen, Eve Maler:
   Extensible Markup Language (XML) 1.0 (Third Edition) W3C Recommendation.
   Feb 2004. See http://www.w3.org/XML
5. Dieter Fensel: Ontologies : A Silver Bullet for Knowledge Management and Electronic Commerce. Springer-Verlag Berlin and Heidelberg GmbH and Co.K, 2004.
6. Graham Klyne, Jeremy Carroll: Resource Description Framework (RDF):
   Concepts and Abstract Syntax W3C Recommendation. Feb 2004. See
   http://www.w3.org/TR/rdf-concepts/.

7. Dan Brickley, R.V. Guha: RDF Vocabulary Description Language 1.0 : RDF Schema W3C Recommendation. Feb 2004. See http://www.w3.org/TR/rdf-schema/.
8. J. Hendler, D. L. McGuinness: The DARPA Agent Markup Language. IEEE Intelligent Systems, vol.15, no.6, pp. 67-73, 2000.
9. I. Horrocks: DAML+OIL: A Description Logic for the Semantic Web. IEEE Bulletin of the Technical Committee on Data Engineering, vol.25, no.1, pp. 4-9, 2002.
10. Kevin Wilkinson, Craig Sayers, Harumi Kuno, Dave Reynolds: Efficient RDF Storage and Retrieval in Jena2. SWDB 2003, pp. 131-150, 2003. Language (XML) 1.0 (Third Edition) W3C Recommendation", Feb 2004. See http://www.w3.org/XML
11. Jeremy Carrol, Brian McBride: The Jena Semantic Web Toolkit. HP-Labs, Bristol, 2001. See http://jena.sourceforge.net/.
12. J. Broekstra, A. Kampman, F. van Harmelen: Sesame: A Generic Architecture for Storing and Querying RDF and RDF Schema. In The Semantic Web - ISWC 2002, volume 2342 of Lecture Notes in Computer Science, pp. 54-68, 2002. See http://openrdf.org/.
13. Kilian Stoffel, Merwyn Taylor, James Hendler: Efficient management of very large ontologies. Proc. 14th Nat'l Conference AAAI, AAAI press, pp. 442-447, 1997.
14. Ramanathan V. Guha, Rob McCool: TAP: a Semantic Web platform. Computer Networks, vol.42, no.5, pp. 557-577, 2003.
15. Kiril Simov, Stanislav Jordanov: BOR: a Pragmatic DAML+OIL Reasoner. On-To-Knowledge project, 2002.
16. Harris, S. and Gibbins, N: 3store: Efficient Bulk RDF Storage. In Proceedings of 1st International Workshop on Practical and Scalable Semantic Systems - PSSS 2003, pp. 1-15, 2003.
17. Zhengxiang Pan, Jeff Heflin: DLDB: Extending Relational Databases to Support Semantic Web Queries. Workshop on Practical and Scalable Semantic Web Systems - ISWC 2003, pp. 109-113, 2003.
18. Alberto Reggiori, Dirk-Willem van Gulik, Zavisa Bjelogrlic: Indexing and retrieving Semantic Web resources: the RDFStore model. Europe Workshop on Semantic Web Storage and Retrieval - SWAD 2003, 2003.

Internet at a Crossroads of Education

Myung Kim[1], Sunsook Noh[2], and Seongmin Cho[2]

[1] Department of Computer Science & Engineering,
[2] Department of Mathematics Education, Ewha Womans University, Seoul Korea
{mkim, noh}@ewha.ac.kr, csminy@ewhain.net

Abstract. The Internet has grown rapidly in the past few years to impact all aspects of modern life. While many areas of the Internet such as commerce has shown tremendous improvements in providing convenient and complex transaction services from shopping to banking, the area of education has seen less development in terms of meeting the potential of the Internet for education. The number of web sites related to education and the types of educational uses have clearly increased on the Internet but the overall consensus is that more should be done in the area of using the Internet to enhance the educational experience of learners. Many technological innovations have been previously touted as a new paradigm for education only to see it disappear from view quietly with time. In order to make sure that the vast potential of the Internet is fully utilized for education, more structured approach and a change in the mindset of educators are needed.

1 Introduction

In a relatively short time, the Internet has radically transformed the world in the way information is handled and communicated. Every aspect of a modern life is impacted from commerce to education by the Internet. Almost overnight, Internet has become an essential part of the daily routine of modern life. Everyday, a person can use the Internet to shop, read newspapers from around the world, carry out bank transactions, watch a TV program, take e-learning classes, socialize with friends, maybe even make new friends and so on. There appears to be no limit to what the Internet could be used for as more and more interesting and creative uses are found everyday. Rapid advancements in both hardware and software technology have truly made the Internet an essential part of the knowledge based society.

From early on, the potential use of the Internet for education was recognized by students, educators and researchers alike. The Internet was widely used first in universities around the world to help researchers communicate with each other. The natural fit between schools and the Internet appeared to be ideal. The Internet possessed the qualities that seemed to be ideal not only for communication but also for teaching and learning. The power of the web interface for multimedia information presentation coupled with ever increasing computer power to run various types of simulation and calculation programs freed the teacher to shift the focus in teaching from lecturing to guiding the students. The students could finally be freed from the traditional learning methods of passively listening to lectures to actively participating

S. Shimojo et al. (Eds.): HSI 2005, LNCS 3597, pp. 85–93, 2005.

in the discovery of knowledge and understanding. The Internet had the potential to provide a new paradigm in teaching and learning that would be available to anyone within the reach of the computer connected to the Internet. All at once, the Internet was the medium that could transform and provide high quality education to all who wished to learn whenever and wherever they are.

2   Challenges for Internet-Based Education

In the year 2000, a report [12] was made in the US by the Web-Based Education Commission to the President and the Congress of the United States. The report stated that while web-based education had extraordinary possibilities, there were key barriers that prevented the realization of the full potential. The 7 areas of barriers were 1) infrastructure, 2) training for educators, 3) research framework for learning on the web, 4) online content development, 5) legal issues, 6) online security and privacy, and 7) funding to support development. In 5 short years, many of the barriers have already been removed or partially removed in the areas of infrastructure, training, legal, security and funding.

For instance, the growth of infrastructure everywhere has been rapid and continuous. In Korea, statistics from the year 2002 compiled by the Korea Network Information Center [5] showed that more than half of the Korean population, 58% or 25 million people, use the Internet at least once a month and 96% of them or 24 million people use the Internet at least once a week. More importantly for education, 94.5% of all students surveyed from elementary school to college were using the Internet and it indicated that almost all students have at least some access to the Internet. The usability of the Internet has also improved in recent years with over 10 million users having broadband access to the Internet which allows more complex web pages and multimedia content to be easily accessed and viewed [5].

For training, teachers are learning about the basics of technology of how to use the computer and the Internet. Not much emphasis has been placed on how to create content and to develop effective use of web sites. Recent study in teaching teachers to develop constructivist use of the Internet showed that most teachers found it useful to understand the theoretical consideration about learning when evaluating web sites for education [1]. Other researchers are also actively engaging in determining how to develop better web sites for education [2].

While the access to the Internet has been made easier, the research framework and the content development appeared to lag behind other developments. One cannot forget that in the end, Web is just another resource for education that must be studied and manipulated appropriately to become a meaningful contributor to education [10]. In fact, the opposite impact can occur if the expectation on the technology was too high in the beginning. Many educational technologies and new ideas have come and gone because the practice did not meet expectation [6]. For instance, the use of the LOGO programming language was once touted as a breakthrough activity in developing mathematical minds in students. Recently, the enthusiasm has diminished greatly with less and less educators using LOGO as an educational tool. [6] suggests that the reason why so many of the educational innovation died away was because there was no theoretical foundation in learning that supported the innovative activities. Even the best tools could be worthless if the user does not understand how the tool works and know what the limitation of the tool is.

The educational use of the Internet has clearly grown in recent years to encompass many aspects of education from administration to course work. Many educational institutions devote time and money to develop attractive web sites since the web site represents the image of the schools. Many of the courses are offered as cyber courses to provide flexibility to the students. While the use of the Internet for educational purpose has increased, the use of the Internet for actual teaching and learning has not made much progress. The promise of the Internet for education was the interactivity of the medium that allowed the students to interact and actively participate in any learning process.

3   Internet at a Crossroads of Education

The growth of the Internet has also allowed the educational use of the Internet to grow rapidly. Only 10 years ago, the primary use of the Internet for education was mostly for communication and data sharing through e-mails and file transfers at the universities and research institutions. The use the Internet for education at the time was limited by availability, cost and user friendliness of the Internet. The introduction of the HTML language and web browsers along with the expanded infrastructure allowed all types of information in a variety of format to be shared by almost anyone with an access to the Internet. Today, students, teachers, school, and institutions provide a multitude of different types of information and services for educational use. In some ways, there is a glut of educational information on the Internet that makes it more difficult to find what you are looking for. The question for education is whether we are heading in the right direction for taking advantage of all the powerful attributes that the Internet has to offer for education.

The use of the internet for education may be categorized into two primary activities. The first is the sharing of information using the Internet and the second is active learning using activities developed specifically for Internet application. Information sharing using the Internet can be described as an extension of distance learning with access to an electronic library. Both students and teachers can use the Internet to communicate and access information required for teaching and learning. The introduction of cyber courses and even cyber schools are examples where the Internet is being used effectively for information sharing for educational use. The interactive learning activity goes one step further by providing and keeping track of activities that require active involvement of the student. Cyber education course can have some aspect of an interactive learning environment but the activity is typically limited to chatting and communicating with students and teachers over the Internet. A true interactive learning activity requires the student to participate in a concrete activity such as graphing, simulation, data search and so on to participate in the process of learning and to develop an understanding of the subject matter. A well designed activity should also provide active feedback to the student based on the response of the student to the lesson to customize the learning activity for each student. In addition, these types of active lessons over the Internet can even develop a database of student activities to be used as a research tool to understand how the student is learning the material. Ideally, a well designed interactive lesson should be valuable for both the student and the teacher with the goal of providing the best possible instruction to each student.

3.1 E-Learning Through EDUNET

A good and successful example of the educational use of the Internet in Korea is the EDUNET site which is an educational portal site maintained by the Ministry of Education & Human Resources of Korea [4]. The main functionality of the website is to provide students with e-learning opportunity as well as to give teachers teaching materials for their offline classes. The membership data shows that there are currently 5.3 million registered EDUNET members, as shown in Table 1. It is considered to be one of the largest educational portal sites in the world. Among the registered members, 3.3 million (or around 62%) users are teachers and students from elementary through high schools nationwide. While the number of registered members indicates a successful use of the Internet to provided educational material to students and teachers, two trends in the data indicate areas for improvement. First, the number of members decreases significantly as you go from elementary school to high school. The drop in participation may indicate a lack of appropriate content material for higher grades or a lack of interest in older students for using the Internet for educational use. The second trend that indicates area for improvement is the general decreasing trend in student and teacher members from year 2001 to 2004. The expectation would have been to observe a steady increase in membership since wider accessibility of the Internet, reduced cost for Internet access and increasing content material for the site should have encouraged greater participation.

Table 1. EDUNET User Statistics

User Category	2001		2002		2003		2004	
	Member	Rate (%)	Member	Rate (%)	Member	Rate (%)	Member	Rate (%)
Elementary School	1,480,172	30	1,831,553	33	994,643	20	1,182,005	22
Middle School	1,026,771	21	1,150,123	21	978,314	19	1,000,895	19
High School	908,183	19	957,270	17	771,728	15	778,601	15
Teacher	320,148	7	346,309	6	290,559	6	299,011	6
Other	1,140,664	23	1,265,682	23	1,995,043	40	2,046,030	38
Total	4,875,938	100	5,550,937	100	5,030,287	100	5,306,542	100

The service of EDUNET can be divided into two categories: e-learning material provisioning and online education of students. EDUNET maintains vast amount of e-learning materials. Table 2 shows the type of materials for teachers. They are mainly for offline classes, i.e., presentation (PowerPoint) files for each lecture, video clips of lecture samples, tools, and software for class management, etc. EDUNET also has self-study materials for teachers. We can see from the monthly retrieval and download numbers that they are heavily used for classes. This is a successful application of using the Internet to help teachers obtain up to date teaching materials.

Table 2. EDUNET - Contents for Teachers

Contents Category	Number of Items	Monthly Usage	
		Number of Retrievals	Number of Downloads
Teaching Materials	182,813	3,035,396	611,880
Video Clips of Lecture Samples	69	24,273	-
Class Management	3,723	11,281	-
General Purpose Materials	49,661	351,305	774,438
Tools	5,591	60,157	-
Self Study Materials for Teachers	92	35,766	-
EDUNET Related Information	10	67,639	-
Total	241,959	3,585,817	1,386,318

Table 3. EDUNET - Contents for Students

Student Category	Number of Subjects/Semesters	Number of Retrievals
Elementary School	81	748,524
Middle School	12	104,903
High School	3	10,528
All	10	30,989
Theme Related Materials	4	127,925
Total	120	1,070,957

Table 3 shows the amount of e-learning materials for students maintained by the EDUNET site. Most materials are for elementary school students. The types of materials are cyber lectures, references for each subject, and materials for reviewing lectures, etc. The lack of materials for higher grade students suggests that more effort is needed to develop content material for the higher grade students.

The interactive online education service provided by EDUNET is called 'cyber home schooling'. The home schooling service is divided into four categories: (1) provisioning of self study materials, (2) cyber service of achievement level evaluation, (3) cyber service of Q&A, and (4) cyber class management. The students can obtain and pace their study by receiving materials for self study through the online education service. The student can then study the material and test their level of achievement through the 'achievement level evaluation service'. The progress of the student is maintained by a database that records and administers the overall progress of the student. For those students who wish to be led by a teacher or a mentor, EDUNET provides a cyber class with about 20 or less students. A teacher or a mentor is assigned to the class to lead the discussion and activities over the Internet. However, the current level of service is not comprehensive enough to fully guide the student through an entire subject matter by the online course. The online education service on EDUNET is geared towards providing a distance education structure to the student with content and administrative functions.

3.2 E-Learning in Mathematics Education

Since most of the education material on EDUNET was not interactive in nature, a survey of web based math instruction sites listed by Yahoo Korea was carried out to further understand how the web sites were being designed specifically for math instruction today [9]. Since Yahoo Korea was one of the most popular search engines in Korea, the listed sites were expected to be somewhat representative of the type of educational web sites that is available in Korea today [5].

The surveyed web sites were categorized based on their content type and level of interactivity to determine the extent with which the web based instruction followed or deviated from traditional classroom experience. At one end of the scale is receiving instruction material over the Internet in a manner not much different from listening to a lecture. On the other end of the scale is participating in an interactive learning environment over the Internet by actively interacting with the computer or a person using the Internet. The traditional approach to teaching will require the student to read, watch or listen to the instructional material and then participate in some assessment activity to determine the level of mastery. A more interactive approach to the lesson would use the power of the computer and the Internet to allow the student to engage in some activity that requires participation by the student. Activity can range from simple JAVA based graphing program to a complex simulation of physical events such as weather forecasting. Math lessons are a good candidate for the interactive approach since learning math requires problem solving and understanding. A student cannot usually read the material and then develop a full understanding of the mathematical concepts behind the material. The student usually needs to actively solve problems and actively generalize the concepts behind the topic to develop a full understanding. A well designed Internet based activity could help to guide the student along the line of reasoning that would help to develop an understanding of the subject matter.

The survey of the Yahoo listed math education sites showed that about 80% of the sites were based on self study using lecture type lesson materials. The lecture materials could be visually interesting and stimulating, but the content was fixed. Similar to the EDUNET site, the lesson materials were mostly classroom instruction materials. A few sites contained interactive inquiry learning materials that were developed by individual educators trying to develop better ways of teaching mathematics. These sites showed progress in the right direction but they were not coordinated in anyway with the curriculum to maximize their effectiveness. A well designed lesson should be structured within the curriculum to provide the right amount of interactivity to the student to help the student develop understanding of the material.

4 Conclusion

An examination of the successful EDUNET education site and a brief survey of the Yahoo listed educational web sites for mathematics education in Korea showed that most of the educational web sites are a reflection of the current teaching environment. The traditional classroom materials were most commonly transferred to the web site in multimedia format for easy access. There were very few sites with interactive activities that could help the student experiment with the learning material. While the presentation and organization of the web sites were well thought out and comprehensive, the sites generally used typical multimedia presentation and assessment tools. The self study web sites were not much different from other distant learning environments with only the advantage of easy access to materials.

With the growth of the Internet, the first phase of using the Internet can be considered a success. The numerous educational websites provide information and lessons that could be used by both students and teachers of all grade levels. The students and teachers have a resource that was not available before the Internet. Now the time has come to take the next step of developing educational content specifically designed to take advantage of the Internet and the power of the computer. The combination of recent educational theories coupled with technology maybe able to provide equal opportunity for customized education to students of all levels and ability regardless of geographic location.

In order to take full advantage of the Internet environment for education, an effort must be made to integrate web based lessons into the curriculum. At Ewha Womans University, a research program in mathematics curriculum design has been in progress for the past 5 years to improve the current curriculum by focusing on promoting creativity in students and also by incorporating technology into the curriculum [8]. The current 7th National Mathematics Curriculum [3] already recommends integrating technology into the curriculum. The research program tried to develop guidelines and specific examples of how technology could be integrated into the curriculum. In the future, more research programs in curriculum design with specific focus on integrating web based instruction should be promoted and supported in order to change the direction of web based instruction.

Ideally, the power of the computer and its ability to collect and analyze data could provide a powerful force for both teaching the students and at the same time learning about how the students learn. One can imagine an integrated instructional strategy where the teacher provides the framework and guidance for the instructional material first and then the student uses the web based lessons to investigate and to develop a deeper understanding of the material. The web based lessons could be designed to use some type of artificial teaching intelligence to provide customized guidance to the student while tracking and recording the student's activities during the lesson. If the activities of all students could be gathered in a large database, a researcher could analyze the data to develop a better understanding about how the students learn. The learning about the students learning could then be incorporated back into the web based lessons to provide a more effective learning environment for the student.

Today's advances in educational theory, psychology, sociology and technology could make the above scenario possible if educators and researchers focus on trying to develop a truly comprehensive Internet based educational system. The time to act is now before the excitement of the Internet wears off and the technology fades away as just another ordinary information medium.

Acknowledgement. Supported by Korea Research Foundation (KRF-2003-005-B00028).

References

1. Gibson, S., and Skaalid, B., "Teacher professional development to promote constructivist uses of the Internet: A study of one graduate-level course," *Journal of Technology and Teacher Education*, Vol. 12, No. 4, pp. 577-592, 2004.
2. Harmon, S. W., and Jones, M. G., "The five levels of web use in education: Factors to consider in online courses," *Educational Technology*, Vol. 39, No. 6, pp. 28-32, 1999.
3. Korea Ministry of Education (KMOE), *The 7th National Mathematics Curriculum*, 1997.
4. Korea Ministry of Education & Human Resources Development (KMOEHRD), & Korea Education & Research Information Service (KERIS), "Adapting Education to the Information Age: Part I – Building a System to Adapt ICT into Elementary and Secondary Education," *2004 White Paper*, 2004.
5. Korea Network Information Center (KRNIC), *2002 Korea Internet Statistics Yearbook*. Seoul, Korea: National Internet Development Agency of Korea (NIDA), 2002.
6. Maddux, C., & Cummmings, R., "Fad, fashion, and the weak role of theory and research in information technology in education," *Journal of Technology and Teacher Education*, Vol. 12, No. 4, pp. 511-533, 2004.
7. Noh, S., "A vision for improving mathematics education in the Internet-based society," *Lecture Notes in Computer Science*, Vol. 2105, pp. 261-272, 2001.
8. Noh, S., Kim, Y., & Kim, M. (Eds.), *Curriculum Development for Mathematics and Information Science in a Knowledge-Based Society*, Seoul, Korea: Ewha Womans University Press, 2003.
9. Noh, S., Kim, Y., Rim, H., & Cho, S., "Evaluation of math education Web sites to develop technology oriented math curriculum," *The Proceedings of SITE(Society for Information Technology and Teacher Education) 2005 Conference*, Phoenix, AZ, March 2005.

10. Reeves, T. C., & Reeves, P. M., "The effective dimensions of interactive learning on the WWW," In B. H. Kahn (Ed.), *Web-Based Instruction*, pp. 59-66, Englewood Cliffs, NJ: Educational Technology, 1997.
11. Stephens, A. C., & Hartmann, C. E., "A Successful Professional Development Project's Failure to Promote Online Discussion about Teaching Mathematics with Technology," *JL of Technology and Teacher Education*, Vol. 12, No. 1, pp. 57-73, 2004.
12. Web-based Education Commission, *Report of the Web-Based Education Commission to the President and the Congress of the United States*. Washington D.C.: The Author, 2000.

Use Case Study of Grid Computing with CGSP[*]

Hai Jin, Xuanhua Shi, and Li Qi

Cluster and Grid Computing Lab,
Huazhong University of Science and Technology, Wuhan, 430074, China
{hjin, xhshi}@hust.edu.cn, quick.qi@gmail.com

Abstract. *ChinaGrid Support Platform* (CGSP) is a grid middleware developed for the deployment of ChinaGrid. CGSP aims to integrate all sorts of heterogeneous resources distributed over CERNET, and provide transparent, high performance, reliable, secure and convenient grid services for scientific researchers and engineers. In addition to supply the portal to ChinaGrid, CGSP offers a whole set of tools for developing and deploying various grid applications. Analyzing large and distributed image dataset is a crucial step in understanding and constructing bioinformatics, military and medical systems. Due to the large scale dataset, such analyzing work is challenging. In this paper, a use case scenario of image processing with CGSP is presented. Such use cases illustrate how to migrate the traditional image process applications to grid systems for different roles of image processing. The purpose of this paper is to introduce the CGSP and let the engineers and scientists from different research areas know how to build a grid testbed with CGSP and how to deploy applications on it smoothly.

1 Introduction

Grid computing presents a new trend to distributed and Internet computing for coordinating large scale heterogeneous resources sharing and problem solving in dynamic, multi-institutional virtual organizations [8], and now the grid technologies are involving towards an *Open Grid Service Architecture* (OGSA) in which a grid provides an extensible set of services that virtual organizations can be aggregated in various ways [7]. According to such philosophy, the resources and services can be accessed with standard interfaces which can be defined, described, registered, discovered and executed. The purpose of grid computing is to eliminate the resource island and to make computing and services ubiquitous.

There are lots of important grid computing projects all over the world, such as TeraGrid [16], IPG [11], DataGrid [15], EGEE [17], UK e-Science Program [19]. ChinaGrid Project is based on the network infrastructure of *China Education and Research Network* (CERNET) [4]. ChinaGrid was launched in 2002 by *China Ministry of Education* (MoE), which is the largest grid computing project in China, aiming to provide the nationwide grid computing platform and services for research and education purpose among 100 key universities in China. The vision for ChinaGrid

---

[*] This paper is supported by ChinaGrid project funded by Ministry of Education, China.

S. Shimojo et al. (Eds.): HSI 2005, LNCS 3597, pp. 94–103, 2005.

project is to deploy the largest, most advanced and most practical grid computing platform in China or even around the world [10].

ChinaGrid Support Platform (CGSP) is a grid middleware developed for the deploying of ChinaGrid [3]. CGSP aims to integrate all sorts of heterogeneous resources distributed over CERNET, and provide transparent, high performance, reliable, secure and convenient grid services for scientific researchers and engineers. In addition to supply the portal to ChinaGrid, CGSP offers a whole set of tools for developing and deploying various grid applications.

There are five important applications over CGSP, image processing is one of them, called image processing grid [5]. Analyzing large and distributed image dataset is a crucial step in understanding and constructing bioinformatics, military and medical systems. Due to the large scale dataset, such analyzing work is challenging. In this paper, a use case scenario of image processing with CGSP is presented. Such use cases illustrate how to migrate the traditional image process applications to grid systems for different roles of image processing. The purpose of this paper is to introduce the CGSP and let the engineers and scientists from different research areas know how to build a grid testbed with CGSP and how to deploy application on it smoothly.

The rest of the paper is organized as follows: in section 2, the related works about use case study in scientific world is introduced. In section 3, the building blocks of CGSP are presented. In section 4, use cases for image processing grid for different roles are studied, and the conclusion is made in section 5.

2 Related Works

Virtually all areas of science and engineering, as well as an increasing number of other fields, are turning to computational science to provide crucial tools to further their disciplines. Cactus is an open source tool with *Common Component Architecture* [2][6]. Globus toolkit is middleware proposed to support scientific applications [1], now it is involving towards WSRF [18]. CoG is a toolkit based on Globus Toolkit which tries to bridge the gap between commodity distributed computing and high-performance grids [12], and the combination of commodity and grid technologies will enhance the functionality, maintenance, and deployment of new developed grid services.

The *Grid Computing Environment* research group is aimed at contributing to the coherence and interoperability of frameworks, portals, PSEs, and other grid-based computing environments by establishing standards that are required to integrate technology implementations and solutions [9]. The *Open Grid Computing Environments* (OGCE) project was established in fall 2003 to foster collaborations and sharable components with portal developers worldwide, which leverages ongoing portals research and development from Argonne National Laboratory, Indiana University, the University of Michigan, the National Center for Supercomputing Applications, and the Texas Advanced Computing Center [13].

For realizing the OGSA vision of a broadly-applicable and adopted framework for distributed system integration, the OGSA working group analyzes a wide variety of grid use case scenarios of both e-science and e-business applications, such use cases cover infrastructure and application scenarios for both commercial and scientific areas [14], and such use cases drive the definition and prioritization of OGSA components. The design and implementation of CGSP follows OGSA, in this paper we will present use case of image-processing applications with building blocks of CGSP.

3 Building Blocks of CGSP

CGSP 1.0 was released in January 2005, and the building blocks for CGSP 1.0 are shown in Fig. 1. The current version is based on the core of Globus Toolkit 3.9.1, which is WSRF compatible. There are five 5 building blocks in CGSP 1.0. They are:

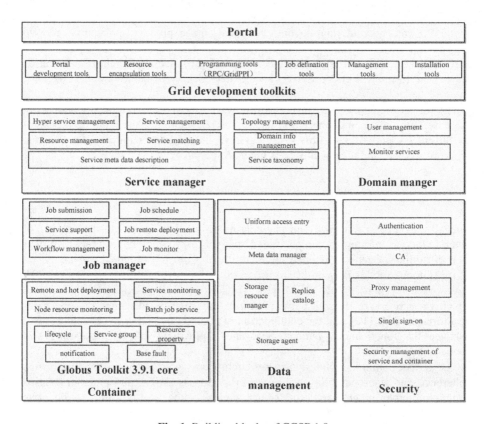

Fig. 1. Building blocks of CGSP 1.0

1. Grid portal: grid portal is the entrance for the end user to use grid services. By using grid portal, users can submit their jobs, monitor the running of jobs, manage and transfer data, inquiry the grid resource information. Grid portal also provides other facilities such as user management and accounting of grid resource usage.

2. Grid development toolkits: they provide toolkit to pack the resource to grid services, the deployment and management toolkit for grid, and programming model to deploy complex grid application in grid environment.

3. Information service: it is responsible for the management of various resources within grid environment, provides a global resource view and grid information services, and updates grid resource information in real time manner. The main purpose is to provide real time information of various grid resources for end users and other modules in grid environment.

4. Grid management: it provides basic support for various jobs in grid environment. It consists four parts:

    ● Service container: it provides a grid service installation, deployment, running, and monitoring environment on each node in grid environment. It also provides necessary support to monitor the real time resources status of each grid node.

    ● Data manager: it is responsible for the management of various storage resources and data files in grid environment. It provides a global file view, so that users can access various data files transparently.

    ● Job manager: based on information services and data management, it provides support for job management, scheduling, and monitoring for end users' computational task, so that data and resources can be accessed transparently within grid and cooperative working among distributed resources.

    ● Domain manager: ChinaGrid is organized in domain. A domain refers to an independent grid system to provide services to the others. A domain can be a specialized grid, or a regional grid. The main function of domain manager is responsible for user management, logging, accounting within domain and interacting with other domains. It makes the domain administrator manage the users, services, and resources within domain easily, and interactive policies among domains.

5. Grid security: it provides user authentication, resources and services authorization, encrypted transmission, and the mapping between users to resources authorization.

4 Use Case for Different Roles of Image Processing

In this section, we first present the use case of customers and their needs, and followed by some scenarios, explaining the some scenarios of image processing on grid, and then illustrate how to fulfill the requirements for the use case.

4.1 Customers

There are five roles of customers in the image processing grid, they are: image processing grid creator, resources provider, end user, domain manager, and grid application developer. The needs for different customers are different.

1. Grid creator: Strictly speaking, the grid creator is not a customer but a provider. However, the grid creator can benefit from the creation of image processing grid to get a single-system-image virtual machine for image processing, and have a creased manageability of the heterogeneous resources. The requirements to grid creator are to increase the utilization of the distributed resources and to provide a uniform access portal to end users. According to several analysts' reports, actual utilization ratio is often less than 20% for scattered resources, increasing to 70% or more when they are consolidated. Also some resources are reserved for failover and provisioning; in other words, they are not put to productive use. It is possible to share such resources among multiple systems, with physical location not being the single determining factor whether sharing is possible or not. Generally, the grid creator is a grid application developer.

2. Resource provider: Resource provider is resource owner who tries to donate usage of resources to end users in ChinaGrid, such as computational resources, storage resources, data resources, software and devices. As the name shows, resource provider is a provider, but it can be regarded as a customer for benefit from increasing utilization of resources and increasing reputation of the resources, especially for software resources. The requirement placed on resource provider is how to provide uniform access to these heterogeneous resources for different users, especially for some heritage resources. Heritage resources are very important software which can not be changed by the end user and application programmer. It should be possible to provide a good resource wrapping method to get uniform access.

3. Domain manager: Domain manager is a very important role in ChinaGrid, as ChinaGrid is organized in different domains. The domains of ChinaGrid are the representations of resource sharing and autonomy. ChinaGrid has two kinds of domains, one is domains of zones, such as ChinaGrid Southeast Domain, ChinaGrid Northeast Domain and ChinaGrid Southwest Domain; the other is logical domain for different application, such as image processing grid domain, bioinformatics grid domain, and CFD grid domain. The requirements for image-grid domain manager are user management, logging, accounting, system monitoring and access control policy making.

4. Application developer: The application developer is the role who tries to construct a problem solving environment for complicated application using APIs of CGSP and to construct grid applications. With the problem solving environment, it is easy for the end user to deploy and run applications on the grid, and the grid application runs across multi-institution with many different services, such as computational services, storage services and data transfer services. The requirement placed on the application developer is to discover the distributed resources and services, and to fully use the distributed resources.

5. End user: The end user regards grid as single-system-image machine, making computing and services ubiquitous. The only requirement for the end user is to know the content about the specific image-processing application, such as the end user of remote sensing image processing should knows the details of image-processing flow and the parameters of each step.

Figure 2 depicts some of the actors described above. The end user interacts with the client devices or portal, the domain manager configures the CGSP components and the domain information to fulfill the functions required by image processing applications, the resource provider wraps the resources for uniform access, the application developer programs with APIs of CGSP, and the grid creator deploys the CGSP on the resources.

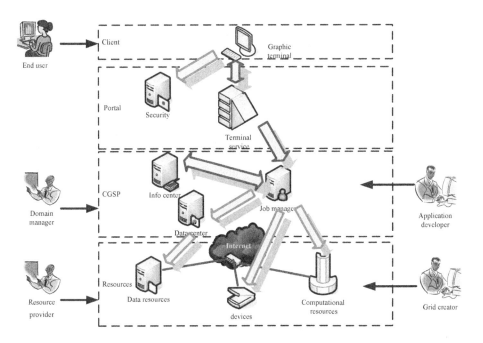

Fig. 2. Image processing grid and its customers

4.2 Scenarios

There are three pilot image processing applications in ChinaGrid, and we consider them as three scenarios.

1. Digital Virtual Human

Virtual human is a three-dimension human fabric in details synthesized by computer, and these data are from true human body. The medical scientists can make medical studies with virtual human instead of true human, by means of controlling the virtual human fabric. State-of-the art researches on virtual human involve use of large-scale slice data for human body. Generally, researches in virtual human have two steps: 1) Reconstruct the data of the slice. This step is both computation-intensive and data-intensive, for there are lots of files of body slices, and the data should be reconstruct to text-style file for romance and display; 2) Romance and display. This step is computation-intensive and includes large number of small files.

For virtual human image processing application, the grid first finds some powerful computational resource which has large storage system to perform the reconstruction action, and then tries to transfer the small files quickly to romance servers. The romance server performs romancing action and the medical scientists can make analysis work on these images.

2. Remote sensing image processing

Remote sensing image processing is widely used in GIS systems. The requirement for remote sensing image processing is coarse granularity programming. For using in GIS or other systems, the images from the remote sensing should be transformed by several steps, and these steps are computation-intensive or data-intensive, or both. Generally, there are four steps in transformation: 1) image grey transformation; 2) image filter transformation; 3) image grey scale transformation; 4) image segment transformation.

As there are large numbers of remote sensing images, and the grid should find different powerful resources for different steps, and this action that the following step get the data for the previous step, should be transparent to the end user or the systems which use the remote sensing images.

3. Medical image processing

Images of various kinds are increasingly important to medical diagnostic processes and difficult problems are encountered in selecting the most appropriate imaging modalities, acquiring optimal quality images, and processing images to obtain the highest quality information. The aim of medical image processing is try to set up a diagnostic system which analyzes the radiology images to improving the diagnostic accuracy and efficiency for doctors. First the hospitals store the available radiology image in different datasets, secondly, when a new patient comes with radiology, the doctor tries to find an available image in these dataset which matches the patient's radiology and make diagnosis. A challenge issue is to query the details of the images in these datasets or even get a subset of one image remotely.

4.3 CGSP Capabilities and Services Utilization

From the scenarios described above, the following functions are required:
   (1) Resources discovery and services discovery. The image processing applications should pick out a perfect resource to deploy the specific programs, and the applications should know where to get the services to fulfill the required function;
   (2) Remote deployment. For uniform access to all kinds of resources, especially software, the resource should be wrapped into services, and when the system finds the perfect hosting environment, the services are able to be deployed remotely;
   (3) Reliable data transfer and data sharing. Image processing is data-intensive;
   (4) Meta-data management. There are large number of data files in the medical image processing and virtual human applications, and the applications require to get these files quickly and correctly;
   (5) Workflow management. Almost all image processing applications work in workflow style, especially the remote sensing image processing application;

(6) Security. All activities in image processing should be secure, such as secure data transfer, authentication, access control;

(7) Monitoring. The customer wants to monitor his/her applications running on the remote environment;

(8) Load balancing. The grid monitors the job performance and adjusts allocated resources to match the load and fairly distributes end users' requests to all the resources;

(9) Virtual organization. Upon the customer job request, the image processing grid creates a VO which provides resources to the job.

CGSP provides the following functions:

1. Resource management. This module in CGSP provides resource register and resource discovery functionality. The customer can pick out the available resource which is qualified for the application.

2. Service management and service matching. These modules in CGSP provide service discovery functionality.

3. Remote and hot deployment. This module in CGSP is based on the core Globus Toolkit 3.9.1. With changing some structure in Globus toolkit and adding some new materials in it, the module provides remote and hot deployment functionality, which means that the customer can deploy applications remotely and does not need to restart the container.

4. Data management. The modules in data management provide reliable data transfer service and meta-data management functionalities. The data transfer service in CGSP is based on a secure FTP protocol, which is reliable and high-speed. The meta-data manager controls all the data in the data space with the help of storage agent.

5. Job management. In CGSP, the job is defined in extended BPEL language, which is a workflow language. The workflow management provides functionalities of workflow creation, workflow execution, workflow monitoring and fault handling. The job management can handle the requirement for workflow management and job monitoring.

6. Job scheduling and hyper service management. Hyper service is a virtual service or an abstract of a group of services that have the same interfaces. For the end user, the hyper service can be revoked like ordinary services if there is any physical service in the grid. The hyper service management modules provide the functionality to dispatch the user invoke to physical services, and the dispatch action is a scheduling method which works together with the job scheduling module to make the grid environment load balanced.

7. Security. The security block provides authentication and authorization services, and with such services, the security requirements for image processing is satisfied.

8. Domain manager. The domain manager provides the functionality to define domains and with the help of security modules, the domain manager can create a VO for image processing applications.

We take remote sensing image processing as an example to illustrate how to deploy services and how to run programs on CGSP, as depicted in Fig. 3. Firstly, the grid creator installs the CGSP on the resources. Second, the resource provider wraps the resources into service with the Service Wrapper in CGSP. Third, the domain manager configures the domains. Fourth, the application developer defines the job, which is a workflow includes four steps, as mentioned in the scenarios sections. Finally, the end user can process the application through the graphic terminals.

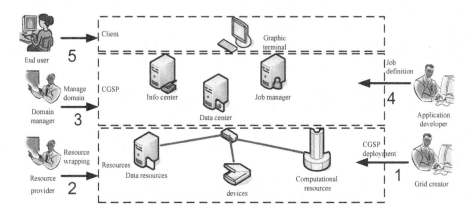

Fig. 3. Flow of image processing with CGSP

4.4 Use Case Situation and Analysis

Sizeable work has been done in the image processing, which works with the traditional HPC methods, and it is not an open architecture for resource collaboration. Several existing cutting-edge technologies and products attempt to solve the workflow style problems, such as WSFL by IBM, XLANG from Microsoft, BEPL4WS derived from both of them, WSCI by SUN, WSCL by HP, and WFMC (*Workflow Management Coalition*) has been working in this field for a long time. In grid computing field, GSFL is proposed by ANL. These techniques are of great help to improve the design and implementation of CGSP.

5 Conclusion

In this paper, we introduce CGSP with use case study of image processing. CGSP is a grid middleware developed for the deploying of ChinaGrid. CGSP aims to integrate all sorts of heterogeneous resources distributed over CERNET, and provide transparent, high performance, reliable, secure and convenient grid services for scientific researchers and engineers. In addition to supply the portal to ChinaGrid, CGSP offers a whole set of tools for developing and deploying various grid applications. Such use cases illustrate how to migrate the traditional image process applications to grid systems for different roles of image processing. Now, all the services over the ChinaGrid can be viewed through the ChinaGrid portal.

References

[1] W. Allcock, A. Chervenak, I. Foster, L. Pearlman, V. Welch, and M. Wilde, "Globus Toolkit Support for Distributed Data-Intensive Science", *Proceedings of Computing in High Energy Physics (CHEP '01)*, September 2001.

[2] Common Component Architecture (CCA) Home Page, http://www.cca-forum.org.

[3] ChinaGrid, http://www.chinagrid.edu.cn

[4] China Education and Research Network, http://www.edu.cn/

[5] ChinaGrid Image Processing Grid, http://grid.hust.edu.cn/ImageGrid/

[6] Cactus Numerical Relativity Community, http://www.cactuscode.org/Community/Relativity.html.

[7] I. Foster, C. Kesselman, J. M. Nick, and S. Tuecke, "The physiology of the grid: An open grid services architecture for distributed systems integration", http://www.gridforum.org/ogsi-wg/drafts/ogsa_draft2.9_2002-06-22.pdf, 2002.

[8] I. Foster, C. Kesselman, and S. Tuecke, "The Anatomy of the Grid: Enabling Scalable Virtual Organizations", *International J. Supercomputer Applications*, 15(3), 200-222, 2001.

[9] GCE-RG, https://forge.gridforum.org/projects/gce-rg

[10] H. Jin, "ChinaGrid: Making Grid Computing a Reality", *Digital Libraries: International Collaboration and Cross-Fertilization - Lecture Notes in Computer Science, Vol.3334*, Springer-Verlag, December 2004, pp.13-24.

[11] W. E. Johnston, D. Gannon, and B. Nitzberg, "Grids as Production Computing Environments: The Engineering Aspects of NASA's Information Power Grid", *Proceedings of 8th IEEE Symposium on High Performance Distributed Computing*, 1999.

[12] G. von Laszewski, I. Foster, J. Gawor, W. Smith, and S. Tuecke, "CoG Kits: A Bridge between Commodity Distributed Computing and High-Performance Grids", *Proceedings of ACM Java Grande 2000 Conference*, pp.97-106, San Francisco, CA, June 2000.

[13] OGCE, http://www.ogce.org/

[14] Open Grid Services Architecture Use Cases, http://www.gridforum.org/documents/GWD-I-E/GFD-I.029v2.pdf

[15] The DataGrid Project, http://eu-datagrid.web.cern.ch/eu-datagrid/

[16] The TeraGrid Project, http://www.teragrid.org/

[17] The EGEE Project, http://egee-intranet.web.cern.ch/egee-intranet/gateway.html

[18] The Web Services Resource Framework, http://www.globus.org/wsrf/.

[19] UK e-Science Programme, http://www.rcuk.ac.uk/escience/

Visual Media Retrieval Framework Using Web Service

Yunmook Nah[1], Bogju Lee[1], and Jungsun Kim[2]

[1] School of Electrical, Electronics, and Computer Engineering, Dankook University,
San 8 Hannam-dong, Yongsan-gu, Seoul 140-714, Korea
{ymnah, blee}@dku.edu
[2] School of Electrical Engineering and Computer Science, Hanyang University,
1271 Sa-dong, Ansan-si, Kyungki-do 425-791, Korea
jskim@cse.hanyang.ac.kr

Abstract. The need for content-based image retrieval from image databases is ever increasing rapidly in many applications, such as electronic art museums, internet shopping malls, internet search engines, and medical information systems. Many such image resources have been previously developed and widely spread over the internet. In this paper, we propose a Web Service-driven architecture, named the HERMES(tHE Retrieval framework for visual MEdia Service), to support effective retrieval on large volumes of visual media resources. We explain how semantic metadata and ontology can be utilized to realize more intelligent content-based retrieval on visual media data.

1 Introduction

Searching image data is one of the essential functions for image database systems (or video database systems) and multimedia database systems, which take important role in majority of emerging IT(information technology) applications, such as electronic art museums, GIS(Geographical Information Systems), digital library, internet e-commerce, EDMS(Electronic Document Management Systems), and medical information systems. The need for content-based image retrieval(CBIR) from image databases is ever increasing rapidly in these applications.

The pioneering work has been done by IBM's QBIC(Query By Image Content) system, which supports queries using color, shape, sketch, and texture features on images, such as post stamps, art pictures, and trademark drawings [1]. The Chabot system was another interesting CBIR system, with high level concepts, such as "light yellow" and "sunset," as well as low level features based on color [2]. One of the most recent research work has been done by the SIMPLIcity system which supports CBIR based on the color, texture, shape features, while increasing matching correctness by utilizing local features on regions [3]. In the medical domain, the KMeD(Knowledge-Based Medical Database) system utilizes semantic modeling focusing on object shapes and spatial relationships between them [4,5]. We developed NERD-IDB, which supports the meaning-based retrieval on neuroscience image databases [6]. We also proposed web catalog image retrieval system, which support intelligent retrieval using keyword, color, texture features and high-level concepts [7,8].

S. Shimojo et al. (Eds.): HSI 2005, LNCS 3597, pp. 104–113, 2005.

Web Services are a standardized way of integrating Web-based applications using open standards including XML, the SOAP(Simple Object Access Protocol), the WSDL(Web Service Description Language), and the UDDI(Universal Description, Discovery, and Integration) specification. XML structures the message, SOAP transfers the message, WSDL describes the available services, and UDDI list them. XML describes both the nature of each self-contained function and the data that flows among systems [9]. The CPXe, proposed by Eastman Kodak, is a Web Service driven photo marketing system, but this system supports simple keyword-based searching only and does not utilize semantics [10]. The SOTA is an ontology-mediated Web Service system for smart office task automation [11]. The previously developed image databases, such as QBIC, Chabot, NERD-IDB, etc, can be considered as image service providers from the viewpoint of Web Services. The main idea of this paper is to exploit the Web Service-based approach to support intelligent retrieval on large volumes of visual media resources, widely distributed over the web.

This paper is an effort to make visual media, such as image and video data, better utilized by visual media consumers. The major purpose of this paper is: 1) to show how visual media, widely spread over the internet, can be effectively searched using Web Service technology and 2) to present how semantic metadata and ontology can be utilized to realize more practical and intelligent content-based retrieval on visual media. The architecture named the HERMES(tHE Retrieval framework for visual MEdia Service) is a Web Service-enabled visual media retrieval framework which consists of HERMES/B node (Web Service broker) and multiple HERMES/P nodes (Web Service providers), each servicing their own visual media resources.

The remainder of this paper is organized as follows. Section 2 describes overview of visual media metadata. Section 3 explains the Web Service-based visual media retrieval framework architecture. In section 4, we show how ontology and metadata are utilized, to allow more intelligent retrieval on visual media data. Section 5 describes Web Service workflow for service registration and query processing. Finally, section 6 summarizes the paper.

2   Visual Media Metadata

In database terms, *formatted data* means traditional data, such as numeric data and character data, and *unformatted data* means new kinds of multimedia data, such as text, image, graphics, audio, video, spatial data, time series data, and document data. Metadata means *data for data*. Let's assume image data is bitmap(or pixelmap) itself, which is usually called *raw data*. Image metadata is *data for image data*. There are two types of basic metadata for images.

- **registration metadata:** Image resolution(width, height), color map, compression ratio, etc are typical examples of registration metadata. This metadata is required to display and manipulate images. In image files, this information is usually hidden within image headers.
- **description metadata:** Image title, caption, keywords, natural language descriptions, and image file names are typical examples of descriptive metadata. This metadata is used to search images, when content-based retrieval operations are not supported.

For content-based retrieval, we can define multiple layers of image metadata on top of raw image data.

- **global feature metadata layer:** Average values or multi-dimensional vectors representing color, texture, and shape of images are examples of global feature metadata. This metadata is heavily used in current content-based retrieval systems.
- **local feature metadata layer:** Average values or multi-dimensional vectors representing color, texture, and shape of each objects or regions belonging to a given image are examples of local feature metadata.
- **semantic contents metadata layer** (or **knowledge layer**): Subjective feelings and knowledges on images, such as concepts, meaning, category, spatial relationships, or other useful interpretations are examples of semantic metadata.

```
<?xml version="1.0" encoding="UTF-8"?>
<dc:COMMON xmlns:dc = "http://purl.org/dc/elements/1.1/"
xmlns:dcterms="http://purl.org/dc/terms/"
xmlns:xsi= "http://www.w3.org/2001/XMLSchema-instance" xsi:SchemaLocation="./dc.xsd">
     <dc:TITLE> Flowers </dc:TITLE>
     <dc:CREATOR> Van Gogh's </dc:CREATOR>
     <dc:RIGHTS> Neue Pinakothek </dc:RIGHTS>
     <dc:DATE> Year 1998 </dc:DATE>
</dc:COMMON>
```

(a) Sample image data   (b) Image metadata expressed in DC standard

Fig. 1. Sample image and its metadata

There are many metadata standards, such as DC(Dublin Core) [13] for electronic cataloging, VRA(Visual Resources Association) [14] for visual art images, and MPEG-7 MDS [15] for video metadata description. Each of these metadata is proposed by different organization with different format. Also, these metadata standards usually put focus on description metadata only. MPEG-7 MDS partly covers global feature, local feature and semantic contents metadata. Figure 1 shows a sample image data and its metadata represented in DC standard.

3 Visual Media Service Architecture

The architecture named the HERMES is a Web Service-enabled visual media retrieval framework architecture which consists of HERMES/B node (Web Service broker) and multiple HERMES/P nodes (Web Service providers), each servicing visual media resources using their own metadata standard format or customized metadata format. The overall HERMES architecture is depicted in Figure 2.

Figure 3 and Figure 4 show the detail architecture of HERMES/B and HERMES/P, respectively. Albeit we did not show in Figure 2, besides the broker and service providers, we assume that there are other entities that provide local and/or global feature extraction services. They are called F.E.S (Feature Extraction Service) Providers. But, HERMES does not exclude the possibility of internal feature extraction services.

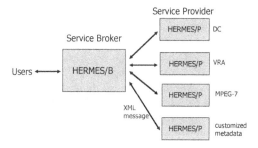

Fig. 2. The HERMES architecture

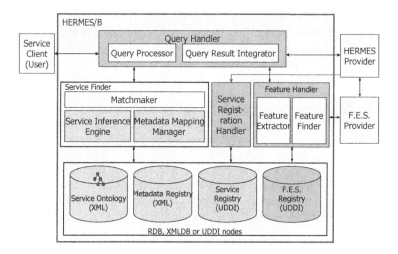

Fig. 3. HERMES Broker architecture

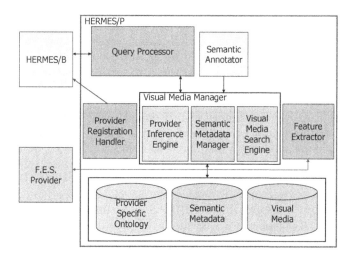

Fig. 4. HERMES Provider architecture

The major functions of HERMES/B modules are as follows. *Query Handler* receives user queries, reformulates queries using metadata and service ontology, and sends the reformulated queries to HERMES/Ps. *Query Processor* transforms query string into provider-specific XML queries. *Query Result Integrator* combines query results and sends them back to users. *Matchmaker* finds best service provider list for the given query. *Service Inference Engine* determines service provider list by using Service Ontology and Service Registry. *Metadata Mapping Manager* transforms query string into provider-specific format by using Metadata Registry. *Service Registration Handler* registers services provided by HERMES/Ps. Provider-specific service and metadata information are stored in Service Registry and Metadata Registry. *Feature Handler* selects suitable F.E.S. Providers and/or obtains features using them.

The major functions of HERMES/P modules are as follows. *Query Processor* receives and extends reformulated queries from HERMES/B. *Visual Media Manager* coordinates image searching processes. *Provider Inference Engine* reformulates user queries by using Provider Specific Ontology. *Semantic Metadata Manager* manages semantic metadata for each image using Semantic Annotator. Semantic metadata consists of description metadata, global feature, local feature and semantic contents metadata. Concepts in query term are transformed into corresponding color values. *Visual Media Search Engine* searches provider images by utilizing description metadata, global feature, local feature and semantic contents metadata. This module performs similarity-based retrieval using multi-dimensional index structures, such as B-trees and R-trees. *Provider Registration Handler* receives image category and common metadata information from HERMES/B. It also reports provider service types and metadata standard types (or its own metadata schema) to HERMES/B. *Semantic Annotator* is a provider-side tool to annotate metadata for each image.

4   Ontology Representation and Metadata Mapping

The representative sample queries are as follows: find 'modern painting' images whose creator is 'Albers' (Q1), find 'passionate' images whose creator is 'Van Gogh' (Q2), find photos of 'Californian' nature (Q3) and find pictures similar with the given image (Q4). Q1-Q3 are example queries, which require ontology-based service site matchmaking and metadata mapping. For Q4, we need to extract global and local features of the sample image by using F.E.S. Providers.

For Q1, we need service ontology to find provider sites related with image, art, painting and modern painting. For Q2, we need definition of concept 'passionate' with related emotion ontology to find 'passionate' images. For Q3, we need service ontology to find sites related with image, photo and scenery. Figure 5 shows Service Ontology, which is used by HERMES/B. The Service Ontology can be viewed as the superset of all the provider-specific ontologies from the HERMES/P. In other words, the provider-specific ontologies of the HERMES/P take the part of the Service Ontology. In this paper, the ontologies are assumed to have the tree form.

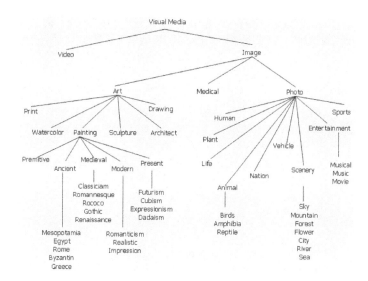

Fig. 5. The ontologies

The Service Ontology is stored in RDF format, as shown in Figure 6. The RDF has the form of subject-property-object which can easily represent various relationships such as 'is-a'.

```
<owl:Ontology rdf:about="">
    <owl:imports rdf:resource="http://purl.org/dc/elements/1.1/"/>
    <owl:imports rdf:resource="http://www.w3.org/2001/XMLSchema"/>
    <owl:imports rdf:resource="http://www.w3.org/2000/01/rdf-schema"/>
    <owl:imports rdf:resource="http://www.w3.org/2002/07/owl"/>
    <owl:imports rdf:resource="http://www.w3.org/1999/02/22-rdf-syntax-ns"/>
</owl:Ontology>
<owl:Class rdf:ID="VisualMedia"> </owl:Class>
<owl:Class rdf:ID="Video"> <rdfs:subClassOf rdf:resource="#VisualMedia"/>
</owl:Class>
<owl:Class rdf:ID="Image"> <rdfs:subClassOf rdf:resource="#VisualMedia"/>
</owl:Class>
<owl:Class rdf:ID="Art"> <rdfs:subClassOf rdf:resource="#Image"/>
</owl:Class>
<owl:Class rdf:ID="Medical"> <rdfs:subClassOf rdf:resource="#Image"/>
</owl:Class>
```

Fig. 6. Service Ontology in RDF format

Each metadata standard and customized metadata can use different element name for the exactly same element. For example, an element 'Creator' can be tagged by different element name 'Creator Name' in another metadata. Metadata Mapping Manager is used to handle these problems. Metadata Registry of HERMES/B consists of ProviderElement table, Mapping table and MDR(MetaData Registry) table. ProviderElement table stores provider-specific metadata information, MDR table stores standard metadata information and Mapping table stores mapping information between metadata formats. During the service registration process (see Section 5.2), when the given metadata schema type of current provider is not yet registered, the corresponding metadata schema information is processed and stored into ProviderElement table, Mapping table and MDR table of Metadata Registry.

```
<Map>
<MDRelement>
<DataElementName> <element>Creator</element> </DataElementName>
<ElementID>DC001</ElementID>
<DataType> <DataTypeName>string</DataTypeName> </DataType>
</MDRelement>
<LocalElement>
<ElementName>CreatorName</ElementName>
<ElementPath> <parent> Image </parent> </ElementPath>
<DataType> <DataTypeName>string</DataTypeName> </DataType>
</LocalElement>
<MappingRule>
<MappingType> <SemanticType>Direct_substitution</SemanticType>
</MappingType>
</MappingRule>
</Map>
```

Fig. 7. Metadata mapping example

Figure 7 is a mapping instance example. This XML instance shows that the 'Creator' element of DC standard is equivalent with 'Creator Name' of MDR element. By using this mapping information, a query with term Creator = 'Albers' can be reformulated as Creator Name = 'Albers.'

5 Web Service Interfaces and Workflow

In this section, we will first describe the Web Service interfaces for HERMES/B, HERMES/P and F.E.S. Providers, and then show the basic service workflow of the system in terms of two important scenarios: service registration and query processing scenarios.

5.1 Web Service Interfaces

For the sake of brevity, we only show externally significant operations in each of the Web interfaces for HERMES/B, HERMES/P and F.E.S. Providers. HERMES/B interface consists of the following operations: *getAllDomains* returns the list of all domains derived from the service ontology; *registerMe* registers a named service provider to HERMES/B together with information about metadata schema; *getFESInfo* returns the list of Feature Extraction Services for a specific domain images; and *acceptQuery* accepts client's query and returns a set of images collected from one or more service providers. HERMES/P interface includes *acceptQuery*, which analyzes reformulated query from HERMES/B and returns appropriate images. Feature Extraction Engine interface includes *GetFeatureInformation*, which receives a list of images and returns the list of extracted features.

5.2 Service Registration Scenario

In this scenario, service providers register themselves on the HERMES/B together with the information about their metadata schema. The service registration occurs in two phases: Service domain search and Service provider registration.

In first phase, the Provider Registration Handler of HERMES/P first calls getAll-Domains() service of HERMES/B and receives visual media service domain information and service ontology from Service Registration Handler of HERMES/B. It then determines its corresponding service domain from the list.

In second phase, the Provider Registration Handler registers itself by calling registerMe() service of HERMES/B, while providing information, such as provider ID, domain list, metadata schema type, metadata schema version and metadata schema. This service call is received by the Service Registration Handler of HERMES/B. The Service Registration Handler then calls registerProvider() service of the Service Finder and stores UDDI-related information, such as ProviderID, Service Key, Service URL and tModel, into Service Registry and service domain list and metadata-related information into Metadata Registry. The service domain list information is stored into Matchmaker Cache table of Metadtata Registry by referencing appropriate Service Ontology and Service Registry.

Service providers can optionally use the Semantic Annotator for their registration for convenience purpose. Also, the Semantic Annotator of HERMES/P provides metadata fill-in form to insert description metadata and semantic contents metadata for each image. The input fields of this semantic annotation form are determined according to the metadata standard used by each HERMES/P. The whole metadata for each image, annotated manually or generated automatically, are stored as the Semantic Metadata of corresponding HERMES/P.

5.3 Query Processing Scenarios

When user(Service Client) fills query form, the query string is received by acceptQuery() service of the Query Handler of HERMES/B. The Query Handler then calls customizedQueryWithProviderList() service of the Service Finder. The Service Finder returns service provider list with provider-specific queries, which are reformulated by using service ontology and metadata mapping information of HERMES/B. For Q1, the appropriate service providers for 'modern painting' is determined by considering Service Ontology, Service Registry and Matchmaker Cache table of Metadata Registry. To find which providers service the 'modern painting', the Service Ontology is traversed from the root to the target node (Visual Meida - Image - Art - Painting - Modern, for Q1). All the nodes under the target node (Romanticism, Realistic, and Impression, for modern painting) are traversed too. Any provider that services any of the resulted node set should be included in the target provider list. The provider-service information is of course located in the Service Registry and Metadata Registry. For example, a provider that services 'Art' is included in the target provider list while the provider that services 'Photo' is not. Q3 is similarly processed: 'Scenery' under 'Photo' is the target node in this case. The query like Q2 is not easy to determine the provider list since there is no provider-specific information in the query. The query is simply transferred to all the providers.

The reformulated queries by HERMES/B are transferred to HERMES/P by calling acceptQuery() service of HERMES/P wrapper interface. A query received by HERMES/P is sent to executeQuery() service of the Visual Media Manager and then reformulated again by considering provider-specific ontology and semantic metadata of HERMES/P. In case of Q1, the 'modern painting' is expanded to {'Romanticism',

'Realistic', and 'Impression'} using the provider-specific ontology in HERMES/P so that the search engine can easily match the target images. In case of Q2, the emotional term 'passionate' is changed to corresponding color values by using Semantic Metadata [16]. The final formulated query is then transferred to the Visual Media Search Engine of HERMES/P. Query results from the participating HERMES/Ps are finally combined, ranked, and returned to the Service Client by the Query Result Integrator of HERMES/B. In case of Q4, the internal workflow of both HERMES/B and HERMES/P are still similar to that of previous query examples, except that interaction with external (possible internal) F.E.S. Providers are required to extract local and global features from the submitted image.

6 Conclusion

In this paper, we proposed HERMES architecture, which is a Web Service-enabled visual media retrieval framework architecture which consists of HERMES/B (broker) and multiple HERMES/P (provider), each servicing visual media resources using their own metadata standard format or customized metadata format. The HERMES architecture intensively uses semantic metadata and ontology to realize more practical and intelligent content-based retrieval on visual media. The proposed architecture can be utilized to effectively search visual media, which are widely spread over the internet, using leading-edge Web Service technology.

Our effort for the experimental implementation of the HERMES architecture is at an early stage. The fuller exposition of implementation details are deferred to subsequent papers. We believe that experimental studies of the performance aspects are highly meaningful subjects for future research.

Acknowledgements

This work was supported by grant No. R01-2003-000-10133-0 from the Basic Research Program of the Korea Science and Engineering Foundation. We would like to thank Chulbum Ahn, Eunyoung Kwon, Sungwoo Lee, Woosang Cho, Sangjin Han, Myoung Mi Yang and Byung Hun Jeong, who are currently developing the prototype of HERMES architecture.

References

1. Flickner, M. et al.: Query by Image and Video Content: The QBIC System. Computer. IEEE CS Press (Sept. 1995) 23-32
2. Ogle, V.E. and Stonebraker, M.: Chabot: Retrieval from a Relational Database of Images. Computer. IEEE CS Press (Sept. 1995) 40-48
3. Wang, J.Z., Li, J., and Wiederhold, G.: SIMPLIcity: Semantics-Sensitive Integrated Matching for Picture Libraries. Transactions on Knowledge and Data Engineering, 23(9). IEEE CS Press (2001)
4. Chu, W.W., Ieong, I.T., and Taira, R.K.: A Semantic Modeling Approach for Image Retrieval by Content. VLDB J., 3. (1994) 445-477

5. Chu, W.W., Hsu, C.-C., Cardenas, A. F., and Taira, R. K.: Knowledge-Based Image Retrieval with Spatial and Temporal Constructs. Transactions on Knowledge and Data Engineering, 10(6). IEEE CS Press (1998) 872-888

6. Nah, Y. and Sheu, P. C.-y.: Image Content Modeling for Neuroscience Databases. Proc. Int'l Conf. on Software Eng. And Knowledge Eng.(SEKE). ACM Press (July 2002) 91-98

7. Lee, B. and Nah, Y.: A Color Ratio based Image Retrieval for e-Catalog Image Databases. Proceedings of SPIE: Internet Multimedia Management Systems II, Vol. 4519. SPIE (August 2001) 97-105

8. Hong, S., Lee, C., and Nah, Y.: An Intelligent Web Image Retrieval System. Proceedings of SPIE: Internet Multimedia Management Systems II, Vol. 4519. SPIE (August 2001) 106-115

9. Chung, J.-Y., Lin, K.-J. and Mathieu, R. G.: Web Services Computing: Advancing Software Interoperability. Computer, 36(10). IEEE CS Press (Oct. 2003) 35-37

10. Thompson, T., Weil, R. and Wood M. D.: CPXe: Web Services for Internet Imaging. Computer, 36(10). IEEE CS Press (Oct. 2003) 54-62

11. Tsai, T.M., Yu, H.-K., et al.: Ontology-Mediated Integration of Intranet Web Services. Computer, 36(10). IEEE CS Press (Oct. 2003) 63-71

12. Nah, Y. and Sheu, P. C.-y.: Searching Image Databases by Content. Proc. KSEA-SC Symposium. CSU, Fullerton (March 2002)

13. Dublin Core Organization: Dublin Core Metadata Initiative.   http://dublincore.org /index.shtml/

14. Visual Resources Association Data Standards Committee: VRA Core Categories Ver. 3.0. http://www.vraweb.org/vracore3.htm

15. ISO IEC JTC1/SC29/WG11: Overview of the MPEG-7 Standard. MPEG2001/N4031, Singapore (March 2001)

16. Hong, S. and Nah, Y.: A Design and Implementation of Intelligent Color Image Retrieval System based on Emotion Information. Proc. Korean Database Conference. (May 2004) 243-250

17. Eakins, J.P. and Graham, M.E.: Content-based Image Retrieval A report to the JISC Technology Applications Programme. (Jan 1999) http://www.unn.ac.uk/iidr/research/ cbir/report.html

18. Lew, M.S.: Next Generation Web Searches for Visual Content. Computer. IEEE CS Press (Nov. 2000) 46-53

Proposal of Social Internetworking

Yukio Okada, Kenji Masui, and Youki Kadobayashi

Internet Engineering Laboratory,
Graduate School of Information Science,
Nara Institute of Science and Technology,
8916-5 Takayama, Ikoma, Nara 630-0192, Japan
{yukio-o, kenji-ma, youki-k}@is.naist.jp

Abstract. Social networks that are built on top of the web, e.g., orkut[9], have been proliferating among online communities. We propose social internetworks, where essential functions of social networks are implemented on top of peer-to-peer networks. Participants and communities are connected through attribute queries and reputation queries; reputation queries are applied to attributes with Secure EigenTrust algorithm[1].

1   Introduction

Since the beginning of 2004, several social networking services (SNSs) have been launched on the web. Participants in SNS can invite their acquaintances as a new user to foster the social network. They can also register their personal information such as real names, living places, and hobbies to show to others. Besides, friends list and communities are essential features of SNS. The list of one's acquaintances is managed and published by friends list. Community is a group of participants with common interest.

Today, every time we participate in a new social network, we have to register similar information repeatedly, and this task often makes us tired. Here, we propose social internetworks that solve the above problem and interconnect social networks.

Social internetworking is implemented in P2P network with distributed hash table (DHT). It consolidates and optimizes information in each social network and provides two search methods based on these information. One is attribute-search, the search method by the attributes attached to users and communities. The other is reputation-search, which considers attributes' reputations from users. The computation of total reputation is based on Secure EigenTrust algorithm[1] proposed by Kamver.

In this paper, we first introduce social network services, P2P applications, and Secure EigenTrust algorithm. Then we propose social internetworking, which includes the integration of information, attribute-search and reputation-search. Finally we evaluate its effectiveness.

S. Shimojo et al. (Eds.): HSI 2005, LNCS 3597, pp. 114–124, 2005.

2   Social Network Services

Social network services (SNSs) provide the management of person-to-person links. In order to participate in a SNS, one has to be invited by anyone else who has already been its member. Once you participate in a SNS, you can register your profile to show to others. Thanks to the real-world communication and the responsibility caused by invitations, the atmosphere of SNSs is relatively peaceful. These elements also contribute to increase the degree of reliability of information in SNSs.

Some major SNSs have unique features. For example, orkut[9] allows its users to rate their acquaintances. In mixi[10], a user can track other users in the access log of one's personal page. In GREE[11] and many other services, a user can write introductory essays of one's friends. As the foundation of these features, two common features are implemented in SNSs: friends list and communities.

2.1   Friends List

One of the common features is "friends list," which lists the users who are registered as one's friends. Since it is visible to everyone, users can use it to trace friend links. In many cases, one's acquaintances are also their acquaintances. So a new participant can find and register one's acquaintances via their friends lists. In order to judge whether the found one is really my acquaintance, one's friends list can be used because it should show my acquaintances. Moreover, users can search their acquaintances by name and add them into the friends lists.

In short, friends list plays roles in the clear indication of relations among participants and the promotion of expansion of the social network.

2.2   Communities

The other common feature is "communities." Participants can express themselves by joining in communities, such as "dog-lovers" community and "*foo-bar* university" community, because the communities to which one belongs can define one's identity. Since everyone can see who belongs to one community, one can find other participants who have similar preferences. Furthermore, communities provide the places for discussions to their participants. They can exchange their opinions and knowledge there.

Communities define one's identity, promote the communication and help to share knowledge among their participants.

2.3   Problems of Current SNSs

SNSs have the above features, but these are not perfect. We will explain the problems of these features here.

Convenience. Every SNS has its information on users and communities in its own style. So we have to register similar information when we participate in a new SNS. This repetitive work may demotivate participants and lead to the uneven distribution of information. For instance, one will actively register and update one's information in one's favorite SNS, but neglect other SNSs.

Broken Friend Links. In case that one participates in SNS A but does not in SNS B, friend links existing in SNS A may not appear in SNS B. This problem can be solved by inviting this person to SNS B. As described above, however, they may not willingly invite their acquaintances because these tasks will be a burden on an introducer. In such a manner, SNSs have the possibilities of losing its own original function.

Explosion of Communities. Communities are categorized by some properties, and participants can use them to search communities. Typically users search communities by following methods:

- Specify certain category.
- Specify some words contained in communities' names.
- Choose from the list of communities to which someone (one's friend in many cases) belongs.

There are over 400,000 communities in active SNS, however, so it is definitely difficult to find all preferable communities by above methods.

In order to solve this problem, SNS providers must find out the effective method for sharing and searching information. Though it could be implemented in the centralized system, we think P2P distributed system is more preferable from the viewpoint of the reduction of initial and maintenance cost.

3   P2P Applications

Originally, the whole Internet was formed in P2P network. However, the lack of resources of hosts and networks has commonized the centralized client-server model in the growth history of the Internet. In recent years, even end nodes have enough resources (e.g., fast CPU, massive storage, and always-on broadband network), so we can easily form global P2P network. As a result, P2P applications such as file sharing and P2P multicast have become common. In such context, researchers have been studying on distributed hash table (DHT), which is a data distribution method. Meanwhile, Secure EigenTrust algorithm, which is a reputation algorithm powered by DHT, is also proposed.

3.1   Data Storage with DHT

DHT is the method of resource distribution in P2P networks. In this method, data is stored in the host allocated by the key calculated from the hash function. Partition of storage area achieves data distribution. DHT have been studied on and several implementations exist: Pastry[2], Chord[3], CAN[4], Kademlia[5], Tapestry[6] and Viceroy[7].

They have regarded propagation latency, search latency, update latency and delete latency as a problem on DHT. However, some improved models including ZFM (zoned federation model)[8] are introduced. Consequently, these contributions close the performance gap of centralized client-server model and distributed P2P model. Now P2P applications have more opportunities to spread than ever before.

3.2   Secure EigenTrust Algorithm

Secure EigenTrust algorithm[1] manages reputation in P2P networks by using DHT. This algorithm is intended for use in P2P file sharing networks. It computes reputation of each shared file from files' ratings by peers.

Secure EigenTrust algorithm is designed with these considerations:

– The system should be *self-policing*.
– The system should maintain *anonymity*.
– The system should not assign any *profit to newcomers*.
– The system should have *minimal overhead* in terms of computation, infrastructure, storage, and message complexity.
– The system should be *robust to malicious collectives* of peers who know one another and attempt to collectively subvert the system.

Additionally, Secure EigenTrust algorithm doesn't need the centralized information about how one peer evaluates one object. With the objective of anonymity and robustness, this property is important. Instead, ScoreManagers, who are selected by the hash function of DHT, collect and store evaluated values. One-way hash function ensures anonymity, and the distribution of ScoreManagers improves the robustness of a system.

Anonymity is especially an important element in rating. In centralized client-server model, server administrators can identify users by inspecting server logs. This model might block honest rating. On the other hand, decentralized P2P system will free users from such uneasiness.

Using these two mechanisms, we can solve the problems of sharing the social network information in P2P networks.

4   Social Internetworks

As a solution to the problems described in section 2.3, we propose social internetworking. The basic concept of social internetworking is to share the information of users and communities by using DHT as shown in figure 1. In addition, some shared attributes are attached to enhance search functions. Figure 2 shows the comparison between existing IP network and our overlay network.

4.1   Advantages of Using DHT

In DHT, each peer backs up its allocated data to the neighbor peers to prevent data loss by an accidental disconnection. This will keep data as long as peers needing it exist. So, by storing the information of friends list and communities with DHT, users need not do the repetitive work even if a certain SNS is closed. On the other hand, one can implement unique features of each SNS such as access logs.

4.2   Scalability of Social Internetworking

Social internetworks will produce new opportunities to existing SNSs. In social
internetworks, we can choose authoritative users by consolidating reputations.
These authoritative users who are allocated some roles will activate communities.
For example, their opinions will be of some help to make a proper decision in a
system.

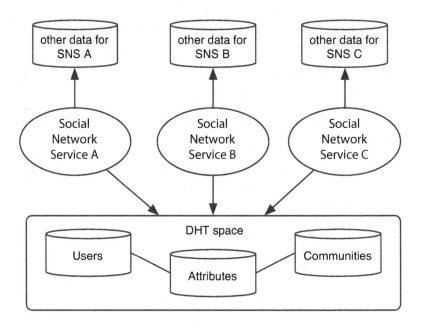

Fig. 1. Social internetworks. SNSs share the information of users, communities and
attributes. They can also have their own data

We can also use XOOPS[12] to interact with social internetworks. XOOPS is
a tool for developing small to large community websites. It provides the features
of user management and forums. A Forum is equal to a community in SNSs. We
can add more features to XOOPS websites by adding modules. So we can make
XOOPS websites join in social internetworks by installing the voting module
which is compatible with social internetworking.

Besides, social internetworks can be adopted in MMORPGs (massive mul-
tiplayer online role playing games) such as Final Fantasy 11[13]. MMORPG is
the network game in which strangers all around the world play collaboratively.
As a result of adopting social internetworks, MMORPG players will be able
to find their companions in the game from their friends lists, communities and
reputations — for example, whether he is a skillful sniper or not.

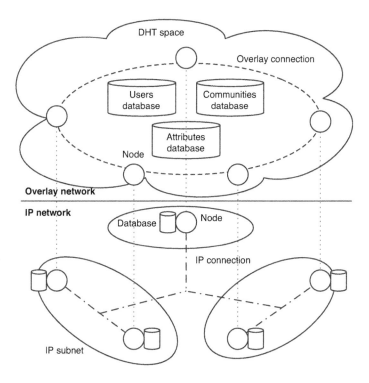

Fig. 2. Comparison between IP network and overlay network. Nodes in IP network have their own databases, but they look like large consolidated databases in overlay network

5   Name-Independent Search Method

In social internetworks, users can use name-independent search methods like attribute-search and reputation-search. Attribute-search uses attributes attached to users and communities, and reputation-search uses reputations calculated from each reputation attached to an attribute. The combination of these two methods enables a user to find other users and communities associated with his preferences.

5.1   Attribute-Search

Attributes define the characteristics of users and communities. "Humorous," "cheerful," "serious" and "energetic" are the examples of user attributes. These attributes can also be applied to communities. User attributes and community attributes are managed separately as shown in figure 3.

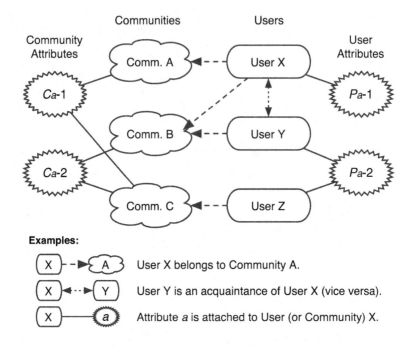

Fig. 3. Attributes attached to users and communities

Attribute-search uses these attributes as search keys. Figure 4 shows the search using an attribute as a key. In case that you want to search "cool" people (user attribute is P_a) and "cool" communities (community attribute is C_a), if you specify "cool" people (P_a) as a search key, you will get the list of users with the attribute "cool." In the same way, if you specify C_a as a search key, you will get the list of communities with the attribute "cool." These attributes may look like categories, but attributes differ in that they can be attached to multiple categories. For example, "Acid Jazz" and "Contemporary Jazz" are the subcategories in the "JAZZ" category and never exist in other categories. On the other hand, "cool" can be applied to multiple categories, like "cool" acid jazz and "cool" contemporary jazz. So attribute-search can be a unique search method of social internetworks.

Additionally, we can interconnect multiple SNSs by treating them as one type of community.

5.2   Reputation-Search

In orkut, a user can make an evaluation of the degree of closeness to his friends like "haven't met," "acquaintance," "friend," "good friend" and "best friend." In social internetworks, the scope of reputation includes attributes. We use Secure EigenTrust algorithm to compute the reputations of attributes. Total reputation

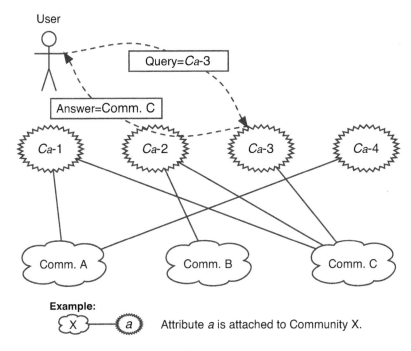

Fig. 4. Attribute-search

of an attribute is computed by its evaluations from each user. Thus we can decide a ranking of users or communities within an attribute, as shown in figure 5.

The targets of reputation are the attributes of users and communities, and attributes themselves. Below is the list of the kinds of reputation. Now we define that R_{C_a} is the communities authorized by the members of C_a-communities. In the same way, R_{P_a} is the users authorized by P_a users. On the other hand, reputation to attributes helps to find proper attributes and prevent a flooding of attributes.

5.3   Query for Name-Independent Search

Name-independent search enables a user to search new objects (users and communities) which have a high reputation and similar attributes to his ones. This search method is implemented in the combination of attribute-search and reputation-search.

We show some examples of the search queries to find "energetic" sport combatives by name-independent search.

Q1. Find the communities with the attribute "energetic". (Query=C_a)

Q2. Find the communities with the authoritative attribute "energetic". (Query=R_{C_a})

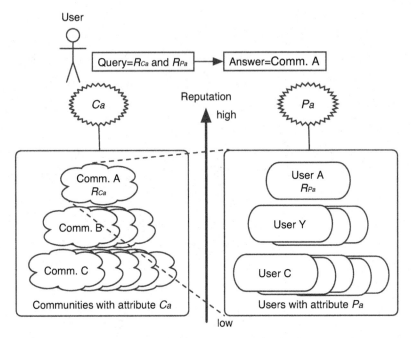

Fig. 5. Combination of attribute-search and reputation-search to find authorized communities

```
// Looking up communities with attribute-search and reputation-search.


// Reputation routine in peer.
1. Specify a community attribute Ca.
2. Evaluate the community from the viewpoint of Ca.


// Automated computation.
1. Computation in SecureEigenTrust.AutomataComp(Ca).


// Search routine.
1. Specify a community attribute Ca.
2. Find authorized communities by the function C = SecureEigenTrust.Lookup(Ca)
3. Find authorized peers P in C by the function P = SecureEigenTrust.Lookup(C).
4. Find peers P joining to the community C = Community.LookupMembers(P).
```

Fig. 6. Pseudo-code for search processes in social internetworks

Q3. Find the R_{C_a}-communities to which the P_a-users belong. (Query=R_{C_a} and P_a)

Q4. Find the R_{C_a}-communities to which the R_{P_a} users belong. (Query=R_{C_a} and R_{P_a})

In general, the authoritative attributes increase the probability of query's providing a proper result. The combination of two search methods also refines a search result. So its order in this example is:

$$Q4 > Q3 > Q2 > Q1.$$

We summarize the sequential processes of search in social internetworks in the pseudo-code of Figure 6.

By using Secure EigenTrust algorithm, name-independent search is achieved with five features of this algorithm.

6   Conclusion

In this paper, we have proposed social internetworking, which expands the capability of social networks.

First, we summarize the value of social internetworking. Social internetworks enable the integrated management of friends list information and communities information over multiple SNSs. Additionally, name-independent search provides a search by friends list, attributes of communities, and their reputation. This method can make troublesome searching compact. Thus, a user can naturally get to know communities which meet his preferences. Our system can be applied to existing SNSs and personal social networks like XOOPS.

However, some problems should be solved before the public use of social internetworking:

- Evaluation criteria to search methods.
- Interconnectivity among SNSs.
- Authentication method for users.
- Authentication method for data exchange.
- User-side control of the usage of his information.
- Incentives for users' information registration.
- A flooding of similar attributes.
- Guess of reputation by repetitive searches.

Along with the implementation of our proposed social internetworking, we will continue to tackle these problems.

Acknowledgments

We thank our labmates Takuji IIMURA and Hiroaki HAZEYAMA for helpful discussions about various topics on social internetworks.

References

1. Sepandar D. Kamvar, Mario T. Schlosser, and Hector Garcia-Molina, "The Eigen-Trust Algorithm for Reputation Management in P2P Networks", In 12th International World Wide Web Conference (WWW2003), May 2003.
2. Antony Rowstron and Peter Druschel, "Pastry: Scalable, decentralized object location and routing for large-scale peer-to-peer systems", Proc of the 18th IFIP/ACM Intl Conf. on Distributed Systems Platforms, 2001.
3. Ion Stoica, Robert Morris, David Karger, M. Frans Kaashoek and Hari Balakrishnan, "Chord: A Scalable Peer-to-peer Lookup Service for Internet Applications", Proceedings of the 2001 Conference on Applications, Technologies, Architectures, and Protocols for Computer Communication, 2001.
4. Sylvia Ratnasamy, Paul Francis, Mark Handley and Richard Karp, "A Scalable Content-Addressable Network", Proceedings of ACM SIGCOMM, 2001.
5. Petar Maymounkov and David Mazières, "Kademlia: A Peer-to-peer Information System Based on the XOR Metric", Proceedings of the 1st International Workshop on Peer-to-Peer Systems, 2002.
6. Kirsten Hildrum, John D. Kubiatowicz, Satish Rao and Ben Y. Zhao, "Distributed Object Location in a Dynamic Network", Proceedings of 14th ACM Symp. on Parallel Algorithms and Architectures (SPAA), 2002.
7. Dahlia Malkhi, Moni Naor and David Ratajczak, "Viceroy: A scalable and dynamic emulation of the butterfly", Proceedings of ACM Principles of Distributed Computing (PODC), 2002.
8. Takuji Iimura, Hiroaki Hazeyama and Youki Kadobayashi, "Zoned Federation of Game Servers: a Peer-to-Peer Approach to Scalable Multi-player Online games", Proc. of ACM SIGCOMM Workshop Network and System Support for Games (NetGames-04), 2004.
9. orkut, Website: http://www.orkut.com/
10. mixi, Website: http://mixi.jp/
11. GREE, Website: http://www.gree.jp/
12. XOOPS, Website: http://www.xoops.org/
13. FINAL FANTASY, Website: http://www.square-enix.co.jp/finalfantasy/

Exploiting Fine Grained Parallelism for Acceleration of Web Retrieval[1]

Junli Yuan[1,2], Chi-Hung Chi[2,3], and Qibin Sun[1]

[1] Institute for Infocomm Research, 21 Heng Mui Keng Terrace, Singapore 119613
{junli, qibin}@i2r.a-star.edu.sg
[2] School of Computing, National University of Singapore, Singapore 117543
{yuanjl, chich}@comp.nus.edu.sg
[3] School of Software, Tsinghua University, Beijing 100084

Abstract. The World Wide Web is the most popular application of the Internet. Web retrieval latency is one of the most important issues in web services and applications. With the increasing number of digital materials appearing in web pages, there emerges a special issue regarding the acceleration of pages containing big web objects. Existing acceleration mechanisms are not effective in this aspect. In this paper, we propose a fine-grained Intra-Object Parallelism (IOP) to address this problem. Our results show that this mechanism can achieve significant improvement on retrieval latency for big objects.

1 Introduction

The *World Wide Web (web)* is the most popular application of the Internet. With the explosive growth of the web, web retrieval latency has become one of the principal concerns to most web users and web content and service providers. Many acceleration mechanisms have been proposed to improve web retrieval performance such as web caching, prefetching, persistent connection, compression and content optimization etc. [1], [2], [3], [4], [5], [6], [7]. However, there emerges a new issue regarding big web objects recently. With the development and proliferation of digital documentation, multimedia materials and web-based applications in the Internet, more and more web pages tend to contain digital materials like image files, pdf files, flash animation files, video and audio files, application executables and so on. As these digital files are usually considerably big in size, they generally take long time to retrieve. For web pages containing big objects, the retrieval of the big objects is often the performance bottleneck for whole page retrieval latency. With the increasing number of big objects appearing in web pages, the need to reduce the retrieval latency of them becomes imperative.

Current acceleration mechanisms are not effective in reducing the retrieval latency of big objects. For web caching [1], its performance is limited due to the low reuse rate of web objects. Since the reuse rate of big objects could be even lower, it is expected that web caching does not have good performance on them. Prefetching [2]

---

[1] This work was supported in part by 2004CB719400.

S. Shimojo et al. (Eds.): HSI 2005, LNCS 3597, pp. 125 – 134, 2005.

suffers from low prediction accuracy and heavy overhead; it may not help much on big objects. As to content optimization [5] [6] and compression [7], they are often difficult to be applied on many big objects due to file format difficulties. For example, compression and content optimization can hardly be applied on pdf files, flash animation files, video and audio files etc. There is parallel fetching in current web system. However, it works only at object-level, so it cannot help big objects either. Therefore, special mechanism is needed in order to accelerate the retrieval process of big objects.

In this paper, we propose a fine-grained parallelism to address the problem of big object retrieval. We extend the concept of parallelism from object level to intra-object level in web retrieval to accelerate the retrieval process of big objects. Our results show that this mechanism can achieve significant improvement on object retrieval latency and whole page latency when big objects are in presence.

2   Background Information

The retrieval process of an object typically involves the following six operations: Request initiation operation r, Location resolution operation l, Network connection operation c, Request sending operation s, Data chunk transfer operation d, and Ending operation e. We can use a directed graph to capture the retrieval process of an object, where vertices represent the operations, arcs represent precedence relationship between two operations, and the weight of an arc represents the time spent in completing the operation represented by the target vertex. Figure 1(a) gives an example graph demonstrating the retrieval process of an object. Note that there may be multiple data chunk transfer operation d in the retrieval process of an object.

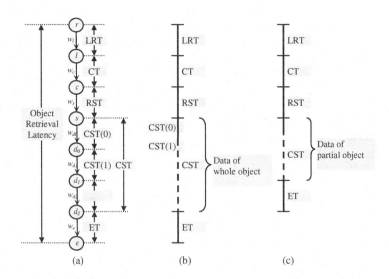

Fig. 1. Representing object retrieval process with graphs

The whole object retrieval latency can be divided into five components based on the six types of operations: Location Resolution Time (LRT), Connection Time (CT), Request Sending Time (RST), Chunk Sequence Time (CST), and Ending Time (ET). These five latency components are also shown in Figure 1(a). For simplicity reason, we will use a simple form of the graph as shown in Figure 1(b) in the rest parts of this paper.

HTTP/1.1 [8] introduces a new HTTP header "Range:" to allow clients to specify and retrieve any part of an object's content. This feature is intended to be used in resuming broken data transfers and retrieving specific parts of objects, e.g. the descriptor fields of multimedia files, the first a few pages of a document, and so on. In this paper, we make use of this feature to implement an intra-object level parallelism to accelerate the retrieval process of big objects. The "Range:" HTTP header specifies desired portions of objects using byte ranges. A byte range request is made like any other normal requests, except with an additional "Range:" header. Although a byte range request may retrieve only part of the object data, it still undergoes all the latency components, especially the CT and RST. Figure 1(c) illustrates this situation.

3 Intra-object Parallelism (IOP)

3.1 Intra-object Parallelism Scheme

The basic idea of *Intra-Object Parallelism (IOP)* is to divide the body of a big object into multiple portions and retrieves them in parallel. Essentially, those different parts of an object can be retrieved using range requests supported by HTTP/1.1. On the whole, the process of IOP is as follows:

When a client retrieves a web object, it first issues a normal request to the server. We refer to the retrieval process associated with this request as *Master Retrieval Thread*. When the server sends back the HTTP headers for the requested object, the client will examine if the server support HTTP/1.1 (i.e. range request) and if there is a "Content-Length" header and if the value of this header exceeds certain threshold. If these conditions are satisfied, IOP will take place. The client will divide the object size into *k* parts based on certain factors. Then, it will trigger *k-1* new requests and let each of them fetch a portion of the object body. These *k-1* new request processes are referred to as *Slave Retrieval Threads*. After the *k-1* Slave Request Threads have been successfully issued, the Master Retrieval Thread will be forced to stop after it receives its portion of the object body. When all the parts are retrieved, they will be assembled together and the original object is got. In IOP, the *k* retrieval processes, 1 master retrieval thread plus *k-1* slave retrieval threads, are carried out in parallel, so the retrieval speed would be much faster than one single retrieval process which fetches the whole object. The above process of IOP is depicted in Figure 2.

Note that IOP is only used to accelerate the retrieval processes of big web objects. It will not affect the correctness of web content. In the situation where partial object is not supported, the IOP will not take place and the master request thread will continue to retrieve the whole body of the object as usual.

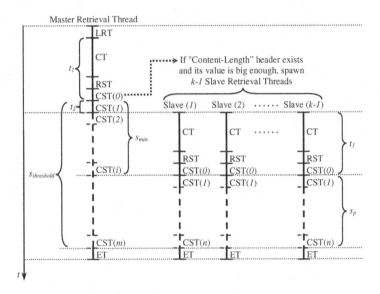

Fig. 2. Retrieval process of Intra-object Parallelism and the relationship between latency components and size ranges

3.2 Prerequisites for IOP

IOP only works with HTTP/1.1-compatible web systems since it requires dealing with partial content of objects. Also, IOP will perform only when there is spare network bandwidth to utilize. Furthermore, IOP can take place only when the size of the object is available and is bigger than a threshold size. The threshold size is determined by multiple factors such as network connection setup time. For example, if connection setup time is long, the threshold size for triggering IOP has to be big. Otherwise, there may not be any benefit at all for doing IOP since the Master Retrieval Thread could have already retrieved the whole object body before the Slave Retrieval Threads have yet finished setting up network connections. So, we would have to answer these questions for IOP: What is the proper threshold size for IOP to take place? How many parts should an object be divided into when it is chosen for IOP?

First, let us look at the number of parts that an object should be divided into. Basically, the more parts an object is divided into, the smaller each part would be, and the shorter the retrieval latency of each part could be. However, to divide an object into too small parts for IOP may not help much in reducing whole page latency because of two reasons:

1) If we divide an object into too small parts, the size of each part could become smaller than other objects in the page. In that case, the page retrieval latency would be dominated by other objects. This suggests that it may not be helpful to divide an object into parts smaller than other objects in the page.
2) Web retrieval process typically undergoes long connection setup time and TCP slow-start effect, which make the retrieval latency for smaller objects often com-

parable to that of bigger objects. This suggests that to divide an object into too small parts is not cost-effective in terms of retrieval latency and resources used.

Taking the above factors into consideration, we would recommend that a large object should be divided into k parts such that the size of each part is around the average size of most commonly seen web objects. Based on the trace in our study, we found that the average size of objects is about 5.71 KBytes. We would suggest using this size as the minimum size of partial objects for IOP mechanism. But this recommendation may vary in different environments.

On the other hand, IOP would impose extra demand on concurrent network connections and server load. If a big object is divided into too many small parts, the burden on network connection and server load could be excessive, which could have negative effects on the performance of web retrieval. To refrain this from happening, we set a maximum value N for k, i.e. $k \leq N$. In our study, we vary the value of N and investigate the effect of it on the performance of IOP.

Now let us look at the threshold size for IOP. As stated earlier, the slave requests would undergo the latency components CT and RST while the master retrieval thread is receiving object data. This put certain constraints on the proper object size for IOP. The relationship between latency components and size ranges in IOP is also shown in Figure 2. Such relations can help us to deduce a formula for calculating proper threshold size for doing IOP.

Because many characteristics about web retrieval vary greatly, e.g. the latency components and chunk size fluctuate considerably due to the status of network and workload on server etc, so it is rather difficult to produce an accurate formula for IOP. But we can develop a rough model for the relationship among the factors based on the following assumptions:

1) No persistent connection is used in IOP, and the connection time is constant for all retrieval processes.
2) All slave retrieval threads have the same CT+RST+CST(0). We represent it as t_1.
3) The first chunk contains HTTP headers.
4) The sizes of all chunks are the same. In this study, we use the statistical average of the chunk size as the size for every chunk, which is about 5.3 Kbytes. We use s_{chk} to denote the size of one chunk: $s_{chk} = 5.3$ Kbytes
5) The latency for every chunk is the same. It is difficult to obtain the latency of the first chunk CST(0) because what we can record is RST+CST(0), so we use the latency of the second chunk CST(1) as the unit latency for transferring one data chunk. We denote this unit chunk latency as t_{chk}. From Figure 2: $t_{chk} = CST(1) = t_2$
6) All slave retrieval threads are started simultaneously.
7) The partial object size s_p assigned to each slave request is the same, and we use the average size of web objects (5.71 KBytes) as the minimum size for each partial object, i.e.: $s_p \geq 5.71$ KBytes

Based on the above assumption and the relationship revealed in Figure 2, we see that the object size satisfies the following formula:

$$s_{object} = s_{min} + k \times s_p \ (k \geq 2).\tag{1}$$

For IOP to happen, k must be greater than or equal to 2. So the minimum object size required for IOP would be:

$$s_{threshold} \geq s_{min} + 2 \times s_p .$$ (2)

Because $s_{min} = i \times s_{chk}$ and $i = (t_l / t_{chk}) + 1$, So, we have:

$$s_{threshold} \geq (t_l / t_{chk}) \times 5.3 + 16.72 \text{ (KBytes) .}$$ (3)

In formula 3, both t_l and t_{chk} can be obtained by monitoring the retrieval process. Therefore, $s_{threshold}$ will be able to be obtained during the retrieval process.

With the above knowledge, we are now able to give some complement description of the IOP mechanism. Client will monitor the retrieval process and record t_l and t_{chk} to calculate the $s_{threshold}$. When IOP is satisfied to take place, it will first use the average web object size (e.g. 5.71 KBytes) as the size of each partial object to calculate an initial k. If k is not greater than N, then the client will use this k and the partial object size to do IOP. Otherwise, k will be set to N and the size of each partial object is calculated based on this new k. By setting up the maximum value N for k, IOP can avoid imposing excessive demand on network connection and server load, while still attains the effectiveness of parallelism.

4   Results and Analysis

4.1 Methodology

To study the performance of IOP, we conducted both simulation experiments and real system tests. For the simulations, we obtained URLs from a NLANR trace [9] dated 12 May 2004 and replayed real retrieval process and recorded detailed operation and chunk level traces for our simulation use. For the real system, we have implemented a working IOP system based on Squid 2.4.STABLE3 [10] to perform the IOP scheme.

4.2 Demand for IOP

When a web page contains large web objects, the retrieval latency of those objects is often the dominant factor to the whole page latency. So, we would like to first investigate the presence of large objects in web pages. Figure 3 plots the distribution of

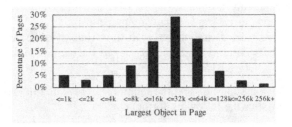

Fig. 3. Distribution of pages w.r.t. size of the largest object in the page

web pages with respect to the largest object size they contain. From this graph, we see that the majority of web pages have objects not bigger than 64 KBytes. However, there are about 10.54% of web pages contain objects bigger than 128 KBytes. As digital documentation, multimedia materials and web-based applications etc. are increasingly distributed over the web, we expect to see the percentage of web pages containing large objects to continuously increase in the future. Nevertheless, the percentage of 10.54% is already significant enough for us to look into effective mechanisms to accelerate the retrieval process of them.

4.3 Threshold Size for IOP

Formula 3 shows that the threshold size $s_{threshold}$ is determined by the time t_l and t_{chk}. So we would like to have a look at them. Figure 4 plots the distribution of the ratio of t_l/t_{chk}. The results show that the values below 15 take up the major portion (more than 85%) of the distribution. However, there exist much bigger values for the ratio, from 50 to up to more than 10,000. Those big values contribute nearly 4% to the overall distribution of t_l/t_{chk}. This put the average value of the ratio to be at about 26.3. In other words, t_l is about 26.3 times bigger than t_{chk} on the average. This result shows that t_l is surprisingly big as compared with t_{chk}. The reason for this phenomenon could be because t_l contains the connection time CT, which is very big in web retrieval.

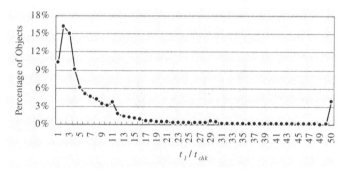

Fig. 4. Distribution of t_l/t_{chk}

The above observation is very important because it implies that IOP is not suitable for medium-sized objects as every retrieval thread will undergo at least t_l, which already equals to the transfer time of many chunks. Using formula 3, we can get the average threshold size for IOP: $s_{threshold} \geq 156.11$ KBytes.

This result indicates that on average, an object should be larger than 156 KBytes to be suitable for IOP to take place.

4.4 Performance of IOP

Figure 5 studies the performance of IOP on retrieval latency of individual objects. Here we set N to be 8. From this graph, we see that the effect of IOP on object retrieval latency is substantial. It can reduce the retrieval latency of big objects dramatically. The simulation results show that the improvement ranges from 77% to 87%

with an average of 83.86%, while the real system testing achieves 68% to 86% improvement with an average of 80.6%. In general, the improvement gets better as the object size increases. This is expected as larger objects have lengthier chunk transfer sequences, which can be effectively improved by IOP.

Note that the performance of real system is often lower than the simulation results. This could be due to the fluctuation of network and server status, which are largely ignored in simulations.

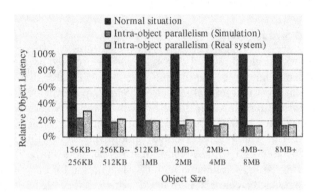

Fig. 5. Effect of Intra-Object Parallelism on retrieval latency of individual objects

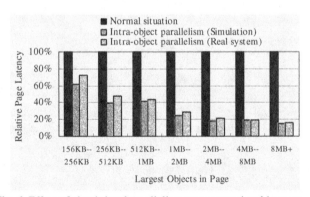

Fig. 6. Effect of chunk-level parallelism on page retrieval latency

Figure 6 plots the effect of IOP on retrieval latency of pages containing big objects. In simulations, IOP improves page retrieval latency from 38% to 85%, with an average of 68.6%. In real system tests, the improvement ranges from 27% to 84%, with an average of 64.5%. Again, we see that the effect of IOP on page retrieval latency is also very significant, and the improvement generally gets better as the size of the largest object in the page increases. This is actually understandable because: For pages containing large objects, the whole page latency will be dominated by those large objects; since IOP can effectively reduce the retrieval latency of large objects, this reduction will inevitably be reflected on whole page latency.

We noticed that the improvement that IOP achieves on page latency is generally lower than that on individual object latency. This could be due to the following reason: When large objects in a page are divided into smaller parts by IOP, the retrieval latencies of other objects in the page may become more important to whole page latency. In other words, there are some other latency contributors that prevent IOP's improvement on individual object latency from being fully reflected on whole page latency.

However, when object size is extremely big (e.g. bigger than 8 MBytes), the improvement on page latency is very close to the improvement on individual object latency. This is because: when page contains object with extremely big objects, the retrieval latency of other objects become very negligible and the page latency is almost solely determined by the extremely big objects even after they have been divided into smaller parts. So, in this situation, the improvement on the extremely big objects will be almost fully mapped into the improvement on whole page latency.

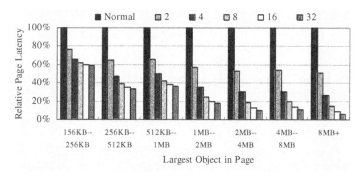

Fig. 7. Effect of N on the performance of Intra-object Parallelism

Figure 7 studies the effect of N on the performance of IOP in terms of page retrieval latency. Here N is the maximum value of k. From the graph, we can see that the performance of IOP generally increases as N increases. However, the relative increase for different N becomes less significant for big values of N. This is more obvious for moderate big objects such as those between 156 to 256 KBytes. This suggests that different values of N should be considered for different sizes in order to achieve the best performance and cost-effectiveness. For moderate big objects, 4 or 8 may be suitable values for N. But for very large objects, bigger values (e.g. 32) should be considered.

We also noticed that the performance gain is far from being directly proportional to the increase in N for pages with relatively smaller objects (e.g. 156 to 256 KBytes objects), while it nearly has the directly proportional relationship for pages with very large objects. This could be due to the same reason stated earlier on: For pages with relatively smaller objects, other objects in the same page could prevent IOP's effect from being fully reflected on whole page latency. But for pages with very large objects, this phenomenon will not be seen since the very large objects would always dominate whole page latency even after they have been divided into smaller parts.

5 Conclusion

In this paper, we exploit fine-grained parallelism for the acceleration of web retrieval. By extending the concept of parallelism to intra-object level, we propose the Intra-Object parallelism (IOP) mechanism to improve web retrieval performance for big objects. Our study reveals some important relations regarding IOP such as the proper threshold size for IOP to take place and different values of N for different object sizes etc. By selecting proper parameters for IOP based on these relations, we have attained high effectiveness of IOP while avoided imposing excessive demand on network connection and server load.

References

1. Wessels, D., Web Caching, O'Reilly Publishing, 2001.
2. Duchamp, D., "Prefetching Hyperlinks," Proceedings of USENIX Symposium on Internet Technologies and Systems, October 1999.
3. E. Cohen, H. Kaplan, and U. Zwick, Connection caching under various models of communication, In Proc. 12th Annual ACM Symposium on Parallel Algorithms and Architectures. ACM, 2000.
4. Craig E. Wills, Mikhail Mikhailov, and Hao Shang, N for the price of 1: Bundling web objects for more efficient content delivery, In Proceedings of the Tenth International World Wide Web Conference, Hong Kong, May 2001
5. Jeffrey Mogul, Fred Douglis, Anja Feldmann, and Balachander Krishnamurthy, Potential Benefits of Delta-encoding and Data Compression for HTTP, In Proceedings of ACM SIGCOMM, pages 181--194, September 1997. An extended and corrected version appears as Research Report 97/4a, Digital Equipment Corporation Western Research Laboratory, December, 1997.
6. Surendar Chandra and Carla Schlatter Ellis, JPEG compression metric as a quality-aware image transcoding, In Proc. USENIX 2nd Symposium on Internet Technology and Systems, pages 81-92, Boulder, CO, Oct. 1999.,
7. Jun-Li Yuan and Chi-Hung Chi, Unveiling the Performance Impact of Lossless Compression to Web Page Content Delivery, In Proc. of the 9th International Workshop on Web Content Caching and Distribution (WCW 2004), Beijing, China, Oct. 2004.
8. Fielding, R., Gettys, J., Mogul, J., Frystyk, H., Masinter, L., Leach, P., Berners-Lee, T., "Hypertext Transfer Protocol -- HTTP/1.1," IETF RFC2616, June 1999.
9. IRCACHE Proxy Traces, http://ircache.nlanr.net
10. Squid Web Proxy Cache, http://www.squid-cache.org/

Semantic Template Generation Based Information Summarization for Mobile Devices

Jason J. Jung[1], Seung-Bo Park[1], and Geun-Sik Jo[2]

[1] Intelligent E-Commerce Systems Laboratory,
School of Computer Engineering, Inha University,
253 Yonghyun-dong, Incheon, Korea 402-751
j2jung@intelligent.pe.kr, molaal@eslab.inha.ac.kr
[2] School of Computer Engineering, Inha University,
253 Yonghyun-dong, Incheon, Korea 402-751
gsjo@inha.ac.kr

Abstract. In contrast with the amount of explosively increasing information on the Web, mobile users are suffering from low hardware capacity, poor interface, and high communication cost of their wireless devices. In this paper, we propose a framework for information summarization on wireless network. More importantly, we have focused on the template generation based on ontology. This system, thereby, can extract and send particular pieces of information relevant to the corresponding users, instead of sending the full texts themselves. Templates can be generated by not only user's manual input but also semantic tagging, which is a process categorizing keywords into the most relevant concepts. Hence, in order to highlight a specific part of documents, these semantic templates can be applied as a set of rules. For conducting experiments, we have designed wireless reverse auction system in which participants can instantly send and receive the bidding messages through their mobile devices.

1 Introduction

Recently, so many people have been concerning about wireless devices, including mobile (cellular) phones and PDAs (Personal Digital Assistant). By the end of 2001, there were over 850 million mobile phone users worldwide. Other devices such as PDAs and pagers will also contribute to the growth of mobile communication [1]. With the hardware development and widely propagated infrastructure, many kinds of wireless messaging services, including e-mail, fax, voice, and video data have been introduced. Ubiquity (or high mobility), so-called "anytime, anywhere," is one of the most beneficial reasons why users have been interested in these mobile services. However, there have been several drawbacks to wireless devices such as low hardware capacity. Especially, poor interface and high communication cost of mobile devices is the main problems that we have been motivated. Because of expensive usage fees, when requesting data on the Web, mobile users often hesitate. Not only the number of accessing

S. Shimojo et al. (Eds.): HSI 2005, LNCS 3597, pp. 135–143, 2005.

times but also the amount of transmitted packets is the main factor determining the total subscription. Moreover, it would make users disappointed to access very long and noisy documents through the small display of mobile devices.

Therefore, we decided to study a template-based information extraction system as a way to send summarized information, instead of a full-text document, to a wireless device. In order to analyze the free or semi-structured text documents such as an e-mail and a particular form of information, there have been many information extraction studies such as the Naive Bayes sliding window model [2], the hidden markov model [3], and the template filling model [4], [5]. Also, with respect to a user's intervention, while most studies needed user involvement [11], wrapper induction [7] was best able to perform automatic information extraction without user supervision.

In this paper, we are focusing on wireless messaging system for reverse auction, which is one of the most famous e-marketplace services. We have tried to summarize messages between auctioneers and bidders by extracting relevant parts of them by using not only user-defined templates but also automatically generated templates. Therefore, in the following section, notations for semantic tagging will be introduced to represent templates and, more importantly, template induction will be described to automatically generate templates.

2   Semantic Template Based Information Extraction

Basically, IE (Information Extraction) identifies the specific pieces of information (or data) in unstructured or semi-structured text documents and transforms this unstructured information from a corpus of documents or web pages into a structured database.

Fig. 1. Template-based Information Extraction

For example, in a financial transaction, an information extraction system could extract the transaction type, date, customer, principal, currency, and interest rate, which would usually be formatted as a database record suitable for subsequent processing such as data trend analyses, summaries, and report generations [6].

For the lightweight use of NLP (Natural Language Processing), as shown in Fig. 1, we have focused on the following two main issues.

- How to *represent* the template class and *generate* template instances
- How to *match* and *select* templates in order to extract relevant information from a particular text

A particular class of documents whose structures are similar is defined as a prototype of a document template. Therefore, a collection of template instances generated from a prototype can extract information by filling slots on these templates.

2.1   Template Representation and Generation

A template class is composed of slots, which contain relevant pieces of information, and two kinds of tags. Tags on the left-hand side and on the right-hand side are the indicators of the beginning and ending of the corresponding slots. Each template class is represented as semantic tagging, which is the process whereby keyphrases (or keywords) in a document are matched with predefined tags. During training by user's supervision, these keyphrases have, in advance, been classified, according to the semantically identical tags. Therefore, a template class T_i is defined as

$$T_i = \{slot_1, slot_2, ..., slot_n\} \tag{1}$$

and a slot S_i in a template instance is represented as

$$S_i = [\{ltag_1, ltag_2, ..., ltag_m\}, \{rtag_1, rtag_2, ..., rtag_n\}] \tag{2}$$

where *ltag* and *rtag* are a set of candidate tags located in left and right sides of $slot_i$, respectively.

There are two approaches to automatically generate template classes, which are frequency measure and lexical entry extraction via dictionary exploration [9]. Similar to CRYSTAL [10], which is a well-known IE system from free text by inducing a conceptual dictionary, we have organized template classes using a bottom up covering algorithm that begins with the most specific rule to cover a seed instance and generalizes the rule by merging it with similar rules.

2.2   Template Matching

A text classifier can most efficiently find out which kinds of information are included in a certain document and what features are extractable from that document. The exact template, therefore, can be instantiated and also easily applied to extract relevant information. On the other hand, when a document fails to be classified, this document should be semantically tagged, in other words, structurized, by referring to a set of predefined tags. The template slot on the document can be expected by matched tag pairs. Then, the similarity between a tagged document *doc* and each template class in a template class repository, as shown in Fig. 1, can be measured by using the following equation

$$Sim(doc, T_i) = \frac{a}{(1 + \alpha^2)(d - a) + (1 + \beta^2)(t - a)} \tag{3}$$

where the d and t are the number of slots in a tagged document *doc* and a template class, respectively. The variable a is the number of common slots in both documents and the coefficients α and β are the factors for weighting. As a result, a template instance is derived from a template class whose similarity with the tagged document is maximum.

3   Application to Wireless Reverse Auction Systems

In order to apply the template-based summarization system to real-world applications, we selected the reverse auction systems based on message-posting bulletin board system. In contrast to traditional auctions, a reverse auction is simply an inverted auction mechanism whereby an auctioneer (buyer) announces an auction item, and then, many bidders (sellers) offer their bids for the item. Due to the domain specific properties of reverse auction, the certain features have to be extracted from a set of bidding messages.

3.1   System Architecture

The system is composed of two main parts, a bidding message management for multiple bidders on wired network and a SMTP-based message transfer system to mobile users.

Fig. 2. System Architecture

According to SMTP (Simple Mail Transfer Protocol), an e-mail consists of two main parts, the headers and the body [8]. While the body of the bidding message is usually unstructured text that needs semantic tagging, the headers already provide tagged information such as sender, subject, and message type.

Therefore, bidding messages can be classified based on extracted features in order to select a proper template class. The mobile user-side system consists of three main components, which are e-mail client, template generator, and template matcher, as shown in Fig. 2. The e-mail client has to be able to classify e-mails based on extracting features such as the headers of each e-mail. Template generator establishes the conceptual dictionary and provide GUI for users' manual coding, then stores them in the template class repository. Template matcher and information extractor can look up the most appropriate template in a template class repository and organize the set of extracted texts in the final message format. Mobile devices have to be, in advance, "wirely synchronized" with the template class repository of template generator. Thereby, a template instance can be effectively derived by receiving messages from the SMS center [14] or the WAP gateway [12], [13].

3.2   Ontology Construction

We designed two essential ontologies for reverse auction processes and LCD monitor. These ontologies are organized in the form of a hierarchical tree.

Fig. 3. Ontology for LCD monitor

Fig. 3 depicts a small part of LCD monitor ontology, which is totally composing of 43 nodes.

3.3   Template Generation and Matching

There are two ways to generate templates, both of which are based on manual coding and, as previously mentioned, inducing a conceptual dictionary. Manual coding, which is the explicit construction of template classes by users, is much more effective for a bidding message that a user has already been waiting for such as "notification of acceptance." This is also effective for private e-mails as well. In this case, all extracted features must be definitely matched with user-defined conditions, for example, "I want to purchase this LCD. The price is 200 dollars". An inductive conceptual dictionary based on e-mail classification is the other way to generate a template class. Features can be extracted by learning the user's categorization patterns. Therefore, e-mails in the same category are lexically analyzed in order to enrich the conceptual dictionary and semantic tagging. For example, by analyzing e-mails posted from a particular mailing-list in a folder, we can recognize sender, subject pattern, and more importantly, the appended user-defined header information.

A template class repository manages these two types of template classes, separately. For template matching, a new e-mail should be semantically tagged and structured, by searching the proper slots. Then, according to the type of features extracted from this e-mail, it is decided which part of the template class repository should be searched and the most suitable template class is obtained by measuring the similarity among template classes in the selected part of the repository.

As an example, a template class "call for bids" and a semantic tag <date> are generated as follows.:

```
(template_class call_for_bids
   <title>                      ; Title of bid
   <date>                       ; Schedule of the bid
   <location>                   ; Place in which the bid will be held
   <submission>
      <submission:deadline>     ; Deadline
      <submission:notification> ; Notification of Acceptance
   <URL>                        ; Website of the bid
   <topics>                     ; Topics of interest for the bid
   <contact>                    ; Contact information
)
(semantic_tag call_for_bid:date
   { "important dates * bid *", "\crlf" }
   { "workshop dates *", "\crlf" }
   { "bid dates *", "\crlf" }
   { "submission deadline * bid *", "\crlf" }
)
```

A template instance can be derived from the matched template class. The detail configuration of this template instance depends on the number of slots and their positions as obtained by semantic tagging. Relevant information, therefore, can be extracted by overlapping this template instance on the tagged e-mail. Another important focus is to refine these pieces of extracted relevant information by reorganizing them and removing redundant words and stop words. More seriously, with respect to communication cost, the limited size of data for one transmission is the maximum length of a fragment for reorganization of the the extracted texts. This refinement is shown in the following algorithm

Algorithm *Refinement*
    Input:
        Set of Extracted Texts, $T = \{t_1, t_2, ..., t_a\}$;
        Maximum Length of a Fragment, L;
        Set of Refined Texts $RT = \{\}$;
    Procedure:
      for each $t_i \in T$ **do**
        if (**not** $IsStopwords(t_i)$)
        then if (**not** $IsRedundant(RT, t_i)$)
          switch $(L - length(t_i))$
            case > 0: $merge(t_i)$
            case < 0: $fragment(t_i)$
            case 0: $RT := RT + \{t_i\}$
      return RT

where the functions *merge* and *fragment* are used to combine residues and then generate residues in order to save null space.

4 Implementation and Experiments

We implemented this system by using Nokia Mobile Internet Toolkit 4.0 [16]. Fig. 4 demonstrates the user interface for mobile users.

Fig. 4. User Interface

In our experiments, we collected bidding messages from the Website Auction [15], which posts product bidding announcement messages and shares this information via e-mails that has been received. Based on the extracted features, we placed these messages into four categories. These messages in this Website additionally contain particularly well-organized headers which support to effective classification such as *X-BID-Message-Type*, *X-BID-Call-For*, *X-BID-Deadline*, and so on. Overall, we collected 250 messages from this Website and split them into two groups, 20% of them as training and the rest of them as testing data. During training for inducing conceptual dictionary, each template class of the corresponding categories was generated.

Table 1. Results of information summarization based on template instance derivation

	Ratio of Summarization $= \frac{size(extracted)}{size(raw)}$	Accuracy of Template Filling $= \frac{number(relevant)}{number(total)}$
Category 1	0.796	0.775
Category 2	0.83	0.926
Category 3	0.812	0.875
Category 4	0.52	0.795

By testing data, we attained the results, as shown in Table 1. We verified that the system was able to remove, an average, 74% of the redundant textual information and that 93% of the template slots were accurately filled.

5   Conclusion and Future Work

Not only hardware limitations of wireless devices but also high communication costs are a serious obstacle to instant accessing of wireless messaging service. We have attempted to summarize e-mails by using template filling. We have thereby proposed the way to generate and match template classes and also derive template instance that is the most suitable for a certain e-mail. Some template class can be manually constructed by user intervention in order to customize adaptive information extraction. The heterogeneous screen specifications of mobile devices and the various communication policies of service providers have also been considered.

We are now developing a GUI system to support users so they can more easily construct template classes based on manual coding. Moreover, we are studying ontologies as background knowledge for semantic analysis of texts.

References

1. Sadeh, N.: M-Commerce: Technologies, Services, and Business Models. Wiley computer publishing (2002)
2. Freitag, D.: Using grammatical inference to improve precision in information extraction. ICML-97 Workshop on Automata Induction, Grammatical Inference, and Language Acquisition (1997)

3. Freitag, D., McCallum, A.: Information extraction using HMMs and shrinkage. Proceedings of the AAAI-99 Workshop on Machine Learning for Information Extraction (1999)

4. Doorenbos, R.B., Etzioni, O., Weld, D.S.: A Scalable Comparison-Shopping Agent for the World Wide Web. Proceedings of Autonomous Agent '97 (1997)

5. Sumita, K., Miike, S., Chino, T.: Automatic Abstract Generation Based on Document Structure Analysis and Its Evaluation as a Document Retreival Presentation Function. Systems and Computers **26**(13) (1995) 32–43

6. Wee, L.K.A., Tong, L.C., Tan, C.L.: A generic information extraction architecture for financial applications. Expert Systems with Applications **16**(4) (1999) 343–356

7. Kushmerick, N., Weld, D.S., Doorenbos, R.: Wrapper Induction for Information Extraction. Intl. Joint Conference on Artificial Intelligence (1997) 729–737

8. Crocker, D.H.: Standard For The Format Of ARPA Internet Text Messages. ftp://ftp.rfc-editor.org/in-notes/rfc822.txt (1982)

9. Maedche, A.: Ontology Learning for the Semantic Web. Kluwer Academic Publishers (2002)

10. Soderland, S., Fisher, D., Aseltine, J., Lehnert, W.: CRYSTAL: Inducing a Conceptual Dictionary. Proceedings of the Fourteenth International Joint Conference on Artificial Intelligence (1995) 1314–1319

11. Ciravegna, F., Petrelli, D.: User involvement in customizing adaptive Information Extraction. Proceedings of the IJCAI-2001 Workshop on Adaptive Text Extraction and Mining (2001)

12. Open Mobile Alliance Ltd. http://www.openmobilealliance.org (2002)

13. WAP 2.0 Specifications. http://www.wapforum.org (2002)

14. Wireless Short Message Service (SMS). http://www.iec.org (2002)

15. Auction Korea, http://www.auction.co.kr

16. Nokia Mobile Internet Toolkit 4.1, http://www.forum.nokia.com/main

A Strategy for Maintaining Client-Based Web Warehouse

Hyuk-Min Lee and Kyung-Chang Kim

Dept of Computer Engineering,
Hongik University, Seoul, Korea
{hmlee, kckim}@cs.hongik.ac.kr

Abstract. Currently there is a common problem of real-time data inconsistency between source transactional systems and data warehouse. ECA, a well-known algorithm, is quite effective in addressing the view maintenance anomaly by making use of compensation queries. However, ECA does not maintain information about the data warehouse, and has to send compensating queries to the source system resulting in performance degradation. This paper proposes a new strategy for maintaining data warehouse in a Web environment without sending update queries to the source system. To maintain consistency in real-time, automatically installed web client program create modify queries for each update query to source system. Modify queries associated with each update query are processed at the web warehouse level without connecting to the source system. Hence the problem of a single modify query having to access multiple source systems disappears and the system performance improves. Through simulation, the performance of the proposed strategy is compared with previous solutions.

1 Introduction

CRM/eCRM has become one of the pivotal issues in the current dynamic business environment. As competition intensifies, companies are transforming themselves from product or price driven organizations into more customer centric organizations. And data warehouse is an example of powerful business tools that support such business transformation.

Thanks to the advancement of Internet technology, many existing legacy client/server systems are becoming web enabled. Following in their footsteps, data warehouse will soon become web enabled as well.

Web warehouse is a web based data warehouse that allows users to connect to data warehouse and perform real-time data analysis through web browser. Consequently, all existing data warehouse services must be reengineered using web interface. Bringing data warehouse to the web means being able to record user's behavior in the data warehouse. It also makes in depth analysis of user behavior and intentions possible by providing a new data source called, click-stream data. This paper also uses click-stream data to predict what queries user might want to perform in advance.

S. Shimojo et al. (Eds.): HSI 2005, LNCS 3597, pp. 144–154, 2005.
© Springer-Verlag Berlin Heidelberg 2005

1.1 Motivation

When an update occurs at the source system, the source system sends a query back to the data warehouse because the source system lacks data warehouse information. The data warehouse, upon receiving a query from the source system, creates a corresponding query to be executed at the source system. This is a common data warehouse maintenance method.

However, if data at the source system changes before the maintenance query has a chance to execute, then the data warehouse is said to have a view maintenance anomaly problem. ECA algorithm is a commonly used solution to this problem. The details of ECA algorithm are discussed in Section 2.

ECA is quite effective in addressing the view maintenance anomaly by making use of compensation queries. However, because ECA itself still does not maintain information about the data warehouse locally, it has to send compensating queries to the source system causing some system performance reduce. In addition, the increasing complexity of compensation queries puts extra burden on the source system's performance.

This paper proposes a new strategy for maintaining data warehouse without sending update queries to the source system. Even if in a multi-source system environment, the new strategy allows real-time maintenance of the data warehouse without accessing source systems.

This paper is organized as follows. Section 2 describes the existing research in data warehouse materialized view maintenance. In Section 3, the real-time data consistency and materialized view maintenance process in a web warehouse is proposed and adapted for multi client/server environment. Finally, Section 4 compares the proposed system against existing systems. The conclusion is given in Section 5

2 Related Work

This section reviews various research topics related to existing data warehouse systems and looks in depth at materialized view maintenance strategy.

[9, 11] proposed an automatic formalization of existing source system ER schema into multi dimensional data warehouse model. [10, 12] tried to improve the query performance by expanding or changing existing SQL. [13, 14] improved the query performance by constructing a query execution plan diagram using AND/OR operators common in many complex queries and making a new materialized view based on finding the location of key nodes.

2.1 ECA (Eager Compensating Algorithm)

ECA [15] is an example of deferred data warehouse maintenance algorithm. When there is a data update to the source system, the source system sends an update query to data warehouse in order to maintain data consistency between systems. If data warehouse lacks the relevant materialized view data, then it sends a return query to the source system to update its materialized view.

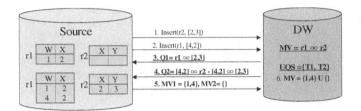

Fig. 1. ECA Processing

Figure 1 is a flow diagram of query T1=insert(r2,[2,3]) and T2=insert(r1,[4,2]) being sent to and from data warehouse and source system with R1(1,2) and R2 tables. If a user sends a T1 query to the source system, then the source systems returns a query back to data warehouse.

In order to maintain consistency of data warehouse, it creates and sends a compensating query $Q1=r1\infty[2,3]$ to the source. Source system processes Q1 then sends the result data MV1={1,4} to data warehouse. Apply the sent data to the data warehouse.

Real-time application of update query is possible. However, as the number of update queries increases, the source system's performance is heavily taxed due to processing of complex compensating queries required to keep data warehouse data consistent.

2.2 Strobe Algorithm

Unlike in ECA where data exist in a single source system, data are usually distributed across many systems in a multi source systems environment. Strobe [6] algorithm is explained in Figure 2.

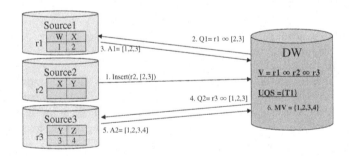

Fig. 2. Strobe Processing

If an update query comes from one source system, then data warehouse sends compensating queries to other source systems then combines the query results.

As the number of update queries increases, the data transfer volume between data warehouse and source systems increases exponentially. And because data warehouse needs to wait for return query results from source system, it is difficult to maintain data consistency of data warehouse real-time.

To overcome the complexity and heavy system load of ECA algorithm as well as the limitation of Strobe algorithm in maintaining data warehouse in real-time, this paper proposes a web warehouse system based on web client.

3 The Proposed System

This section proposes an optimal solution that addresses the problem of maintaining historical data in data warehouse in real time and performance improvement issues.

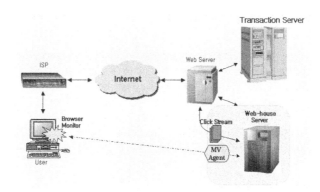

Fig. 3. The propose system environment

Figure 3 is an overview of the of the proposed system environment. It assumes that all users connect to source system and web warehouse (used interchangeably with data warehouse) via web browser and explains the difference between the update query and the modify query. Update query is a transaction query requested from web browser to source system. Modify query is created automatically by web client program to be applied to materialized view of web warehouse and is used interchangeably with compensating query in ECA.

If users connect to web server via web browser, web based client program (Browser Monitor) is automatically installed. Browser monitor not only stores users' click-stream data in web warehouse but also creates necessary modify queries in order for update queries to be applied to data warehouse using web warehouse metadata.

Web warehouse metadata is information about mapping source system to data warehouse and it helps browser monitor determine whether modify query is needed for each update query.

Materialized view agent (MV Agent) performs real time storage of click-stream data sent by browser monitor. It also requests modify queries to web warehouse and perform recovery procedure in case of client failure.

3.1 Maintenance Process for Web Warehouse Consistency

When user's update query (OLTP) is processed by source system, browser monitor creates modify queries in real time and updates web warehouse automatically.

The following are detailed steps in processing update queries and maintaining web warehouse consistent. Users create and send update queries to source system via web browser. Browser monitor uses web warehouse metadata to create modify queries and sends them to MV agent that in turn executes the queries against web warehouse.

When source system sends the requested query result to users, browser monitor captures the even message "query processed result".

If an update query is successful, browser monitor "Commit" modify query to be applied to web warehouse otherwise 'Roll Back' the query.

Example 1. There are R1 (1,2) and R2(2,3) tables in the source system and web warehouse is MV=R1∞R2. Let us take a look at queries T1=insert(r1,[4,2]) and T2=delete(r1,[1,2]).

1. When a user requests t1 and t2 to the source system, browser monitor reviews the queries and determine its impact on the web warehouse. And then it requests modify queries (r1[4,2]∞MV[X,2]) to the web warehouse and records it in TQ.
2. If T1 results is received from the source system, browser monitor requests to store the modify query result ([4,2,3]) and deletes it from TQ.
3. T2 uses delete operator (deleteMV[1,2]) to delete "W=1 and X=2" records in web warehouse and deletes T2 from TQ.

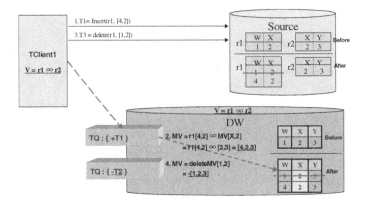

Fig. 4. Example 1 detailed steps

Example 2. There are R1(1,2) and R2(2,3) tables in the source system and web warehouse is MV=R1∞R2. Let us take a look at queries T1=insert(r1,[4,2]), T2=insert(r2,[3,5]), and T3=insert(r1, [6,3]).

1. When a user requests t1, t2 and t3 to the source system, browser monitor reviews the queries and determine its impact on the web warehouse. And then it requests modify query (r1[4,2]∞MV[X,2]) to the web warehouse and records {+T1,+T2,+T3} in TQ.
2. If t1 results is received from the source system, browser monitor requests to store the modify query result ([4,2,3]) and deletes it from TQ.
3. Because there isn't "X=3" record in web warehouse, t2 is left in TQ.

4. T3 and t2 are combined ([6,2,3]) in TQ, joined against "X=3" data in web warehouse ([6,2,3]), and then deleted from TQ.

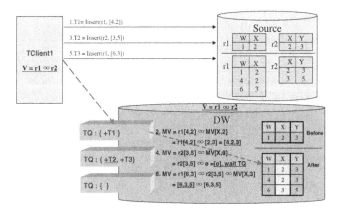

Fig. 5. Example 2 detailed steps

3.2 Web Warehouse Maintenance Algorithm

In ECA materialized view, there was a performance problem with source system because data warehouse uses source system to process modified data.

As in figure 6, because there is a copy of source system's data in the web warehouse, there is no need to access the source system for processing of unchanged data (MV0=A0∞B0). For data that has changed (Δ), web client automatically updates the data warehouse so that real time maintenance algorithm is simplified. Therefore, source system performance is improved because processing of modify queries is eliminated.

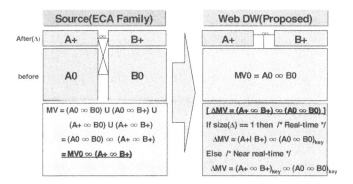

Fig. 6. The concept of Proposed system

Explanations of the following key variables are provided below in order to help understand the web warehouse maintenance algorithm.

Variables	Description
t1, t2, …	update query input
TQ (Transaction Queue)	pool of queries affecting web warehouse
T (final Modify query)	pool of intermediate result set of queries in TQ that can be combined.(incremental changes)
MV(Attr, Value)	intermediate result set satisfying applicable "Attr=Value" condition in web warehouse. . Attr: name of field to be used as key in web warehouse. . Value: field value to be used in web warehouse

This is an example of web warehouse maintenance algorithm.

```
Proc   MVM(t1, MV)
{
     TQ[] = t1;   // t1 = insert(r1,[4,2])
     MergeT(TQ, t1, T);
      for( i=0; T.count >= i; i++)
              •MV = joinT(MV, T[i].value);
      if(MV == NULL) return 0;
      MV = MV + • MV;
}


MergeT(TQ, t1, T)
{
     for( i=0; TQ.count-1 > i; i++)
             if(cmp(TQ[i].attr, t1.attr) == 0) {
          T = TQ[i];
               delete_TQ(i);
      }
}
```

Incoming query t1 is recorded in TQ. If there is a same key query of t1 in TQ, then merge applicable queries in T. Select only the applicable data from web warehouse, then join them using the final modify query T and, finally apply them to web warehouse.

3.3 Maintaining Consistency In Real Time In Multi Source System Environment

The most difficult problem in expanding a single source system into multi source system is that of system performance. The main difficulty lies in multiple source systems maintaining separate data and data warehouse having to query each source system separately and then pooling the results of queries. On the other hand, the proposed system accesses web warehouse rather than source system for existing base data sets. And for updated data set, web client automatically updates them to web warehouse so that the number of source systems has very little impact on overall system performance.

However, the issue of maintaining query serialization becomes rather important and it is addressed below:

1. When users request an update query to source system and receive the result, browser monitor receives "time of update query completion" message from web server.
2. After confirming successful query completion, browser monitor sends "Commit/Abort + time of update query completion" message to MV agent.
3. If multiple update queries try to update same data set, TQ compares the time of update query completion to determine the order of queries to be processed.

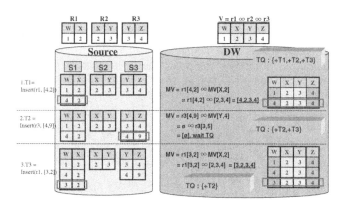

Fig. 7. Example 3 detailed steps

Example 3. Tables S1[R1(1,2)], S2[R2(2,3)] and S3[R3(3,4)] exist in each source system, and web warehouse is MV=R1∞R2∞R3. Let us take a look at queries T1=insert(r1,[4,2]), T2=insert(r3,[4,9]) and T3=insert(r1,[3,2]).

1. When users request t1, t2, t3 to each source system, each user's browser monitor reviews the queries and determines their impact on web warehouse. Then it records {+T1, +T2, +T3} in TQ and creates modify query (r1[4,2]∞MV[X,2]) and sends them to web warehouse.
2. Upon receiving T1 result from source system, browser monitor requests to save the modify query result([4,2,3,4]) and deletes {+T1} from TQ.

3. T2 is left at TQ because there is no "Y=4" record in web warehouse.
4. Because T3 and T2 cannot be combined at TQ, Modify query(r1[3,2]∞MV[X,2]) for T3 is created and requested to web warehouse.
5. After joining "X=2" data in web warehouse ([2,3,4]), update T3 modify query result([3,2,3,4]) then delete {+T3} from TQ.

4   Performance Comparison

Arena simulation program is used for evaluating the performance of the proposed (CWH) system and previous systems. Taking into account the time it takes to process update and modify queries between web warehouse and source system, the simulation assumes the following:

- Source system query processing time: 0.01-0.1/sec
- Web warehouse query processing time: 0.5-1.5/sec
- Update query inflow interval: exponential function
- Proportion of incoming update queries against modify queries: 70%
- The number of update query: 10000 - 1000000

Strobe algorithm assumes 3 separate source systems. Figure 8 displays source system's performance varying the number of update queries. Because source system processes both update and modify queries in ECA, its performance deteriorates rapidly as the number of queries increases. As in ECA, the system performance of Strobe is poor because each source system has to execute both update and compensating queries separately. On the other hand, the proposed system's distributed handling of queries improves the performance 7 fold against Strobe algorithm and 2.5 fold against ECA.

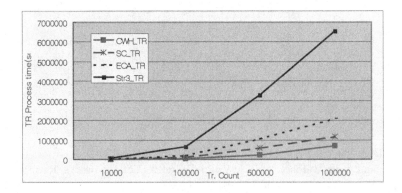

Fig. 8. Source system's performance comparison

Figure 9 displays the processing time of modify queries varying the number of requested update queries. Because modify queries are handled by source system in ECA, web warehouse performance is superior, but source system is taxed heavily. In case of Strobe algorithm, it takes longer to process queries because the number of modify queries to source systems increases as the number of update queries increases.

On the other hand, the proposed system shows performance comparable to SC (Store Copies) having duplicate copy of data and to ECA without processing modify queries.

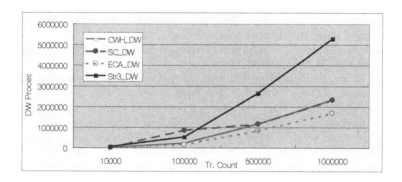

Fig. 9. Web warehouse's performance comparison

5 Conclusion

This paper tries to solve the data warehouse real time data consistency problem and address the multi source system performance issue.

To maintain consistency in real time, automatically installed web client program create modify queries for each update query to the source system.

Modify queries for each update queries are processed at the web warehouse level without connecting to source system. Hence the problem of a single modify query having to access multiple source systems disappears and the system performance improves.

All web client programs are automatically installed and maintained thus program maintenance is kept simple. Also implementation is simple without taxing source systems or installing additional programs.

In the future, a recovery method in case of system failure will be proposed. Finally the proposed system's application as an eCRM system will be carefully considered.

References

[1] Q. Luo, J. F. Naughton, R. Krishnamurthy, P. Cao, and Y. Li. "Active Query caching for database Web servers", In Proc. of the International Workshop on Web and Databases (WebDB), pp.29-34, 2000

[2] A. Labrinidis, N. Roussopoulos, "WebView Materialization", In Proc. of the ACM SIGMOD Conference, pp.367-378, May 2000

[3] Alexandros Labrinidis, Nick Roussopoulos, "On the Materialization of Webviews", ACM SIGMOD Workshop on the Web and Databases, pp.79-84, June 1999

[4] Y. Kotidis, N. Roussopoulos, "DynaMat: A Dynamic View Management system of Data Warehouses", In Proc. of the ACM SIGMOD Conference, Philadelphia, pp.371-382, 1999

[5] Budzik, J., Bradshaw, S., Fu, X., and Hammond, K. J.,"Watson : Anticipating and Contextualizing Information Needs", In Proc. of the 62 Annual Meeting of the American Society for IS., 1999.

[6] Y.Zhuge, H. Garcia-Molina, Janet L. Wiener,"The Strobe Algorithms for Multi-Source Warehouse Consistency", In proc. the International Conference on Parallel and Distributed Information system, pp146-157, 1997

[7] Elke A. Rundensteiner, "DyDa : DW Maintenance in fully concurrent Environments", In Proc. ACM SIGMOD pp94-103, 2001

[8] Ralph Kimball, Richard Merz, "The Data Webhouse Toolkit", John Wiley & Sons, 2000.

[9] M.Golfarelli, D.Maio, S.Rizzi, "Conceptual Design of Data Warehouses from ER Schemes", In proc. the Hawaii International Conference, 1998

[10] D.Chatziantoniou, K. A. Ross, "Querying Multiple Features of Groups in Relational Databases", In Proc. the 22th VLDB Conference, pp.295-306, 1996

[11] Luca Cabibbo and Riccardo Torlone, "From a Procedural to a Visual Query Language for OLAP", In Proc. 10th International Conference on Scientific and Statistical Database Management, pp.77-83, July, 1998

[12] Chang Li, X.Sean Wang, "A Data Model for Supporting On-line Analytical Processing", In Pro. the Fifth International Conference on Information and Knowledge Management, pp.81-88, Nov., 1996

[13] D.Theodoratos, T. Sellis, "Dynamic Data Warehouse Design" , In Proc. 1st International Conference on Data Warehousing and Knowledge Discovery, pp.1-10, August, 1999

[14] W.J.Labio, R.Terneni, H. Garcia-Molina, "Shrinking the Warehouse Update Window", In Proc. ACM SIGMOD International Conference on Management of Data, pp.383-394, June, 1999

[15] Y.Zhuge, H. Garcia-Molina, J.Hammer, J.Widom, "View Maintenance in a Warehousing Environment", In SIGMOD 1995

A Groupware Design for Supporting International Medical Collaboration over the Internet

Duminda Nishantha[1], Yukuo Hayashida[1], Takeshi Katsuki[2], Masaaki Goto[2], Koichiro Ihara[2], and Jayantha Weerasinghe[3]

[1] Department of Information Science, Saga University, Japan
[2] Department of Oral and Maxillofacial Surgery, Saga University, Japan
[3] Department of Oral Surgery, University of Peradeniya, Sri Lanka
{duminda, yukuo}@fu.is.saga-u.ac.jp,
{gotohm, ihara}@cc.saga-u.ac.jp, juw@pdn.ac.lk

Abstract. A groupware that integrates synchronous and asynchronous collaboration paradigms is developed to support international medical collaboration activities carried out among Japan, Sri Lanka and other countries in Asia. Synchronous medical collaboration activities are facilitated through high-quality image transmission and through an interactive shared-workspace. A web based asynchronous collaboration environment facilitates file uploading, editing and reviewing functions. Provisions such as multi-stream session recording, enhanced object linkage of collaboration contents, and persistent data sharing, harness the integrated collaborative environment. Adaptive M-JPEG transmission, application level multicasting and mirrored database architecture enables efficient data transmission among heterogeneous groups connected through wide range of network channels.

1 Introduction

As a training center in *oral and maxillofacial* [1] surgery in Sri Lanka, the Department of Oral Surgery of Faculty of Dental Sciences, University of Peradeniya has been engaged in offering surgical care, training and research in the fields of oral cancer and maxillofacial trauma in the country, with the expertise from Department of Oral and Maxillofacial Surgery, Saga University in Japan. This work has been immensely supported by a telemedicine system over the Internet developed by the authors previously [1], and several success stories have been reported [2][3]. Currently the above collaborative work between Japan and Sri Lanka has evolved into a *third country project,* in which University of Peradeniya in Sri Lanka is assigned to perform as a training center for several developing countries in Asia (Maldives, Nepal, Bhutan, Bangladesh etc.) under the supervision of JICA experts (Japan International Cooperation Agency). In view of supporting this activity, we have been developing a group collaboration system that can be used to facilitate synchronous and asynchronous collaboration activities among heterogeneous groups in different countries.

---

[1] Oral & Maxillofacial Surgery has incorporated the principles of plastic and reconstructive surgery for the treatment of problems such as cleft lip & palate, oral carcinoma, and implant related prosthetic dentistry.

S. Shimojo et al. (Eds.): HSI 2005, LNCS 3597, pp. 155 – 164, 2005.
© Springer-Verlag Berlin Heidelberg 2005

Existing group collaboration systems [4] fail to support the intended telemedicine activities due to several problems. Firstly, the existing applications do not guarantee the quality of images, especially at low speed networks, because the employed streaming technologies only concern the preservation of continuity of images rather than the quality. The designed system introduces an adaptive M-JPEG streaming mechanism over a multicast overlay to preserve the high-quality of image frames even through low bandwidth channels (e.g. the network path between Saga and Peradeniya is an 18-hop channel with average round-trip-time (RTT) greater than 350 ms, and an average available bandwidth less than 40kbps). Secondly, the non-existence or apparent disassociation of asynchronous collaboration framework in existing collaboration tools should be improved or redesigned to suit modern and future collaboration requirements. Finally, the clinicians would prefer a user-friendly operating environment with sufficient software artifacts specifically designed for telemedicine related to maxillofacial activities.

Many researches have worked on integrating synchronous and asynchronous collaboration paradigms. Geyer *et. al.* [5] claims for bringing email based add hoc collaboration to a more structured activity centric paradigm, but only limited to textual contents. Changtao *et. al.* [6] uses *Web-based Distributed Authoring and Versioning* (WebDAV) to implement a document centric web based groupware, but their mechanism to use asynchronous content for real-time sessions is through an independent set of commercial applications. A general framework for synchronous collaboration application design introduced in [7] uses reusable agents to replace scattered MBONE applications. It also introduces media getaways to handle adaptive delivery, however, this design is heavily dependent on IP multicast and could not be practically realized in absence of IPv6 to achieve most of its objectives.

These problems motivated the authors to develop a novel system to support collaboration among heterogeneous groups with particular emphasis to international medical collaboration. The designed system provides an integrated fully functional collaboration environment with following features.

- The system integrates transmission strategies capable of adapting from narrowband to broadband Internet access channels while preserving the high quality of real-time image and voice, facilitating multiple participants to collaborate from any where in the world.
- Synchronous session recording and integration with a web based asynchronous collaboration system link asynchronous and synchronous collaboration paradigms effectively resulting efficient utilization of human and material resources.
- No special devices are required for synchronous clients. Only a personal computer (preferably over 1GHz CPU and 512MB memory), a camera (DV camcorder preferred), microphone, and the access components to the Internet (LAN card or modem) are required.
- Provision of tools such as shared-board, graphically pointing on the patient's images, and shared web-browser gives useful supplementary support for synchronous collaboration.
- Operations of software are simple and straightforward, enabling users such as doctors who lack special knowledge and skills in computer technologies to use our system in daily life frequently and actively.

- The system accommodates ubiquitous connectivity of group members irrespective of the dynamics of IP addresses. Most cases of firewalls and local proxies are also supportive to our design.

The rest of this paper is organized as follows. In Section 2, we explain the architecture of the designed system in detail. Section 3 describes the practical deployment scenarios of the system. Conclusion and future work will appear at Section 4.

2 Architecture of the Designed Collaboration System

The synchronous collaboration environment has been designed by extending our previous peer-to-peer collaboration system [1] to support group communication. While the synchronous system is targeted for Windows clients, the asynchronous collaboration system is designed as a web based application to support multiplatform compatibility. Fig.1 illustrates the overall design architecture of the collaboration system. Detail design issues related to synchronous and asynchronous systems are described in following sections.

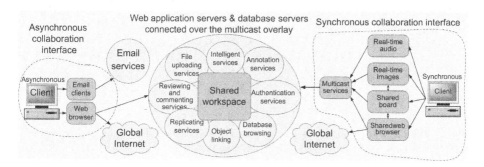

Fig. 1. Architecture of the designed collaboration system

2.1 Synchronous Collaboration System

As shown in Fig. 1, the interaction among the group members is in the form of exchanging real-time images, interactive audio, and shared transactions. The core of the system facilitates multicast services and access to persistent database through web application servers. Important design issues are described in detail below.

Session Management. A valid member (pre-assigned) can join a synchronous session either as a *passive member* (receiver only) or as an *active member* (both transmit and receive) after a user authentication process. Essentially, one active member is assigned as the *leader* of a particular session at the logging process. The session leader is assigned authority to select a *speaker* to directly communicate with. In this case, all other members will be synchronized to the speaker's viewing state.

Real-time Multimedia Delivery. Voice quality can be selected (GSM, MP3 etc.) according to the availability of bandwidth and quality requirements of the collaboration context. Generally, all the voice streams are mixed to form a single voice stream at the multicast servers. However, receiver has an option to mute unwanted voice channels when increasing clarity of particular voice channel/channels is required. Real-time images are transmitted as a series of JPEG images (M-JPEG streaming) with flexibility to exploit video quality-smoothness tradeoff. Unlike voice reception, all members receive multiple image streams from all active members, where only two image streams are displayed in high quality (i.e. image streams from session leaders and speaker). All other image streams are received as small size image frames (thumbnails) to serve member awareness to the group.

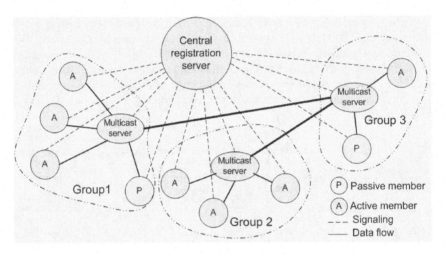

Fig. 2. Illustration of the application level multicast mechanism. Through signaling with the central registration server, multicast servers self organize into a Steiner tree while the members group around their nearest multicast server

Application Level Multicast: Although, network level multicast support (e.g. IPV6 multicast) is considered to be very promising in realizing group collaboration systems, absence of such ubiquitous framework severely hinders its practical deployment. Realistically, global multicast ubiquity will not be seen for another decade or more, especially in the developing world. In our design, we use application level multicast where, as illustrated in Fig. 2, application level servers at rendezvous points are used in connection with a static central registration server to implement network efficient data transport. All the members and multicast servers perform a lightweight communication (signaling) with the registration server exchanging a parameter metric (IP address, user name, round trip delay, and hop count etc) and form the multicast tree according to a method similar to narada [8] protocol.

Application Level Rate Adaptive M-JPEG Streaming: The application level adaptive delivery mechanism used in this system overcomes several potential technical problems in M-JPEG streaming. The authors have extended their previous work [9], which addressed point to point adaptation, to multipoint to multipoint scenario. This adaptation is three-fold: (a) M-JPEG source adapts to its CPU performance, channel bandwidth, and peer receiver's receiving status by changing the frame rate, frame size and compression quality; (b) The multicast server allows session leader and speaker to exchange image frames at maximum possible frame rates at a given quality; (c) Multicast server synchronizes the frame rate of leader and speaker to the rest of the members changing compression quality and frame size to suit available channel bandwidth of the peer members.

Shared board and Shared Web Browser. The shared board and the shared web browser constitute the system's shared workspace. An image of interest (IOI) can be loaded onto the shared board by an active member and all active members are able to make suggestions and comments through audio communication as well as marking on the image using appropriate colors and symbols. Zooming and panning of the shared-board, replication and deletion of markers, and clipboard integration are some of the important functions integrated to the shared board.

Shared web-browser brings web resources (identified by a URL address) to the shared workspace for group discussion. Shared web browser is the key for accessing the system database during synchronous sessions. The system database can be browsed on the shared workspace to find documents related to the ongoing discussion. Moreover, shared web browser is indispensable for conducting remote presentations (PowerPoint slides, MPEG playback etc.).

Collaboration Recording. It is a multiple stream recording that involves incoming/ outgoing audio streams, incoming/outgoing image streams and all incoming thumbnail streams. Session playback produces a four-window output for transmit image, receive image, shared board and shared web browser respectively. Besides, all thumbnails are displayed on a separate panel. To handle multiple streams with flexibility and to preserve original image quality of patient images, we have developed a customized MJPEG codec [3]. However, to stay intact with the portability issues, we have facilitated trans-coding to MPEG-4 format.

2.2 Asynchronous Collaboration System

The asynchronous collaboration system has been implemented as a web application driven by a tomcat web application server as shown in Fig. 3. Following functions are currently supported through the asynchronous collaboration interface:

- *Multiple file uploading:* Multiple file uploading and folder-wise uploading are both possible. Duplicate file names will be treated through an internal renaming policy.
- *Custom layout:* User can create custom sub-folders to build a preferred tree layout. Page layouts (viewing status) can also be customized to user preferences.
- *Enhanced file linking:* Files can be uploaded with links to existing files. Exiting files can be pre and post linked (forward and backward links) to other files. Two-dimensional hierarchical links as well as random links are also possible. This provides maximum information sharing (disk space), provisions for intelligent processing, and convenient object navigation.
- *Reviewing and commenting:* Uploaded files can be commented through a separate comment-page linked to each object. Use of hypermedia (hypertext and voice) for commenting enhances reviewing quality as well as efficiency.

- *Server side intelligence:* Server alarms possible mistakes on patient IDs, mistaken reference to objects (by matching contextual key words), and also provides access statistics of the object history.

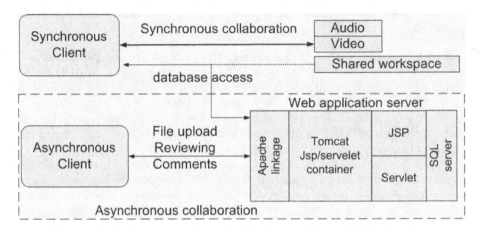

Fig. 3. Interaction between asynchronous and synchronous collaboration systems

2.3 Integration of Synchronous/Asynchronous Collaboration

Mutual interaction between asynchronous and synchronous collaboration paradigms enhances the overall collaboration efficiency in terms of material and human resource utilization. The designed collaboration system achieves this integration by allowing synchronous clients and asynchronous clients to access a common database as illustrated in Fig. 3 and described below.

- Collaboration contents (i.e. high resolution still face images, pictures of study models, radiographs, PowerPoint files, voice clips etc.) generated by asynchronous sessions are stored in the persistent system database and readily accessible during subsequent synchronous sessions without overloading the network.
- Access to the system database during synchronous sessions is facilitated through shared web browser which is an integrated artifact of the system. This enables the group members to browse the system database in a common workspace.
- Synchronous sessions are recorded using a multi-stream motion-JPEG codec developed by the authors. These session records are automatically posted to the system database enabling the asynchronous users to review missed session.
- Tedious ad hoc email based session negotiation method has been replaced by a well structured asynchronous email based procedure for notifying proposed future sessions to the potential participants.

3   Collaboration Scenario

Using the designed group collaboration system presented in this paper, several experts can participate a collaborative session from geographically different locations in the world, while several trainee/recipient groups may participate from their respective countries.

3.1 Nature of Collaboration

The intended medical collaboration activities are presently rooted on the process that medical experts visit recipient countries to give practical training for the local surgeons by conducting surgeries on some pre-selected problem cases. Through Internet collaboration, experts' number of visits to recipient countries can be reduced curtailing the cost significantly, and thereby enabling fast and effective medical technology transfer to needy countries. Moreover, Internet collaboration brings a valuable opportunity for the whole group of medical personnel from different countries to share the experience and come up with group solutions to the problem cases. Following are the main activities facilitated by the designed system.

- *Pre-observation:* Specialists in donor countries, who wish to go to recipient countries for teaching through surgeries and other training programs, can get accustomed to the situation (patients, instruments available etc.) in the recipient country before hand, enabling proper planning before leaving to recipient countries.
- *Post-observations:* when returned to the home country after completing the mission, the medical experts can observe the patients operated remotely and prescribe necessary treatment and advice.
- *Trainee evaluation and remote lecturing:* The trainees in recipient countries can present their performance to the experts through PowerPoint presentations, video recording and showing actual patients they operated. The experts on the other hand can arrange Internet training sessions in a regular basis to the trainee groups through similar methods.
- *Remote medical expert services:* The surgeons in recipient countries are able to acquire experts' service to solve problems in emergency clinical cases. The experts can offer their service from convenient locations at convenient times due to asynchronous collaboration framework and ubiquitous connectivity.
- *Social relationship development:* Besides the medical collaboration activities, this collaboration system will be immensely helpful to build up personal acquaintance and relationships, creating an environment with high-spirited groups motivated for development of health of the global community.

3.2 Synchronous Collaboration Scenario

A snap shot of the synchronous groupware is shown in Fig. 4. The control panel and main menu shown on the top of the figure contains controls for software operations. Other windows below the control panel accommodates transmit image, received image, shared board and share web browser. *IPhone*, the window shown in the bottom, is an independent application used for audio communication and session initiation. The snap-shot illustrates a scene where a Japanese medical expert evaluating a maxillofacial case handled by a Sri Lankan medical surgeon.

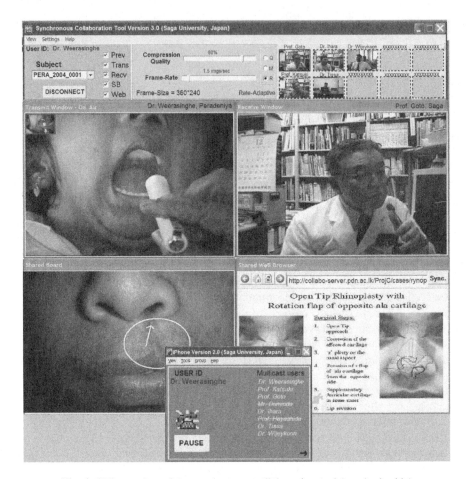

Fig. 4. GUI snapshot of the synchronous collaboration tool (speaker's side)

3.3 Asynchronous Collaboration Scenario

Asynchronous collaboration is facilitated through a web-based interface that provides context aware data representation. Fig. 5 illustrates a sample view of particular patient data page stored in the system. The elliptical shapes represent file objects whereas boxed shapes represent subfolders which group a collection of other objects. Still images are displayed as thumbnails on a configurable horizontal or vertical layout for easy comparison. Provisions are given for searching, sorting and customizing the view to client's preferences. The interface for adding new threads, editing and updating images, adding comments, and navigation through the database is self explanatory. Collaborators who already have some knowledge of the problem cases can share there knowledge suggesting solutions and sometimes inviting for a synchronous session to observe the patient in real-time. Fig. 6 illustrates how session records are stored in the system. A particular session is stored as a serious of clips belonging to different patients and cases. External access points and internal object linkage are illustrated in the figure.

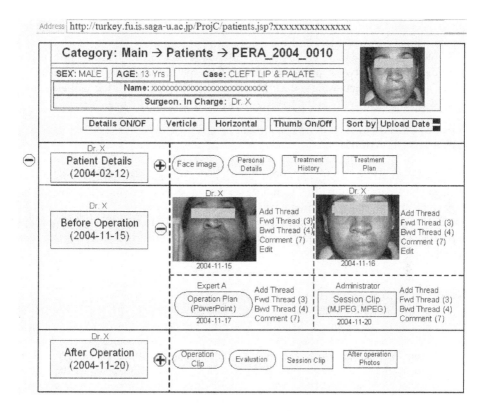

Fig. 5. A sample of a customized page view accessed by an asynchronous client

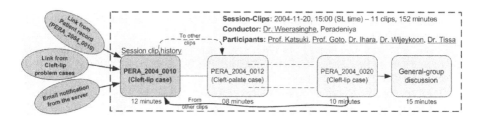

Fig. 6. Illustration of a session recording in the database with corresponding access links

4   Conclusions and Future Work

The design rationale of the integrated collaboration system for group collaboration was discussed and its deployment scenarios were presented giving practical examples. By using our software with its unique features, especially in international medical collaboration activities, geographically dispersed groups have been able to engage in co-operate activities effectively. We anticipate our system will motivate the international community towards expanding cooperate activities to groups with low bandwidth internet facilities, and also to harness internet collaborative activities among groups with access to the fast Internet.

We will investigate more closely on the efficiency of application level multicasting in terms of both network performance and CPU performance aspects. Enhancing server intelligence, increasing robustness and efficient server mirroring will also considered in future research.

Acknowledgements

The would like to thank Mr. Ranjith of University of Peradenya, and Dr. Shigematsu of Saga University for providing technical support in session activities. Dr. Parakrama Wijekoon of University of Peradeniya is also acknowledged for his contribution in conducting collaboration sessions. Authors would also like to take this opportunity to express gratitude to the President of Saga University for offering research grants and resources to conduct this project.

References

[1] Nishantha, D., Hayashida, Y., Hayashi, T., Katsuki, T., Goto, M., Ihara, K., Amaratunga, N., Weerasinghe, J., and Tokura, N.: Multimedia Medical Collaboration over the Internet between Sri Lanka and Japan. The Journal of Information and Systems in Education, Vol. 1. Japanese Society for Information and Systems in Education, Japan (2002) 98-108

[2] Nishantha, D.: Internet-based Communication for Transferring Technology to Developing Countries. International Cooperation Research – Research Contest for University Students, Vol. 6. Japan International Cooperation Agency, Japan (2003).

[3] Home page of the telemedicine project at Saga University. http://turkey.fu.is.saga-u. ac.jp/education/project/Collabo1.html

[4] Singh, M. P.: Practical Handbook of Internet Computing. Chapman Hall & CRC Press, Baton Rouge (2004)

[5] Geyer, W., Vogel, J., Cheng, T., and Muller M.: Supporting Activity Centric Collaboration through Peer-to-Peer Shared Objects. SIGGROUP Bull., Vol. 24. ACM Press, New York, NY, USA (2003) 9-18

[6] Qu, C., Nejdl, W.: Constructing a Web-based Asynchronous and Synchronous Collaboration Environment using WebDAV and Lotus Sametime. Proc. of the 29th annual ACM SIGUCCS conference on user services, ACM Press, New York, NY, USA (2003) 142-149

[7] Parnes, P., Synnes, K., and Schefström, D.: mSTAR: Enabling Collaborative Applications on the Internet. IEEE Internet Computing, Vol. 4. IEEE (September/October 2000) 32-39

[8] Chu, Y., Rao, S.G., Seshan, S., and Zhang, H.: A Case For End System Multicast. IEEE Journal on Selected Areas in Communications, Vol. 20, IEEE (2002) 1456-1471

[9] Nishantha, D., Hayashida, Y., and Hayashi T.: Application Level Rate Enhancement of Motion-JPEG Transmission for Medical Collaboration Systems. Proc. of the 24th IEEE International Conference on Distributed Computing Systems Workshops, IEEE Computer Society (2004) 64-69

Towards the Construction of the Information Infrastructure for Genome Medicine

Norihiro Sakamoto and Jun Nakaya

Department of Clinical Genome Informatics,
Graduate School of Medicine, Kobe University,
7-5-2, Kusunoki-cho, Chuo-ku, Kobe, Japan
{nori, junnaka}@med.kobe-u.ac.jp

Abstract. One of the most expected applications of the human genome information is the development of genome medicine. Towards this goal, basic and applied biomedical laboratory researches and developments have been steadily in progress. However, clinical genome informatics and its applications in practice have been making slower progress compared to biomedical laboratory works. In order to facilitate the progress of clinical genome informatics and its powerful application to the development of genome medicine, the construction of the information infrastructure for genome medicine calls for urgent attention. In this paper, we propose the architecture of the information infrastructure for genome medicine. It is required to provide three essential features: security mechanisms, comprehensive information models, and intelligent analyzers. To implement these features, we employed PKI as the security mechanisms and the HL7 Version 3 as the information models. To analyze information, knowledge discovery tools are expected to be implemented in addition to a lot of clinical and genetic statistical functions.

1 Introduction

The Human Genome Project has produced the detailed map and the comprehensive dictionary concerning the human genome on a basis of about 3 billion nucleotide sequences. These results have changed the way researchers approach the life sciences and have pushed them to the post genomic era.

1.1 Clinical Genome Informatics

The major research topics in the post genomic era contain proteomics, system biology, genome-based drug discovery and other advanced life science areas. Among them, the research and development of genome medicine is one of the most expected applications of the human genome information. The research and development of genome medicine need both high throughput biological laboratory works and high performance computational power. Towards realizing genome medicine, basic and applied biomedical laboratory researches and developments have been steadily in progress so far. However, informatics for genome medicine and its applications in practice have

S. Shimojo et al. (Eds.): HSI 2005, LNCS 3597, pp. 165 – 178, 2005.

been making slower progress compared to biomedical laboratory works. Bioinformatics is the critical research field and the key information technology that supports genome medicine. Although bioinformatics seems to have been active in basic life science and genome based drug discovery among wide range of its scope, its activity in the application field of genome medicine seems to be lower. We have taken up and focused this research field of bioinformatics that supports the development of genome medicine and named it clinical genome informatics. In order to facilitate the progress of clinical genome informatics and its powerful application to the development of genome medicine, we consider that the construction of the information infrastructure for genome medicine calls for urgent attention. Towards the construction, we describe the architecture of the information infrastructure for genome medicine in this paper.

1.2   Research and Development Processes of Genome Medicine

As the first step of the research and development of genome medicine, genomic analyses for detecting disease susceptibility genes have been popular. The genomic analyses are mainly categorized into the following two approaches: the candidate gene approach and the whole genome scan approach. The whole genome scan approach for detecting disease susceptibility genes makes more use of the human genome information, particularly the single nucleotide polymorphisms (SNPs) and microsatellites (MSs), than the candidate gene approach. The whole genome scan approach is further categorized into the following subgroups based on the methodology of genetic statistics: the linkage analysis and the linkage disequilibrium analysis or the association study. In order to determine a disease susceptibility gene, the linkage analysis usually requires 10-200 samples or patients that are members of a few large families while the linkage disequilibrium analysis requires 200-2,000.

The main targets of genome medicine are so called common diseases that are very popular in today's society, for example, diabetes mellitus, hypertension, heart disease, cancer and so forth. The association analysis is more suitable for the genome analyses of such common diseases because it is easier to collect a large number of samples of the common disease than to get a large family. The millennium genome project employed the approach based on the association study. The millennium genome project started in 2000 in order to detect susceptibility genes of the common diseases. The project consists of the following 5 subgroups: Alzheimer's disease, asthma, cancer, diabetes mellitus (DM), and hypertension. The DM subgroup has been led by Prof. Masato Kasuga from Kobe University and we have been involved in it. Each of subgroups has collected and analyzed more than 200 patients (cases) and 200 normal controls on average. The DM subgroup collected 178 cases for the first screening and 752 cases and controls of the same number for the second and third screening. More than 15 medical schools have been cooperating to collect such a large number of cases and controls. This cooperation has been strongly facilitated by using the Internet. We have set up a home page and shared analysis results. The accesses to the home page are secured through SSL.

Another example of such a large study was reported in the research paper on an affected sib pair study on DM from Kyushu University [1]. They collected more than 100 cases and their siblings from more than 30 medical facilities. It is clear that the secure communication infrastructure through the Internet is indispensable to connect the participant medical facilities and researchers and share the information.

We need to handle various types of information in the research and development of genome medicine. Theses pieces of information include genome sequences, genomic structures such as promoters, exons and introns, amino acid sequences, protein structures and functions, genomic polymorphisms such as SNPs and MSs, metabolic pathways, signal transductions, and so forth. In the public biological databases, a part of them are usually managed in relational database systems. Such management is appropriate for the purposes of retrieving and browsing pieces of information. However, the efficient research and development of genome medicine requires the integrated management and analyses of the whole of those pieces of information. For this purpose, a relational model is not necessarily suitable but more powerful data model such as an object model is preferable. Health Level Seven (HL7) is the international standards for the messaging and communications in the fields of healthcare and provides the reference information model (RIM). HL7 is now extending its scope to the filed of clinical genomics.

The common diseases are usually considered as a multifactorial disease. More than 10 genes in addition to environmental factors are involved in the development process of the disease. The extent of the involvement of each gene varies from case to case. According to such difference, a case shows different phenotypes or clinical symptoms. Therefore, efficient analyses of disease susceptibility genes require the combined analyses of the genome information and the clinical information. The genome information and the clinical information have been usually analyzed separately. In the typical genome analyses of disease susceptibility genes, the clinical information is used only when cases are diagnosed. However, in the genome analyses regarding the common diseases, patients of which present different phenotypes, any pieces of clinical information are required to be used in order to categorize the cases into subgroups. The combined information of the genome information and the clinical information also requires the combined method of clinical statistics, genetic statistics, and data mining. Such integrated intelligent approaches are critical for the efficient research and development of genome medicine.

1.3 Intelligent Database

To summarize the above requirements, the architecture of the information infrastructure for genome medicine shall possess the following features: security mechanisms, comprehensive information models, and intelligent analyzers. We recognize the information infrastructure for genome medicine with these features as a natural extension of the intelligent database.

The intelligent database represents the state of the art in the evolution of database technology [2]. The intelligent database handles a variety of functions ranging from data modeling and management to information discovery, summarization, and presentation. The basic architecture of the intelligent database consists of three layers: the intelligent database engine, the object model, and a set of high-level tools that tend to vary somewhat according to the application [3]. The intelligent database handles the storage, retrieval and management of information. It also handles extraction of data from heterogeneous databases and the various communication and transaction protocols required by this activity. In terms of the intelligent database, the information framework for genome medicine is the clinical genome specific one featured by secure communication on the Internet. Therefore, the architecture of the information framework for genome medicine can be primarily a natural extension of the intelligent database.

2 Method

We designed the architecture of the information framework for genome medicine based on the concept of the extended intelligent database. Here, we describe the approaches of design and implementation for the three outstanding features: the security mechanisms, the comprehensive information models and the intelligent analyzers.

2.1 Security Mechanisms

For making use of the genome information and clinical information across healthcare institutes, standardization of data formats and vocabularies of representing the information are essential. The detail regarding this issue is described in the next subsection. In addition to them, digital signature is a critical key technology for making the information to be exchanged secure and trustworthy [4]. Especially for the genome information, digital signature is much more important because of its reusability. Efficient exchanges of authorized information with a digital signature in healthcare information networks require a construction of a public key infrastructure (PKI).

The necessity of PKI in the healthcare domain has been internationally discussed and recognized [5]. However, there have been few reports on the implementation and practical use of PKI for healthcare. A plan to use PKI for out-patients' prescription is under way in Korea [6]. Japan is ahead in a point of view of implementation of PKI because some of the EPR projects have already implemented a PKI and been operating a CA for different purposes [7]. One of the purposes of using a PKI is user authentication. A second is an access control and privilege management. A third is a digital signature on clinical information. A composite usage of them can be a forth purpose. We employed a PKI for the security mechanism for the construction of the information infrastructure for genome medicine because it provides these various security solutions.

2.1.1 Community of the PKI

The community of a PKI is composed of the following entities: the root CA (Certification Authority), the sub CAs, and end entities. The end entities are in turn categorized into subscribers and verifiers.

- Root CA: The root CA authorizes the sub CAs by means of issuing PKCs (Public Key Certificates) for digital signature to them. It also authorizes itself as the root CA by a self-issued PKC.
- Sub CAs: The sub CAs authorize end entities by means of issuing end entity PKCs for digital signature. In this study, there are no intermediate sub CAs that issue PKCs to subjects that are CAs.
- Subscribers: The subscribers are end entities that are the subjects of PKCs, hold the PKCs and sign pieces of genome information and clinical information by using them. In terms of healthcare, they are referring doctors that send clinical information to a referred doctor.
- Verifiers: The verifiers are end entities that make use of PKCs and verify digital signatures. In terms of healthcare, they are research leaders that receive clinical information and genome information signed by a participant researcher of different medical institutes.

2.1.2 Policies and Statements

In order to manage the hierarchical PKI, coordinated security policies are essential. We defined the security policies to manage both the root CA and the sub CAs as two kinds of documents. These documents are referred to as Certificate Policy (CP) and Certification Practices Statement (CPS) [8].

A policy is a set of rules established to govern a certain aspect of organizational behavior. The CP addresses the components of a PKI in total. It describes the goals, responsibilities, and overall requirements for the protection of the CAs, PKCs and their supporting components. It is a high-level document that describes a security policy for issuing PKCs and maintaining certificate status information. This security policy describes the operation of the CA, as well as the users' responsibilities for the requesting, using, and handling of PKCs and keys.

Compared to the CP, the CPS is a highly detailed document that describes how a CA implements a specific CP. The CPS identifies the CP and specifies the mechanisms and procedures that are used to achieve the security policy. Each CPS applies to a single CA. The CPS may be considered the overall operations manual for the CA.

The policy information is indicated in the three policy extensions of the PKC: certificate policies, policy mapping, and policy constraints. Now, we have prepared the secure mechanism based on the PKI. Next we describe the comprehensive model that defines the forms of information to be communicated.

2.2 Comprehensive Information Models

The architecture of the intelligent database proposes the adoption of the object model to handle complex data. In the area of healthcare, HL7 is the international standards and have entirely adapted the object oriented technologies for the latest version, HL7 Version 3. Therefore, the architecture of the information structure for genome medicine is expected to follow HL7 Version 3. However, HL7 Version 3 has been strongly focusing on the clinical information. The HL7 information model for the genome information is not completed. Hence, in this paper we devise and propose the comprehensive information models that integrate the genome information and the clinical information by extending HL7 Version 3.

2.2.1 HL7 Version 3

HL7 Version 3 has been developed to cater for the more complex requirements of today's healthcare information systems [9]. It defines the communication protocols between healthcare information systems as a set of messages. HL7 Version 3 also provides a comprehensive information model, Reference Information Model (RIM) in the healthcare field.

The RIM is a coherent, shared information model that is the source for the data content of all HL7 Version 3 messages. It provides an explicit representation of the semantic and lexical connections that exist between the information carried in the fields of HL7 Version 3 messages by using UML. Sixty-four classes are defined in the RIM 2.04. The RIM represents all information involved in clinical events as relationships among the six core classes; Entity, Role, Participation, Act, ActRelationship, and RoleLink.

Entity class represents a physical thing or organization and grouping of physical things. Person class is a subclass of Entity. Role class represents a role that an Entity plays. For example, "patient" or "physician" is a role for a person. Act class is an intentional action in the business domain of HL7. Examples include orders of laboratory tests and medication, care plan, procedure and document service. A physician who is an actor in a healthcare act and patient who is a target of the act are represented as Entities participated (Participation class) in the Act class that corresponds to the service with particular role (Role class).

2.2.2 EHR Projects Based on HL7 Version 3

Although the HL7 Version 3 is still under development, various national projects of EHR based on HL7 Version 3 are ongoing in several countries in the world. An example of such projects is the National Health Service (NHS) National Programme for Information Technology (NPfIT) project [10] that is responsible for major IT initiatives to support health care delivery in United Kingdom. The NPfIT has chosen the HL7 Version 3 as a base standard for its national and regional projects. Another example is the Canadian Institute for Health Information (CIHI) National e-Claims Standard (NeCST) project in Canada [11]. The goal of the NeCST is to facilitate and support the development of a national electronic claims messaging standard for exchanging electronic health claims information across Canada, for private and public sector payers and for health service providers. Other examples include The Medication Supply Registry Project in the Netherlands [12] and the Center for Disease Control and Prevention (CDC) Public Health Information Network (PHIN) [13] that enables consistent exchange of response, health, and disease tracking data between public health partners. In Japan, the Japanese Ministry of Health, Labor and Welfare recommends the use of HL7 Version 3 as one of the standard protocols for exchanging clinical information.

As stated above, HL7 Version 3 RIM is the most appropriate basis for developing the comprehensive information models that integrate the genome information and the clinical information though HL7 Version 3 is still working for providing a complete information model for the genome information.

2.3 Intelligent Analyzers

The genome information and the clinical information require their specific analysis methods respectively. Namely, they are genetic statistics and clinical statistics. For efficient analyses of both the genome information and the clinical information, the analyzing system should provide the various kinds of statistical analysis functions.

2.3.1 Genetic Statistical Functions

The following functions are primary genetic statistical functions that the intelligent analyzers are expected to provide.

- Hardy-Weinberg Equilibrium
- Case-Control study
- Linkage Disequilibrium Analysis
- Haplotype Inference
- others

2.3.2 Clinical Statistical Functions

The following functions are primary clinical statistical functions that the intelligent analyzers are expected to provide.

- Paired t-test
- Student t-test
- Welch t-test
- Mann-Whitney U-test
- others

In addition to these traditional statistical analysis methods, a sort of knowledge discovery approaches or data mining approaches are known to be powerful for efficient analyses of the integrated genome and clinical information. Among the data mining approaches, we employed machine learning approach and back propagation neural network approach.

3 Results

Towards the construction of the information infrastructure for genome medicine, we implemented some software components for PKI and HL7. Then we developed a prototype system based on the architecture that was described in the above and evaluated it.

3.1 PKI Components

3.1.1 Configuration of the Root CA

The root CA was installed in the Medical Information System Developing Center (MEDIS-DC). The X.500 distinguished name (DN) for it was set to 'c=JP, o=MEDIS-DC, cn=MD-HPKI-01-MEDIS -TopCA-for-CAs-and-TSAs'.

The primary functions of the root CA are 1) issue of the certificate signing certificate to the root CA (the root CA signing certificate), 2) issue of the certificate signing certificates to the sub CAs (the sub CA signing certificates), 3) revocation of the sub CA signing certificates, 4) distribution of the authority revocation list (ARL) that lists the revoked sub CA signing certificates, and 5) distribution of the certificate revocation list (CRL) that lists the end entity signing certificates that are revoked by each sub CA. The certificate validity period of the root CA signing certificate is set to 8 years. That of the sub CA signing certificates is also set to 8 years. Distribution of ARLs and CRLs are made via HTTP protocol.

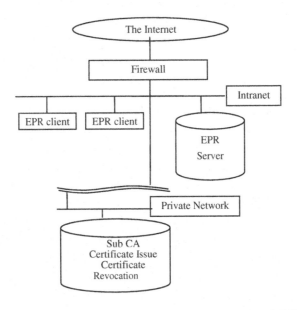

Fig. 1. The system architecture of the root CA installed in MEDIS-DC

The system architecture of the root CA is illustrated in Figure 1. Since it shall be operated in top level secure way, the CA system that generates PKCs and ARL is installed on the private network that is isolated from either the intranet of MEDIS-DC or the Internet. The web server for distributing ARLs and CRLs is installed on the demilitarized zone (DMZ).

3.1.2 Configuration of the Sub CA

The sub CAs were installed on the private networks in Kobe University Hospital and Kobe Translational Research Informatics Center. The DN for Kobe University Hospital was set to 'c=JP, o=Kobe University Hospital, ou=Kobe University Hospital, cn=MD-HPKI-01-KUH-CA-for-non -Repudiation'. The DN of the end entities were, for example, identified by a DN like 'c=JP, o=Kobe University Hospital, ou= regulated health professional, cd=Real Name' where 'Real Name' is a doctor's real name.

The primary functions of the sub CA are 1) issue of the clinical document signing certificates to end entities (the end entity signing certificate), 2) revocation of the end entity signing certificates, 3) registration of the CRL to the CRL distribution point on the web server of the root CA. The certificate validity period of the end entity signing certificate is set to 4 years that is a half of that of the sub CA signing certificates.

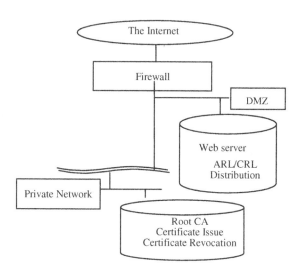

Fig. 2. The system architecture of the sub CA installed in Kobe University Hospital

The system architecture of the sub CA is illustrated in Figure 2. The CA system that generates PKCs and CRLs is installed on the private network that is isolated from either the intranet of each EPR project where EPR servers and EPR clients are running or the Internet.

3.2 HL7 Components

The clinical documents including individual genome information are composed of two components. The first component is clinical information and genome information itself. We designed the format of those information of a patient according to the

Table 1. J-MIX items that are used for the description of clinical information and genome information

Item code	XML element name	Data type
MD0010050	Patient.WholeName	String
MD0010110	Patient.Birthday	Date
MD0010120	Patient.Sex	Category
MD0010150	Patient.WholeAddress	String
MD0020180	Referral.Date	Date
MD0020220	Referring.Provider.Name	String
MD0020410	Referring.Physician.WholeName	String
MD0020480	ReferredTo.Provider.Name	String
MD0020670	ReferredTo.Physician.WholeName	String
MD0020730	ReferralNote	Text

Table 2. A part of XML scheme for a clinical document described in HL7 Version 3 format with a digitall signature

```
<?xml version="1.0" encoding="UTF-8" standalone="no" ?>
- <xs:schema targetNamespace="urn:hl7-org:v3"
elementFormDefault="qualified"
xmlns:fo="http://www.w3.org/1999/XSL/Format"
xmlns:msg="urn:hl7-org:v3/mif" xmlns:hl7="urn:hl7-org:v3"
xmlns:voc="urn:hl7-org:v3/voc" xmlns="urn:hl7-org:v3"
xmlns:my="http://schemas.microsoft.com/office/infopath/2003/myXSD/20
04-02-20T09:07:01" xmlns:xs="http://www.w3.org/2001/XMLSchema">
  <xs:element name="OutcomeResearchReport"
type="UUDD_MT990100.OutcomeResearchReport" />
- <xs:complexType name="UUDD_MT990100.OutcomeResearchReport">
- <xs:sequence>
  <xs:element name="id" type="II" />
  <xs:element name="recordTarget" type="UUDD_MT990100.RecordTarget" />
  <xs:element name="component" type="UUDD_MT990100.Component" />
  <xs:element name="signature" type="my:SignatureType" />
  </xs:sequence>
  <xs:attribute name="classCode" type="ActClass" />
  <xs:attribute name="moodCode" type="ActMood" />
  </xs:complexType>
- <xs:complexType name="UUDD_MT990100.RecordTarget">
- <xs:sequence>
  <xs:element name="patient" type="UUDD_MT990100.Patient" />
  </xs:sequence>
  <xs:attribute name="typeCode" type="ParticipationType" />
  </xs:complexType>
```

Japanese Set of Identifiers for Medical Record Information Exchange (J-MIX) [14] and HL7 Version 3. The items and their XML elements are listed in Table 1. We exchanged the clinical information and the genome information as an XML document in conformity to J-MIX and HL7 Version 3.

The second component of the clinical documents is a digital signature and its related information. Digital signatures are usually transferred with the signer's PKC that is used for verifying the digital signature and the CA PKCs that are necessary for building the certification path to validate the signer's PKC.

There are various choices regarding the format of the digital signatures and signed document formats. An XML signature is one of the most possible choices because we use J-MIX and HL7 Version 3 in an XML format. However, the implementation of the XML format is not straightforward. For example, it requires a lot of preprocessing of XML documents such as canonicalization. PKCS #7 is another possible choice. It is the de facto standard specification for protecting information with digital signature.

The basic PKCS #7 message format has two fields: the content type and the content. The content types defined by PKCS #7 are data, signedData, envelopedData, signedAndEnvelopedData, digestedData, and encryptedData. Since PKCS #7 is a basic building block for cryptographic applications, such as the S/MIME v2 electronic mail security protocol, there are already a lot of libraries or modules available on many platforms. Since this means the ease of implementation, we chose PKCS #7 as the signature format in this study. A part of the XML scheme for the clinical information and genome information described in HL7 Version 3 format with a digital signature is illustrated in Table 2.

3.3 Prototype System

We developed a prototype system by using the above components and evaluated it in Kobe University Hospital and Kobe Translational Research Informatics Center. The system was developed using with Microsoft Internet Information Servers, Microsoft InfoPath, and Microsoft .Net C#. The overall system architecture was illustrated in Figure 3.

About 60 users participated in using the prototype system. First they applied for registration through the registration web page to the sub CA either in Kobe University Hospital or Translational Research Informatics Center depending on their affiliation. The sub CA verified the registration and issued a private key and the corresponding public key certificate stored in a USB token. The users generated pieces of translational research information that contained SNP information in some cases in an HL7 Version 3 format and signed it with the USB token. The signed documents were uploaded through the Internet by using SSL to the Translational Research Information System that was maintained in Translational Research Informatics Center. The system was running successfully and the system architecture we proposed in this paper was evaluated to be appropriate.

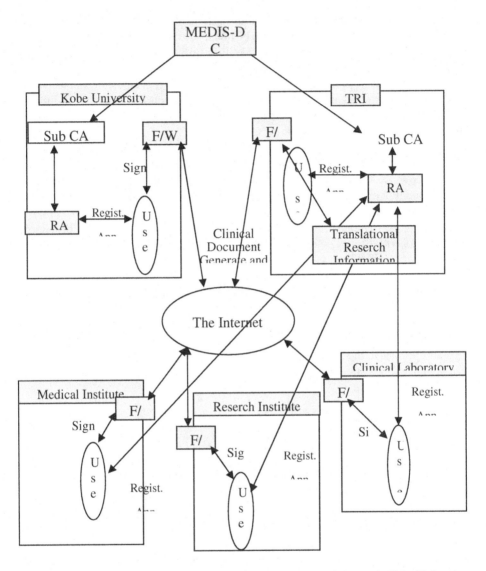

Fig. 3. The overall system architecture of the prototype system. The users in Kobe University Hospital posses the PKC that was issued by the sub CA installed in Kobe University Hospital while the other users possess the PKC that was issued by the sub CA installed in TRI

4 Discussion

During the evaluation process of the prototype system, we had no technical problems and the system was running without any troubles. The most difficult part of the process was in the steps of registration of users and issuing their public key certificates because these steps required a lot of collaboration of the users who didn't know much about

PKI. We needed to ask them to bring forward their resident's card for the personal identification and their medical license for conformation of their qualification, This procedure put a burden on the users and it took about seven days for half of them to get a complete set of the papers. In order to make these steps much speedier and easier, social infrastructure for digital application should be developed. Especially, the development of nation wide PKI that is specific for the healthcare field and assert healthcare professionals is a pressing issue.

The cost of issuing the public key certificate is another serious problem. One PKC stored in a USB token cost about 24,000 yen or 220 USD. It is obviously higher compared to current seals and handwritten signature. Though this problem about the cost is the one that is expected to be solved as PKI becomes popular and the number of the PKC in use increases, it is another pressing issue.

We succeeded in the development of the comprehensive information models for clinical information and genome information on a basis of HL7 Version 3. However, the more comprehensive the information models are getting, the more complicated the implementations becomes. In the development of the prototype system, the implementation of the clinical document of HL7 Version 7 XML format took the longest time (man month) in the whole implementation processes. A development of a set of software tools that supports the HL7 Version 3 is an urgent business for the construction of the information infrastructure for genome medicine.

We pointed out the importance of the intelligent analyzers that provide a lot of statistical functions for the information infrastructure for genome medicine and its essential components. However, its implementations are still in progress and were not included in the prototype system. In order to make the prototype system much more practical, we need to work hard for its implementations.

5   Conclusion

The Internet is providing the powerful foundation for the construction of the information infrastructure for genome medicine because the Internet is now stable, trustworthy and fast. The Public Key Infrastructure is adding another good feature, namely security, to the Internet. PKI is expected to be more popular through the Internet society in the near future, which will provide more sound foundation for the construction of the information infrastructure for genome medicine.

Though PKI is one of the key technologies that is critical for all of those who want to use the Internet in safety, other methods that are specific for the development of genome medicine should be devised by the research community of clinical genome informatics. Among those methods, comprehensive information models and intelligent analyzers are most essential. In this paper, we proposed an implementation of the information models based on the HL7 Version 3 and demonstrated the integrated architecture of the models and the PKI. The architecture was evaluated to work well and we consider that the architecture gives the basis for the construction of the information framework for genome medicine.

Acknowledgment

This work was partially supported by the research fund of the Japanese Ministry of Health, Labor, and Welfare.

References

1. Nawata, H., et. al: Genome-wide linkage analysis of type 2 diabetes mellitus reconfirms the susceptibility locus on 11p13–p12 in Japanese. Journal of Human Genetics, Vol. 49, No.11 (2004) 629-34
2. Parsaye, K., Chignell, M.: Intelligent Database Tools & Applications: Hyperinformation Access, Data Quality, Visualization, Automatic Discovery. New York: John Wiley & Sons, Inc. (1993)
3. Parsaye, K., Chingnell, M.H., Khoshafian, S., Wong, H.K.T.: Intelligent Databases: Object-Oriented, Deductive Hypermedia Technologies. New York: John Wiley & Sons (1989)
4. Takeda, H., et. al: Architecture for networked electronic patient record system. International Journal of Medical Informatics Vol. 60, No.2 (1999) 161-167
5. Blobel, B.: Advanced tool kits for EPR security. Int. Journal of Medical Informatics Vol.60, No.2, (1999) 169-175
6. Park, Y.M., et. al: A Method to Implementing the Extended Order Communication System Using the Public Key Infrastructure (PKI) through the Patient Certification System (PCS), CJKMI '2001 Tokyo, Japan (2001)
7. Sakamoto, N.: The Construction of a Public Key Infrastructure for Healthcare Information Networks in Japan. MEDINFO 2001, V.Patel et al. (Eds), Amsterdam IOS Press, © 2001 IMIA (2001) 1276-1280
8. Housley, R., et. al: Internet X.509 Public Key Infrastructure Certificate and CRL Profile, RFC 2459 (1999)
9. Hinchley, A.: Understanding Version 3: A primer on the HL7 Version 3 Communication Standard. Munich, Germany: Alexander Moench Publishing (2003)
10. Jones, T.: NPfIT interoperability - the role of HL7 version 3. HL7 UK 2003, 2003. Available at http: //www.hl7.org.uk/HL7UKConferenceSite/HL7UK2003Papers.htm. Accessed Dec 12, 2004 (2003)
11. The NeCST Progress Report. 2003. Available at http://secure.cihi.ca/cihiweb/en/ downloads/infostand_eclaims _prog2003 _e.pdf. Accessed Dec 12, 2004. (2003)
12. de Jong, T.: Medication Supply Registry Project and Demonstration in the Netherlands. Available at http://www.hl7.org.uk/HL7UKConferenceSite/HL7UK2003Papers.htm. Accessed Dec 12, 2004. (2003)
13. William, B.L., Trigg, B.K.: Information System Architectures for Syndromic Surveillance. Morbidity and Mortality Weekly Report. 2004; 53(Suppl) (2004) 203-208
14. The Medical Information System Development Center: The Japanese Set of Identifiers for Medical Record Information Exchange (J-MIX) (in Japanese) http://www.medis.or.jp/ Accessed Dec 12, 2004 (2000)

Establishment and Assessment of Wide Area Medical Information Network System in Hokkaido

Hirofumi Akashi[1,*], Hajime Tokura[1,*], Hirofumi Ohnishi[1], Kenji Nishikage[2], Tokuzo Yamaguchi[1], Kazuyoku Saijo[1], Takahiko Shinmi[3], Masahiro Nakamura[3], Masashi Nakayama[2], and Haruyuki Tatsumi[3]

[1] Information Center of Computer Communications, Sapporo Medical University, Sapporo, Japan
[2] Non profit organization NORTH, Sapporo, Japan
[3] Biological Informatics and Anatomy, Sapporo Medical University, Sapporo, Japan
hakashi@sapmed.ac.jp

Abstract. To support regional medicine in rural area of Hokkaido, we have tried to establish advanced medical information network system. At first we connected two rural town hospitals with SMU (Sapporo Medical University) and performed medical data transmission via the Internet. We used IPsec and regional Internet exchange (IX) for ensuring security and stability. As a second stage, we established a Metropolitan Area Network (MAN), a gigabit network with a 120 km radius in order to connect three medical schools (Hokkaido University, Asahikawa Medical College and SMU) with 10 hospitals. These experiments were performed with Internet technology such as VoIP (voice over IP), VPN, IPsec. As a third stage, we have coined VGN (Virtual Global Network) a concept, which includes IPv6 Topological Addressing Policy. According to the policy we established the IPv6 network to connect SMU with Obihiro area hospitals and a preschool for disabled children. Here, we described details of these experiments in terms of applications and network technologies.

1 Introduction

In Hokkaido Island, people are spread over a very wide area, but medical infrastructure and manpower is concentrated in the urban areas. Therefore, there is a large discrepancy between rural and urban area in terms of medical services. We thought that our answer to these problems was to offer support with information technology. Nowadays, information infrastructure is rapidly being promoted in Hokkaido Island as well as in other areas of Japan. We can utilize a high-speed Internet connection and CUG (Closed Users Group) services with commercial access lines (optical fibers or xDSL) over almost the whole area of Hokkaido Island. And some lease line services such as L2L services or optical fibers laid by the government are also available. We attempted to use these infrastructures and information

---

* Hirofumi Akashi and Hajime Tokura contributed equally to this work.

S. Shimojo et al. (Eds.): HSI 2005, LNCS 3597, pp. 179–189, 2005.

technologies and, in particular, Internet Technology (TCP/IP) to develop a medical information network system. Some problems existed in using the Internet for medical fields, including network security and network stability[1-14]. Recently, security threats on the Internet have been increasing dramatically. We used IPsec or VPN (virtual private network) technologies to assure security. Since Hokkaido is far from national IX (Internet exchange) (NSPIXP2) in Tokyo, the pathway of the packet among nearby hospitals is longer than in any other areas of Japan. This situation results in increasing disruption of the communication. Consequently, we tried to construct a regional IX in Hokkaido to avoid this problem. Another problem is depletion of IPv4 global address and abuse of NAT (Network Address Translation) technology. This led to interruption of peer to peer connections and resulted in some applications being to put out of service. By using IPv6, we attempted to resolve this problem. The optical fibers laid by the government have some good and bad points and there are some problems of application for medical support, usability, user training and so on, which we discuss here.

2 Methods (Network Design and Application)

In this paper, we focus mainly on the "Hokkaido Wide Area Medical Network System" project, that was financed by the MLIT (Ministry of Land, Infrastructure and Transport) budget for developing Hokkaido Island and undertaken from 1999 to 2003. The project is divided to three stages in terms of experiment theme.

2.1 IPsec and Regional IX (From 1999 to 2000)

In 1999, we connected two rural town hospitals with SMU (Sapporo Medical University) and performed DICOM (Digital Imaging and Communication in Medicine) transmission and interactive teleconference via the Internet with IPsec security and regional IX. We chose OCN (NTT communications Co. Ltd.) as an ISP (Internet Service Provider) and selected one of OCN's services, "Super OCN", which supports a steady bandwidth for applications. We were able to use a 256 kbps uplink bandwidth for the Internet in SMU and 128 kbps in town hospitals (Kikonai and Honbetsu). We ensured security of communications by S-box (Nextech Co. Ltd.), which support IPsec and VPN. In order to establish a robust network, we have experimentally made a regional IX. The regional IX is based on the fruits of the G7 project and uses BGP4 routing protocol. We performed BGP4 routing among NORTH (AS7661)[15], OCN (AS4713) and Tokyo Net (AS2551). We analyzed the time course in which the pathway changed from default path to substitute one, after artificial physical link down of network was done by switching off DSU in SMU. And the effect of the regional IX was measured by counting the number of hops and the time of ping response before and after the change of the routing. Medical applications tested were DICOM transmission and interactive teleconference. We tested if DICOM transmission via Internet was able to achieve the same quality (image quality and required time) as via ISDN link (bulk 128kbps). We performed interactive teleconference with popular software, NetMeeting, CU-SeeMe Pro.

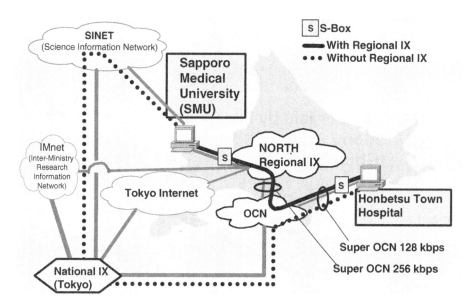

Fig. 1. Network and experiment design of stage 1 (IX)

2.2 MAN (Metropolitan Area Network: Gigabit Network with 120 km) (From 2001 to 2002)

As a second stage, we established a Metropolitan Area Network (MAN), a gigabit network with a 120 km radius in order to connect three medical schools (Hokkaido University, Asahikawa Medical College and SMU) with 10 hospitals. This stage was divided into two phases. In the first phase (2001), we constructed a gigabit backbone using optical fibers laid by MLIT and Gigabit switches. This backbone was then connected with 3 universities (SMU, Hokkaido University, Asahikawa Medical College) and 10 hospitals (Mikasa City hospital, Akabira City hospital, Sunagawa City hospital, Takiwa City hospital, Bibai City hospital, Keiyu-kai Hospital, Shirakaba-dai hospital, Bibai Rosai Hospital, Sapporo Kousei Hospital, Sapporo Shakai-hoken Sougou Hospital) using lease line(1 Gbps Ethernet , 76 Mbps or 9 Mbps ATM, 1.5M digital access) or outdoor wireless LAN system (between Bibai City Hospital and Bibai Rosai Hospital). In the second phase (2002), we connected the above facilities via Internet using VPN to ensure security, and used commercial access lines (optical fibers or ADSL). We tested a lot of advanced medical applications, including a tele-conference, tele-lecture, network-based genetic diagnosis, tele-pathology, tele-radiology, tele-dermatology and tele-fundus examination. At this time, we performed interactive conference using Medasis DxMM as a pointing device, IP phone (Amigate) as VoIP and e-Watch as a visual communications tool. In tele-lecture, we used MPEG2 encoder (VNP) and e-watch to retransmit the video of an academic conference, DDW Japan (Digestive Disease Week Japan). In DICOM transmission, we constructed full mirror sever of Mikasa City Hospital's DICOM server in SMU. Other projects used dedicated systems, such as Genetic Labo system for tele-genetic diagnosis, TFX-2000 (Visual Technology Inc.) for tele-pathology, HIROX microscope for tele-dermatology and ImageNet2000 (TOPCON Inc.) for tele-fundus examination.

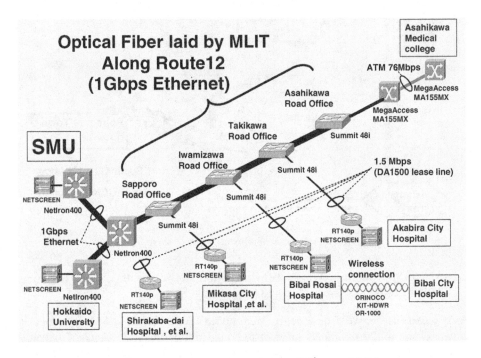

Fig. 2. Network and experiment design of 2nd stage (MAN)

2.3 IPv6 Network (From 2002 to 2003)

As a third stage, we have coined the Virtual Global Network (VGN) concept, which includes IPv6 Topological Addressing Policy. According to the policy, we established the IPv6 network to connect SMU with Obihiro area hospitals, clinics, Guidance Center for Children, nursing school and a preschool for disabled children. As a health promotion program, we provided a virtual racing system for walking, which was IPv6 and IPv4 Internet compliant. In this stage, we constructed a 100 Mbps backbone between SMU and Obihiro area using HOTnet L2L services and connected this backbone with 1 university (SMU), 3 hospitals (Obihiro kyoukai hospital, Obihiro Kousei Hospital, Hokuto Hospital), 2 clinics (Koseki clinic, Adachi Clinic), 2 schools (Tsubasa preschool and Obihiro Koutou nursing school), Obihiro Guidance Center for Children and 2 general households. And we used 100 Mbps or 10 Mbps wide area ethernet services (HOTnet and OCTV), using optical fibers or coaxial cablesrespectively, and outdoor wireless LAN system (general households) as access lines. In this stage, we chose a variety of medical applications for estimating usability of IPv6 networks, exploring potentiality of extraordinary broadband networks and expanding ranges of support to non-hospital facilities and households. Practically, we performed live video transmission of neurosurgery operation, teleconference on rehabilitation and bronchoscope, tele-dermatology and tele-lecture with DVTS (digital video transfer system) under 100 Mbps IPv6 connections. To care for handicapped children, we carried out multipoint meetings among university, preschool and Guidance Center using multipoint video conference system (Polycom ViewStation MP) and IP TV phone (i-See), and also performed real time consultation by SMU's experts using Polycom. We tried to support home medical cares using IP TV phone, IPv6 pressure sensor that detect heartbeat and breaths, and home rehabilitations using Polycom. We also constructed the patient-registration systems to investigate the incidence and the prognosis of patients with cancer and cardiovascular disease in Tokachi-area. Virtual Medical Museum System was created with WebObect and Oracle data base for medical and biological resources to be utilized from remote site. DICOM transmission and tele-fundus examination were advanced type of prior ones, which could be used between clinics and community-based hospitals.

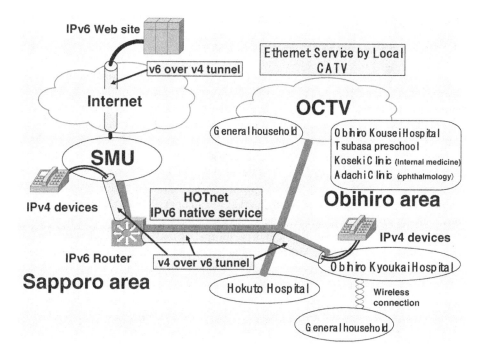

Fig. 3. Network and experiment design of stage 3 (IPv6)

3   Results

Table 1. List of Applications tested in this project

stages	applications	facilities	bandwidth
1	01 teleconference	KikonaiTown Hospital	128kbps
	02 DICOM transmission	HonbetsuTown Hospital	128kbps
2	03 tele-pathology	SunagawaCity Hospital et al.	1.5Mbps
	04 tele-genetic diagnosis	KeiyukaiHospital et al.	1.5Mbps
	05 DICOM transmission	MiaksaCity Hospital	1.5Mbps
	06 teleconference	MikasaCity Hospital	1.5Mbps
	07 tele-rehabiritationconference	AkabiraCity Hospitaet al.I	1.5Mbps
	08 tele-fundusexamination	AkabiraCity Hospitaet al.	1.5Mbps
	09 tele-dermatology	AkabiraCity Hospital et al.	1.5Mbps
	10 tele-lecture	Shirakabadai Hospital	1.5Mbps
3	11 tele-rehabilitation conference	ObihiroKyoukaiHospital et al.	100Mbps
	12 home medical care	General households	3Mbps
	13 caring handicapped children	Tsubasapreschool	100Mbps
	14 live of neurosurgical operation	HokutoHospital et al.	100Mbps
	15 tele-lecture	KosekiClinic et al.	100Mbps
	16 tele-bronchoscope conference	ObihiroKyoukaiHospital	100Mbps
	17 Virtual Medical Museum	ObihiroNursing School	3Mbps
	18 Webbase patients registration for cancer	ObihiroKyoukaiHospital et al.	100Mbps
	19 Web based patients registration for cardiovascular disease	ObihiroKouseiHospital et al.	100Mbps
	20 tele-dermatology	ObihiroKyoukaiHospital	100Mbps
	21 tele-fundusexamination	Adachi Clinic	100Mbps
	22 DICOM transmission	ObihiroKyoukaiHospital et al.	100Mbps

3.1   IPsec and Regional IX (From 1999 to 2000)

We observed a reduction in the number of hops and ping response time with variable packet size after establishing the regional IX. For the evaluation of the redundancy of the routing, we tested the fail-safe system of the network by disconnecting the OCN Link at the IX. Even in such circumstances, we could still achieve communication between SMU and Honbetsu town Hospital in 98 second via Tokyo Net. Subsequently, by restoring the OCN connection at the IX, the normal routing via OCN was returned in 58 seconds. We could transmit DICOM data via Internet in same quality and speed as via ISDN. Transmission speeds were 116.6kbps with ISDN Dial-up (128 kbps), 102.7 kbps with Internet (128 kbps) without regional IX, 110.3 kbps with Internet (128 kbps) with regional IX. Also we could perform interactive teleconference in secure conditions and useful discussions were had. Three clinical cases presented by Kikonai town Hospital's doctors were discussed. Clear and definitive suggestions were given by some specialists in SMU. But, there were some practical problems in used. At first, handling of software to be used was difficult for medical doctors to set up. Second, preparation for teleconference is tiresome because the input/output devices are not connected with the network and there are no electric records for patients. Ultimately, 128 kbps bandwidth was not enough to do an interactive teleconference using shared whiteboard displaying medical images[16].

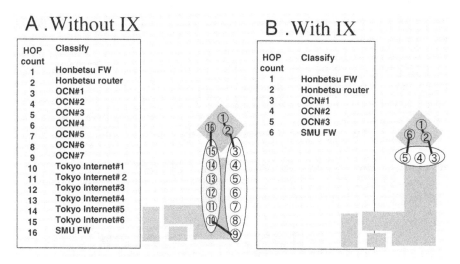

HOP count	Classify
1	Honbetsu FW
2	Honbetsu router
3	OCN#1
4	OCN#2
5	OCN#3
6	OCN#4
7	OCN#5
8	OCN#6
9	OCN#7
10	Tokyo Internet#1
11	Tokyo Internet# 2
12	Tokyo Internet#3
13	Tokyo Internet#4
14	Tokyo Internet#5
15	Tokyo Internet#6
16	SMU FW

HOP count	Classify
1	Honbetsu FW
2	Honbetsu router
3	OCN#1
4	OCN#2
5	OCN#3
6	SMU FW

Fig. 4. Effects of regional IX in Hokkaido. IX reduced hop counts to destination site

3.2   MAN(Metropolitan Area Network: Gigabit Network with 120 km) (From 2001 to 2002)

In this stage, the available bandwidth became 15 times wider than was available in the previous stage and thus many interactive communications could be performed more comfortably. An interactive clinical conference between SMU and Mikasa City hospital was held using Medasis DxMM, e-Watch and IP phone. Many doctors participating in this conference admired this system's audio and image quality, and in particular they liked the DxMM device for sharing medical images. In the rehabilitation conference between SMU and Akabira City Hospital, we used e-watch and IP phone. On this occasion, we sent a video image from Akabira (patient side) to SMU (consultant) and because this transmission used up almost the whole bandwidth (1.5 Mbps), we could not send a video images of the consultant. In this way, we were able to transmit the patient's video image smoothly enough to make a diagnosis. Also we could transmit MRI or CT image with e-watch by taking images of these films on the view box, and these images were enough to use as reference images. This system was regarded as practical enough to use in clinical situations, but participating medical staff in Akabira Hospital had complaints about being unable to see images of consultants. Rural areas are lacking specialists such as dermatologists, ophthalmologists, clinical pathologists, gene therapists or genetic counselors and radiologists. Our projects were designed to assist with diagnoses including remote diagnoses in these rural areas and to create consulting systems to support various fields via tele-dermatology, tele-fundus examination, tele-pathology, tele-gene diagnosis and DICOM transmission system.   All of these were performed almost perfectly, especially DICOM transfer system which is still used today, because Mikasa City Hospital has PACS and can transmit DICOM images automatically, seamlessly and no extra work is required of medical staff. Unfortunately, other systems were not established on a permanent basis, because of difficulties of preparation and low cost-benefit ratio. Because many facilities was participating in and preparing for the second phase (using Internet), we encrypted the transmission by IPsec (using NetScreen). Nonetheless, all the above projects were performed smoothly. In the first phase, because MLIT's optical fibers were used as the backbone and we only paid the fee for renting switches. However, due to the fact that the connection point was limited to MLIT road offices, the connection fee for access lines between the backbone and the various facilities was very expensive and no other, cheaper services for access line was available in the rural area. In the second phase, we used ADSL line or Optical fibers without support for steady bandwidth as access lines to the Internet, and security was controlled via the Internet connection by using IPsec. We could perform the above medical applications achieving the same quality as in first phase and no problems were encountered.

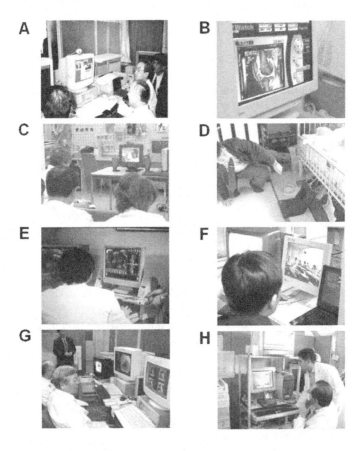

Fig. 5. Images of experiments A: Clinical teleconference with DxMM. B: tele-rehabilitation conference with e-Watch and IP phone. C: tele-rehabilitation conference with DVTS. D: Home medical care with IPv6 bio sensor. E. Live of neurosurgical microscopic operation with DVTS. F. Tele-lecture on "Health behavior theory" with DVTS. G: Teleconference on bronchoscope image with DVTS, DxMM and Polycom. H: Tele-dermatology with HIROX camera and DVTS

3.3 IPv6 Network (From 2002 to 2003)

In this stage, we constructed an IPv6 native network with HOTnet IPv6 L3 service. We assigned IPv6 addresses according to the Topological Addressing Policy. This policy is an epoch-making concept for assigning IPv6 addresses. In this policy, we tried to divide Japan to 8 areas and to assign IPv6 addresses according to geographical location. Additionally, flags were embedded to represent medical emergency capacity in IPv6 addresses. This policy will be useful for constructing regional IX, especially, MDX (Medical internet exchange) and "Medical-Care Initiatives (SDMCI)". In this stage, we performed huge data transmission using bidirectional DVTS (total 70 Mbps) and tested performance limitations of the network devices. We had to tune all intermediary switches ports' link speed and duplex mode fixing 100 full mode. In this condition, we successfully transmitted DV data from neurosurgical operation, bronchoscope conference, rehabilitation conference and tele-lecture on "Health Behavior Theory", successfully. DVTS had only a 200 msec delay, and that suggested the possibility of using it practically for real time guidance in neurosurgical operations. In conference and tele-lecture, we could emulate real conferences and lectures almost perfectly. Home medical care was also performed successfully, but data transmissions from micronode or bio-sensor and communications by IP TV phone were not established on a permanent basis. Within the experimental period, the patient-registration systems contained data on about 30 patients, and these projects have to be continued in years to come. Fortunately, these systems do not require a wide band network and it is possible to continue using them using low-cost network connections. DICOM transmission and tele-fundus examination may represent model methods for cooperation between hospitals and clinics. Considered as a whole, the projects including caring for handicapped children and the Virtual Medical Museum, represent a model of medical support for the whole community through use of information technologies.

4 Discussion

We successfully performed experiments on transferring medical information and constructing an experimental "Hokkaido Wide Area Medical Network Systems". The information infrastructure in rural areas of Hokkaido Island has improved dramatically since we started this project, but the digital divide between rural and urban areas still persists. We speculate that public support is required to resolve these problems and to promote the IT infrastructure in rural areas. It is important to keep security in medical information systems, and many people mentioned "network security". But to maintain total security, we have to pay attention not only to the information system but also the physical situation, for example, monitoring who is entering and leaving the computer room. This standpoint is absolutely lacking in the perspective of many people involved in medical information systems. Furthermore, we tend to talk about real time clinical teleconference and its telemedicine applications as through it were completely new, but many systems previously existed for this purpose are simply not utilized effectively. From now, we have to plan the projects on the basis of user needs, which are not necessarily direct medical support such as teleconference or tele-diagnosis, but may be indirect support such as improvement of provision of information or educational environment.

We are implementing tele-lecture, tele-radiology and tele-clinico-pathological conferences (CPC) with CUG (Closed Users Group) lines on the basis of the results of the experiments and discussion above. Through our work and studies outlined above, we have created the idea of, "Strategic Defensive Medical-Care Initiatives (SDMCI)" for health promotion in the forthcoming highly advanced aging society. Multi-lateral preparations for the SDMCI programs are on going.

Acknowledgements

This work was supported in part by Ministry of Land, Infrastructure and Transport (MLIT), Ministry of Education, Culture, Sports, Science and Technology (MEXT) and Ministry of Health, Labour and Welfare in Japan

Reference

[1] Tatusmi H. Advanced Internet Computing from the Standpoint of Life Science. Advanced Technology Seminor Text, pp45, International Conference on Network Protocols (1995).

[2] Tatsumi H. Computer Utilization and the Internet in Academic Activities. Med. Imag. Tech. 14 :151-163 (1996).

[3] Nogawa H, Ohkawa Y, Nakamura M, Tatsumi H. Prototype of Sophisticated System for 3D reconstruction. Proceedings of The Second China-Japan Joint Symposium on Medical Informatics 140-144 (1997).

[4] Tatsumi H, Nakamura M, Ohkawa Y, Nogawa H, Takaoki E and Kato Y. Medical education at a distance – a future vision for the way to study medicine. Program and Book of Abstracts, 85 The 3rd International Conference on the Medical Aspects of Telemedicine (1997).

[5] Nogawa H, Tatsumi H, Nakamura H, Kato Y and Takaoki E. An Application of End-User- Computing Environment for VHP. The Second Visible Human Project Conference. 9-100 (1998).

[6] Tatsumi H, Thomas G, Gill M, Ackerman MJ. Visible Human Anatomical Co-laboratory. At The Workshop: Bridging the Gap from Network Technology to Applications, NASA Ames Research Center. (1999).

[7] Aoki F, Tatsumi H, Nogawa H, Akashi H, Nakahashi N, Xin G. A Parallel Approach for VHP Image Viewer. International Workshop 2000, Proceedings on Medical Session-I, 209-214 (2000).

[8] Aoki F, Tatsumi H, Nogawa H, Akashi H, Nakahashi N. Distributed Processing for Large Medical Image Database. JAMIT Annual Meeting 2000, Proceedings, 58-59 (2000).

[9] Aoki F, Nogawa H, Tatsumi H, Akashi H, Maeda T. Distributed Computing Approach for High Resolution Medical Images. 16th World Computer Congress 2000, Proceedings on Software: Theory and Practice, 611-618 (2000).

[10] Nogawa H, Aoki F, Akashi H, Nakahashi N, Tatsumi H. Network Design and Management for Medical Institutes: a Case in Sapporo Medical University. International Workshop 2000, Proceedings on Medical Session-II, 221-226 (2000).

[11] Aoki F, Akashi H, Goudge M, Toyota M, Sasaki Y, Guo X, Li SJ, Tokino T, Tatsumi H: Post-Genome Applications Based on Multi-Parallel Computing over High Performance Network. ibid. 61-67 (2001).

[12] Nogawa H, Tatsumi H, Kobayashi S, Kawai S, Ohishi N, Akiba S. Configurations of the Internet Server with Multi-Home Environment for E-mail Robustness. 1999 Internet Workshop (ISBN 0-7803-5925-9) by IEEE, Inc. 61-68 (1999).

[13] Nishinaga N, Tatsumi H, Gill M, Akashi H, Nogawa H, Reategi I. Trans-Pacific Demonstration of Visible Human (TPD-VH), Space Communications 17: 303-311 (2001).

[14] Maruyama R, Akashi H, Toyota M, Aoki F, Sasaki Y, Mita H, Akino K, Tatsumi H, Imai K, Tokino T.Identification of p53 target sequences by network parallel computing. Proceedings 95th Annual Meeting of American Association for Cancer Res. 45:1108 (2004).

[15] http://www.north.ad.jp

[16] Akashi H, Nakahashi N, Aoki F, Goudge M, Nakamura M, Kobayashi S, Nakayama M, Nishikage K, Imai K, Hareyama M, Tatsumi H: Development and Implementation of an Experimental Medical Network System in Hokkaido, Taking Advantage of the Results of NGI Project. International Workshop 2001, Proceedings on Bio-Medical Applications, 19-22 (2001).

A Multimedia Service Implementation Using MJPEG and QCELP in Wireless Handset

Gu-Min Jeong[1], Seung-Won Na[2], Doo-Hee Jung[3], Jun-Ho Kang[4],
and Gu-Pil Jeong[5]

[1] Dept. of Electrical Engineering, Kookmin University, Korea
gm1004@kookmin.ac.kr
[2] Terminal Development Team, SK Telecom, Korea
nasw@sktelecom.com
[3] Dept. of Electronic Engineering, Korea Polytechnic University, Korea
doohee@kpu.ac.kr
[4] NeoMtel Cooperation, Korea
jhkang@neomtel.com
[5] School of Electrical Engineering and Computer Engineering,
Chungbuk National University, Korea
fec3homme@nate.com

Abstract. In this paper, a fast implementation of JPEG is discussed and its application to multimedia service is presented for mobile wireless internet. A fast JPEG player is developed based on several fast algorithms for wireless handset. In the color transformation, RCT is adopted instead of ICT for JPEG source. For the most time-consuming DCT part, the binDCT can reduce the decoding time. In upsampling and RGB conversion, the transformation from YC_bC_r to RGB 16 bit is made at one time. In some parts, assembly language is applied for high-speed. Also, an implementation of multimedia in wireless handset is described using MJPEG (Motion JPEG) and QCELP(Qualcomm Code Excited Linear Prediction Coding). MJPEG and QCELP are used for video and sound, which are synchronized in handset. For the play of MJPEG, the decoder is implemented as a SW upon the MSM 5500 baseband chip using the fast JPEG decoder. For the play of QCELP, the embedded QCELP player in handset is used. The implemented multimedia player has a fast speed preserving the image quality.

1 Introduction

The development of wireless network and wireless handset makes it possible to implement various multimedia solutions in handset. 3GPP and 3GPP2 make a standard of multimedia codecs and recommend the service providers to apply them. However, several limitations of wireless handset make it difficult to utilize the multimedia codecs. In addition, the characteristics of multimedia in wireless handsets are different from those in PC. Main characteristics of handset can be summarized as low processing power, limited memory, and narrow network bandwidth, which should be considered in the wireless handset services.

S. Shimojo et al. (Eds.): HSI 2005, LNCS 3597, pp. 190–199, 2005.

Especially, in wireless handset, the speed of codec must be fast and the compressed size must be small. Nowadays, one of the most popular multimedia codec is MPEG. However, DSP chip is essential since it is difficult to implement MPEG as a SW in wireless handset. In this paper, an implementation of a multimedia using QCELP [6] and MJPEG is presented. MJPEG extends JPEG [1] by supporting videos and each frame in the video is stored with the JPEG format. For the play of MJPEG, it is required to implement fast JPEG decoder. QCELP is a vocoder which is widely used for a voice call in CDMA network. It is embedded in CDMA handset where playing sound is possible using QCELP if API's are provided to application. One can implement a multimedia using QCELP and MJPEG without any HW. In this paper, the multimedia player is ported on BREW environment [8] in a CDMA handset with MSM 5500 baseband chipset. The fast JPEG decoder is developed using IJG open source [4]. QCELP player is made out using KTF extension in BREW. Comparing with the fast QCELP API which is processed on DSP, JPEG is implemented as a SW and can be slow.

In this paper, fast JPEG player is developed based on several fast algorithms considering the characteristics of wireless handset. In some time-consuming parts, assembly language is used for high speed. The implemented codec has a high speed preserving the image quality and it makes wireless multimedia service possible in wireless handset. It has a performance of 4-5 frames per second for 128×96 images and similar quality comparing to conventional JPEG player. Also, if the well-known R-D optimization scheme [9] or its variation for high speed [10] are used, the proposed codec can have more improved performance. An implementation of a multimedia using QCELP and MJPEG is presented using the proposed codec. The remainder of this paper is organized as follows. In Section 2, the MJPEG and QCELP are briefly summarized. Also the test environment is described. In Section 3, the fast implementation methods of JPEG decoder are presented. In Section 4, implementation results are presented and the conclusion follows in Section 5.

2   MJPEG, QCELP and System Settings

The methods for porting multimedia player in handset can be divided into 3 categories. The first one is using SW player that runs over baseband chipset. It is used for low end handset or usual handset. The next one is using ASIC chip. Some JPEG players in camera module or some midi players are applied as a HW ASIC chip. The last one is using application CPU and DSP. The multimedia solutions like MPEG or 3D are developed on those environments. It should be noted that if there is another HW chipset, the handset becomes expensive. In this paper, the player is ported on the baseband chipset for all of the handsets. Baseband chipset mainly performs the wireless communications. Full use of the baseband chipset cannot be achieved for the application such as multimedia player. If the player needs to be implemented on the baseband chipset, fast player is essential. The fast player proposed in this paper also can be used in ASIC or DSP. In mobile multimedia services, the handset must have functions of decoder or player. The encoder may be in PC, server or handset. In some services such as MMS, the encoder is in handset. However in most of services, the contents are encoded in PC or server and played in handset. In this paper, we propose a design for encoder and decoder. But the implementation in handset is done only for the decoder part.

2.1   MJPEG

MJPEG is a video format extending JPEG [1]. It has only intraframe coding JPEG without interframe coding. Thus the code structure is very simple, and it is easier to port the decoder than MPEG decoder. Fast implementation of JPEG is needed for fast MJPEG player. JPEG decoder can be divided into several parts such as entropy coding, dequantization, IDCT and color space transformation. It is important to optimize each part for fast decoder. Especially, the IDCT part is most time-consuming and the display part for handset LCD is also time-consuming.

In this paper, IJG open source is used for the JPEG decoder. Fast JPEG decoder is developed on BREW and MJPEG decoder is implemented with QCELP player.

Table 1. Test environment

Settings	
Network	CDMA 1x EVDO
Baseband Chipset	MSM 5500 (ARM 7 core)
Image	MJPEG
Sound	QCELP
Image size	128×96
LCD size	128×160
LCD bit depth	16 bit
Memory size	1M bytes
Heap memory size	200k bytes
Porting environment	Qualcomm BREW
Target FPS	3-5 fps

2.2   QCELP

For the voice communication, vocoder is developed and used in handset. In CDMA, there are two vocoders, EVRC and QCELP [6]. QCELP is one of the CELP vocoder developed by Qualcomm. QCELP 8 kbps and QCELP 13 kbps are used respectively. QCELP 13 kbps is generally used for the voice quality. QCELP uses 20 ms as the data frame size. Each frame may be encoded at one of four different data rates: full rate, 1/2 rate, 1/4 rate, and 1/8 rate and variable rate is also supported. Vocoder is essential for the voice communication. For the high compression, complex algorithms are used in vocoder and it is implemented on DSP. If the vocoder API's are provided for applications, one can play the vocoder data. Since QCELP uses 20ms as the data frame size, it is good to streaming or synchronization. In this paper, the QCELP player is implemented using QCELP extension API's over the BREW environment. QCELP is played on DSP and the decoder speed is very fast. So, for the implementation of MJPEG and QCELP, it is important to implement fast JPEG decoder.

2.3   System Settings

CDMA handset with MSM 5500 is used in this paper. MSM 5500 has ARM 7 core and the CPU clock is up to about 40 MHz. The multimedia player is developed and runs over BREW platform. LCD size is 128×160 and the bit depth of LCD is 16 bit. Target speed of JPEG is about 3-5 fps. Table 1 shows the system settings in this paper.

3   Fast Implementation of JPEG

3.1   JPEG Porting in Handset Using IJG Source

The JPEG can be easily ported using IJG open source. Actually, the decoding time depends on CPU speed, the memory access time or other environment. In our porting of IJG JPEG decoder based on the system setting of Table 1, it takes about 300 ms to decode 1 frame whose size is 128×96. To implement fast decoder, the analysis of decoding time is shown in Table 2. Table 2 shows the time ratio required for IJG JPEG decoding in handset with MSM 5500. In this test, quality factor is set to 75 and $Y : C_b : C_r$ is set to 4 : 2 : 0. As shown in Table 2, the portion of IDCT is about 30 %.

3.2   Main Direction of Codec Design

As discussed before, the fast decoder with preserving image quality is required for wireless handset. Several parts in Table 2 are implemented by use of fast algorithms. In the color transformation, RCT is adopted instead of ICT. For the most time-consuming DCT part, binDCT can reduce the decoding time. In upsampling and RGB conversion, the transformation from YC_bC_r to RGB 16 bit is made at one time. In some parts, assembly language is applied.

3.3   IDCT Part

DCT has been adopted in many standards such as JPEG, MPEG and H. 26x. Though DCT is good for compression, it requires a great amount of computation. Thus various fast algorithms have been proposed. Especially, Arai et. al. [5] have proposed the fast algorithm for DCT, which is adopted in IJG JPEG open source. In ARM [7], multiplication processing time is 4 times larger than that of addition (multiplication 8 clock, addition 2 clock, shift 2 clock). If we use multiplierless fast algorithms, the decoding time can be reduced. Recently, Liang and Tran [2] have proposed fast multiplierless DCT algorithms. The proposed DCT algorithm, binDCT, approximates the DCT with shift and addition using lifting structure. There is a tradeoff between image quality and speed for the

Table 2. Ratio of required time in JPEG decoding

Part	Time(ms)	Ratio(%)
IDCT	84	29
Decoding MCU	58	20
Upsampling and RGB conversion	84	29
The rest	64	22
Total	290	100

Table 3. Forward and inverse transform matrix of binDCT C7

1	1	1	1	1	1	1	1
15/16	101/128	35/64	1/4	-1/4	-35/64	-101/128	-15/16
3/4	1/2	-1/2	-3/4	-3/4	-1/2	1/2	3/4
1/2	3/32	-11/16	-1/2	1/2	11/16	-3/32	-1/2
1/2	-1/2	-1/2	1/2	1/2	-1/2	-1/2	1/2
1	-23/16	-1/8	1	-1	1/8	23/16	-1
1/2	-1	1	-1/2	-1/2	1	-1	1/2
1/4	-21/32	13/16	-1	1	-13/16	21/32	-1/4

1/2	1	1	1	1	1/2	1/2	1/4
1/2	13/16	1/2	1/8	-1	-11/16	-3/4	-35/64
1/2	21/32	-1/2	-23/16	-1	-3/32	3/4	101/128
1/2	1/4	-1	-1	1	1/2	-1/2	-15/16
1/2	-1/4	-1	1	1	-1/2	-1/2	15/16
1/2	-21/32	-1/2	23/16	-1	3/32	3/4	-101/128
1/2	-13/16	1/2	-1/8	-1	11/16	-3/4	35/64
1/2	-1	1	-1	1	-1/2	1/2	-1/4

approximation. Through several tests from binDCT C1 to binDCT C9, we select binDCT C7 for this implementation. binDCT C7 has 9 shifts and 28 additions preserving coding gain. Table 3 shows the transform matrices of binDCT C7.

3.4   Color Transformation

In JPEG, color space conversion transforms RGB pixels into YC_bC_r. In IJG source [4], ICT (Irreversible Component Transformation) has been implemented. The forward ICT is defined as

$$Y = 0.229R + 0.587G + 0.114B,$$
$$C_b = -0.16875R - 0.33126G + 0.5B,$$
$$C_r = 0.5R - 0.41869G - 0.0813B$$

(1)

There is another transformation called RCT (Reversible Component Transformation) [3]. RCT approximates the ICT and the implementation can be done using only shift and addition. The forward and inverse RCT is defined as

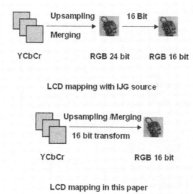

Fig. 1. LCD mapping

Fig. 2. Test images

$$Y' = 0.25R + 0.5G + 0.5B,$$
$$C_r{}' = R - G,$$
$$C_b{}' = B - G \tag{2}$$
$$G = Y' - 0.25C_b{}' - 0.25C_r{}'$$
$$R = C_r{}' + G$$
$$B = C_b{}' + G \tag{3}$$

Using RCT, the color transformation can be made faster than ICT.

3.5   LCD Mapping

The test handset has 16 bit LCD. Many handsets have 16 bit LCD since it is easier to handle the memory structure with 2 bytes. In JPEG, 24 bit display is supported. When using 24 bit in handset, the decoder consumes 2 times bigger memory than 16 bit LCD. As image quality degradation in 16 bit is not so big, 16 bit LCD is widely applied. The LCD in test handset has 5, 6 and 5 bits for RGB respectively. In JPEG decoding and display, color transform should be made from YC_bC_r 24 bit to RGB 24 bit and next RGB 24 bit should be converted to 16 bit as in Fig. 2. These all processes are also time-consuming. In this paper, the whole transformation is made at once by one function. As a result, the decoding time can be reduced.

4   Implementation Results

4.1   JPEG Decoder

Table 4 shows the decoding time of the proposed implementation with C in each part. Comparing to Table 2, the decoding time is 25 % faster than that of Table 2. The run-time memory size required for the codec is smaller than 80K bytes (25K bytes for the coder and 42K bytes for input and output buffer). The coder size is about 42K bytes in case of C implementation and is about 41K bytes if some parts are implemented using assembly.

If assembly language is applied for certain parts, the decoding time can be faster. It can be seen in Table 4. IDCT, upsampling and RGB transformation is programmed with assembly. As in Table 4, the total decoding time is 40 % faster than the original IJG source porting. Using this implementation JPEG can be decoded with the speed 4-5 fps. In this paper, Decoding MCU parts has not been changed. If some algorithms such as [11] are applied, better results may be achieved.

To check the image quality and size, we use the images in Fig. 2 with size 128×128. Table 5 shows the image quality and bpp (bit per pixel) for IJG source and the proposed method. The quality is measured by PSNR such as $PSNR(dB) = 10\log_{10}\frac{255^2}{\sigma^2}$, where $\sigma^2 = \frac{1}{3N}\sum_{n=1}^{N}\{(R_a - R_b)^2 + (G_a - G_b)^2 + (B_a - B_b)^2\}$.

Table 4. Decoding time with the proposed implementation with C and assembly

	With C		With C and assembly	
Part	Time(ms)	Ratio(%)	Time(ms)	Ratio(%)
IDCT	66	30	41	23
Decoding MCU	77	36	77	42
Upsampling and RGB conversion	38	18	28	16
The rest	34	16	34	19
Total	215	100	181	100

Table 5. Image quality and size (for 128×128)

Test image	IJG source		Proposed method	
	Quality(dB)	bpp	Quality(dB)	bpp
Image 1	21.40	0.0617	21.77	0.0607
Image 2	25.59	0.0303	25.52	0.0294
Image 3	23.07	0.0510	23.20	0.0502
Image 4	25.73	0.0553	25.73	0.0548

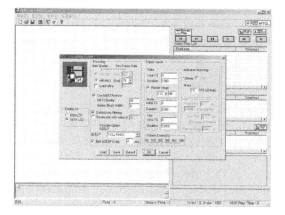

Fig. 3. The Multimedia Encoder

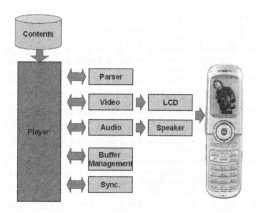

Fig. 4. Structure of the Multimedia player

Image size in the proposed method is slightly smaller than that of IJG. In image quality, there are no significant differences. It should be noted that the decoder has a fast speed preserving the image quality and size.

4.2   Performance Improvement of the Designed Codec

R-D optimization [9] is an algorithm to optimize rate-quality tradeoffs in an image-specific way. If this scheme is adopted for the proposed codec, more improvement in image quality and rate can be obtained. Generally, it takes too much time to calculate optimized quantization table. In some applications of wireless handset, the contents is made beforehand and downloaded afterwards. In this case, R-D optimization can be utilized as it is acceptable to take more time for encoding.

If the fast encoding is essential and the images have similar characteristics, the quantization table design technique in [10] can be adopted.

In [10], only photos with face are considered. For these images, the filesize of the images is 10%–20% smaller than that of JPEG, preserving similar image quality.

4.3   MJPEG and QCELP

Fig. 3 and Fig. 4 show the encoder and the total structure of the multimedia player, respectively. MJPEG player works on BREW with C code or assembly code. QCELP player use the QCELP API. QCELP is played over DSP and it does not affect JPEG decoding too much. Syncronization of sound and image is done by dividing the QCELP data based on the data rate. In this implementation, JPEG decoding and display time is smaller than 200 ms. It is possible to display the video with 4-5 fps. For 3 fps, total file size is about 300-400K bytes with JPEG (quality 75) and QCELP (full rate) for 1 minute.

5   Conclusion

In this paper, a multimedia implementation has been discussed in wireless handset using MJPEG and QCELP. MJPEG has been used for an image with QCELP for a sound. Considering slow CPU in wireless handset, fast player has been developed. For each part of JPEG decoder, fast algorithms have been adopted. Some parts have been implemented using assembly code. In color transformation, RCT has been adopted instead of ICT in JPEG source. In most time-consuming DCT part, the decoding time has been reduced using binDCT. In upsampling and RGB conversion, the transformation from YC_bC_r to RGB 16 bit has been made at once. This implementation has been made using CDMA handset with the CPU MSM5500 and 16 bit LCD size. The implemented multimedia has a performance of 4-5 frames per second for 128×96 images. The designed decoder for JPEG has fast speed while preserving good image quality similar to JPEG. The performance of proposed design can be improved using R-D optimization or similar quantization design technique.

Acknowledgments

This work was supported in part by the research program 2005 of Kookmin University in Korea.

References

1. G. K. Wallace, The JPEG still-picture compression standard, Commun. ACM, vol. 34, pp. 30-44, Apr. 1991.
2. J. Liang and T. D. Tran, Fast multiplierless approximations of the DCT with the lifting scheme, IEEE Trans. on Signal Processing, vol. 49, no. 12, pp 3032-3044, Dec., 2001.
3. M. D. Adams, The JPEG-2000 Still Image Compression Standard , ISO/IEC JTC 1/SC 29/WG 1 N 2412, Dec. 2002.
4. Independent JPEG Group, http://www.ijg.org.
5. Y. Arai, T. Agui, and N. Nakajima, A few DCT-SQ scheme for images, Trans. IEICE, vol. E71, pp. 1095-1097, 1988.
6. Rate Speech Service Option 17 for Wideband Spread Spectrum Communication Systems, TIA/EIA/IS-733, March 1998.
7. ARM, http://www.arm.com
8. BREW, http://brew.qualcomm.com/brew/en/
9. M. Crouse and K. Ramchandran , Joint thresholding and Quantizer Selection for Transform Image Coding : Entropy-Constrained Analysis and Application to Baseline JPEG. IEEE Trans. on Image Processing, vol. 6, no. 2, Feb, 1997.
10. Gu-Min Jeong, Jun-Ho Kang, Yong-Su Mun and Doo-Hee Jung, JPEG Quantization Table Design for Photos with Face in Wireless Handset, Lecture Notes in Computer Science, vol. 3333, pp.681-688, Dec. 2004.
11. Gopal Lakhani, Modified JPEG Huffman Coding, IEEE Trans. on Image Processing, vol. 12, no. 2, Feb, 2003.

On a Video Surveillance System with a DSP by the LDA Algorithm

Jin Ok Kim[1], Jin Soo Kim[2], Chin Hyun Chung[2], and Jun Hwang[3]

[1] Faculty of Multimedia, Daegu Haany University,
290, Yugok-dong, Gyeongsan-si, Gyeongsangbuk-do, 712-715, Korea
bit@dhu.ac.kr
[2] Department of Information and Control Engineering, Kwangwoon University,
447-1, Wolgye-dong, Nowon-gu, Seoul, 139-701, Korea
chung@kw.ac.kr
[3] Division of Information and Communication Eng., Seoul Women's University,
126, Kongnung2-dong, Nowon-gu, Seoul, 139-774, Korea
hjun@swu.ac.kr

Abstract. As face recognition algorithms move from research labs to real world product, power consumption and cost become critical issues, and DSP-based implementations become more attractive. Also, "real-time" automatic personal identification system should meet the conflicting dual requirements of accuracy and response time. In addition, it also should be user-friendly. This paper proposes a method of face recognition by the LDA Algorithm with the facial feature extracted by chrominance component in color images. We designed a face recognition system based on a DSP. At first, we apply a lighting compensation algorithm with contrast-limited adaptive histogram equalization to the input image according to the variation of light condition. While we project the face image from the original vector space to a face subspace via PCA , we use the LDA to obtain the best linear classifier. The experimental results with real-time input video show that the algorithm has a pretty good performance on a DSP-based face recognition system. And then, we estimate the Euclidian distances between the input image's feature vector and trained image's feature vector.

1   Introduction

Machine face recognition is a research field of fast increasing interest [1]. The strong need for user-friendly systems that can secure our assets and protect our privacy without losing our identity in a sea of numbers is obvious. At present, one needs a personal identification number (PIN) to get cash from an ATM, a password for a computer, a dozen others to access the internet, and so on [2] [3]. Although extremely reliable methods of biometric personal identification exist, e.g., fingerprint analysis and retinal or iris scans, these methods rely on the cooperation of the participants, whereas a personal identification system based on analysis of frontal or profile images of the face is often effective without

S. Shimojo et al. (Eds.): HSI 2005, LNCS 3597, pp. 200–207, 2005.

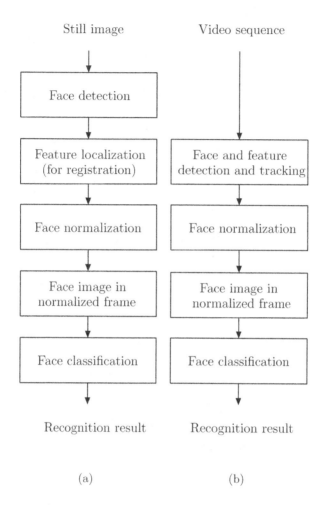

Fig. 1. Two approaches to face recognition: (a) Face recognition from still images (b) Face recognition from video

the participant's cooperation or knowledge [4] [5]. Phillips [6] described in the advantages/disadvantages of different biometrics.

We implemented a fully automatic DSP-based face recognition system that works on video [7]. Our implementation follows the block diagram shown in Fig. 1(b). Our system consists of a face detection and tracking block, an skin tone extract block, a face normalization block, and face classification blocks.

2   Face Detection System

Face detection algorithms have primary factors that decrease a detection ratio: variation by lighting effect, location and rotation, distance of object, complex

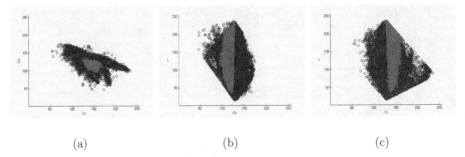

(a)   (b)   (c)

Fig. 2. The YC_bC_r color space and the skin tone color model (red dots represent skin color samples): (a) 2D projection in the $CbCr$ subspace (b) 2D projection in the YCb subspace (c) 2D projection in the YCr subspace

background. Due to variations in illumination, background, visual angle and facial expressions, the problem of machine face detection is complex.

An overview of our face detection algorithm contains two major modules: 1) face segmentation for finding face candidates and 2) facial feature extraction for verifying detected face candidates. Our approach for face localization is based on the observation that human faces are characterized by their oval shape and skin color, also in the case of varying light conditions. Therefore, we locate face-like regions on the base of shape and color information. We employ the YC_bC_r color space by using the RGB to YC_bC_r transformation. We extract facial features based on the observation that eyes and mouth differ from the rest of the face in chrominance because of their conflictive response to C_b, C_r.

We adopt the YC_bC_r space since it is perceptually uniform, is widely used in video compression standards, and it is similar to the TSL(Tint-saturation-luminance) space in terms of the separation of luminance and chrominance as well as the compactness of the skin cluster. Many research studies assume that the chrominance components of the skin-tone color are independent of the luminance component [8] [9].

However, in practice, the skin-tone color is nonlinearly dependent on luminance. We demonstrate the luminance dependency of skin-tone color in different color spaces in Fig. 2, based on skin patches collected from IMDB [10] in the Intelligent Multimedia Laboratory image database. These pixels from an elongated cluster that shrinks at high and low luminance in the YC_bC_r space are shown in Fig. 2(b) and Fig. 2(c). Detecting skin tone based on the cluster of training samples in the C_bC_r subspace is shown in Fig. 2(a).

3   Face Region Segmentation

Region labeling uses two different process. One is region growing algorithm using seed point extraction and another one is flood fill operation [11]. The other method is shown Fig. 3(b).

We choose face candidate region that has a suitable distribution of pixel. Result is shown Fig. 3(c).

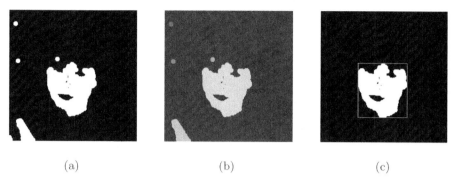

(a)   (b)   (c)

Fig. 3. Connected component labeling: (a) Segmented image (b) Labeled image (c) Facial candidate region

4   Linear Discriminant Analysis

Linear discriminant analysis (LDA) easily handles the case where the within-class frequencies are un equal and their performances has been examined on test data generated randomly. This method maximizes the ratio of between-class variance to the within-class variance in any particular data set thereby guaranteeing maximal separability [12] [13].

The LDA for data classification is applied to classification problem in speech recognition and face recognition. We implement an algorithm for LDA in hopes of providing better classification. The prime difference between LDA and PCA is that PCA does more of feature representation and LDA does data classification. In PCA, the shape and location of the original data sets change when

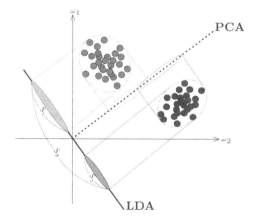

Fig. 4. A comparison of PCA and Fisher's linear discriminant (FLD) for a two class problem

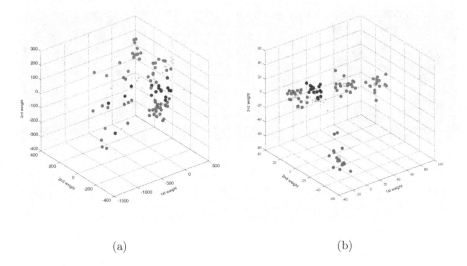

(a)   (b)

Fig. 5. Distribution of facial features: (a) feature space by PCA method (b) feature space by LDA method

transformed to a different space whereas LDA doesn't change the location but only tries to provide more class separability and draw a decision region between the given classes. This method also helps to better understand the distribution of the feature data. Figure 4 will be used as an example to explain and illustrate the theory of LDA.

5   Experimental Result

We use the response to a chrominance component in order to find eye and mouth. In a general, images like digital photos have problems (e.g., complex background, variation of lighting condition). Thus it is difficult to determine skin-tone's special features and to find location of eye and mouth. Nevertheless we can make to efficiency algorithm that robustness to variation lighting condition to use chrominance component in YC_bC_r color space. Also we can remove a fragment regions by using morphological process and connected component labeling operation. We find eye and mouth location use vertical and horizontal projection. This method is useful and shows that operation speed is fast.

Fig. 6 demonstrates that our face detection algorithm can successfully detect facial candidate region. The face detections and recognitions on the POSTECH image database [10] are presented in Fig. 7. The POSTECH image database contains 951 images, each of size 255×255 pixels. Lighting conditions (including overhead light and side lights) change from one image to another.

This system can detect a face and recognize a person at 10 fps. This speed is measured from user-input to final stage with the result being dependent on

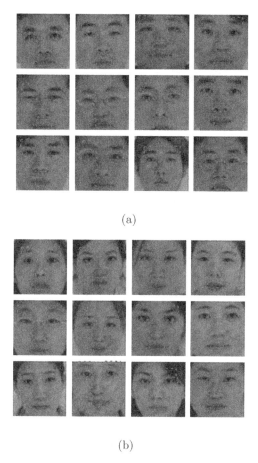

(a)

(b)

Fig. 6. Some face and facial component extraction: (a) Male (b) Female

the number of objects in an image. The system captures a frame through IDK, preprocessed it, detects a face, extracts feature vectors and identifies a person.

6   Conclusion

Our face detection method detects skin regions over the entire image, and then generates face candidates based on the spatial spatial arrangement of these skin patches. Our algorithm constructs maps of eye and mouth to detect the eyes, mouth, and face region. Detection results on several photo collections are shown in Fig. 6. The PCA and LDA method presented here is a linear pattern recognition method. Compared with nonlinear models, a linear model is rather robust against noise and most likely will not over-fit. Although it is shown that distribution of face patterns is complex in most cases, linear methods are still able to provide cost effective solutions. Fig. 7 shows that he effectiveness of the proposed

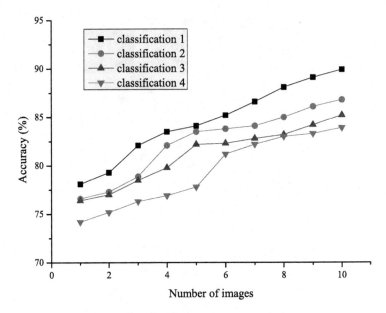

Fig. 7. Result of recognition experiments

method is demonstrated through experimentation by using the POSTECH face database. Especially, the results of several experiments in real life show that the system works well and is applicable to real-time tasks. In spite of the worst case, the complete system requires only about 100 ms per a frame. The experimental performance is achieved through a careful system design of both software and hardware for the possibility of various applications. It is a future work to make the training stage faster or to make code optimize for efficiency vectors calculation and face recognition. Also hardware integration may be considered for faster system.

Acknowledgements. The present Research has been conducted by the Research Grant of Kwangwoon University in 2005.

References

1. Feraud, R., Bernier, O., Viallet, J.E., Collobert, M.: A fast and accurate face detection based on neural network. IEEE Trans. Pattern Analysis and Machine Intelligence **23** (2001) 42–53
2. Yang, M.H.: Kernel eigenfaces vs. kernel fisherfaces : face recognition using kernel method. Automatic Face and Gesture Recognition, 2002. Proceedings. 4th IEEE International Conference (2002) 208–213
3. Pratt, K, W.: Digital Image Processing Third Edition. John Wiley & Sons, United States (2001)

4. Moritz, S.: Computer Vision and Human Skin Colour. PhD thesis, Electrical Engineering, Technical University of Berlin, Germany (2004)
5. Vezhnevets, V., Sazonov, V., Andreeva, A.: A survey on pixel-based skin color detection techniques. GraphiCon, Moscow, Russia (Sept. 2003)
6. Phillips, P.J., McCabe, R.M., Chellappa, R.: Biometric image processing and recognition. Proceedings, European Signal Processing Conference (1998)
7. Texas Instrument: TMS320C6000 Imaging Developer's Kit programmer's Guide. (2001)
8. Menser, B., Brunig, M.: Locating human faces in color images with complex background. Intelligent Signal Processing and Comm. Systems (1999) 533–536
9. Saber, E., Tekalp, A.: Frontal-view face detection and facial feature extraction using color, shape and symmetry based cost functions. Pattern Recognition Letters **19** (1998) 669–680
10. IMDB. Intelligent Multimedia Laboratory, POSTECH, KOREA. (2001)
11. Mathworks: Image Processing Toolbox User's Guide. The MathWorks (2002)
12. Belnumeur, P.N., Hespanha, J.P., Kriegman, D.J.: Eigenfaces vs. fisherfaces: Recognition using class specific linear projection. IEEE Trans. on PAMI (1997)
13. Duda, R.O., Hart, P.E., Stork, D.G.: Pattern Classification 2nd Ed. John Wiley & sons, New York (2001)

A Web Service-Based Molecular Modeling System Using a Distributed Processing System

Sungjun Park[1], Bosoon Kim[1], and Jee-In Kim[2,*]

[1] Department of Computer Science & Engineering , Konkuk University,
Seoul, Korea
hcipsj@konkuk.ac.kr, foxgap@dreamwiz.com
[2] Department of Internet & Multimedia, Konkuk University, Seoul, Korea
jnkm@konkuk.ac.kr

Abstract. Molecular Modeling is based on analysis of three dimensional structures of molecules. It can be used in developing new materials, new drugs, and
environmental catalyzers. We propose a molecular modeling system based on
web services. It visualizes three dimensional models of molecules and allows
scientists observe and manipulate the molecular models directly through the
web. Scientists can examine, magnify, translate, rotate, combine and split the
three dimensional molecular models. The real-time simulations are executed in
order to validate the operations. We developed a distributed processing system
for the real-time simulation. The proposed communication scheme reduces data
traffics in the distributed processing system. The new job scheduling algorithm
enhances the performance of the system. Therefore, the real-time simulation for
molecular modeling can be exercised through the web. For the experiments,
HIV-1 (Human Immunodeficiency Virus) was selected as a receptor and fifteen
candidate materials were used as ligands. An experiment of measuring performance of the system showed that the proposed system was good enough to be
used in molecular modeling on the web.

1 Introduction

Molecular modeling is based on analysis of three dimensional structures of molecules.
It can be used in developing new materials, new drugs, and environmental catalyzers.
Scientists use character strings in order to symbolize molecules in molecular modeling. The character strings are translated into three dimensional structures of molecules. Then, scientists examine such three dimensional structures in terms of their
shapes, features, and their stability. They perform a docking procedure through which
a *receptor* combines with a *ligand* at a special position called an *active site*[1]. A real-
time simulation is required, Since it can computationally prove or disprove if such a
chemical operation is val id. The simulation is basically calculating energy minimization equations[1,2].

---

[*] Corresponding author.
[1] The term "receptor" is used to describe any molecule which interacts with and subsequently
holds onto some other molecule. The receptor is the "hand" and the object held by the "hand"
is commonly named, the *ligand.*

S. Shimojo et al. (Eds.): HSI 2005, LNCS 3597, pp. 208 – 217, 2005.

There have been many researches and tools for molecular modeling. Scientists can access some of the tools through the web. Most of them focus on visualizing structures of molecules in three dimensions. However, molecular modeling procedures require scientists to examine and manipulate three dimensional models of molecules. During a docking procedure, for example, the shapes of a receptor and a ligand should be visually represented, carefully examined and interactively manipulated by scientists. Since three dimensional structures of most molecular models look quite similar, it is very difficult for scientists to differentiate the structures. It follows that scientists should be able to manipulate three dimensional models in order to examine different views of the models. For example, operations of translation, rotation, magnification, selection, split, etc. can be exercised to examine different views of three dimensional models. However, the current web based modeling tools do not provide direct manipulation methods for the operations. That is, scientists must use a set of commands to manipulate the models by typing commands using a keyboard. Experiences demonstrate that such command based operations require more time and efforts than direct manipulation of models. Therefore, more convenient and more intuitive methods of manipulation must be developed.

It is required to execute real-time simulations during molecular modeling. Since the size of molecules is large and their structures are complicated, the computations require huge computing power. Super computers must be helpful. However, many scientists cannot afford to use them. As computer technologies develop, a high performance computing system can be implemented using a set of personal computers.

We develop a distributed computing system for real-time simulation which can be accessed through web services via the Internet. Scientists can use the system as a real-time simulation tool for molecular modeling. Also, the proposed system visualizes three dimensional molecular models through the web and provides a direct manipulation method of the molecular models.

2 Related Works

RASMOL[3]is a molecular modeling tool and mainly visualizes three dimensional structures of molecular models. It is widely used, because it provides fast and simple ways of examining three dimensional structures of molecules through visualization. But it does not provide direct manipulation methods of molecular structures. No real-time simulation function is provided by RASMOL, either. Scientists use character strings in order to symbolize molecules in molecular modeling. The character strings are translated into three dimensional structures of molecules.

MDL enhanced RASMOL and developed *Chime* which is a plug-in for a web browser and enabled three dimensional structures of molecules to be visualized through the web. Chime has its own script language and its users issue a command to view three dimensional structures and manipulate the visualized models. This feature makes the Chime plug-in lighter and more portable. Also, it could be useful for experts. However, such a text based manipulation method is not helpful for general users. If direct manipulation methods were added, users of the tool could be more productive and more satisfied.

Protein Explorer, Noncovalent Bond Finder, DNA Structure, MHC, Identifying Spectral, and *Modes* are web based tools for molecular modeling and they use the Chime plug-in. Protein Explorer is the most popular and widely used tool among them. Protein Explorer[4] has various functions such as presents chemical information of a molecule, displays three dimensional structures of a molecule. Since it can display only one molecular structure at a given time, we cannot visually compare several molecules through the window. It follows that a docking procedure of merging a receptor and a ligand cannot be displayed on the window. Since it does not have a simulation capability, we cannot complete a molecular modeling procedure such as a docking procedure using Protein Explorer. We probably need *Insight II* [5] which was commercialized by *Accelys*. Unfortunately, Insight II is not accessible on the web.

As we summarize in Table 1, the tools have different features. Since we would like to develop a molecular modeling system which is affordable and accessible, we propose a web service based system and call it *MMWeb*. It offers new features such as direct manipulation, distributed processing and web service.

Table 1. Comparison of features of tools for molecular modeling

Molecular Modeling Systems \ Functions	3D Visualization	Direct Manipulation	Web-based Molecular Docking	Distributed Processing	Web Sevice
RASMOL	O	X	X	X	X
Chime Plug-In	O	X	X	X	X
VMD	O	X	X	O	X
Protein Explorer	O	X	X	X	X
Insight II	O	O	X	X	X
MMWeb	O	O	O	O	O

3   System

3.1   Overview

We propose a system of molecular modeling using the web service as shown in Figure 1. The molecular modeling system based on the web (called *MMWeb*) consists of clients, a server and a database. The client is a web browser for scientists. The server performs real-time simulations of molecular modeling. The client accesses the server through web services. The database stores and manages files and information about molecules.

The client (*Web Browser*) has four components. *File Manager* reads data about molecules from PDB (*Protein Data Base*) files/Database and exercises parsing the data. *Operation Manager* arranges the parsed data in order to compute energy equations. The results are arranged to be properly displayed by *Rendering Engine* which visualizes three dimensional models of molecules using graphical libraries like OpenGL. Various rendering algorithms are implemented. *Computing Engine* computes energy equations which are essential in the simulation.

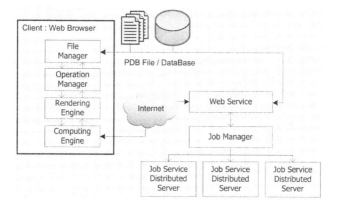

Fig. 1. System Overview

The *Job Service Distributed Servers* communicate with the clients (*Web Browser*) through *Computing Engines* in a form of *Web Services*. They perform real-time simulations of molecular modeling. The computations are basically minimization of energy for molecules. *Job Manager* creates jobs for energy minimization and delivers them to the distributed servers. PDB files and information about molecules are loaded from the database to the servers. The simulation results are sent to the client through web services.

3.2   Web Browser – The Client

We developed Web Browser using OpenGL[6]. The Chime plug-in was not used because we needed to support loading multiple molecular models, docking procedures, bonding and non-bonding procedures, etc.

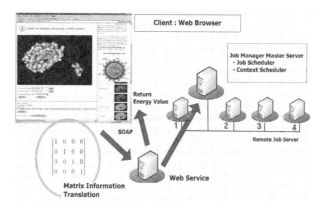

Fig. 2. Web Browser sends information of transformation to the servers and receives simulation results through Web Service

As shown in Figure 2, the client (Web Browser) displays three dimensional structures of molecular models and allows scientists manipulate the models in interactive
and intuitive ways using a mouse[7]. This feature makes the browser more usable
than the Chime based browsers which use script language commands to manipulate
the models. When the positions and the orientations of the models change, a matrix of
transformation is sent to *Web Service*. The matrix becomes an input for real-time
simulations. The web service supplies the matrix to the servers each of which has
loaded data of molecules from the database and executes computations of energy
minimization using the matrix.

3.3 Distributed Processing System

MMWeb requires a high performance computing system in order to exercise real-time
simulations. We developed a distributed processing system[8,9].

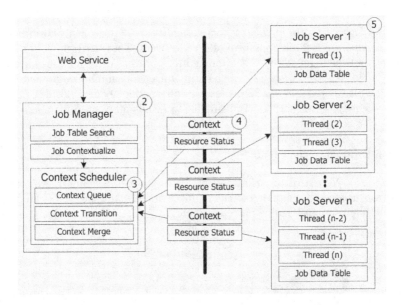

Fig. 3. A distributed processing system

Web Service(① in Fig. 3) is a gateway which transfers information from the client
(*Web Browser*) to *Job Servers* (⑤ in Fig. 3) and returns the simulation results from
the servers to the client. The information from the clients includes a transformation
matrix of molecular models, and information about a receptor and a ligand. SOAP
(Simple Object Access Protocol) is used for the communication.

Job Manager (② in Fig. 3) is a master server and manages the distributed computing resources. It receives information from the Web Service component and searches
a proper job from lookup tables (*Job Table Search* in Fig. 3). Then, it partitions the
job found in the table into jobs which can be executed by the servers. *Job Manager*
also contextualizes the jobs. The procedure aims to store information of processing

resources into each job. That is, *Job Contextualizer* assigns status of processing resources for each job. *Context Scheduler* (③ in Fig. 3) performs job scheduling tasks. There are many jobs from multiple clients. A job of a user is partitioned and contextualized. Then, the contextualized jobs are stored in *Context Queue*. *Context Scheduler* allocates a thread for each job depending on its scheduling policy. The contextualized jobs (④ in Fig. 3) are sent to *Job Servers* (⑤ in Fig. 3). After the computations, the results from the servers are sent back to the client through *Web Service*.

Context Transition means state transition of contexts while they are processed as shown in Fig. 4-(a). The context, *C1*, in *Ready Hash Table* is allocated to a resource and stored into *Running Hash Table*. The context, *C2*, in *Running Hash Table* completes its tasks and goes into *Done Hash Table*. The context, *C3*, in *Done Hash Table* is finished. The Contexts, *C4,..., Cn*, in *Ready Hash Table* are waiting for their corresponding resources. When all contexts are processed as shown in Fig. 4-(b), they are merged and sent back to the client.

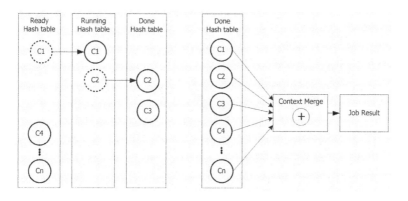

Fig. 4. (a) State Transition of Contexts. (b) Merge the processed Contexts

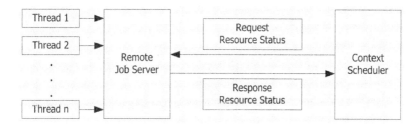

Fig. 5. The status of a resources denotes information about a resource for processing contextualized jobs

As shown in Fig. 5, *Resource Status* represents the status of resources of the servers and shows whether the resources are available for processing contextualized jobs. *Context Scheduler* periodically asks *Job Server* for the status of resources of the server. Then, the server sends a list of status of its resources. The scheduler examines the list and allocates an available resource to a job selected from *Context Queue*.

4 Experiments

In these experiments, we check (i) if MMWeb computes reliable values after simulation, (ii) if MMWeb performs fast enough to exercise real-time simulations. We exercised a docking procedure. HIV-1 (Human Immunodeficiency Virus)[10,11,12] was selected as a receptor. Fifteen materials related to reproduction of HIV-1 were chosen as ligands.

Table 2. Simulated values of energy calculation using Insight II and MMWeb

$T = Elec + Vdw$

PDB code	Insight II Energy Value				MMWeb Energy Value			
	ΔE^{Vdw}	ΔE^{elec}	ΔE^{T}	RMSD (A)	ΔE^{Vdw}	ΔE^{elec}	ΔE^{T}	RMSD (A)
1gno	-7.63	-0.32	-7.95	1.02	-9.08	-0.46	-9.54	0.98
1hbv	-14.73	-1.24	-15.97	0.92	-14.21	-1.14	-15.35	0.86
1hps	-16.87	0.74	-16.13	2.41	-14.64	1.10	-13.54	3.15
1hpv	-10.15	-0.93	-11.08	0.36	-10.28	-0.74	-11.02	0.42
1hvj	-11.85	-0.11	-11.96	1.25	-10.85	-0.21	-11.06	1.28
1hvk	-16.25	0.55	-15.70	0.37	-14.21	0.65	-13.56	0.89
1hvl	-15.43	-1.20	-16.63	0.35	-15.35	-0.98	-16.33	0.39
1hvs	-12.31	-0.24	-12.55	1.66	-11.28	-0.34	-11.62	1.93
1hte	-1.24	-0.23	-1.47	0.39	-1.89	-0.65	-2.54	0.98
1htf	-22.61	-2.30	-24.91	0.32	-18.87	-2.15	-21.02	0.94
1htg	-17.46	-1.23	-18.69	0.49	-18.31	-1.24	-19.55	0.44
1pro	-9.95	0.67	-9.28	1.04	-9.70	0.62	-9.08	1.26
1sbg	-11.29	0.08	-11.21	2.01	-12.99	0.13	-12.86	1.36
2upj	-10.80	0.49	-10.31	1.59	-10.87	0.98	-9.89	1.89
4phv	-17.43	-0.98	-18.41	0.67	-15.64	-1.12	-16.76	0.92

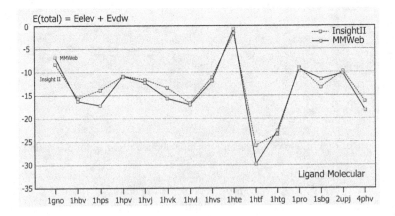

Fig. 6. Energy values of fifteen ligands

First, we checked the reliability of the simulation values. That is, the values of computing energy equations for binding the fifteen ligands with the receptor were calculated. We compared MMWeb with Insight II which is the most popular tool of molecular modeling. RMSD(Root Mean Squared Deviation) is used as a measure for the reliability. Table 2 and Fig. 6 compare energy values of fifteen ligands which are simulated using Insight II and MMWeb. The results show that there are no significant differences between the values of computing energy equations using Insight II and those using MMWeb. Therefore, the results of docking procedures using the two tools would not be significantly different.

Secondly, we measured processing times of simulations with a distributed processing system. We compared processing times with respect to different sized receptors, different number of computers for the distributed system, and different number of threads per computer. We used receptors of 3000 atoms, 6000 atoms and 12000 atoms. The ligand had 100 atoms. The numbers of computers were one, two, and four in

Table 3. Processing times were measured with different receptor sizes vs. Number of computers of the distributed processing system

Receptor Size	Threads Per Computer No.	Localhost			1 Computer			2 Computers			4 Computers		
		1	2	4	1	2	4	1	2	4	1	2	4
3000	1	0.922	0.969	0.937	1.011	0.811	1.002	0.711	0.621	0.711	0.501	0.410	0.511
	2	0.968	0.953	0.938	0.811	1.000	0.911	0.501	0.511	0.611	0.410	0.511	0.510
	3	0.891	0.875	0.969	0.912	0.912	1.012	0.510	0.511	0.711	0.411	0.511	0.410
	4	0.891	0.969	0.921	0.811	0.911	1.012	0.611	0.611	0.711	0.410	0.511	0.511
	5	0.907	0.969	0.938	0.911	0.911	0.901	0.511	0.511	0.711	0.411	0.410	0.510
6000	1	1.671	1.625	1.594	1.612	1.713	1.712	0.902	0.901	1.011	0.611	0.621	0.611
	2	1.578	1.640	1.594	1.612	1.613	1.612	0.912	0.911	1.031	0.501	0.721	0.611
	3	1.562	1.640	1.641	1.522	1.613	1.612	0.811	0.911	1.111	0.611	0.611	0.610
	4	1.531	1.688	1.625	1.612	1.713	1.722	0.911	0.901	1.011	0.611	0.621	0.731
	5	1.563	1.625	1.609	1.713	1.712	1.712	0.821	0.911	1.011	0.511	0.611	0.721
12000	1	3.031	3.047	3.203	2.914	3.315	3.024	1.612	1.622	1.812	1.012	1.022	1.211
	2	2.985	3.000	3.25	2.924	3.224	3.014	1.512	1.713	1.723	1.012	1.122	1.111
	3	2.984	3.016	3.281	3.015	3.115	3.215	1.613	1.622	1.913	0.932	1.282	1.122
	4	2.953	3.281	3.266	2.914	3.115	3.215	1.613	1.612	1.813	0.911	1.282	1.112
	5	2.984	3.204	3.219	2.914	2.925	3.225	1.712	1.622	1.923	1.011	1.122	1.311

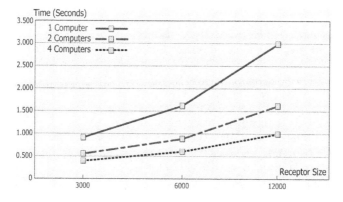

Fig. 7. Average processing times of the distributed system with different numbers of computers and atoms in a molecule

the distributed system. The numbers of threads were one, two, and four. For each receptor, a computation of energy equations was executed five times. The results are summarized in Table 3.

Notice that there is a 0.5 second difference between the case with one computer and the case with four computers in their processing times, when the number of atoms was 3000 in the receptor as shown Table 2. The difference becomes 2 seconds when the number of atoms was 12000. It means that the processing time reduces faster as the number of computer increases when the number of atoms in a molecule is large. Fig. 7 graphically shows the fact.

5 Concluding Remarks

In this paper, we proposed a web service based molecular modeling system. Our motivations are 1) to provide a molecular modeling system accessible through the web, 2) to offer direct manipulation methods of molecular models rather than command-based manipulation methods, 3) to develop an affordable high-performance computing system for real-time simulation of molecular modeling. The key features of the system are three dimensional visualization and direct manipulation of molecular models, and real-time simulations. A distributed processing system was developed for the simulations. We executed experiments to validate the simulation results and to evaluate the performances of the system.

As a future work, we would like to enhance the proposed system in terms of its interaction methods with scientists. More natural and convenient ways of interacting between the scientists and the system should be researched in order to improve the productivity of the scientists. Secondly, the computing power of the system should be improved. Since the simulation requires high performance computing, we plan to develop faster and more powerful computing system. Thirdly, we are focusing on developing a new algorithm for a docking procedure. The algorithm for calculating the energy equations is expected to be enhanced.

Acknowledgements

This work was supported by the Ministry of Information & Communications, Korea, under the Information Technology Research Center(ITRC) Support Program.

References

1. CHARMm Principles Http://www.hhmi.swmed.edu/
2. B.R.Brooks, R.E.Bruccoleri, B.D.Olafson, D. Vid J. States, S. Swaminathan, and M.Karplus. CHARMM: A program for macromolecular energy, minimization, and dynamics calculations. J.Comp. Chem., 4:187-217, (1983)
3. RASMOL Http://www.umass.edu/rasmol
4. Protein Explorer Http://www.umass.edu/micobio/chime/index.html
5. Insight II Http://www.accelrys.com

6. Gans J, Shalloway, Qmol: A program for molecular visualization on Windows based PCs Journal of Molecular Graphics and Modelling, Vol.19, pp. 557-559, 2001.
7. Sungjun Park, Jun Lee, and Jee-In Kim, A Molecular Modeling System based on Dynamic Gesture, ICCSA 2005, LNCS 3480, pp.886-895, 2005
8. Alois Ferscha, Michael Richter, Java based conservative distributed simulation, Proceedings of the Winter Simulation Conference, p381-388, 1997
9. James   C.Phillips,   Gengbin   Zheng,   Sameer   Kumar,   Laxmikant   V.Kale, NAMD:Biomolecular Simulation on Thousands of Processors, IEEE, pp36, 2002
10. Earl Rutenber, Eric B.Fauman, Robert J.Keenan, Susan Fong, Paul S.Furth, Paul R.Ortiz de Montellano, Elaine Meng, Irwin D.Kuntz, Dianne L.DeCamp, Rafael Salto, Jason R.Rose, Charles S.Craik, and Robert M.Stroud, Structure of a Non-peptide Inhibitor Complexed with HIV-1 Protease, The Journal of Biological Chemistry, Vol. 268, No. 21, pp.15343-15346, 1993.
11. Junmei Wang, Paul Morin, Wei Wang, and Peter A. Kollman, Use of MM-PBSA in Reproducing the Binding Free Energies to HIV-1 RT of TIBO Derivatives and Predicting the Binding Mode to HIV-1 RT of Efavirenz by Docking and MM-PBSA, Journal of American Chemical Society, Vol. 123, pp. 5221-5320, 2001.
12. Ekachai Jenwitheesuk and Ram Samudrala, Improved prediction of HIV-1 protease-inhibitor binding energies by molecular dynamics simulations, BMC Structured Biology, 3:2, (2003)

Automatic Generation and Use of Negative Terms to Evaluate Topic-Related Web Pages

Young-Tae Byun[1], Yong-Ho Choi[2], and Kee-Cheol Lee[1]

[1] Department of Computer Engineering Hong-Ik University, Seoul, Korea
{byun, lee}@cs.hongik.ac.kr
[2] Cyber Terror Response Center Korean National Police Agency, Seoul, Korea
kumdoin@naver.com

Abstract. Deciding the relevance of Web pages to a query or a topic is very important in serving Web users. For clustering and classifying Web pages the similar decisions need to be made. Most of work usually uses positively related terms in one form or another. Once a topic is given or focused, we suggest using negative terms to the topic for the relevance decision. A method to generate negative terms automatically by using DMOZ, Google and WordNet, is discussed, and formulas to decide the relevance using the negative terms are also given in this paper. Experiments convince us of the usefulness of the negative terms against the topic. This work also helps to solve the polysemy problem. Since generating negative terms to any topic is automatic, this work may help many studies for the service improvement in the Web.

1 Introduction

Since the Web has increased very rapidly and provides the abundance of information in every field, it becomes very popular to everyone who can access it. However it does not mean that everyone uses it very conveniently and efficiently. We may have hard time to find what we are looking for, because there are not only relevant information sources but also irrelevant ones as search results. The word sense ambiguity or polysemy problem may cause general search engines to provide us with too many irrelevant information sources as well as relevant ones.

There are several types of Web sites and pages such as general search engines, portal sites, private or public organization Web sites, and personal Web pages. We can address a topic issue regardless of types, because most pages of all types have information related to a topic or a set of several topics. For instance, a Web site or a page may have information about biology and/or weather, whereas another one may be related to culture and/or education. Therefore, we may need to do topic-related research.

There are many studies to classify or cluster a set of documents into subsets of documents where each subset has a common topic. Association rules, K-means methods, decision trees, Bayesian networks, LSA(Latent Semantic Analysis), and variations of these methods have been studied for topical classification or clustering. For the Web, we need to consider the incremental environment. Web crawlers or Web robots of search engines or portal sites navigate the Web and need to continuously

S. Shimojo et al. (Eds.): HSI 2005, LNCS 3597, pp. 218–227, 2005.

find new Web pages, classify them, and update the old page information when necessary. They may need to decide which topic(s) new pages are mostly related to. The topical Web crawling research has been done in [6, 11, 12, 14]. A topic or topics are decided first and then finding relevant pages is done in the topical Web crawling research. No matter what approaches are used, we need to evaluate the relevance of Web pages to a topic or topics. [1] and [7] used terms and link information for the relevance decision. [9] focused only link information.

In order to select pages relevant to a single keyword or a set of keywords, the extension possibly with weights is used so that the keyword(s) and the extension words cause relevant pages to get higher relevance scores than before the extension[2, 8, 13]. Irrelevant pages have no score change in most cases, since the extension words may not appear in irrelevant pages. As relevant ones get higher scores by the extension, it may be reasonable for irrelevant pages to get lower scores by the extension. It is obvious that the positively relevant words, called positive terms, used in the extension are related to a keyword or a topic. In the same sense, we believe it is possible for the extension words to include terms, called negative terms, by which irrelevant pages get lower relevance scores than before the extension.

As a test bed, we choose one topic, 'Mammal' in DMOZ of the Open Directory Project[15]. Since DMOZ is less commercial, "open resources", and maintained by several thousands of reasonably-qualified volunteer editors, we prefer to use it as sources of well classified Web information. When the word 'tiger' is given to a general search engine, the result has not only pages having information of animal 'tiger' but also pages of 'Tiger Woods' or some manufacturing company names. Once the topic Mammal is given, golf or companies having no relation with the topic must stay out of the topic scope, and commonly used words except 'tiger' in those pages can be negative terms. Examples of negative terms are 'golf', 'swing', 'score', 'cost', 'productivity', 'price', 'sale', etc.

We present a method automatically deriving a set of negative terms to a topic by using Google[16], DMOZ and WordNet[17], and show the result of relevance evaluation of using negative terms as well as positive terms. Although we show the result with the topic Mammal, the method can be used for any topic. The importance of using negative terms has been studied in several studies. [5] showed that negative terms can be used for better correctness of document relevance than positive terms. [3] showed a method to cluster positive and negative terms by using LSA. A method to classify positive terms and negative terms based on the contribution of document similarity given keywords, was developed in [4]. However, a method similar to ours was not studied.

2   Automatic Generation of Negative Terms

We present in this section how to decide automatically negative term sets. Words in the topic Mammal are used to get many Web pages both from DMOZ and from Google, and we get the difference of (term, term-frequency) between the pages from DMOZ and the pages from Google. Based on WordNet, several functions and threshold values are defined to get negative term sets. Test results are also shown.

2.1 Web Pages from DMOZ and Google

We select 29 keywords like bats, dogs, cats, tigers and whales among 86 words from the page for mammal in DMOZ[15]. The number of links that each keyword has varies from a few to several dozens. We follow the links and preprocess the pages. The preprocessing includes removing HTML tags, stemming, stopping, and selecting only correct English nouns. A set of pairs of a term and term frequency, (t, tf), is the result of preprocessing a page. We do not consider strings of two or more words. In other words, no collocation in WordNet is considered. The total number of pairs, i.e. the number of collected terms in all pages from DMOZ, is 5,305, and the total number of term frequency is 53,832.

We give the same 29 keywords to Google and gather top 100 links from each, and approximately 2900 pages are visited and preprocessed as done in the DMOZ case. The total number of pairs is 17,264 and the total number of term frequency is 588,819. Table 1 shows a set of terms with high frequency in DMOZ and Google. Although we use the same keywords, the high frequency terms are different. The parentheses in the table are used to show original full words which are modified by stemming.

Table 1. Several high frequency terms from DMOZ and Google

DMOZ		Google	
Term	Frequency	Term	Frequency
Cat	2393	Hors(e)	717
Time	2305	Bat	457
Inform(ation)	2212	Speci(ness)	392
Lion	1975	Anim(al)	353
Hors(e)	1959	Hyena	346
Anim(al)	1944	Femal(e)	290
Link	1894	Eleph(ant)	273
Dog	1817	Pig	266

2.2 Using WordNet

After we collect a set of (t, tf) from DMOZ, we record each term frequency on corresponding words in synsets in WordNet, called $WordNet_{DMOZ}$. We get $WordNet_{Google}$ in the same way. And then we make $WordNet_{tf-diff}$ to show the term frequency difference between $WordNet_{DMOZ}$ and $WordNet_{Google}$ after the adjustment so that the total numbers of term frequencies are almost the same for both cases, i.e. $WordNet_{tf-diff} = WordNet_{Google} - floor((588,819/53,832) * WordNet_{DMOZ})$.

Nouns in WordNet have a hierarchy based on the hypernymy/hyponymy relation between synsets. There are 40269 words (78904 words – 38635 collocations) in WordNet, since we do not consider collocations in WordNet in this research as mentioned earlier. It is obvious that $WordNet_{tf-diff}$ has the same noun hierarchy of Word-

Net except collocations and their synsets. We here introduce additional terms and notations related to WordNet$_{tf\text{-}diff}$.

A terminal synset : A synset having no hyponym (subordinate)
A subgraph of a synset : it consists of
1)   the synset itself
2)   if it is not a terminal synset,
      i.   all its hyponym synsets and hypernym-hyponym relations
      ii.   all subgraphs of each hyponym synset
$\#S(s1)$: Number of all synsets in a subgraph of synset s1
$\#W(s1)$: Number of words of all synsets in a subgraph of synset s1
$Depth(s1)$: Maximum depth (maximum number of consequent hyponym
          relations from s1 to any terminal synset) of a subgraph of synset s1
$Total\_tf(s1)$: Sum of all term frequencies in a subgraph of synset s1

$$Avg\_tf(s1) : \frac{Total\_tf(s1)}{\#W(s1)}$$

$$Stand\_dev(s1) : \sqrt{\frac{\sum (tf\_of\_each\_word\_in\_s1 - Avg\_tf(s1))^2}{\#W(s1)}}$$

2.3 Finding Negative Topics

WordNet$_{tf\text{-}diff}$ has many words whose frequency difference is positive as well as many words whose frequency difference is negative. Positive frequency-difference words can be ones which appear many times in pages from Google and appear much less in pages from DMOZ. It means that Google provides pages irrelevant to the topic mammal in spite of using the same keywords. Those irrelevant topics can be sports, electronic companies, or some products like furniture. Similarly, negative frequency-difference words can be words which appear many times in pages from DMOZ and appear much less in pages from Google. It means that Google does not provide relevant pages which are provided by DMOZ. We concentrate on the negative terms against the topic, i.e. positive frequency-difference words in WordNet$_{tf\text{-}diff}$, in this study. Since WordNet$_{tf\text{-}diff}$ = WordNet$_{Google}$ - floor((588,819/53,832) * WordNet$_{DMOZ}$) is used, positive frequency-difference words are negative terms against the topic.

Remember that we use only dozens of words and information from Web pages having those words. Since they are only a small portion of information of a topic, we want to find groups, i.e. topics, in reasonable size to which those positive frequency-difference words belong. A group in reasonable size can be a topic. Examples may be 'Sports', 'Furniture', 'Device', etc. The topics can be the ones in which one or more polysemous words are used with the topic 'Mammal'. If we identify those irrelevant groups or topics, many words in the topics can be used to reject pages having those words. It means we can use those words as negative terms against the topic 'Mammal'. We now need to define some measures to identify those topics, i.e. subgraphs of synsets in WordNet. Unique-beginner mentioned below is the noun synset with no superordinate, i.e. the root 'Entity' of WordNet.

θ_1 : *Minimum value of* $\dfrac{Total\_tf(s1\ of\ WordNet_{tf-diff})}{Max(Total\_tf\ for\ all\ subgraphs\ in\ WordNet_{tf-diff})}$

θ_2 : *Minimum value of* $Avg\_tf(s1)$ θ_4 : *Minimum value of* $\#S(s1)$

θ_3 : *Minimum value of* $Stand\_dev(s1)$ θ_5 : *Minimum value of* $\#W(s1)$

θ_1 is used to find a subgraph s1 of WordNet$_{tf-diff}$ in which the ratio of the total frequency of s1 with respect to the maximum frequency of the whole WordNet$_{tf-diff}$ is greater than a certain value. It means that the words in the subgraph s1 need to appear at least with a certain frequency ratio. However, if a synset s1 is located near to the unique beginner of WordNet, Total_tf(s1) may be big enough to be greater than θ_1. Although the ratio of Total_tf(s1) is greater than θ_1, if there are too many words in the subgraph s1, most of the words may appear less frequently than the average. We want to identify a concentrated subgraph in which many words appear more frequently than others in outside. Therefore we use θ_2 so that we find such subgraphs in which Avg_tf is greater than some value, and we can say that those groups are negative topics against the given topic where polysemous words are used in common.

Although θ_1 and θ_2 are satisfied by a subgraph(s1), a subpart s2 of s1 may have words appearing very frequently and the rest subpart of s1 may have words appearing much less frequently. It is unbalanced in terms of frequency. In this case, the sub-

Table 2. A part of possible negative topics when $((\theta_1 = 0.015), (\theta_2 = 0.0085), (\theta_3 = 30), (\theta_4 = 30), (\theta_5 = 30))$ is used

Hypernym	Synset	WordNet$_{tf-diff}$
Device	memory device, storage device	2854
Creation	product, production	7858
Part, portion	Component, constituent, element	3546
Means	Medium(2)	2725
instrumentality, instrumentation	Means	2725
work, piece of work	Publication	4926
Product, production	work, piece of work	5018
Equipment	electronic equipment	1753
State(2), province	American state	3290
Publication	Book	2217
Device	Conductor	1255
Leader	head, chief, top dog	1313
Device	Electronic device	1797
Point	position, place(6)	1681
artifact, artifact	Article	2280
Instrumentality, instrumentation	System	3439
Ware	Tableware	1744

graph s1 may not be a proper negative topic, but the subgraph s2 may be. θ_3 is used to decide a topic at a reasonable level in a sense that each words, not a part of words in a subgraph, contributes to be in a negative topic group.

Possible negative topic groups can be too small since θ_2 and θ_3 require the concentration of a subgraph. Even if θ_1 is used, the groups may still be too small in a special case. Since we want to find topics comparable to the given topic, or topics are generally used in our society, each negative topic needs to have a certain amount of synsets and words. Therefore, θ_4 and θ_5 are used to guarantee the certain size of a subgraph. We show a part of subgraphs which we use in this study with a set of threshold values

3   Evaluating Web Page Relevance with Negative Terms

A function to decide the relevance of a Web page to the topic 'Mammal' in this research is supposed to use negative terms mentioned in the previous section. We propose a method to get the proper relevance evaluation function using manually classified data. Then the test results using the function are given in this section.

3.1   Data Sets

Since we use a topic-relevant positive term set discussed in the following subsection and a negative term set generated automatically as mentioned in Section 2, we need to derive a relevance evaluation formula using two sets associated with weights. When the value of the relevance evaluation function of a Web page is greater than some threshold value, the page is decided to be relevant to the topic. In order to derive the formula, we need a set of pre-classified Web pages by men. A few of 29 keywords used in section 2 and several different keywords are used to collect a set of Web pages for the test. 713 Web pages, called Set W, are collected and 209, called Set M_{rel}, out of 713 Web pages are manually classified as relevant ones and 514 Web pages, called Set M_{irr}, are manually classified as irrelevant ones.

As usual, stemming and removal of stopping words are done and only legal words in dictionary are collected. In addition, we use a weighting strategy for words between certain HTML tags [10]. For instance, the frequency of words in a title tag is increased 14 times. It means that words in certain tags are more meaningful usually than others.

3.2   Positive Terms

Although we get a positive term set of subgraphs in which many words are related to or used in common with the topic Mammal, we do not use the positive term set in this paper, because we want to focus only on the effect of negative terms to a topic. Instead, we use as positive terms i) all words in the subgraph Mammal in WordNet, ii) attributes used for mammal like length, weight, size, etc, and iii) attribute value units like km, m, cm, mm, gram, g, kg, etc. Appearance of the words in the positive term set increases the relevance of a Web page. We used the same positive set in the previous research[10] in which we tried to find what term set is proper as a positive term set for the topic.

3.3 Negative Terms

As mentioned in Section 2., a set of subgraphs are automatically derived by using Google, DMOZ, and several measures. Depending on several threshold values, the set of subgraphs varies. We use the subgraphs in Table 2 in this research. Of course, appearance of the words in the negative term set decreases the relevance of a Web page.

3.4 Formulas for Relevance Evaluation

Since we have the positive term set and the negative term set, we need to formulate a relevance evaluation function of a Web page using two sets with weights. As mentioned earlier, a Web page turns into a set of pairs (t, tf). The term t in (t, tf) can be positive, negative, or nothing.

$$\mathbf{Rel}(\text{page}) = Wp * \sum (tf_u \ / \ tf_{\max}) - Wn * \sum (tf_v \ / \ tf_{\max}) \tag{1}$$

tf_u : Frequency of a positive term t_u in a page
tf_v : Frequency of a negative term t_v in a page
tf_{max} : Max tf in a page
w_p : Weight for positive terms
w_n : Weight for negative terms

$$\mathbf{Rel}(\text{page}) \ge \theta : \text{a page relevant to a topic, o/w irrelevant.} \tag{2}$$

$$|M_{rel} \cap F_{rel}| / |M_{rel}| \ + \ |M_{irr} \cap F_{irr}| / |M_{irr}| \tag{3}$$

$$|M_{rel} \cap F_{rel}| / |M_{rel}| \ * \ |M_{irr} \cap F_{irr}| / |M_{irr}| \tag{4}$$

M_{rel} : A set of relevant Web pages classified manually
M_{irr} : A set of irrelevant Web pages classified manually
F_{rel} : A set of relevant Web pages classified by the formula
F_{irr} : A set of irrelevant Web pages classified by the formula

The relevance classification of Web pages in our system is desired to be the same as that of manual classification by men as much as possible. In other words, we want that the intersection of F_{rel} and M_{rel} is as large as possible and that of F_{irr} and M_{irr} is also as large as possible. If it becomes true, using negative terms is very effective in the topic-relevance classification, and the automatic generation of negative terms against a topic is very valuable. What we need to decide now is the weights w_p and w_n , and the threshold value θ used in deciding the relevance so that Formula 3 gets a high value near to the maximum value 2, or Formula 4 gets a high value near to the maximum value 1.

Whereas W, $M_{rel,}$ and M_{irr} are given as mentioned in Section 3.1, F_{rel} and F_{irr} need to be decided by Formula 1 and 2. Since two weights and the threshold are not decided at this point, we use the ratio of two weights in order to reduce the number of unknown values with the constraint that the sum is 1. Now in Figure 1, the ratio and

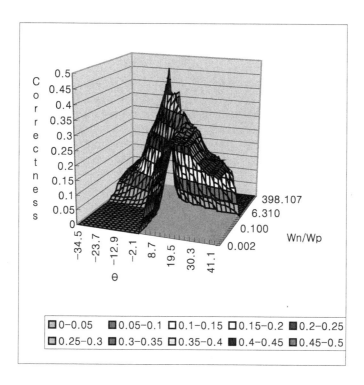

Fig. 1. Value change of Formula 4 with respect to w_p/w_n and θ values

the threshold are on X and Y axis, respectively, and the result of Formula 4 is on Z axis. There is a peak where Formula 4 gets the highest value which is approximately 0.5. Our final decision is $w_p = 0.3077$, $w_n = 0.6922$, and $\theta = 0.870$. We get the almost same result by using Formula 3. With these values and test data sets, the precision of Formula 2 can be approximately 71%.

3.5 Evaluation

In order to confirm the usefulness of using negative terms and the formulas, we get more data about mammal from Altavista, Yahoo, and Google and check the result of relevance classification. We collect about 3000 Web pages from the search engines and classify them manually, and let the system do its own work. The precision of all search engines is approximately 0.23. The precision of relevant pages of our system, i.e. $|\ M_{rel} \cap F_{rel}\ |\ /\ |\ M_{rel}\ |$, is 0.67 and that of irrelevant pages is 0.90. The result using only positive terms is also worse than this. Once a topic is focused, this result says using negative terms can do better service. We cannot say that ours is much better than search engines or other methods, because we use positive and negative terms along with a keyword whereas they use only keywords or positively extended keywords. There is none directly comparable with our method at the moment.

4 Conclusions

The more the Web grows, the more Web users use it and request better services. Keyword service and directory service are provided to users. Clustering and classification of Web pages have been studied for several reasons, and the relevance of a Web page to a topic and the similarity of Web pages should be decided correctly and efficiently as much as possible. Hence it becomes very important to decide the relevance of Web pages to a query or a topic in serving Web users.

A keyword is extended in several studies in order to select pages related to it. This can cause relevant pages to get higher relevance scores than before the extension. However, there is no action taken for irrelevant pages to get lower relevance scores. We suggest using negative terms as well as positive terms to a topic.

The topic Mammal has been chosen in this study. We first present a method automatically deriving a set of negative terms to the topic by using Google, DMOZ and WordNet. 29 words in the topic Mammal are used to get many Web pages both from DMOZ and from Google, and we get the difference of (t, tf) between the pages from DMOZ and those from Google. Based on WordNet, several functions and threshold values are defined to get negative term sets. Reasonable results are shown.

We then present several formulas for the relevance evaluation, and show the result of relevance evaluation of using negative terms. The results show the usefulness of negative terms. Although the reasonable comparison cannot be made, we compare the results of our method with other search engines. Since generating negative terms to any topic is automatic and our method is not restricted to the topic 'Mammal', this work may help many studies for the service improvement in the Web.

The positive terms as well as the negative terms can be automatically generated. We did not study the effect of automatically generated positive terms in the current research. Using positive terms generated automatically and the comparison between this and the current positive terms, which are selected by domain heuristics, will be studied. Meta data and link information in Web pages may need to be considered in the near future.

Acknowledgements

This research was supported by the 2003 Hongik University Academic Research Support Fund. We would like to thank C. H. Ahn, a undergraduate student at Hongik University, for implementation and tests of a part of this work.

References

1. G. Attardi, A. Gulli, and F. Sebastiani, " Automatic Web Page Categorization by Link and Context Analysis", In Proc. of THAI'99, European Symposium on Telematics, Hypermedia and Artificial Intellignece, 1999
2. R. Baeza-Yates and B. Ribeiro-Neto, "Modern Information Retrieval", Addison-Wesley, 1999
3. A. Kontostathis and W. M. Pottenger, "Improving Retrieval Performance with Positive and Negative Equivalence Classes of Terms", TR in Lehigh Univ., 2002

4. K. Hoashi, K. Matsumoto, N. Inoue, and K. Hashimoto, "Experiments on the TREC-8 Filtering Track", In Proc. of SIGIR'00, 2000
5. C.T. Yu, G. Salton, and M.K.Siu, "Effective Automatic Indexing Using Term Addition and Deletion", JACM, Vol.25, 1978
6. S. Chakrabarti, M. van den Berg, and B. Dom. "Focused crawling: A new approach to topic-specific Web resource discovery", In Proc. of the 8th International WWW Conference, 1999
7. S. Chakrabarti et al., " Automatic Resource Compilation by Analyzing Hyperline Structure and Associated Text", In Proc. of the 7th International WWW Conference, 1998
8. K. Eguchi, "Incremental query expansion using local information of clusters", In Proc. of the 4th World Multiconference on Systems, Cybernetics and Informatics, 2000
9. J. Kleinberg, "Authoritative sources in a hyperlinked environment", In Proc. of ACM-SIAM Symposium on Discrete Algorithms, 1998
10. S. Kim, "Improving the Performance of an Information Agent for a Specific Domain on the WWW". Master thesis, Hongik Graudate School, 2002
11. F. Menzcer, G. Pant, and M. Ruiz, "Evaluation Topic-Driven Web Crawlers", In Proc. of SIGIR'01, 2001
12. F. Menzcer, G. Pant, and P. Srinivasan, "Topical Web Crawlers: Evaluating Adaptive Algorithms", ACM Transactions on Internet Technology, Vol V, Feb, 2003
13. G. Miller, "Wordnet: An online lexical database", International Journal of Lexicography, Vol 3, 1997
14. G. Pant and F. Menzcer, "MySpiders: Evolve Your Own Intelligent Web Crawlers", Autonomous Agents and Multi-Agent Systems, Vol. 5, 2002
15. [DMOZ]   http://www.dmoz.org/Kids_and_Teens/School_Time/Science/Living_Thing/Animals/ Mammals/
16. [Google] http://www.google.com/
17. [Wordnet] http://www.cogsci.princeton.edu/~wn/

How to Evaluate the Effectiveness of URL Normalizations[†]

Sang Ho Lee[1], Sung Jin Kim[2], and Hyo Sook Jeong[1]

[1] School of Computing, Soongsil University, Seoul, Korea
shlee@computing.ssu.ac.kr, hsjeong@ssu.ac.kr
[2] School of Computer Science and Engineering, Seoul National University,
San 56-1 Shinlim-dong Kwanak-gu Seoul 151-744 Korea
sjkim@oopsla.snu.ac.kr

Abstract. Syntactically different URLs could represent the same web page on the World Wide Web, and duplicate representation for web pages causes web applications to handle a large amount of same web pages unnecessarily. In the standard communities, there are on-going efforts to define the URL normalization that helps eliminate duplicate URLs. On the other hand, there are research efforts to extend the standard URL normalization methods to reduce false negatives further while allowing false positives on a limited level. This paper presents a method that evaluates the effectiveness of a URL normalization method in terms of page loss/gain/change and the URL reduction. Over 94 million URLs were extracted from web pages for our experiment and interesting statistical results are reported in this paper.

1 Introduction

A Uniform Resource Locator (URL) is a string that represents a web resource (here, a web page). Given a URL, we can identify a corresponding web page on the World Wide Web (WWW). If more than two URLs locate the same web page on the WWW, we call them equivalent URLs in this paper.

One of the most common operations on URLs is simple comparison to determine if the two URLs are equivalent without using the URLs to access their web pages. For example, a web crawler [1][2][3][4] encounters millions of URLs during its collection of web pages on the WWW, and it needs to determine if a newly found URL is equivalent to any previously crawled URLs to avoid requesting the same page repeatedly. The inability to recognize two equivalent URLs as being equivalent gives rise to a large amount of processing overhead; a web crawler requests, downloads, and stores the same page repeatedly, consuming unnecessary network bandwidth, disk I/Os, disk space, and so on.

It is possible to determine that two URLs are equivalent, but it is never possible to be sure that two URLs represent different web pages. For example, an owner of two

---

[†] This work was supported by grant number KRF-2004-005-D00172 from the Korea Science and Engineering Foundation.

S. Shimojo et al. (Eds.): HSI 2005, LNCS 3597, pp. 228–237, 2005.

different domain names could decide to serve the same resource from both, resulting in two different URLs. The term "false negative" is used to refer determining equivalent URLs not to be equivalent (hence not being able to transform equivalent URLs into a syntactically identical string). The term "false positive" is used to refer determining non-equivalent URLs to be equivalent. Even though any URL normalization methods are subject to causing occurrences of false negatives, we would like to have URL normalization methods that transform equivalent URLs into an identical string as many as possible (i.e., reducing the occurrences of false negatives as few as possible).

In the standard body [5], there are on-going efforts to define URL normalizations that transform syntactically different but equivalent URLs into a syntactically identical string. Burners-Lee et al. defined the three types of URL normalizations, namely the syntax-based normalization, the scheme-based normalization, and the protocol-based normalization. The first two types of normalizations reduce false negatives while strictly avoiding false positives (they never transform non-equivalent URLs into a syntactically identical string).

Lee and Kim [6] argued the necessity of extending the standard normalization methods and explored the probability of extending normalization methods beyond the standard normalizations. They noticed that the standard community does not give specific methods for the protocol-based normalization. They presented four types of extended normalization methods. Discussed are changing letters in the path component into the lower-case letters or into the upper-case letters, attaching and eliminating the "www" prefix to URLs with and without the prefix in the host component, eliminating the last slash symbol from URLs whose path component is not the slash symbol, eliminating default page names in the path component.

Once a URL normalization method is developed, we need to evaluate the effectiveness of an URL normalization method in a systematic way. This paper presents a scheme to evaluate the effectiveness of URL normalization methods in terms of two aspects (URL reduction rate and web page loss/gain/change rate). A normalization method may allow false positives to occur, and in these cases we may lose, gain, or change web pages unintentionally. The evident advantage of an extended URL normalization method is to reduce the number of total URLs in operation, which would mean, for example, the number of page requests for web crawlers.

An experiment on the effectiveness of extended normalization methods has been carried out. The evaluation was done over 94 million URLs, which were extracted from the 20,799 web sites in Korea. We applied the standard and extended URL normalization methods to the URLs, requested web pages with the normalized URLs, and compared the download results before and after each normalization method. We evaluated the effects of the normalizations on the basis of the metrics we propose. Our work can help developers select which normalizations should be used for their applications.

Our paper is organized as follows. In section 2, the standard URL normalizations and the extended normalizations are discussed. In section 3, we propose the metrics for evaluating the effectiveness of URL normalizations. Section 4 presents the experimental results. Section 5 contains the closing remarks.

2 URL Normalizations

A URL is composed of five components: the scheme, authority, path, query, and fragment components. Fig. 1 shows all the components of a URL.

Fig. 1. URL Example

The scheme component contains a protocol (here, Hypertext Transfer Protocol) that is used for communicating between a web server and a client. The authority component has three subcomponents: user information, host, and port. The user information may consist of a user name and, optionally, scheme-specific information about how to gain authorization to access the resource. The user information, if present, is followed by a commercial at-sign ("@") that delimits it from the host. The host component contains the location of a web server. The location can be described as either a domain name or IP (Internet Protocol) address. A port number can be specified in the component. The colon symbol (":") should be prefixed prior to the port number. For instance, the port number of the example URL is 8042.

The path component contains directories, including a web page and a file name of the page. The query component contains parameter names and values that may be supplied to web applications. The query string starts with the question mark symbol ("?"). A parameter name and a parameter value are separated by the equals symbol ("="). For instance, in Fig. 1, the value of the "name" parameter is "ferret". The fragment component is used for indicating a particular part of a document. The fragment string starts with the sharp symbol ("#"). For instance, the example URL denotes a particular part (here, "nose") on the "there" page.

A percent-encoding mechanism is used to represent a data octet in a URL component when that octet's corresponding character is outside the allowed set or is being used as a delimiter of, or within, the component. A percent-encoded octet is encoded as a character triplet, consisting of the percent character "%" followed by the two hexadecimal digits representing that octet's numeric value. For example, "%20" is the percent-encoding for the binary octet "00100000", which corresponds to the space character in US-ASCII.

2.1 Standard URL Normalizations

The URL normalization is a process that transforms a URL into a canonical form. During the URL normalization, syntactically different URLs that are equivalent should be transformed into a syntactically identical URL (simply the same URL string), and URLs that are not equivalent should not be transformed into a syntactically identical URL. The standard document [5] describes three types of standard   URL   normalizations: syntax-based   normalization,   scheme-based normalization, and protocol-based normalization.

The syntax-based normalization uses logic based on the URL definitions. First, the normalization transforms all characters within the triplet into upper-case letters for the digits A-F, and transforms characters in the scheme and host components into lower-case   letters.   For   example,   "HTTP://EXAMPLE.com"   is   transformed   into "http://example.com/". Second, all unreserved characters (i.e., uppercase and lowercase letters, decimal digits, hyphens, periods, underscores, and tildes) should be decoded.   For   example,   "http://example.com/%7Esmith"   is   transform   into "http://example.com/~smith". Third, the path segment "." and ".." are removed appropriately. For example, "http://example.com/a/b/./../c.htm" is normalized into "http://example.com/a/c.htm".

The URL normalization may use scheme-specific rules (we consider the "http" scheme in this paper). First, the default port number (i.e., 80 for the "http" scheme) is truncated from the URL, since two URLs with or without the default port number represent the same page. For example, "http://example.com:80/" is normalized into "http://example.com/". Second, if a path string is null, then the path string is transformed into "/". For example, "http://example.com" is transformed into "http://example.com/". Third, the fragment in the URL is truncated. For example, "http://example.com/list.htm#chap1" is transformed into "http://example.com/list.htm".

The protocol-based normalization is only appropriate when equivalence is clearly indicated by both the result of accessing the resources and the common conventions of their scheme's dereference algorithm (in this case, use of redirection by HTTP origin servers to avoid problems with relative references). For example, "http://example.com/a/b" (if the path segment "b" represents a directory) is very likely to be redirected into "http://example.com/a/b/".

2.2   Extended URL Normalizations

One striking feature of standard URL normalizations is that no false positive is allowed during the normalization process. The benefits of this feature is that the standard normalizations always transform equivalent, yet syntactically different, URLs into a syntactically identical URL. The downside is that this strict policy often results in high possibility of false negatives (in other words, not being able to transform equivalent URLs into a syntactically identical string). In web applications (such as web crawlers) that handle a huge number of URLs, reducing the possibility of false negatives implies reduction of URLs that need to be considered.   Such reduction can save a lot of processing efforts that would be repeated otherwise.

For example, consider the two URLs: u1 (http://www.acm.org/) and u2 (http://www.acm.org/index.html). u1 requests a default page in the root directory, and u2 explicitly expresses the default page in the URL string. In reality, any file name could be designated as a default page. However, we may take a chance to assume that the default page of the directory is "index.html", so we drop off the specification of the default page. A possible extended normalization method could eliminate "index.html" in the URL path.   Similarly another extended normalization method could be to eliminate "default.htm" in the URL path, since "default.htm" is also a popular default file name. The idea behind the extended normalizations is that we want to significantly reduce the possibility of false negatives while allowing false positives on a limited level.

One can conceive many extended normalization methods. Enumerating a number of extended normalization methods is indeed simple. A person with average web developing experiences can list several extended normalization methods without difficulty. The important thing is how to evaluate the effectiveness of an extended normalization method precisely. The evaluation methods allow us to choose good extended normalization methods that can be used in practice.

3   Evaluation of a URL Normalization Method

This section presents how to evaluate the effectiveness of a URL normalization method. The effectiveness of the normalization is analyzed in two different points of view: how much URLs are reduced due to true positives and how many pages are lost, gained, or changed due to false positives.

Suppose we transform a given URL u1 in the original form into a URL u2 in a canonical form. Also suppose that the u1 and u2 locate web pages p1 and p2 on the web, respectively. There are totally ten cases to consider, depending on existence of p1 and p2, whether u2 is already known to us, and whether p1 and p2 are of the same page. All the above discussions are summarized in the table 1.

(1) Page p1 exists on the web

    (A) Page p2 does not exist on the web (case 4 and case 9): This case implies that the normalization method incorrectly transformed u1 into u2 (false positive takes place). As a result, we lose one page p1 on a crawling process.

    (B) Page p2 exists on the web, and p1 and p2 are of the same page (case 1 and case 6): This case implies that the normalization method works well (no false positive). By transforming u1 to u2, we can save one page request (without the normalization, we would make two page requests with u1 and u2)

    (C) Page p2 exists on the web, and p1 and p2 are not of the same page: This case implies that false positive takes place. Due to the incorrect normalization method, we lose one page (here, p1). There are two sub-cases. If u2 is not known beforehand (i.e., u2 is new, as shown case 7), then we can gain a new page p2 by accessing u2 even though p2 is not the same as p1. If u2 is already known to us (i.e., u1 is transformed to one of URLs we know of, as shown case 2), the pure effect of the normalization is that we lose one page regardless of availability of p2 on the web.

(2) Page p1 does not exist on the web

    (A) URL u2 is already known to us (i.e. u2 is in a database of URLs): In this case, we do not lose any web pages. In addition, we can reduce the number of page requests by one, because page request with u2 is subject to execution anyway. These are denoted by case 3 and case 5.

    (B) URL u2 is not known to us (i.e. u2 is not in a database of URLs): In this case, there are two sub-cases. If p2 exists on the web (case 8), we can gain one web page. If p2 does not exist on the web (case 10), we lose nothing anyway. In both sub-cases, the number of page requests remains unchanged

Table 1. Effects of a normalization method

u1 (given) / u2 (normalized)		Page exists		Page not exists
u2 in databases	Page exists	Identical	Non-loss (1)	Non-loss (3)
		Different	Loss (2)	
	Page not exists	Loss (4)		Non-loss (5)
u2 not in databases	Page exists	Identical	Non-loss (6)	Gain (8)
		Different	Change (7) (= loss+gain)	
	Page not exists	Loss (9)		Non-loss (10)

Due to a normalization method, we can lose a web page (cases 2, 4 and 9), gain a web page (case 8) or get a different web page (case 7). In case 7, we miss the intended page due to the normalization, but we able to get a new page instead. Negative false takes place in cases 2, 4, 7, 8, and 9. In other cases, the normalization method does not lose intended pages at all, leaving a possibility of reducing the number of URLs.

The effectiveness of the URL normalizations is two-fold. First, by transforming URLs into a canonical form of URLs, we can significantly reduce the number of URLs in operation. Second, in the course of URL normalization, we may lose (or gain) pages that should be crawled (or not be crawled, respectively). For evaluating the effectiveness of the URL normalization, we propose a number of metrics that shows the effectiveness of a normalization method. Let N be the total number of URLs that are considered.

- Page loss rate = the total number of lost pages / N
- Page gain rate = the total number of gain pages / N
- Page change rate = the total number of change pages / N
- Page non-loss rate = the total number of non-lost pages / N

Note that the sum of all the four rates is always 1. Regarding reduction of URLs, we define the URL reduction rate as below:

- URL reduction rate = 1 − (the unique number of URLs after normalization / the unique number of URLs before normalization)

For example, if we normalize 100 distinct URLs into 90 distinct URLs, we say that the URL reduction rate is 0.1 (1 − 90/100, or 10%). A good normalization method should exhibit a high value of URL reduction rate, and low values of page loss/gain/change.

4 Empirical Evaluation

In this section, we introduce the five extended normalization methods (i.e., EN1, EN2, ..., EN5), apply those methods into real URLs, and evaluate the methods with our metrics. The extended normalizations reduce false negatives more strictly at the cost of allowing false positives than the standard normalizations do.

The path component of a URL is case-sensitive in principle. However, in a web server working on the Windows operating system, URLs representing the same resource can be composed with various combinations of the upper-case and lower-case letters. This is why the file systems (such as FAT, FAT32, and NTFS), which the Windows operating system use, manage names of directories and files in a case-insensitive fashion. For instance, "http://www.nasdaq.com/asp/ownership.asp" and "http://www.nasdaq.com/ASP/ownership.asp" are equivalent. Let us suppose that there is a URL composed of upper-case and lower-case letters. If we assume that the URL is used to access a web page in case-insensitive file system, then we can consider the following extended normalization.

- EN 1: Change letters in the path component into the lower-case letters

We consider the last slash symbol at the non-empty path component of URL. A URL with the last slash symbol represents a directory. When sending web servers such URL, web clients get either a default page in the requested directory or a temporarily created page showing all files in the directory. Users requesting a directory often omit specifying the last slash symbol in a URL. What really happens in this case is that web servers are likely to redirect the URL into a URL including the last slash symbol. For instance, "http://acm.org/pubs" is redirected into "http://acm.org/pubs/". We can consider the following normalization.

- EN 2: A URL with the last slash symbol is transformed into a URL without the last slash symbol

A default page is a file to look for, when a client requests a directory. The default page can be specified in a URL. For instance, "http://www.acm.org/" and "http://www.acm.org/index.htm" represent the same page on the site (acm.org), which sets the designation of a default page as "index.htm". In reality, any file name could be designated as a default page. It is reported [7] that only two web servers (the Apache web server, the MS IIS web server) comprise over 85% of all the installed web servers in the world. The default pages of those web servers are "index.htm", "index.html", or "default.htm", when they are installed by default. We consider the three file names, i.e., "index.htm", "index.html", and "default.htm", as default pages in our experiment. We consider the following three normalizations.

- EN 3: Eliminate the default file name "index.htm" in the path component
- EN 4: Eliminate the default file name "index.html" in the path component
- EN 5: Eliminate the default file name "default.htm" in the path component

Our experiment is organized of the following six steps. First, the robot [3] collected web pages. Second, we extracted raw URLs (URL strings as found) from the collected web pages. Third, we eliminated duplicate URLs with simple string comparison operations to get a set of URLs that are subject to be normalized. This step is simply to get a set of URLs that are syntactically different with each other, irrespective of URL normalizations. Fourth, we applied the syntax-based normalization and the scheme-based normalization of the standard URL normalizations to the set of URLs obtained in the third step. We call the URLs obtained during this step RFC-normalized URLs. Fifth, the five extended normalizations (will be described later in this section) are applied to the RFC-normalized URLs. Sixth, with the RFC-normalized URLs we requested web pages. Also we requested pages with URLs we obtained during the extended normalizations.

We randomly selected 20,799 Korean sites. The web robot collected 748,632 web pages from the sites in November 2004. The robot was allowed to crawl a maximum of 3,000 pages for each site. We got 94 million raw URLs from the collected pages. We eliminated duplicate URLs without any URL normalization (only with simple string comparison) as follows. We eliminated duplicates of syntactically identical, raw URLs that are found on the same web page, that start the slash symbol (it means that these URLs are expressed as an absolute path) and are found on the same site, or that start with the "http:" prefix. After the third step, we got 24.7 million URLs.

Next, we eliminated duplicate URLs with the standard URL normalization: the syntax-based normalization and the scheme-based normalization. In our experiment, transforming a relative URL, in which some components of a URL are omitted, into an absolute URL is regarded as one part of the standard URL normalization. After raw URLs are transformed into RFC-normalized URLs, we eliminated duplicate URLs with the string comparison method. Finally, we got 4,337,220 unique RFC-normalized URLs.

We need to say which URLs are used for showing the effectiveness of the extended URL normalizations. We included the RFC-normalized URLs belonging to the 20,799 sites in our experiment. Also, we excluded the RFC-normalized URLs including the question mark symbol. The reason is that those URLs usually represent dynamic pages that are generated differently whenever the pages are referred to. Dynamic pages make our experiment difficult to handle, because we cannot be sure that an extended normalization produces a wrong URL even though both the contents before and after an extended normalization are different. Totally, 1,588,021 RFC-normalized URLs were used for evaluating the effectiveness of the extended URL normalizations.

Table 2. Number of unique URLs before and after each of the extended normalizations

Normalizations	Unique URLs before normalization	Unique URLs after normalization	URL reduction rate
EN1	302,902	280,399	7.43%
EN2	36,539	29,701	18.71%
EN3	3,761	3,164	15.87%
EN4	105,118	102,394	2.59%
EN5	120	110	8.33%

Table 2 shows how many RFC-normalized URLs participated in each of the normalization methods and how many URLs are reduced by each extended normalizations. EN1 is applied to 302,902 URLs containing more than one upper-case letter. After EN1 was applied, 7.43% of the URLs were removed. EN2 eliminated the last slash symbols in 36,539 URLs. 18.71% of the applied URLs were removed. EN3, EN4, and EN5 removed 15.87%, 2.59%, and 8.3% of the applied URLs, respectively.

Fig. 2 shows how much percents of the applied URLs caused page non-loss, loss, gain, and change. The page non-loss means that false positives do not happen in an extended normalization. The page loss, gain, and change mean that false positives happened. 97% of the URLs to which EN4 was applied were transformed without false positives. In the EN4, only a small number of the URLs (3%) caused false positives. 12% of the URLs to which EN3 were applied caused false positives.

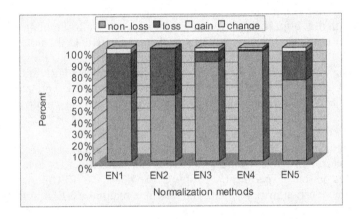

Fig. 2. Percent of page non-loss, loss, gain, and change

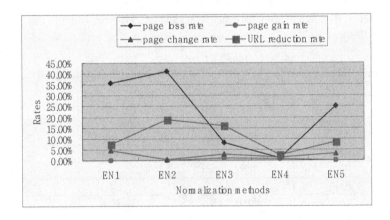

Fig. 3. Effectiveness of normalization methods

Fig. 3 shows the summarized results. In EN1, EN2, and EN5, the page loss rates are more than 10%, which means that the normalizations often transform some correct URLs into wrong URLs. The page gain rates of all of the normalizations are less than one or two percent. The extended normalization methods did not likely to get new pages accidentally. The page change rates were less than 5%. The URL reduction rates ranged from 3% to 19%. This figure precisely shows how many URL requests we can reduce at the cost of false positives.

5   Conclusions and Future Works

In this paper, we have proposed a number of evaluation metrics: the loss rate, the gain rate, the change rate, and the URL reduction rate. The metrics are used to evaluate a URL normalization method, which can be applied in real-world web applications. With the metrics proposed, we have analyzed the effectiveness of the illustrative extended normalization methods. Some method exhibits acceptable performance rates good enough to be applied in real applications.

The contributions of this paper are to present an analytic way to evaluate the effectiveness of a URL normalization method. In practice, URL normalization methods have been treated heuristically so far in that each normalization method is primarily devised on a basis of developer experiences. We need to have a systematic way to evaluate each URL normalization method. We believe that our research would pave the way to development of efficient web applications.

Dynamic pages were troublesome in our experiment. Even though both the contents before and after applying an extended URL normalization are different, we cannot be sure that the extended normalization produces a wrong URL. To conduct a stable experiment, we had to use static URLs only. How to determine page updates effectively remains as future work.

References

1. Burner, M.: Crawling Towards Eternity: Building an Archive of the World Wide Web, Web Techniques Magazine, Vol. 2. No. 5. (1997) 37-40
2. Heydon, A. and Najork, M., 1999. Mercator: A Scalable, Extensible Web Crawler, International Journal of WWW, Vol. 2. No. 4. (1999) 219-229
3. Kim, S.J. and Lee, S.H.: Implementation of a Web Robot and Statistics on the Korean Web, Springer-Verlag Lecture Notes in Computer Science, Vol. 2713. (2003) 341-350
4. Shkapenyuk, V. and Suel, T.: Design and Implementation of a High-performance Distributed Web Crawler, In Proceedings of 18th Data Engineering Conference, (2002) 357-368.
5. Berners-Lee, T., Fielding, R., and Masinter, L.: Uniform Resource Identifiers (URI): Generic Syntax, http://gbiv.com/protocols/uri/rev-2002/rfc2396bis.html, (2004)
6. Lee, S.H. and Kim, S.J.: On URL Normalization, to appear in Proceedings of the Workshop on Ubiquitous Web Systems and Intelligence (2005)
7. Netcraft: Web Server Survey, http://news.netcraft.com/archives/web_server_survey.html, (2004)

A New Approach for Semi-supervised Online News Classification*

Hon-Man Ko and Wai Lam

Department of Systems Engineering and Engineering Management,
The Chinese University of Hong Kong, Hong Kong
{hmko, wlam}@se.cuhk.edu.hk

Abstract. Due to the dramatic increasing of information on the Web, text categorization becomes a useful tool to organize the information. Traditional text categorization problem uses a training set from online sources with pre-defined class labels for text documents. Typically a large amount of online training news should be provided in order to learn a satisfactory categorization scheme. We investigate an innovative way to alleviate the problem. For each category, only a small amount of positive training examples for a set of the major concepts associated with the category are needed. We develop a technique which makes use of unlabeled documents since those documents can be easily collected, such as online news from the Web. Our technique exploits the inherent structure in the set of positive training documents guided by the provided concepts of the category. An algorithm for training document adaptation is developed for automatically seeking representative training examples from the unlabeled data collected from the new online source. Some preliminary experiments on real-world news collection have been conducted to demonstrate the effectiveness of our approach.

1 Introduction

Automatic text categorization (TC) has been an active research area and it has a large number of applications. It is different from search engines, like Yahoo! The functionality of search engines is to collect the target information for Internet user efficiently and accurately. Instead of forming a query by several keywords, the query for TC problem will be a full document. Based on the query, search engines find out all documents with exact keyword matching. Meanwhile TC systems identify a class label to the full document and relax the constraint of exact matching. Labeling the unseen documents organizes the main idea for the document group with the same class label.

---

* The work described in this paper was substantially supported by grants from the Research Grant Council of the Hong Kong Special Administrative Region, China (Project Nos: CUHK 4187/01E, CUHK 4179/03E, and CUHK 4193/04E) and CUHK Strategic Grant (No: 4410001).

S. Shimojo et al. (Eds.): HSI 2005, LNCS 3597, pp. 238–247, 2005.

The traditonal TC problem relies on a reasonable amount of documents for training the classifiers [6, 8]. Typically, the set of training documents contains both positive and negative training examples. In some practical situations, a small amount of positive sample documents is available for each category. Besides, there is some information regarding the set of major concepts associated with the category [7]. Sometimes we can get those concepts by automated summaries [5]. However, the concept labels for each positive sample document are not known. The documents in such a new collection are unlabeled. For example, a user may already have a small amount of previously collected news about "Election". This category "Election" consists of news about different kinds of election events such as election preparation, candidate campaign, voter turnout, and so on. Given another new, different online news source, this user needs an automatic categorization system which can categorize news stories about election. Typically it is easy to collect a relatively large volume of unlabeled documents from this new source.

This TC problem setting is different from traditional problems. In essence, if we consider a particular category K, only positive training examples while no negative training examples are given. Note that examples from other categories (not K) cannot be reliably served as negative examples for K since these documents are only labeled as positive examples for the corresponding categories (not K) and their membership for K is unknown. This categorisation problem can be regarded as a kind of semi-supervised learning. Traditional text categorization learning techniques are not suitable for this semi-supervised setting since the success of traditional TC classifier is based on the reliable positive and negative examples.

We propose a technique called Example Adaptation for Text categorization (EAT). The technique is able to exploit the available positive examples and the information about the major concepts associated with the category. It seeks reliable positive examples from the unlabeled data collected from the new target online source. The goal is to learn a categorization scheme which can classify documents coming from this new source.

Our approach will identify more positive examples from the unlabeled documents first in order to build a more accurate classifier. Users only need to provide a small amount of representing examples for each concepts. It is also quite common that the user has a brief idea of what kinds of concepts are covered for the category. The concepts are not necessarily complete or exhaustive. We call these concepts as "Topic Descriptions". For example, a category about "Election" may be associated with concepts such as "Political Campaign", "Voters' Turnout", etc. One issue is how to utilize this information to improve the categorization performance. Given the new, different online news source, it is common that a relatively large set of unlabeled documents can be easily obtained. Therefore, another issue is how the unlabeled data can be utilized so that a new classifier suitable for the new source can be effectively learned.

Our approach is quite different with relevance feedback and adaptive filtering [9, 10]. The purpose of EAT is to autoamtically boost the discriminative power of classifier whereas the other two tasks are learning the behaviours of users by their relevance judgement. Moreover, pseudo relevance feedback does not make use of inherent structure for category while EAT does.

2   Related Work

There have been some previous works focusing on TC problems for which only a small amount of labeled examples are needed [2, 12]. These methods can exploit the information found in the unlabeled data, but they still require some negative examples. Some recent approaches attempted to tackle this kind of semi-supervised text categorization problems mentioned above. Blum and Mitchell [1] proposed a Co-Training methodology to extract the class information given a large set of unlabeled examples and a small set of labeled one. Nigam et al. [14] applies EM algorithm to calculate the probabilistically-weighted mixture components for the labeled documents. Each components can be treated as sub-classes. However, there is no clear definition on the mixture components since EM is an unsupervised learning process. Both positive and negative examples are used in the above algorithm. Besides the above, there are some state-of-the-art algorithms using positive labeled examples only. Yu. et al. [16] proposed an approach called PEBL which employs Support Vector Machines (SVM) for building a classifier for Web pages. PEBL is, unfortunately, sensitive to the number of positive examples. Small number of positive examples will seriously affect PEBL performance since noise may be dominant. Li and Liu [11] proposed a technique based on Rocchio algorithm and SVM. These two approaches share a common idea of automatically identifying good negative training examples from the unlabeled data and then learning a classifier. Liu et al. [13] have shown that identifying negative examples from unlabeled set helps to build a more accurate classifier. Different from their works, our approach identifies potentially positive examples from the unlabeled documents. We have conducted a preliminary experiment on a real-world online news corpus composed news from different sources. The experimental results illustrate that our proposed solution can significantly enhance the performance.

3   Background and Motivation

Conceptually, a separate binary classifier can be learned for each category. After the classifiers for all categories have been learned, they can be combined to conduct m-ary categorization task. Generally, it is allowed to assign more than one categories for a document.

Consider a particular category K, the categorization problem can be formulated as binary classification where the goal is to decide whether a document belongs to K. Some of positive training examples and a set of major concepts for the category K are available. Typically, there should be some positive training examples associated with each concept. It is also possible that some positive training examples are not associated with any concepts. For example, the category "Election" may be associated with the concepts such as "political campaign", "election day coverage", "inauguration", "voter turnouts", "election results", "protest", "reaction", "candidate intention", and "nomination". A positive training example may belong to some of these given concepts or may not belong to any given concepts. This concept membership information is, however, generally not given or labeled. From a new target document source which is different from where the training example originates, a collection of unlabeled documents is available. In practice, this kind of unlabeled documents can be easily obtained. Thus the size of the unlabeled document set is usually relatively large. The goal is to build a good classifier for this target document source.

The basic idea of our proposed approach EAT is to automatically seek potentially positive training examples from the unlabeled document set. The rationale is that representative training examples extracted from the target document source can greatly improve the classifier construction. This capability can be viewed as a kind of training example adaptation. In the classification process, the quality of positive examples is extremely crucial. Poor quality of the positive examples will greatly degrade the performance, especially when the original training set is relatively small.

A major component in EAT is to identify positive examples based on the existing labeled positive examples and the information of the concepts of the category. Our technique attempts to exploit the inherent structure of the existing set of positive examples guided by the related concepts of the category. As a preliminary study, we investigate a clustering model taking into account the category concepts. Then a positive example seeking algorithm from unlabeled data is developed. Finally a set of classifiers which base on different number of positive exmaples extracted will be built iteratively until we can select a good classifier from the set.

4   The Proposed Approach

This section describes a new approach for semi-supervised online news classification, which consists of two steps : (1) extracting a set of potentially positive examples from the unlabeled set, (2) generating a set of classifiers iteratively with increasing the number of positve examples until the classifier reaches its local maximum accuracy level. The first subsection shows how EAT extracts positive examples and the second subsection explains how EAT automatically determines the number of positive examples that should be extracted.

4.1   Example Adaption for Text Categorization

This method processes on each category separately. Consider a particular category K, there is a set of concepts related to the category. The first step is to manually identify a sample document for each concept from the pool of positive training documents. This only imposes a very small amount of manual effort which can be easily done in practice. The next step is to make use of an unsupervised learning algorithm to cluster the whole pool of positive training documents. The final step is to identify a good classifier for new online source. The clustering process will also take into account of the sample document in each concept. The unsupervised learning is derived from a nearest neighbor clustering. The details of the unsupervised learning algorithm are given as follows:

1. Let φ be a set of clusters found and it is initialized to $\{\varphi_1, \ldots, \varphi_k\}$ where φ_i denotes the centroid of the initial cluster formed by the seed document.
2. Let t_j be the term weight calculated by td-idf weighting scheme. For each document D from the positive training document set, calculate the Euclidean distance d_i between D and the centroid φ_i of each cluster

$$d_i = \sqrt{\sum_j (W(D, t_j) - W(\varphi_i, t_j))^2} \tag{1}$$

where $W(D, t_j)$ and $W(\varphi_i, t_j)$ are the normalized feature weight of t_j for document D and centroid φ_i respectively.
   (a) For any cluster φ_i, if the Euclidean distance d_i is less than a threshold λ, D will be assigned to that cluster.
   (b) If D cannot be assigned to any cluster, it will be the initial seed for a new cluster.

After the clustering process, those clusters containing more than τ documents are considered as informative clusters.

Next, we develop a positive example seeking algorithm which processes each informative cluster one by one. Consider a particular informative cluster P. Let U be a set of unlabeled documents collected from the target source. The positive example seeking algorithm is presented below.

1. Initially, let all documents in U be negative examples and those in the informative cluster P be positive examples. Let P_i be a document in P and the normalized weight of a term t_k in P_i be $W(P_i, t_k)$. Let U_j be a document in U. The normalized weight of a term t_k in U_j is $W(U_j, t_k)$.
2. Let the set of newly sought positive example set be M which is initialized to empty.
3. Two concept vectors, Q and N, corresponding to positive and negative concepts respectively, are learned by Rocchio algorithm as follows:
   (a) For each feature t_k, we define

$$\theta = \sum_{P_i \forall P} W(P_i, t_k) \text{ and } \phi = \sum_{U_j \forall U} W(U_j, t_k) \tag{2}$$

   (b) Calculate the positive concept vector:

$$W(Q, t_k) = \frac{1}{|P|} \alpha\theta - \frac{1}{|U|} \beta\phi \tag{3}$$

(c) Calculate the negative concept vector:

$$W(N, t_k) = \frac{1}{|U|}\alpha\phi - \frac{1}{|P|}\beta\theta \qquad (4)$$

where $W(Q, t_k)$ and $W(N, t_k)$ are the feature scores in the positive and negative concept vectors respectively. α and β are the Rocchio classifier parameters controlling the weighting of positive and negative concept vectors.

4. For each unlabeled document U_j,
   (a) Calculate the similarity score $\Delta_Q(U_j)$ of U_j to the positive concept vector as follows:

   $$\Delta_Q(U_j) = \sum_k W(Q, t_k)W(U_j, t_k) \qquad (5)$$

   (b) Similarly we calculate the similarity score $\Delta_N(U_j)$ of U_j to the negative concept vector as follows:

   $$\Delta_N(U_j) = \sum_k W(N, t_k)W(U_j, t_k) \qquad (6)$$

   (c) Set $\delta = \Delta_Q(U_j) - \Delta_N(U_j)$ and get its normalized value $\delta_{norm} = \delta/(\delta_{max} - \delta_{min})$. If δ_{norm} is larger than a threshold η and U_j is not in M, then move U_j into M.

The above steps are repeated for each informative cluster. After all the newly sought positive examples are found, they are merged together as well as the original positive examples to form the final set of positive example training set.

4.2   Classifier Construction

The next step is to determine the number of potentially positive exmaples to be extracted. Cohen et la. [3] showed that extracting more labeled examples may suffer a performance degradation. But this problem can be solved if the number of unlabeled examples is appropriately controlled. We propose a methodology to identify a good categorization scheme from a set of classifiers trained by different number of potentially positive examples.

The final classifier is constructed by running a particular categorization scheme iteratively with different size of Z_k, which is the set of original positive examples plus extracted positive examples. The algorithm for classifier construction is given in Figure 1.

The score δ_{norm} is in the interval $[0,1]$ since it is normalized. Decreasing η by a small constant , the number of document in M_n keeps increasing. To facilitate the classifier construction process, we introduce a parameter ϵ and make sure that a signifcant number of unlabeled examples is added to M_n. For building classifers S_n, we let Z_n be the positive training set and those labeled documents which is not in category K (non-K class) be negative training set. Based on the accuracy of S_n, the algorithm will automatically select the best classifier with local maximum accuracy.

Input: Set $n = 1$, $\eta = 1.0$
         M_0 = a empty set of potentially positive labeled exmaples
         S_0 = a classifier built by P as positive set and non-K class
            documents as negative one
         R_0 = accuracy of S_0 on P

1. Initialise $R_{max} = R_0$
2. Loop
3.   Loop
4.   decrement η by a small constant
5.   apply EAT to obtain M_n
6.   Until $|M_n|$ - $|M_{n-1}| \geq \epsilon$
7. $Z_n = P \bigcup M_n$
8.   use Z_n as positive set and non-K class documents as
      negative set to build classifier S_n
9. R_n = accuracy of S_n on P
10.   if ($R_n \geq R_{max}$)
       $R_{max} = R_n$
11.   increment n by 1
12. Until $R_{n-1} < R_{max}$

Fig. 1. The outline of classifier construction method

The idea of this classifer construction method is to select a well-performed classifier automatically. Docuemnt U_j which has higher score δ_{norm} in the informative clusters P_i will be used to build the classifier first. The algorithm will continue until it finds a good classifier achieving the local maximum accuracy. The accuracy of S_n should keep increasing until the classifiers are biased to the noise.

5   Experimental Results

We have conducted some experiments on a real-world news collection extracted from the Topic Detection and Tracking (TDT) evaluation project. It contains news stories from different sources. We extracted English news stories labeled with some broad categories in our experiments. The number of stories in the training set is 28,806.

We investigate the binary classification of four categories, namely, "Election", "Accidents", "Legal/Criminal Cases", and "Sports". The numbers of corresponding positive examples are 130, 96, 182, and 528 respectively and the remaining stories are treated as unlabeled documents. The concepts associated with the categories "Election" , "Accident", "Legal/Criminal" and "Sports News" are shown in Table 1. The total number of new source documents is 1,267,

Table 1. The Topic Description for Different Categories

Category	Topic Description
Election	"political campaign", "election day coverage", "inauguration", "voter turnouts", "election results", "protest", "reaction", "candidate intention", "nomination"
Accident	"accident description", "death tolls and injuries", "economics losses", "compensation for accident", "investigation", "legal proceeding"
Legal / Criminal Cases	"case description", "arrest", "investigation", "legal proceeding", "verdicts and sentencing", "law making process"
Sports	"preparation of competition", "game description", "result announcement", "player injury", "retirement"

Table 2. The categorization performance, measured by F-measure, of EAT and other methods

Category	Original number of positive examples	Baseline	EAT	Roc-SVM
Election	130	0.547	0.824	0.7
Accident	96	0.698	0.698	0.866
Legal / Criminal Cases	182	0.788	0.852	0.855
Sports	528	0.726	0.842	0.773
	Macro-Average	0.690	0.804	0.797

which are inside TDT3 corpus. The vocabulary size of the whole document collection is 19,513.

The data pre-processing steps involved stopword removal and stemming. Information gain [15] was used for feature selection. For the algorithm used for learning a classifier, we employed Support Vector Machine (SVM) [4] with linear kernel. We reserved 20% of training documents as the tuning set in order to select automatically suitable parameter values. F-measure evaluation metric which considers both recall and precision is used for measuring the performance.

The performance of our proposed EAT method is shown in Table 2. We also present the performance of a baseline method commonly used in traditional methods. "EAT" stands for using our approach to extract positive examples and selecting a representative classifier. For the traditional classifier building process, we simply treats those documents labeled to other categories as negative examples. The parameter settings are distance threshold λ is 1.0; minimum number of document in cluster τ is 10 and ϵ is 10 for classifier selection. "Roc-SVM" stands for the algorithm for extracting negative examples, which is proposed by Li and Liu [11]. From the result, we observe that collecting more representative positive examples from the unlabeled document set generally improves the categorization performance. Although the classifiers cannot obtain global optimal accuracy on P, the performance can reach a satisfactory level of 27.7% at category "Election". For category "Election", automatically seeking 260 more positive documents improves the F-measrue by 27.7%. For category "Legal/Criminal Cases", automatically seeking 105 more positive documents improves the F-measure by 6.4%. For category "Sport News", automatically seeking 132 more positive documents improves the F-measure by 11.6%. Comparing with baseline, EAT obtains a great improvement on SVM model. The reason is that EAT performs well for the sparse distribution over the categroy K document space. Extracting more positive examples boosts those weak classifiers by improving the compactness of the document space. Moreover, EAT obtains higher F-measure scores than Roc-SVM on most of the categories and the overall average performance.

6   Conclusions and Future Work

This paper presents a novel approach for solving a non-traditional text categorization problem. In this problem setting, only positive examples are available. Besides, some information about the major concepts of a category is given. The goal is to learn a new classifier to conduct categorization for a new different source. It also makes use of the unlabeled documents easily collected from the new source. The idea of our approach is to exploit the inherent structure of the positive training document set. Then we develop an algorithm for adapting the training set by automatically seeking useful positive document examples from the unlabeled data. The experimental results show that our proposed approach can improve the categorization performance.

In the future, we intend to further investigate several directions. The first direction is to develop a sophisticated approach for learning the inherent structure of the existing set of positive examples guided by the related concepts of the category. The second direction is to develop a more formal mechanism to tackle this semi-supervised learning problem.

References

1. A. Blum and T. Mitchell. Combining labeled and unlabeled data with co-training. In *Proceedings of the Eleventh Annual Conference on Computational Learning Theory*, pages 92–100, 1998.
2. J. Bockhorst and M. Craven. Exploiting relations among concepts to acquire weakly labeled training data. In *Proceedings of the IEEE International Conference on Machine Learning*, pages 43–50, 2002.
3. I. Cohen, F. Cozman, N. Sebe, M. Cirelo, and T. Huang. Semisupervised learning of classifiers: Theory, algorithms, and their application to human computer interaction. *IEEE Transaction on Pattern Analysis and Machine Intelligence*, 26(12):1553–1567, 2004.
4. T. Joachims. Text categorization with support vector machines: Learning with many relevant features. In *Proceedings of 10th European Conference on Machine Learning*, pages 137–142, 1998.
5. W. Lam, K. Chan, D. Radev, H. Saggion, and S. Teufel. Context-based generic cross-lingual retrieval of documents and automated summaries. *Journal of American Society for Information Science and Technology*, pages 129–139, 2005.

6. W. Lam and Y. Han. Automatic textual document categorization based on generalised instance sets and a metamodel. *IEEE Transaction on Pattern Analysis and Machine Intelligence*, 25(5):628–633, 2003.

7. W. Lam, C. Keung, and D Liu. Discovering useful concept prototypes for classification based on filtering and abstraction. *IEEE Transaction on Pattern Analysis and Machine Intelligence*, 24(8):1075–1090, 2002.

8. W. Lam, M. Ruiz, and P. Srinivasan. Automatic text categorization and its application to text retrieval. *IEEE Transaction on Knowledge and Data Engineering*, 11(6):865–879, 1999.

9. W. Lam, W. Wang, and C. Yue. Web discovery and filtering based on textual relevance feedback learning. *Computational Intelligence*, 19(2):136–163, 2003.

10. W. Lam and K. Yu. High-dimensional learning framework for adaptive document filtering. *Computational Intelligence*, 19(1):42–63, 2003.

11. X. Li and B. Liu. Learning to classify texts using positive and unlabeled data. In *Proceedings of Eighteenth Internatinoal Joint Conferences on Artifical Intelligence*, pages 587–594, 2003.

12. B. Liu, W. Lee, P. Yu, and X .Li. Partially supervised classification of text documents. In *Proceedings of the IEEE International Conference on Machine Learning*, pages 387–394, 2002.

13. B. Liu, D. Yang, X.Li, W. Lee, and P. Yu. Building text classifiers using positive and unlabeled examples. In *Proceedings of the IEEE International Conference on Data Mining*, pages 179–188, 2003.

14. K. Nigam, A. McCallum, S. Thrun, and T. Mitchell. Text classification from labeled and unlabeled documents using em. *Machine Learning*, 39(2):103–134, 2000.

15. Y. Yang and J. Pedersen. A comparative study on feature selection in text categorization. In *Proceedings of the IEEE International Conference on Machine Learning*, pages 412–420, 1997.

16. H. Yu, J. Han, and K. Chang. PEBL : Positive examples based learning for web page classification using svm. In *Proceedings of the ACM SIGKDD International Conference on Knowledge Discovery and Data Mining*, pages 239–248, 2002.

Automatic Generation of Web-Based Mathematical Courseware for Solving Simultaneous Equations

Yukari Shirota

Faculty of Economics, Gakushuin University,
1-5-1 Mejiro, Toshima-ku, Tokyo 171-8588, Japan
yukari.shirota@gakushuin.ac.jp

Abstract. This paper presents an efficient method to generate teacher's guidance and presentation materials for mathematical education, especially for solving simultaneous equations. Using XSL translations on presentation templates named the guidance plans and incorporating the output of a mathematical symbolic processor such as Maple, the presentation materials can be dynamically generated.

1 Introduction

Today, Web-based courseware is widely used in the field of education. However, teachers face a cost problem when developing Web-based learning materials. It takes much time, practice, and devotion to design and develop the learning materials. Our research target is the automation of interactive Web-based courseware for mathematical education, especially for economical mathematics education. The generated courseware must be of the same high quality as the teaching of the teacher best suited to instruct each student. Furthermore, development costs should be low and development time short. To meet these requirements, we have introduced XML[1] technologies and mathematical symbolic processors to develop Web-based courseware. Using XSL translations on presentation templates named the guidance plans and incorporating the output of a mathematical symbolic processor, the presentation materials can be dynamically generated.

In general, the advantages of automatic updates using XML and XSLT are their low cost and speedy turnaround time. Meanwhile, their disadvantage is that they produce Web pages of uniform appearance whose content, layout and generated dialogues can thus be tedious for the viewer. To solve the problems, we have introduced a metadata framework for learning material generations. First we define the metadata for important concepts in the given mathematical word problem. From the metadata, our developed courseware automation system named e-Math Interaction Agent generates various kinds of learning materials. The formats of the generated presentation materials include (1) In words explanations by a virtual teacher, (2) Visual materials, such as graphs and animations, (3) Mathematical symbolic equations, and, (4) Concrete values after mathematical computations. In the generated courseware, the virtual teacher explains in words economical and mathematical relationships between data

S. Shimojo et al. (Eds.): HSI 2005, LNCS 3597, pp. 248–259, 2005.

repeatedly and in various ways until students can understand them. In addition, many graphs can be automated so that students can see the relationships visually from various angles.

The paper describes automatic generation of Web-based courseware for teaching simultaneous equations. Especially, we shall focus on the following three kinds of simultaneous equations: (1) national income determination problems, (2) supply and demand problems, and (3) crane-turtle problems. In the next section, a system model of our proposed courseware generation will be described. In Section 3, the generation processes are explained using the national income determination problem as the sample problem. In Section 4, we shall show the same solution plan can be shared for generation of the supply and demand problems and the crane-turtle problems. The existing related work will be described in Section 5. Discussions and conclusions are given in the last section.

2 Automatic Generation Process Model

In the section, we shall explain our proposed model of the automatic generation processes[2]. The input file is the definition data of a mathematical word problem. These data consist of "What is the given data?" "What is the given condition?" "What is the unknown data?" and "What do you want to seek?" We call the definition data file a 'metalevel description file'. In the following section, a sample of the metalevel description file will be shown. All a human teacher has to do there to generate his/her learning materials is just only to write this metalevel description file. All the left processes can be executed automatically by our system e-Math Interaction Agent.

The important parts of this model are (1) solution plan, and (2) guidance plan. The solution plan is a definition of the mathematical (logical) solution plan and describes how to mathematically solve the given problem. The guidance plan is a definition of the presentation templates and defines what a virtual teacher dialogues with a student and how the virtual teacher guides a student using various kinds of presentation materials. These two kinds of plans must be defined in advance by a "system supervisor" who is both a computer expert and a mathematical teaching specialist well-versed in solving the problems and teaching them to students. The "system supervisor" at first classifies a set of similar problems as being of the same problem type. Problems of the same type can share the same solution plan. The solution plan is defined for the problem type, not for each problem, at a metalevel using metadata of the concepts. The same are the guidance plans as the solution plans.

So far we have already defined the following two problem types: (a) optimization of single variable functions and (b) solving simultaneous equations. Concerning the optimization problems, the application fields include optimization problems for business, in economics, in life science, and in social science, and high school students' geometrical optimization problems. We have reported our system can successfully automate the learning materials for these wide application fields[3]. In this paper, we shall focus on the (b) solving simultaneous equations. This application range is much broader than that of the optimization, because every "find-to-a-solution" type math problem belongs to this problem type.

In our approach, we define the term "concept" to be some important concepts appeared in the given mathematical word problem. The concept is the metadata and defined for the problem type to express the contents of the mathematical word problems. Thus, a concept has some mathematical/economical semantics. Each concept can be seen from the following three different angles:

(1) Economical concept: for example, revenue, cost, profit, investment, demand, its total, average, and marginal.
(2) Mathematical concept: for example, solution, cross point, stationary point (max, min, or inflection), the first-order partial derivative, multiplier, domain/range of a function.
(3) The word problem context related concept: for example, a set of equations, the main equilibrium equation, unknown variable, the equilibrium value, effect of the variable xxx.

Our courseware automation system "e-Math Interaction Agent"[4] has the following new features:

(1) Definition of a solution plan and a guidance plan by Document Type Definition (DTD) documents, using semantic metadata called concepts.
(2) Breakdown of the generation process into the generation of mathematical contents and that of presentation materials.

The guidance plan has been separated from the solution plan as a presentation template on a presentation layer. The advantages of such a layer division are: (a) Increased flexibility of presentation formats for the same mathematical solution plan, and (b) Increased reusability of a solution plan at the mathematical concept level.

3   Generation Processes

In this section, we shall explain the generation processes in our proposed method. As a problem type for solving simultaneous equations, we have defined 'equilibrium' problem type. In this problem type, the equilibrium level of the unknown variable is finally calculated under the condition of the main equilibrium equation. For example, an equation *total-supply* = *total-demand* is the main equilibrium equation. Thus, we defined the following key concepts for the problem type: (1) the unknown variable, (2) the left part of the main equilibrium equation, and (3) the right part of the main equilibrium equation. The application field of this problem type is broad. For example, there are lots of economical supply and demand problems that belong to this problem type where the main equilibrium equation is *supply* = *demand*. Another example is a national income determination problem where the main equilibrium equation concerning the nation is *total-supply* = *total-demand*. In this section, we use a simple two-sector model ($Yd=C+I$) national income determination problem as an example problem[4].

First, we shall explain the generation processes of mathematical contents. As shown in Figure 1, the input file to the system is a metalevel-description file (See

Figure 2). In the 'equilibrium' problem type, the equilibrium level of the unknown variable is finally calculated.

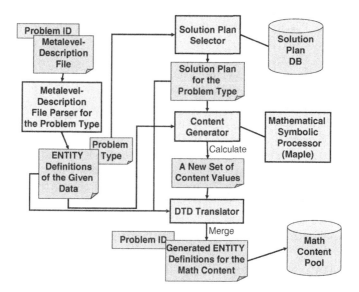

Fig. 1. Generation processes of mathematical contents

```
<!-- Metalevel-Description File  for an "Equilibrium" Type Problem        -->
<!-- equilibrium(var, eq)                                       -->
<!--  var: equilibrium variable (ex. Y)          -->
<!--  eq:  main equilibrium equation             -->
<!--     (ex. "Ys(Y)=Yd(Y)")                     -->
title: problem 1-a
problem-words: &problem1-a.txt
data: national income, Y, , Y>0
data: total supply, Ys, , Ys>0
data: total demand, Yd, , Yd>0
data: consumption, C, C=0.8*Y+100
data: investment, I, I=50
relationship: Ys=Y, Yd=C+I
find: equilibrium(Y, Ys=Yd)
```

Fig. 2. A sample metalevel-description file

Thus, the key concepts are: (1) the unknown variable, (2) the left part of the main equilibrium equation, and (3) the right part of the main equilibrium equation. These three concepts are represented by the concept names (a) equilibrium, (b) balance-left, and (3) balance-right, in the solution plan (See Figure 3). Then, the content generator generates a new set of content values by calculating the given functions, such as 'solve' and 'split-eqs,' using the mathematical symbolic processor Maple[6]. The defined function 'solve' is used to solve the given simultaneous equations.

```
<!-- Solution Plan for "Equilibrium" Type Problems    -->
<!-- solve(eqs, var[, param])                          -->
<!-- eqs:       a set of equations to be solved        -->
<!-- var:       an unknown variable                    -->
<!-- param:     a parameter of the unknown             -->
<!ENTITY all-eqs.eq        'relationships.eq, given-eqs.eq'>
<!ENTITY left-sided-eqs.eq        split-eqs(all-eqs.eq, balance-left.var )>
<!ENTITY right-sided-eqs.eq       split-eqs(all-eqs.eq, balance-right.var )>
<!ENTITY left-sided-eq.eq         solve(left-sided-eqs.eq,balance-eft.var,equilibrium.var)>
<!ENTITY right-sided-eq.eq     solve(right-sided-eqs.eq,balance-right.var,equilibrium.var)>
<!ENTITY balance-eq.eq            'balance-left.var=balance-right.var'>
<!ENTITY equilibrium.value        solve('all-eqs.eq, balance-eq.eq', equilibrium.var)>
```

Fig. 3. A solution plan for problem type 'equilibrium'

```
<!ENTITY problem-type          "equilibrium">
<!ENTITY problem-words         &problem1-a.txt>
<!ENTITY given-eqs.eq                  "C=0.8*Y+100, I=50">
<!ENTITY relationships.eq      "Ys=Y, Yd=C+I">
<!ENTITY equilibrium.id        "national income">
<!ENTITY equilibrium.var       "Y">
<!ENTITY balance-left.id       "total supply">
<!ENTITY balance-left.var      "Ys">
         ...........................
<!ENTITY all-eqs.eq            "Ys=Y, Yd=C+I, C=0.8*Y+100, I=50">
<!ENTITY left-sided-eqs.eq     "Ys=Y">
<!ENTITY right-sided-eqs.eq    "Yd=C+I, C=0.8*Y+100, I=50">
<!ENTITY left-sided-eq.eq      "Ys=Y">
<!ENTITY right-sided-eq.eq     "Yd=0.8*Y+150">
<!ENTITY balance-eq.eq         "Ys=Yd">
<!ENTITY equilibrium.value     "750">
```

Fig. 4. Generated ENTITY definitions for the mathematical contents

Finally, the DTD translator embeds the calculated values and equations to the ENTITY definition parts of the given data. For example, the calculated equilibrium level of the unknown variable 750 is embedded there, as shown in Figure 4.

Next the process of creating presentation materials is explained. The materials to be generated are XML files, graph files named Maplets, and equation image files, such as 'jpeg' files. The generated file names are embedded as the return values of the file generation functions such as 'makeCrossGraph' to the guidance plan (See Figure 5).

```
<!-- Guidance Plan for "Equilibrium" Type Problems        -->
<!-- Page # 5, Black Board Window                          -->
<!ELEMENT           blackboard(statement, relationship, balance)>
<!ELEMENT           statement        item>
<!ELEMENT           item      (#PCDATA)>

....

<!ENTITY   _item 'Find the equilibrium point between balance-eq.eq'>
<!ENTITY   _variable 'balance-left.id balance-left.var -related equations'>
<!-- String "$eq$" is translated to the equation image file name      -->
<!-- makeCrossGraph(x, y1, y2, y1(x), y2(x))                  -->
<!--    x:      a variable of the horizontal axis             -->
<!--    y1, y2:       two variables of the vertical axis             -->
<!--    y1(x), y2(x):  two functions to be drawn             -->
<!ENTITY   _url
    makeCrossGraph(equilibrium.var, balance-left.var, balance-right.var, bal-
    ance-left.eq, balance-right.eq)>
<blackboard>
 <statement>
  <item>_item</item>
 <relationship>
  <variable>_variable</variable>
  <equation>
   <image><src>$left-sided-eq.eq$</src>
   <alt>left-sided-eq.eq</alt>
  </equation>
  ........................
 <balance>
  <button><name>graph</name>
   <url>_url</url>
  ...........................
</blackboard>
```

Fig. 5. A guidance plan for problem type 'equilibrium'

Finally the Web page generator combines the various kinds of materials to generate the final XML files. The XML files are displayed through a XSLT stylesheet on a Web browser.

4 Sample Courseware

We shall show in the section that our e-Math Interaction Agent can generate learning materials for the supply and demand problems and the early Japanese solution method of crane-turtle problems with the same solution/guidance plans of the 'equilibrium' problem type.

4.1 Supply and Demand Problem

In this section, we present sample learning materials for a supply and demand problem. Let us first outline the sample problem. When we teach a supply and demand problem, we begin by describing how to set up a simple model of the economic model

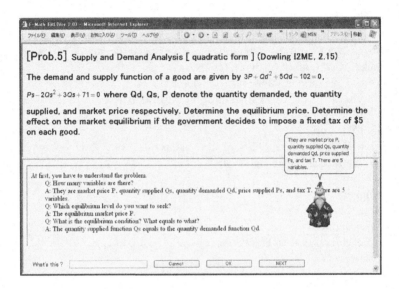

Fig. 6. A sample supply and demand problem

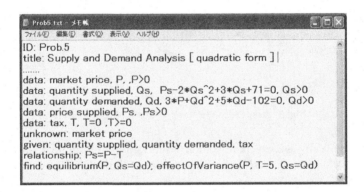

Fig. 7. A metalevel description file of the supply and demand problem in Figure 6

as a set of simultaneous equations. In terms of the process, it is important to make students to understand the problem, namely, "what are the given data, what is the unknown, and what are the relationships between data?" The teacher must repeatedly explain the economic model in various ways until the student can identify the following things: (a) the endogenous and exdogenous variables in the economic model, and

(b) the linear/non-linear demand and supply function. A supply and demand problem with non-linear simultaneous equations is used as the example here (See Figure 6). The solution/guidance plans are those for the 'equilibrium' problem type that have been already defined in Figures 3 and 5 in the previous section. The metalevel description file of this supply and demand problem is shown in Figure 7.

In addition, we would like to explain to students the effect of an increase in the other variables on the equilibrium level of P (market price) and Q (quantity). For example, suppose that the given problem is "What is the effect of an increase in tax T on the equilibrium level of market price P?" To explain this effect problem, a new problem type 'effectOfVariance' is defined and new solution/guidance plans for the problem type are also defined and stored in system databases in the same manner as the 'equilibrium' problem type.

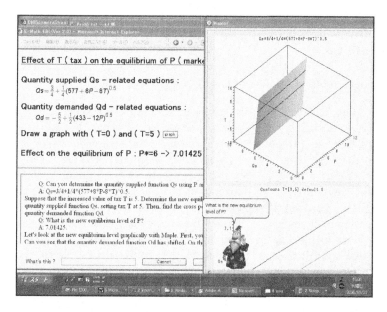

Fig. 8. The automated Web page on which a virtual teacher explains the effect of an increase in T on P

The generated Web page on which a virtual teacher explains the effect of an increase in T on P is shown in Figure 8. The key part of the problem is mathematical function shifts. On the page shown in Figure 8, the three graphs are displayed when the student clicks on the "graph" button. Students can interact with the 3D graph by moving their viewpoints. The two contour lines correspond to the conditions $T=0$ and $T=5$ on the function $Qs=Qs(P, T)$. The students can move his/her viewpoints interactively to map the contour lines to a 2D plane of Qs-P. Visual and interactive explanations of the changed value effect help students understand the relationships visually. To explain the effect of the other variable, mathematical differentiation and partial differentiation are useful. Because our system can invoke Maple, the system can calculate the difference values both by symbols and concrete values. In the generated animation page, the virtual teacher explains how to spread the effect of the starting variable (T) to the unknown variable (P), using the concrete differential values (See Figure 9).

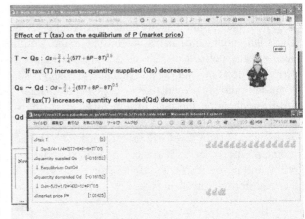

Fig. 9. The generated animation page that illustrates how to spread the effect of the starting variable to the unknown variable

4.2 Japanese Solution Method of Crane-Turtle Problems

The crane-turtle method is an early Japanese calculus method focusing on the difference between the numbers of legs possessed by each creature: a crane has two legs and a turtle has four. The given data are *the total number of given cranes and turtles* and *the total number of legs of the given cranes and turtles*. The unknown variable is *the number of turtles* or *the number of cranes*. There are two solution methods for this kind of problems: (1) this early Japanese method, and (2) the simultaneous equation method. The former method supposes firstly that all creatures are cranes if the unknown variable is the number of turtles. It then calculates the difference of the total number of crane legs and the given number of legs. Lastly, it divides the difference by two. This two is the difference of the number of legs between a turtle and a crane. On the other hand, in the latter (2) normal simultaneous equation methods, the following equation is set up where "*x*" represents the number of turtles:

$4*x + 2*(\ [the\ total\ number\ of\ creatures]\ -x) = [the\ given\ number\ of\ total\ legs].$

We generate the learning materials for crane-turtle problems by these two solution methods. Figure 10 shows the learning materials by the early Japanese calculus method of the problem. It is easier to solve the problem using this early Japanese method than by using simultaneous equation methods. The defined concepts in the Japanese method are (1) the number of legs if all are cranes ('*A*'), (2) the difference of the number of legs between a turtle and a crane ('*d*'). The following given data are also defined as concepts: (3) the number of legs a crane /turtle has (2 or 4), (4) the total number of given cranes and turtles ('*H*'), and (5) the total number of legs of the given cranes and turtles ('*L*'). The value of variable '*A*' is calculated by $A=2*H$.

As shown here, our proposed courseware definition method can also be applied to non-simultaneous equation-based solution processes, such as early Asian

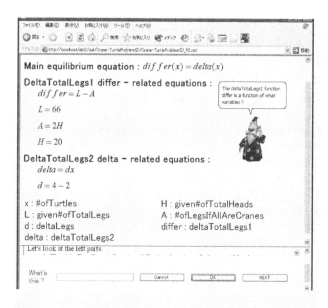

Fig. 10. The generated Web page for the crane-turtle problem by the Japanese early method

calculus methods as far as the problem is not a proof type math problem. Various interesting solution plans other than sets of simultaneous equations can be used to solve a mathematical word problem. We would like to also implement such a traditional Japanese solution plan in our e-Math system.

We showed that our e-Math Interaction Agent can generate learning materials for the three kinds of problems that are a national income determination problem, a supply and demand problem, and an early Japanese solution method of crane-turtle problems with the same solution/guidance plan of the 'equilibrium' problem type. As the examples show, this solution plan/guidance plan is applicable to many types of simultaneous equation problems.

5 Related Work

In the section, we discuss work related to mathematical documentation, in particular, OMDoc and OpenMath, in order to clarify the difference between the research goal of this work and our own. OpenMath is a standard for representing mathematical objects with their semantics, allowing the exchange of these objects between computer programs, storage in databases, or publication on the Web[6, 7]. OpenMath has a strong relationship to the MathML recommendation from the Worldwide Web Consortium[1]. MathML deals principally with the presentation of mathematical objects, while OpenMath is solely concerned with their semantic meaning or content. Although MathML facilities for dealing with content are somewhat limited, they allow semantic information encoded in OpenMath to be embedded inside a MathML structure. Thus, the two technologies may be seen as very complementary[6]. Content Dictionaries (CDs) in OpenMath are used to assign informal and formal semantics to all symbols used in OpenMath objects. They define the symbols used to represent concepts arising in a particular area of mathematics. For example, differentiation and integration symbols are contributed as the CD symbols, as follows (See http://www.openmath.org/cocoon/openmath/cdfiles2/cd/):

- nthdiff: the nth-iterated ordinary differentiation of a unary function.
- partialdiff: partial differentiation of a function of more than one variable.
- int: integration of unary functions.
- defint: definite integration of unary functions.

As the above CD examples show, CDs provide definitions of mathematical formulas, not mathematical procedures (algorithms). As Kohlhase described, CDs are largely informal because the OpenMath framework offers no support for ensuring their consistency, conciseness, or manipulation[9]. In addition, OpenMath has no means of structuring the content of a mathematical document by dividing it into logical units, such as "definition," "theorem," and "proof"[10].

OMDoc is an extension of the OpenMath and MathML standards. It extends these formats using markup for the document and theory levels of mathematical documents so that the document author can specify them and the consumer (an OMDoc reader or a mathematical software system) can take advantage of them[11]. For example, OMDoc offers the following elements:

- Metadata: in Dublin Core and other formats, such as RDF.
- Statements: namely, definitions, theorems, axioms, examples, et cetera.
- Proofs: structured from hypotheses, conclusions, methods et cetera.

In terms of education systems, the interesting OMDoc modules are as follows:

- Presentation: OMDoc allows the user to specify notations for content mathematical objects using XSLT.
- Applet: programs that can be executed in some way in a web browser during manipulation. The applet is called an "omlet" in OMDoc.
- Exercise/Quiz: to make OMDoc a viable format for educational and course materials.

As shown here, one extension of OMDoc is used to transform an OMDoc document into interactive courseware. These extensions have been developed by certain projects. MBASE is an open mathematical knowledge base founded on OMDoc[12, 13]. ActiveMath, which is a web-based learning system, also uses OMDoc format and can dynamically generate interactive mathematical courseware[14, 15]. However, OMDoc elements, such as "theorem," "example" and "proof" correspond to grammatical objects, not content objects.

Our target is metadata even higher than the targets of OMDoc. Our defined concept expresses semantics for the given word problem. For example, the given number of the total creatures is defined as a concept in the crane-turtle problem. Therefore we can say that our defined concepts correspond to semantics in a still higher application layer.

6 Conclusions

In this paper, we have explained our developed automatic courseware generation system named e-Math Interaction Agent, especially its functions of creating learning materials to teach simultaneous equations. We showed that our e-Math Interaction Agent can successfully generate learning materials for the following kinds of simultaneous equation solving problems with the same solution/guidance plan: they are (1) national income determination problems, (2) supply and demand problems, and (3) an early Japanese solution method of crane-turtle problems. As the examples show, this solution plan and the guidance plan are applicable to many types of simultaneous equation problems and are helpful for mathematical teachers to develop their learning materials.

Acknowledgements

This research is supported in part by the Japanese Ministry of Education, Science, Sports, and Culture under Grant-in-Aid for Scientific Research (C) (2)15606014.

References

1. XML: http://www.w3c.org/TR/xmlschema-2/.
2. Yukari Shirota: "Design of Automation Systems for Web Based Courseware using XML and XSLT," Proc. of Workshop on Databases in Networked Information Systems: 4th International Workshop, DNIS 2005, Springer Lecture Notes in Computer Science (3433), University of Aizu, Japan, March 28 - 30, 2005, pp. 186-203.
3. Yukari Shirota: "Knowledge-Based Automation of Web-Based Learning Materials Using Semantic Web Technologies," Proc. of The Second International Conference on Creating, Connecting and Collaborating through Computing (C5), Kyoto, Japan, January 29-30, 2004, pp.26-33.
4. Yukari Shirota: "A Semantic Explanation and Symbolic Computation Approach for Designing Mathematical Courseware," Proc. of The Third International Conference on Creating, Connecting and Collaborating through Computing (C5), Kyoto, Japan, January 28-29, 2005, pp.158-165.
5. MapleSoft: Maple, http://www.maplesoft.com/.
6. The OpenMath Society: The OpenMath website at http://www.openmath.org/cocoon/ openmath/ overview/index.html.
7. The OpenMath Society:"The OpenMath Standard," 2004 at http://www.openmath.org/cocoon/ openmath//standard/om20/index.html.
8. Worldwide Web Consortium: "W3C Math Home" at http://www.w3.org/Math/.
9. Michael Kohlhase: "OMDoc: an infrastructure for OpenMath content dictionary information," ACM SIGSAM Bulletin, Vol. 34, No. 2, June 2000, pp. 43-48.
10. Erica Melis, Jochen Büdenbender, Georgi Goguadze, Paul Libbrecht, and Carsten Ullrich: "Semantics for Web-Based Mathematical Education Systems," Proc. of the WWW2002 International Workshop on the Semantic Web, Hawaii, May 7, 2002.
11. OMDoc: http://www.mathweb.org/omdoc/.
12. The MBase Mathematical Knowledge Base: http://www.mathweb.org/mbase/.
13. Michael Kohlhase and Andreas Franke: "MBase: Representing Knowledge and Context for the Integration of Mathematical Software Systems," Journal of Symbolic Computation Vol.23, No.4, 2001, pp. 365 - 402.
14. ActiveMath: http://www.activemath.org/.
15. The ActiveMath group: Erica Melis, Jochen Büdenbender, George Goguadze, Paul Libbrecht and Carsten Ullrich: "Knowledge Representation and Management in ActiveMath," Annals of Mathematics and Artificial Intelligence , Vol.38, No.1□3, 2003, pp.47-64.

Intercultural and Multilingual E-Learning to Bridge the Digital Divide

Elena Verdú[1], María Jesús Verdú[2], Luisa M. Regueras[2], and Juan Pablo de Castro[2]

[1] CEDETEL, Parque Tecnológico de Boecillo,
47151 Valladolid, Spain
everdu@cedetel.es
[2] University of Valladolid, ETSI Telecomunicación, Camino del Cementerio s/n,
47011 Valladolid, Spain
{marver, luireg, jpdecastro}@tel.uva.es

Abstract. The Internet is changing the economy, the society and the culture. But an inequality in access to information exits and is creating an information digital divide. This article describes the ODISEAME project as an effort to extend the use of the Internet to several very different countries of the Euro-Mediterranean area. One of the main achievements of the project is to share and transfer technology and knowledge, with the aim of reducing the existing barriers for digital inclusion. ODISEAME is an intercultural and multilingual project, which is focused on the application of Information and Communication Technologies to the learning process in the context of University Education. The article firstly examines the barriers of digital inclusion: cost of infrastructure and lack of contents in the mother tongue. It then describes the ODISEAME project and the e-learning experiences, before discussing how the project promotes digital inclusion.

1 Introduction

The Information Society is a rapidly changing social environment. On the one hand, Information and Communication Technologies (ICTs) have changed the way people work, live and learn. On the other hand, globalization of the economy reflects this change: markets expand as fast as barriers disappear and, consequently, competition at all levels and within all fields is continuously increasing. In this changing environment, tele-learning is an appealing and ideal solution to new training needs.

Besides, the dialogue among cultures and the exchange of scientific and technological knowledge is an essential factor in bringing people closer. ICTs can play an important role in this process and promote the collaboration among institutions in different countries, developing the dissemination of new technologies and contributing to improved integration of all countries into the Information Society environment.

In the Euro-Mediterranean area several countries (countries from the European Union and MEDA countries[1]) are making an effort in order to get that dialogue, partici-

---

[1] MEDA countries are those which belong to the Mediterranean coast and are not member states of the European Union: Algeria, Egypt, Israel, Jordan, Lebanon, Morocco, Syria, Palestine, Tunisia and Turkey.

S. Shimojo et al. (Eds.): HSI 2005, LNCS 3597, pp. 260–269, 2005.

pating in pilot projects of application of ICTs in priority sectors like education. ODISEAME (Open Distance Inter-university Synergies between Europe, Africa and Middle East) is an interdisciplinary, intercultural and multilingual project, which is focused on the application of ICTs to the learning process in the context of University Education.

This article describes the ODISEAME project as an effort to extend the use of the Internet, and technologies, services and applications related to it, to several very different countries. One of the main achievements of the project is to share and transfer technology and knowledge, with the aim of reducing the existing barriers for digital inclusion.

The article firstly examines the barriers of digital inclusion. It then describes the ODISEAME project and the e-learning experiences, before discussing how the project promotes digital inclusion.

2 Digital Inclusion

One of the main objectives of the European Union (EU) and other policy organizations is the digital inclusion or not exclusion of neither groups nor countries in the use of new technologies. Digital inclusion could probably prevent further social exclusion [1], which is owing to unemployment, low income, low educational attainment or lack of access to essential services.

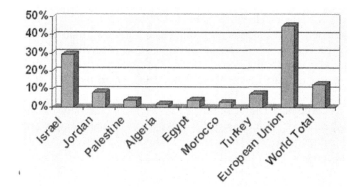

Fig. 1. Internet penetration in MEDA countries vs. European Union countries: percentage over the total population in December 2004. Source: own elaboration with Internet World Stats data(http://www.internetworldstats.com)

It is clear that digital divide exists between citizens of the EU Member States and those of most MEDA countries. MEDA countries are clearly under-equipped compared to their neighbors in the European Union and their network infrastructure is inadequate, although there is an exception in Israel. Computers are a rare resource in most settings and the costs of an adequate system for the Internet access are out of the purchasing power of the individuals. As a consequence, the percentage of population connected to the Internet in these countries is much lower than in Europe as it is shown in Fig. 1. However, although the Internet penetration is low, fortunately the use from 2000 to 2004 in those countries has increased substantially; for example, Algeria and Morocco have had a growth in the use of 900 percent and 700 percent respectively.

Besides, while the Internet penetration continues growing, certain segments of the population are being left behind: the disabled, women and those living in rural areas [1].

When explaining the low Internet penetration and the lack of digital inclusion in big populations like the Arab world, there are two reasons that seem to be the most important ones [2] [3]:

- High cost of infrastructure (hardware and Internet access).
- Few or lack of contents and web sites in the mother tongue.

2.1 The Economical and Technological Barrier

The MEDA region, as a whole, has made progress in the access to and use of ICTs. However, the infrastructure to access the Internet is still inadequate. With a number of telephones per inhabitant below 10 percent in most countries [3], the MEDA countries are clearly under-equipped. The need for investment has become even more critical by the fact that, in many cases, ageing equipment must be replaced.

Rapid growth in mobile phones has compensated for the relative underequipment in fixed lines but has, at the same time, slowed the establishment of the infrastructure needed for the Internet [3]. Internet access is related to the availability and cost of fixed phone lines, since most technologies for accessing the Internet are based on the PSTN (Public Switched Telephone Network). Wireless technologies are more expensive, and the entry barrier is therefore higher. In addition to the cost of communications and of purchasing a computer, subscribing to a service provider is the main impediment today. So, the Internet is beyond the financial means of an important part of the population in most of the MEDA countries where the GDP (Gross Domestic Product) per capita is less than $ 4,500.

But the technological and economical barrier is not the only drawback for these countries. While Gulf State countries possess the financial strength and state-of-the-art information technologies, the number of Internet users is growing more slowly than in some countries with far less economic capacities [3] [4].

2.2 The Language Barrier in the Internet

One of the most obvious obstacles to the universal access to the Internet in the Arab world is the fact that the Internet has been an English-dominated medium. Many of the MEDA countries share a common language, Arabic. As it is shown in Fig. 2, although Arabic is one of the most widely spoken languages in the world, only two per cent of the Arabic-speaking population is connected to the Internet. The dominance of the English language has hindered the penetration of the Internet into schools and homes, which reinforces the opinion that it is not designed by or for Arabic-speaking cultures, whereas, from a technical standpoint, the use of Arabic presents no major impediment.

Within that 2 % of Arabic users that are on-line, most of them are young, highly educated and have a good command of English [5].

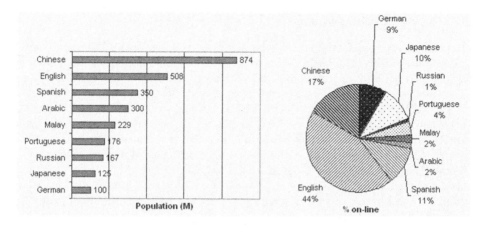

Fig. 2. Internet penetration by languages (native speakers), September 2004. Source: own elaboration with Global Reach data (http://www.global-reach.biz)

Likewise, many Asian countries are at a disadvantage in the use of the Internet and the access to western websites, because of the different characters of their writing. Moreover the command of English is also an unfinished business there [6]. This gap means a worse penetration of Internet services like e-learning, strongly based on the contents. However, the language is not an obstacle when using communication services like videoconference, chat or e-mail, which are extensively used and growing. This is the reason why some researchers think that connectivity to the Internet does not depend on proficiency in English, because these services are language independent [7] [8].

However, when thinking about contents, with few web-pages in Arabic and more than 80 % in English, the command of this language seems fundamental to increase the Internet use rates in these countries. The most favourable research estimate that the Arab world will take at least one decade to access advantages of ICTs in a widespread way [2].

The ODISEAME project is one of the attempts to improve that situation, through multilingual e-learning experiences.

3   ODISEAME: An E-Learning Project

The popularity of the World Wide Web and its development has enabled the creation and implementation of Web-based learning. The evolving new generation of education environment leads to a revolution in traditional teaching methods.

E-learning can be a priority for some regions. For example, the region of Castilla y León, in Spain, is a rural, vast and sparsely populated region, with a lot of small towns and villages. So, the sparse population lives far from traditional education centres. Some students decide to change residence and others go every day to another town to attend the courses. Education independent from space is critical in this case and that independence can be provided by e-learning.

3.1 Objectives and Description

The ODISEAME project (http://www.odiseame.org) is funded by the European Union (EUMEDIS initiative). Its main goal is to carry out several multilingual and multidisciplinary virtual learning experiences in an efficient way, using a web-based multilingual virtual space for collaborative learning focused on higher education.

The project is coordinated by CEDETEL (Centro para el Desarrollo de las Telecomunicaciones de Castilla y León) and other 14 institutions from Europe and MEDA countries are involved as partners: University of Salamanca (Spain), University of Granada (Spain), Fachhochschule für Technik und Wirtschaft (Germany), Islamic University of Gaza (Palestinian Authority), University of Jordan (Jordan), Institut Supérieur de Gestion et de Planification (Algeria), University of Malta (Malta), Anadolu University (Turkey), University of Cyprus (Cyprus), Institute Agronomique et Vétérinaire Hassan II (Morocco), Hebrew University of Jerusalem (Israel), Jordan University of Science and Technology (Jordan), Frederick Institute of Technology (Cyprus) and University of Valladolid (Spain).

The base of this project is an interdisciplinary research on the application of the ICTs to the different aspects of the learning process, including the delivery of contents, its creation, and the interaction of students and teachers. This has been a shared research with the involvement of students, teachers, contents providers, service providers, pedagogues, technicians, etc. Other aspects that have been present in the whole project are the intercultural and multilingual ones, especially in the virtual learning experiences that are being shared by students and teachers from the different countries of the partner institutions.

The project started in September of 2002 and it will finish in December of 2005. It started with the analysis of the current situation of the participants, taking into account their available network infrastructure as well as general aspects of the participating institutions. This analysis was the base for a number of recommendations about the development of the distance learning experiences, the type of communication (synchronous or asynchronous) and the kind of contents (text, voice, image, video, etc) to be exchanged [9]. The analysis was followed by the design and implementation of a multilingual virtual learning space and the design of several training modules.

3.2 The E-Learning Platform

The contents of the training modules have been integrated into a collaborative e-learning space. The platform focuses on providing university teachers with the flexibility they need to organize the learning process in the more adequate way for them. As a consequence, both synchronous and asynchronous communications are possible. Asynchronous communication provides freedom from the constraints of time and place and it involves more reflective thinking [10]. The synchronous contact when provided by videoconference provides a human face and dimension to the distance communication, which is so important in an educational environment [11].

Thereby, a tool called *Conference Centre* is available; teachers can offer live and recorded conferences. An *area for exchange of documents* is also provided as well as a *Content Generator* that enables the teacher to generate his own didactic units.

Finally, tools for *Assessment and Tracking* of the student allow teachers to create assessment and self-assessment tests.

3.3 Beta-Test Training

At the end of the first year of the project each partner had to select the courses for the virtual learning experiences and design them taking as a basis the analysis of situation previously done. In the particular case of the University of Valladolid the courses selected were the following: "TCP/IP", "Internetworking Devices", "IPv6 Protocol" and "E-Spanish Interactive". For each course we initially gave a general description with objectives, timing, assessment, language, etc. and later a more detailed description with contents, format, development and so on would also be done. It is important to point out that all this process was accomplished taking always into account the particular distance learning context instead the traditional one, since the most important point when designing any learning process is to identify students' needs and the focus should be always on the learner. All the training modules were evaluated by an interdisciplinary group of experts so that the final versions were done based on their changes and suggestions.

The training modules were implemented and integrated in the virtual learning space before some beta-test training experiences. The beta-test training experiences aimed at evaluating the courses implemented and improving them according to the changes suggested by teachers and students who participated in them. A questionnaire was used in order to pick up the suggestions and evaluation results. For each course, at least two students and two teachers took part in the beta-test experiences, checked the electronic contents and filled in the questionnaire. The most important conclusions for the courses of the University of Valladolid drawn from the above evaluation were:

– The courses are well structured and designed. So, we can conclude that the methodology used is suitable for this kind of learning.
– Users have valued the interactivity as one of the most positive points.
– It is useful to divide the self-assessment tests in several difficulty levels.
– The combination of different media and methods has turned out to be a suitable way to stimulate students.
– Real-time reviews are very useful for students.
– Students have been more critical regarding the quality of contents than teachers. It is important to point that problems with the educational material can be overcome only by enhancing student-tutor communication and by improving communication means and frequency of communication [12].

Once the collaborative virtual learning space and the training modules are ready, several pilot experiences should take place within ODISEAME. These pilot experiences would consist of a number of intercultural virtual learning experiences.

4 Intercultural and Multilingual Learning Experiences

The development and evaluation of the learning experiences is taking place during 2005. The learning experiences, in English and in the mother tongue of the partners, count on the participation of students and teachers from more than one partner institution.

In order to evaluate these experiences, the quality of the e-learning service is being monitored and, at the end, the participants will fill in a questionnaire to measure their satisfaction with the service as well as with the experience in general. In this study, we are taking into account both pedagogical and technical aspects. The objective of these mixed training experiences is not only to learn how to teach or how to learn in a virtual space, or to acquire some new knowledge, but also to live an intercultural and multilingual experience with a view that will help to establish stronger ties among the partner institutions in the format of teachers and students exchanges, shared research projects, etc.

5   Benefits and Results

The most interesting results of the ODISEAME project could be summarized as follows:

- A multilingual virtual learning space.
- Several higher education courses for virtual learning.
- A handbook about how to design and implement virtual learning experiences.
- A book describing the experience accumulated during the intercultural tele-learning experiences.
- A group of teachers and students all over Europe and the Mediterranean border with the ability to successfully carry out intercultural virtual learning experiences.
- A demo effect for the rest of students and teachers of the partner institutions who do not take part in the virtual learning experiences.

Next, the most important benefits in order to bridge the digital divide are going to be discussed.

5.1   Flexibility of E-Learning

The main strength of virtual learning is flexibility, since it makes the learning process independent from space and time. Flexibility provides a whole range of options. By not requiring the student to be physically present at the same location and during the same time as the instructor, virtual learning takes advantage of the information age and overcome the obstacles posed by societal changes.

One example of this flexibility, related to physical distance problems, is the case of the Islamic University of Gaza which is offering the developed courses at its three campuses synchronously through the e-learning platform. This allows students to get lectures within their areas without having to travel to the main campus.

Another example of the importance and use of e-learning within the University community in order to provide universal access to University degree education has been the one of Cyprus. In Cyprus there are 4 major cities (Nicosia, Limassol, Larnaca, and Paphos). All the universities offering accrediting bachelor degrees are located in Nicosia. Two colleges in Limassol offer accredited diplomas. Students in Larnaca can choose to attend schools in Nicosia (45 minutes away by car) without having to rent an apartment in Nicosia. Therefore the cost of living of students from Larnaca is negligible. However, students in Limassol and Paphos have to move to Nicosia and thus their cost of education is higher (around $ 6,000 per year are needed just for rent). Hence, for students from Limassol and Paphos the concept of e-learning could be a great opportunity.

Besides, the project has proved that e-learning is very suitable for people who have not the time to enter full higher education. So, e-learning facilitates the education for a growing heterogeneity of pupils and especially for students who may have been excluded from traditional learning due to different reasons (time, physical distance, cultural or economic barriers, etc). This feature makes virtual learning suitable for a lot of sectors of the society such as people living in rural areas, people with physical disabilities, people lacking time as workers and housewives, etc.

5.2 Transfer of Knowledge and Technology

It is known that some of the barriers of digital inclusion are the different levels of knowledge and technology. ODISEAME project has had a strong component in transfer of knowledge, know-how and technology.

The contents have been designed by interdisciplinary workgroups of different specialists including pedagogues and psychologists, telecommunication and computing engineers, graphical designers and experts on the contents to be delivered. The partners with no previous experience in the design of virtual learning projects have been assisted by the experienced partners, like University of Valladolid, in relation to, for example, adapting contents for the available infrastructure.

The project is also a clear example of an international technology transfer from European Union countries to their MEDA counterparts. Moreover, the technical courses, open to students from all the countries, and the use of an e-learning platform, involves a training in ICTs, that can improve the technological level of those countries.

However, an important barrier is that most of the territory of these countries is a desert, and people who live there have no access to computer equipment. Moreover, connection to the Internet in these regions is practically impossible or shows great difficulties. For example, it is being difficult for veterinary practitioners in remote areas to attend the courses of the Institute Agronomique et Vétérinaire Hassan II, because they do not have access to the Web is these areas. Some measures have already been taken to overcome these barriers. For example the EUMEDconnect project (http://www.eumedconnect.net/) is being developed to improve the network connection between the European Union and the MEDA countries.

5.3 The International and Multilingual View

Internet is a global means, which demands global software, so internationalization plays more and more a fundamental role in the construction of applications for the network. Besides, some experiences have shown that writing for an international audience improves the usability of a site [13].

One of the main aims of the development of the e-learning platform was that each partner could visualize the courses in their mother tongue. So, a multilingual and multi-skin platform has been developed. Internationalization allows users to see the tool taking into account their preferences (language and appearance). The platform is currently available in the following languages: Arabic, English, French, German, Greek, Spanish and Turkish, and it will shortly be also available in Hebrew. As this platform has been designed taking into account its multilingual nature as essential from the beginning, it is easily adaptable to other languages.

As it has been said, the courses should be imparted in English and in the mother tongue of the partners. However, in a number of partner institutions, such as the Islamic University of Gaza, the regular courses are given in English and not in the mother tongue. This happens especially with the technical courses, where the terminology, references and bibliography are usually in English. Some other partners have set out the same situation previously, for example, the University of Jordan, whose course is only given in English within its institution, although a translated version into Arabic is also available for this project. Nevertheless, all the non-technical courses (and some technical too) are being imparted in the mother tongue.

6 Conclusions and Outlook

This paper has presented the ODISEAME project as an effort to combat the low Internet penetration in some MEDA countries. The high cost of infrastructure (hardware and Internet access) and lack of contents in the mother tongue seem to be important points for digital inclusion in big populations like the Arab world.

An intercultural and multilingual e-learning platform based on Web has been successfully used for delivering higher-education courses with students and teachers from countries as diverse as Cyprus, Egypt, Israel, Germany or Spain.

It has been shown that the ODISEAME is contributing to the development attempts of Mediterranean countries and to the integration process of MEDA countries with the European Union and is providing important benefits in order to bridge the digital divide.

It is expected that the final evaluation of the whole project will provide interesting knowledge and experience to all the participants. The objective of these mixed training experiences is not only to acquire some new knowledge, new technologies or skills in e-learning, but also to live an intercultural experience and, as a consequence, become more tolerant and establish ties among the different countries and cultures.

References

1. Alakeson, V., Aldrich, T., Goodman, J., Jorgensen, B., Millar, P.: Social Responsibility in the Information Society. Digital Europe Final Project Report. European Commission (2003)
2. Cáceres, S.: Los Países Árabes y la Sociedad de la Información. Fundación Auna. Madrid (2003)
3. Aubert, J., Reiffers, J.: Knowledge Economies in the Middle East and North Africa. The World Bank. Washington, DC (2003)
4. Abbi, R.: Internet in the Arab World. UNESCO Observatory of the Information Society (2002)

5. Al Rostamani, N.: Arabs lag in Internet use. Gulf News on-line edition (2003, October 23)
6. Babot, I.: Elearning en el Mundo: Realidad Actual. SEDIC (2003, November 27)
7. Maceviciute, E.: Multilingual Virtual World: Languages on the Internet. Razón y palabra. 42 (2004)
8. Xiaoming, H., Kay, C.S.: Factors affecting Internet development: an Asian survey. First Monday. 9 (2). USA (2004)
9. Verdú, M.J., Regueras, L.M., de Castro, J.P., Verdú, E.: ODISEAME Project: an Approach to a Web-based Multilingual and Collaborative Learning. In Cantoni, L., McLoughlin C. (eds.): Proceedings of ED-MEDIA 2004, World Conference on Educational Multimedia, Hypermedia & Telecommunications. AACE. USA (2004) 4857-4862
10. Pulkkinen, J.: Pedagogical foundations of open learning environments. In Selinger, M., Pearson, J. (eds.): Telematics in Education: Trends and Issues. Elsevier Science. The Netherlands (1999) 76-87
11. Wright, N., Cordeaux, C.: Desktop video-conferencing: Telematic learning, In Selinger, M., Pearson, J. (eds.): Telematics in Education: Trends and Issues. Elsevier Science. The Netherlands (1999) 167-177
12. Pierrakeas, C., Xenos, M., Pintelas, P.: Evaluating and Improving Educational Material and Tutoring Aspects of Distance Learning Systems. Studies in Educational Evaluation. 29 (2003) 335-349
13. Kjell, B., Gailer, H.: Enhancing Usability by International Students of a Distance Learning Web Site. In Proceedings of International Symposium on Technology and Society (ISTAS). IEEE (2004) 104-106

SMIL-Based eLearning Wrapper for Incorporating Computer Games on Personalized Multimedia Course Materials

Elvis Wai Chung Leung[1], Frederick W.B. Li[2], Qing Li[1], and Rynson W.H. Lau[1]

[1] City University of Hong Kong
{iteleung, itqli, itrlau}@cityu.edu.hk
[2] The Hong Kong Polytechnic University
csbor@comp.polyu.edu.hk

Abstract. A dramatic increase in the development of technology-based teaching and learning has been witnessed in the past decade. Many universities and corporations have started to rethink the design and implementation of learning systems. In particular, these systems do not have powerful multimedia retrieval features for responding to student enquiries based on individual students' background and interests. In this paper, we present a SMIL-based approach to manage text, graphics, audios, and videos for incorporating computer games on personalized media-based course materials to satisfy the needs of individual students. In particular, we incorporate computer games in the personalized course materials so as to further promote learning interest, motivate thinking, and retain students learning on the Internet. The facilities and capabilities of user profiles, XML, game engine, and SMIL are incorporated and utilized in a prototype system that has been presented by RealOne on the PC platform.

1 Introduction

Life-long learning is encouraged to enhance the personal abilities to cope with the new challenges. To meet with the increasing trend of learning demand, a dramatic increase in the development of technology-based teaching and learning has been witnessed in the past decade. Many universities and corporations have started to rethink the design and implementation of learning systems [10, 12].

Among the multimedia-based projects for eLearning, *Classroom 2000* [1] is designed to automate the authoring of multimedia documents from live events. The researchers have outfitted a classroom at Georgia Institute of Technology with electronic whiteboards, cameras, and other data collection devices that collect data during the lecture, and combined these facilities to create a multimedia document to describe the class activities. *Cornell Lecture Browser* from Cornell University [2] captures a structured environment (a university lecture). It automatically produces a document that contains synchronized and edited audios, videos, images and text, so as to synchronize the video footage in the live classroom with pre-recorded slides used in the class. *MANIC,* from University of Massachusetts [3], discusses the ways of effectively utilizing WWW-based, stored materials and presentation paradigms. It proposes that students should be given the opportunity to browse the materials, stopping and starting the audio at their own pace.

S. Shimojo et al. (Eds.): HSI 2005, LNCS 3597, pp. 270–281, 2005.

Although online course materials have many advantages over traditional textbooks and lecture notes, they still have a number of generic deficiencies as follows:

- Distribution of media-based course materials on the Internet is comparatively slow.
- Development of course materials does not cater for individual student's needs.
- Pre-programming for combination of text and multimedia in a presentation is required.

Currently, a high student dropout rate and low satisfaction with the learning processes remain to be the drawbacks. Not surprisingly, failing to consider students' attributes and instructional strategies seems to cause ineffectiveness even with the technologically advanced e-Learning system being developed. To make eLearning more attractive and retain students learning on the Internet, the introduction and incorporation of computer games is one possible solution. Research in education and psychology has shown that play is an important part of the human social, psychological and mental development cycle as well as a powerful mediator for learning throughout a person's life [15, 16]. Individual gaming can promote thinking, reflecting, and creativity. Collaborative gaming allows players to interact, have sense of belonging, and become part of a group that shares similar concerns, interests and goals [15]. In response to the above-mentioned issues in the technology-based learning, we have engaged in developing a *Personalized eLearning System* (**Peels**) over the last few years [4, 6].

1.1 Paper Objective and Organization

To easily manage, store and retrieve course materials and generate media-based course materials that are interoperable, we propose an innovative mechanism that incorporates *user profile, dynamic conceptual network, game engine,* and *SMIL-based wrapper* to manipulate course materials. Through designing the conceptual framework and algorithms, we aim to address the following main topic in this paper: *How to effectively distribute the personalized multimedia course materials incorporating games to serve individual student needs and interests?*

The rest of this paper is organized as follows. Section 2 reviews relevant work to this research. Section 3 presents in detail the specific features of the proposed framework and algorithms. Finally, Section 4 concludes this paper and makes suggestions for further research.

2 Background of Research

To address the problem of slow access to the online course materials on the Internet, *decentralizing approach for the multimedia application* [13, 14] is a possible solution. In particular, the overall course materials management in Peels is centrally controlled and the course materials (e.g., text, graphics, audios, and videos) are distributed directly to individual students on demand [5, 11]. To advocate the concept of distributed course materials, standardized methodologies and languages for annotation of hypermedia information are required. The following are such technologies employed by Peels.

XML (Extensible Markup Language) is designed for content publishing on the Internet. The ambition of XML provides some advantages that are not available in HTML, such as DTD (Document Type Definition). XML is adopted for storing the course materials in the server-side of our proposed Peels. To make it successful, standardization for course materials development becomes a critical factor.

In order to encourage the standardization and interoperating course materials, a common standard is required in building the eLearning course materials. One possibility is the IEEE's Standard for Learning Object Metadata (LOM) [7] that describes data structures for providing interoperability content. In the course materials development, XML metadata has become the de-facto standard for indexing, defining and searching learning objects and all of the repositories mentioned above use metadata standards developed under LOM.

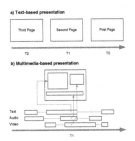

Fig. 1. Presentation layout

Through SMIL (Synchronized Multimedia Integration Language), multimedia data can be played on the Internet in a synchronized manner. One important reason for developing SMIL-based course materials presentation is that the needs for the multimedia spatial layout model are different from those of the text-based documents. As shown in Figure 1(a), the layout of text-based documents (e.g. HTML) is based on one-dimensional text-flow. The transformation from one to two dimensions is typically through scrolling. In Figure 1(b), multimedia spatial layout is inherently two dimensional with little or no transformation from the document structure to the final display space. It helps students to manage the text and multimedia presentation simultaneously and simulates the classroom environment.

In (e-)education, games have become an important tool for learning and teaching. The rationale for using games is that they help create a classroom atmosphere in which students at various levels of ability can collaborate in order to promote interest, enhance critical thinking and decision-making skills, and help remember information [15][17].

3   Media-Based Course Materials Generation Mechanism

Figure 2 shows the overall mechanism for course materials generation. The major components include the *Dynamic Conceptual Network* (DCN), *Analytic Hierarchy Process* (AHP), *Game Engine*, and *SMIL Wrapper*.

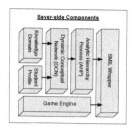

Fig. 2. Overall mechanism for course materials generation

Basically, the Dynamic Conceptual Network (DCN) [4] is to manage course materials by a hierarchical tree and to generate the personalized course materials through some pre-defined rules and mechanism. As for *Knowledge Domain*, it is the primary repository for all course materials and multimedia lessons. The relevant course materials are extracted from the Knowledge Domain in providing a suitable lesson to the students. The retrieval operation is based on the index server to locate the expected multimedia lessons/course materials for a given lesson.

To provide the best course materials to individual student, Analytic Hierarchy Process (AHP) [9] is used as the selection mechanism based on *student profiles*, which are the primary storage for all student-specific information such as study history, personal information, and study status. They provide relevant information for determining the related concepts for a lesson. Normally, a user profile can provide the latest student's information on demand.

To implement the interactive learning environment, the media-based course materials and selected computer game(s) are distributed by the SMIL wrapper. The functions of the SMIL wrapper are to manage all the provided course materials from AHP [9], and to identify the most suitable SMIL presentation template for generating the multimedia presentation as well as associated game(s) to individual students. The detailed mechanisms for each component are discussed next.

3.1 Dynamic Conceptual Network

Definition: The Dynamic Conceptual Network (DCN) is a *hierarchical tree* to develop *dependent-relationships* among *learning concepts*. Each learning concept is stored as a *concept node* (Figure 3(a)) of the dynamic conceptual network.

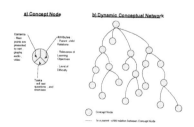

Fig. 3. Dynamic conceptual network

As depicted in Figure 3(b), the DCN is composed of concept nodes. Each concept node has a unique identity for easy reference. As shown in Figure 3(a), a concept node includes *contents, tasks, and attributes*. The contents are represented by text, graphs, audios, and videos. Tasks include self-test questions and exercises. In order to provide facilities for building up the relationships among the concept nodes, three attributes are defined in each concept node: *parent-child relations, relevance of learning objectives*, and *level of difficulty*. The semantics of each attribute are explained as follows.

- Parent-child Relations. These inter-concept links are for building up the dynamic conceptual network. Each relation contains a *parent link* and *child link,* which refer to the identities of the other concept nodes.
- Relevance of Learning Objectives. This is the information for identifying the relevant concepts of a particular learning objective.
- Level of Difficulty. As a means to serve the concept of personalization, this attribute is a parameter to determine whether the course materials are suitable for a targeted student group.

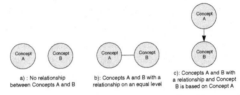

Fig. 4. Inter-concept-node relationships

Based on the above attributes, we now explain the process of concept node mapping for generation of the DCN. Figure 4 shows three possible scenarios among the concept nodes, i.e., no relationship between concepts, concepts A and B have a relationship on an equal level (level of difficulty), and concepts A and B have a relationship and concept B is based on concept A. A rule-based mechanism [8] is employed for the concept node mapping according to the following rules.

- **Rule I:** // Figure 4a shows that no relation exists between concepts A and B.
    IF <no equal of parent-child attributes for the concept nodes A and B>
        THEN <No relation between A and B>
- **Rule II:** // Figure 4b shows that concepts A and B are of a relationship on an equal level.
    IF <the parent links of concepts A and B in their parent-child attributes are of the same object reference>
        THEN <A and B are of the relation on an equal level>
- **Rule III:** // Figure 4c shows that concepts A and B are of relationship and concept B is based on concept A.
    IF <the parent link of concept node B is of the same object reference as that of concept node A's child link >
        THEN <A and B are of the parent-child relation; concept node A is the parent and concept node B is the child>

Based on these mechanisms, the course materials can be built up by a hierarchical framework for manipulation. To implement the DCN, XML is adopted to construct the course materials. The detailed course materials development has been explained in [4]. The determination of the best-fit materials for a particular student through AHP will be explained in the following section.

3.2 Analytic Hierarchy Process

The Analytic Hierarchy Process (AHP), developed at the Wharton School of Business by Thomas Saaty [9], allows decision makers to model a complex problem in a hierarchical structure showing the relationships of the goal, objectives (criteria), sub-objectives, and alternatives. AHP is a decision-making method that helps find the candidate out of a set of alternatives to best satisfy a set of criteria. The criteria may be divided into sub-criteria and so on, thus forming a hierarchical criteria tree. Basically, the first step of AHP is to define the objective of the task and then select some criteria to judge the alternatives for achieving the objective.

For illustration, we assume that *the objective is to identify the best course materials for student A in a particular subject.* The selected criteria to judge the alternatives (course materials) include related subject knowledge, current study workload, and learning initiative. This information can be extracted from the individual student profiles for evaluation [6]. The alternatives contain Course Materials A (CMA), Course Materials B (CMB), and Course Materials C (CMC). These course materials are stored in XML files through the DCN.

CMA includes some revisions for the past learning concepts and additional examples / illustrations to explain the new learning concept. Meanwhile, the provided number of new learning concepts is less than the standard course materials (e.g., CMC) in order to fit for a student who needs more assistance. CMB includes some additional advanced topics and challenging exercises to cater for a student with good learning ability. CMC is a standard course material which is suitable for the middle-level ability students. According to the profile of a student (say, student Tom) and Saaty's scale of relative importance table (Table 1), the criteria matrix and alternative matrix are calculated, as shown in Tables 2 and 3, for judging the alternatives.

Table 1. Saaty's scale of relative importance [9]

Comparative Importance	Definition	Explanation
1	Equally important	Two decision elements (e.g., indicators) equally influence the parent decision element.
3	Moderately more important	One decision element is moderately more influential than the other.
5	Strongly more important	One decision element has stronger influence than the other.
7	Very strongly more important	One decision element has significantly more influence over the other.
9	Extremely more important	The difference between influences of the two decision elements is extremely significant.
2, 4, 6, 8	Intermediate judgment values	Judgment values between equally, moderately, strongly, very strongly, and extremely.

Table 2. Criteria matrix

Selection criteria

	Related subject knowledge	Current study workload	Learning initiative
Related subject knowledge	1	1/3	1/5
Current study workload	3	1	1/4
Learning initiative	5	4	1

Selection criteria after normalization

	Related subject	Current study workload	Learning initiative	Average
Related subject knowledge	0.111	0.063	0.138	0.104
Current study workload	0.333	0.188	0.172	0.231
Learning initiative	0.556	0.750	0.690	0.665

Table 3. Alternative matrix

Related subject knowledge

	CMA	CMB	CMC
CMA	1	1/2	1/3
CMB	2	1	1/2
CMC	3	2	1

Related subject knowledge after normalization

	CMA	CMB	CMC	Average
CMA	0.111	0.095	0.109	0.105
CMB	0.222	0.188	0.137	0.182
CMC	0.333	0.375	0.690	0.466

Current study workload

	CMA	CMB	CMC
CMA	1	1/3	1/9
CMB	3	1	1/6
CMC	9	6	1

Current study workload after normalization

	CMA	CMB	CMC	Average
CMA	0.111	0.045	0.157	0.104
CMB	0.333	0.188	0.196	0.239
CMC	1.000	1.125	0.690	0.938

Learning initiative

	CMA	CMB	CMC
CMA	1	1/2	1/5
CMB	2	1	1/4
CMC	5	4	1

Learning initiative after normalization

	CMA	CMB	CMC	Average
CMA	0.111	0.061	0.138	0.103
CMB	0.222	0.188	0.172	0.194
CMC	0.556	0.750	0.690	0.665

By calculating priority weights for each matrix and linearly combining them, the following priority vector is developed: CMA is 0.363, CMB is 0.69, and CMC is 0.498. Referring to the AHP's definition, the alternative with the highest priority weight is the best choice. In result of this case, course material B is the best choice (for student Tom) with an overall priority weight of 0.69. Thus, course materials B should be provided for Tom. Once identified, the relevant course materials will be transferred to the SMIL wrapper (to be detailed in section 3.4) for composition and distribution to the student.

3.3 Game Engine

To simplify the program and improve real-time performance, existing game systems are primarily based on a full replication approach, i.e., the complete game content is installed at the player's machine prior to game playing. However, as the content of a game is usually large in size (especially if it is 3D), such an approach generally imposes a long download time. In our system, computer games are managed by a game engine and distributed through the SMIL wrapper (ref. Figure 2). Instead of replicating the complete game content in the user machine, we progressively distribute the game content to the user machine according to the location of the user in the game scene. Our approach to game content delivery offers two major advantages. First, it requires a very short startup time. Second, it makes it possible to adjust the visual quality of the game, i.e., the amount of data needed to be transferred, according to the available network bandwidth and local memory of the user machine.

Our game engine manages the game content in two levels, *scene-level* and *model-level*. At scene-level, the game content is organized in a two-dimensional game space, where each game object in the space can be indexed and retrieved by its (x, y) coordinates. In addition, to model the visibility of a game object, we associate each object with an *object scope*, which is a circular region defining how far the object can be seen. At the model-level, different types of game objects, including deformable models, rigid models and texture images, are arranged into a unified data structure to support progressive transmission, i.e., they are arranged to be sent in parts, and the partially received information may be incrementally refined to improve their semantic details or qualities at the user during visualization.

To encode 3D game objects in a progressive format, each object U is represented as a tuple of a *base record* U^0 and an ordered list P of *progressive records* $\{p_1, p_2, ..., p_{|P|}\}$. The base record U^0 contains the minimal and most critical information for a game object U to be visualized by the user. By applying each progressive record p_n, for $1 \leq n \leq |P|$, one by one onto U^0 using the function $\Omega(u, p)$, a series of representations of different levels of detail of U, $\{U^0, U^1, U^2, ..., U^{|U|}\}$, are obtained, where $U^n = \Omega(U^{n-1}, p_n)$. Each U^n in the series improves the quality or the detail of U^{n-1} with a finite amount and the final $U^{|P|}$ in the series is implicitly equivalent to U, i.e., $U = U^{|P|}$. When transmitting a U to a user, we first transmit the base record U^0. Such record may alert the user the existence of the object. Whenever it is necessary, the subsequent progressive records may be transmitted progressively to the user to enhance the quality or detail of the object.

To perform content delivery, the game engine retrieves required game objects from the game database and determines their priorities and details for delivery to users, based on their relevancies to the users. However, due to network latency, when these objects are received by the user, it may already be too late for them to be useful. To resolve such a problem, we have developed a prioritized content delivery method. We model the interest of a user on certain game contents in the game scene by a *viewer scope*. Consequently, a game object is visible to a user only if its object scope overlaps with the viewer scope of the user. A viewer scope consists of three regions, $Q1$, $Q2$ and $Q3$. $Q1$ collects the current visible game objects of the user, while $Q2$ collects the potentially visible game objects of the user. All objects within it are not immediately visible to the user but will become visible if the user simply moves forward or turns its head around in the game scene. $Q3$ collects the least important game objects of the user. Normally, it will take sometime before objects within $Q3$ become visible to the user. Hence, we would prefetch them to the user machine if extra network bandwidth is available. For content delivery, individual queues for regions $Q1$, $Q2$ and $Q3$ are setup for each user. The priorities of the three queues for transmission are: $Q1 > Q2 > Q3$. Objects placed in a lower priority queue may be considered for delivery to the user only if all higher priority queues are empty.

3.4 SMIL Wrapper and Its Implementation

Referring to Figure 2, the SMIL wrapper is to coordinate the game engine, all the data sources (i.e., text, graphics, audios, and videos) from AHP, and the related SMIL-based presentation template to generate the media-based course materials to individual student. As shown in Figure 5, the SMIL wrapper contains 4 layers: *Presentation Layer* (PL), *Generation Layer* (GL), *Spatial Layer* (SL), and *Input Layer* (IL). The abstraction of each layer is as follows.

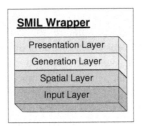

Fig. 5. SMIL Wrapper

Input Layer (IL). It is the input layer that communicates with Analytic Hierarchy Process (AHP) to get the course materials. The related parameters of each course material will be captured and transferred to each of the upper layers for further processing.

Spatial Layer (SL). To identify the sequence relationship among the course materials in a synchronized presentation, it is required to extract the spatio-temporal parameters of each course material. The sequence relation between the text and videos in a presentation is an example.

Generation Layer (GL). It is required to identify which SMIL template is fit for the presentation based on the timeline information from SL. The pre-defined SMIL template is stored in a repository. Meanwhile, the SMIL template is required to update the presentation. For example, the *seq tag* and *URL* will be updated to capture both the sources of course materials and the presentation sequence, based on the timeline information and the parameters from the input layer.

Fig. 6. Sample of presentation template

A sample presentation layout is shown in Figure 6(a). The presentation (screen) includes 3 regions, video, slide, and text. Video region is designed for video presentation, slide region is for displaying text-based course materials, and text region is for displaying the supplement information. In the SMIL template (Figure 6(b)), the media and synchronization information is defined in the *body* tag. The temporal structuring can be specified by *seq* and *par* tags. In this example, all media components are contained in a par tag. Likewise, the media type and related URL are specified inside the temporal structuring tags.

Presentation Layer (PL). It includes a presentation interface through which a student can input some parameters (e.g., course code, topic) to request the lesson content through HTTP on the Internet. If PL receives the related result, then it will deliver the media-based course materials via the SMIL file which defines all the presentation schedule of each course material. Otherwise, the student is required to re-input the request.

In overall processing, PL receives a request from a student and transfers it to DCN for course materials generation. Then IL identifies the sources (course materials) to include in the presentation based on the result of AHP. Meanwhile, SL generates a presentation timeline to define the sequence of each course material based on each source's parameter. Subsequently, GL identifies the most suitable SMIL template for this presentation based on the presentation timeline and the available SMIL presentation templates. According to the timeline and template, GL generates a SMIL file to present the course materials. Finally, PL distributes the media-based course materials to the student.

Fig. 7. Sample screen of personalized course materials

Based on the result from section 3.2, the media-based course materials are constructed as a SMIL file by the SMIL wrapper. A sample screen as shown in Figure 7 is captured from the media-based presentation which is played by RealOne on the PC platform. This screen is in conformance with the template of three elements (video region, slide region, and text region) shown in Figure 6. In this example, course title information is displayed in the text region. The text-based learning materials are provided in the slide region. In order to enhance the learning effectiveness, the multimedia contents displayed in the video region are also incorporated to simulate the face-to-face learning environment. Finally, the user can click "play game" at any time, to invoke the underlying game engine to start a game which is either relevant or simulative to the topic of the current course material.

As an example, Figure 8 shows an online first person fighting game developed on the game engine. This game allows multiple players to navigate in a shared game scene to fight with each other and some automated opponents. By connecting to the game engine via the SMIL wrapper, an initial content package, which contains the geometry information of the objects surrounding the player, is transmitted to the player. After receiving the package, the player may start to play the game. Additional content is then progressively streamed to the player based on the location of the player in the game.

Fig. 8. Screen shots of computer game

4 Conclusions and Future Research

In this paper, we have presented a SMIL-based approach to manage multimedia data for course materials generation. Through the hybrid use of Dynamic Conceptual Network, Analytic Hierarchy Process, user-profiles, XML, SMIL, and Java technologies, our personalized e-learning system (Peels) aims at generating personalized media contents and incorporating computer games to accommodate individual student needs and interests. Among the many desirable features offered by Peels, the following building blocks are particularly worth mentioning:

- Dynamic Conceptual Network. It provides a hierarchical tree for developing the inter-relations among individual course materials. Through the student user profile, the best course materials can be determined by the Analytic Hierarchy Process.
- SMIL-based multimedia course materials incorporating games. Pertinent media-based course materials incorporating computer games are retrieved and composed based on individual student's expectation and learning goals, which support the ideas of personalization and interactive learning effectively. As a result, the attraction of the lessons can be increased and, thus, continuous learning on the Internet can be maintained more satisfactorily.

Currently, the SMIL-based approach for distributing multimedia course materials and incorporating games is being incorporated into our Peels prototype system [6]. In our subsequent work, we plan to make our system Web-enabled so as to collect real user comments and perform user analysis on the Internet for consolidated research.

References

[1] Pimentel, M.G.C., Abowd, G.D. and Ishiguro, Y., Linking by Interacting: a Paradigm for Authoring Hypertext, Proceedings of ACM Hypertext, May 2000
[2] Mukhopadhyay, S. and Smith, B., Passive Capture and Structuring of Lectures, Proceedings of ACM Multimedia, pp.477-487, October 1999
[3] Stern, M., Steinberg, J., Lee, H. I., Padhye, J. and Kurose, J.F., MANIC: Multimedia Asynchronous Networked Individualized Courseware, Proceedings of Educational Multimedia and Hypermedia, pp.1002-1007, 1997
[4] Leung, E. and Li, Q., Dynamic Conceptual Network Mechanism for a Web-based Authoring System, Proceeding of the Second Human Society and the Internet, LNCS 2713, pp.442-453, Korea, 2003.
[5] Leung, E. and Li, Q., XML-based Agent Communication in a Distributed Learning Environment. Proceedings of the Third International Conference on Web-based Learning, LNCS 3143, pp.136-146, China, Aug 2004.
[6] Leung, E. and Li, Q., Towards a Personalized eLearning System. Encyclopedia of International Computer-Based Learning. (To be published by Ideas Pub. in 2005.)
[7] IEEE Standard 1484.12.1 for Learning Object Metadata, http://ltsc.ieee.org/wg12
[8] Riley, G., CLIPS, A Tool for Building Expert Systems. http://www.ghg.net/clips/CLIPS.html
[9] Saaty, T.L., The Analytic Hierarchy Process, New York, N.Y., McGraw Hill, 1980.

[10] Jonassen, D.H., Supporting Communities of Learners with Technology: A Vision for Integrating Technology with Learning in Schools. Educational Technology, 35(2). 60-63, 1995

[11] Lesser, V.R., Cooperative Multiagent Systems: A Personal View of the State of the Art, IEEE Transactions on Knowledge and Data Engineering, vol. 11, no.11, Jan –Feb 1999

[12] Johnson, D.W. and Johnson, R.T. Cooperative learning: where we have been, where we are going. Cooperative Learning and College Teaching. Vol 3, No.2, Winter, 1993.

[13] Duffield, N., Ramakrishnan, K., and Reibman, A. S., An Algorithm for Smoothed Adaptive Video over Explicit Rate Networks. IEEE Transactions on Networking 6, 717–728, 1998.

[14] Goncalves, P. A. S., Rezende, J. F., and Duarte, O. C. M. B., An Active Service for Multicast Video Distribution. Journal of the Brazilian Computer Society 7, 43–51, 2000.

[15] BECTA, Computer Games in Education Project (CGE). British Educational Communications and Technology Agency, 2001. Available online: http://www.becta.org.uk/technology/ software/curriculum/computergames/index.html

[16] Kirriemuir, J, Video Gaming, Education and Digital Learning Technologies: D-Lib Magazine, Vol. 8, #2, February 2002. Available online: http://www.dlib.org/dlib/february02/kirriemuir/02kirriemuir.html

[17] Avedon, E. & Sutton-Smith, B, The Study of Games: A Source Book. Teachers College, Columbia University. Robert E. Krieger Publishing: Huntington, NY, 1979.

A Novel Conference Key Distribution System with Re-keying Protocol

Hui-Feng Huang[1] and Chin-Chen Chang[2]

[1] Department of Information Management,
National Taichung Institute of Technology, Taichung 404, Taiwan
phoenix@ntit.edu.tw
[2] Department of Information Engineering and Computer Science,
Feng Chia University, Taichung 40724, Taiwan
ccc@cs.ccu.edu.tw

Abstract. A conference key distribution system is designed to establish a common secret key so that a group of people are able to hold a conference securely. However, the existing conference distribution schemes do not consider the situation that a user may be in a conference for only a period of time. If a user resigned from this session and premeditatedly eavesdropped on data transmissions, he could then also decrypt the data. Thus, all messages are likely to be compromised during the span of the system. In this paper, we propose a new conference key distribution scheme with re-keying protocol in which all conference keys in a conference are different for each time period. Our goal is to minimize the potential damages over a public network. Once the time period has elapsed the participants in a conference cannot access any messages with previously used common keys. Therefore, if a user resigns from a conference and premeditatedly eavesdrops on later messages, he cannot decrypt the message with his old keys. Moreover, in our proposed scheme, we do not require a chairman (or trusted center) and any interactive protocols among all participants in order to construct the common conference key for each time period. It can be easily implemented to a dynamic conference key distribution system because other participants' information items of the system need not be immediately changed once a participant is added or deleted.

1   Introduction

A conference key distribution system is designed to establish a secret key so that a group of people are able to hold conference a securely. The conference key is a common secret key in which one can encrypt and decrypt messages to communicate with others in the group. The first type of conference key protocol is that a chairman selects a conference key and distributes the key to all participants [1, 2, 3, 7]. The second type of conference key protocol is that all participants together compute a common key without a chairman [5, 6, 8]. The latter one is suitable for distributed environments. There have been many investigations

S. Shimojo et al. (Eds.): HSI 2005, LNCS 3597, pp. 282–290, 2005.
© Springer-Verlag Berlin Heidelberg 2005

done on conference key distribution systems. Most proposed schemes focus on the privacy of conference keys and compute the conference keys efficiently. However, they do not consider the situation that a participant may be in a session for only a period of time. If a participant resigned or left the conference and he premeditatedly eavesdropped on data transmissions, he could then also decrypt the data. Thus, all messages are likely to be compromised during the span of the system. Therefore, it is unable to implement a dynamic conference key distribution system because the whole system has to be reestablished once a participant addition or deletion occurs.

In this article, based on ElGamal's [4] public key system, we propose a novel conference key distribution system with re-keying (key updating) protocol in which conference keys in a conference is different for each time period. It means the common conference key is updated or re-keyed by all participants periodically. Our goal is to minimize the potential damages over a public network. Once the time period has elapsed the participants in a conference cannot access any data with previously used common keys. Therefore, as a user resigned or was deleted from a conference and eavesdropped on later messages, he could not then decrypt the message with old conference keys. The time is not necessarily a real time. We actually divide the total time into t time periods, starting with 1. Suppose that a participant of the conference has an expiration time of w, then he can compute the secret conference key $f(z)$ if and only if the time period $z \leq w$. Once the time period $z \leq w$ elapses, he cannot decrypt any data to obtain any useful messages. So, our conference key is constrained by the time period. Our purpose is to protect future messages. To the best of our knowledge, all existing conference key distribution schemes need a chairman (or trusted center) or several interactive communications in order to generate the common conference key [1, 2, 3, 5, 6, 7, 8]. Thus, it will result in a further communication burden and inconvenience. In our scheme, no chairman (or trusted center) or interactive protocol among participants is required to construct the common conference key for each time period. Our proposed method has the following three properties.

1. Conference key generation and re-keying (key updating) algorithm are quite simple.
2. It can be easily implemented to a dynamic conference key distribution system because other participants' information items need not be immediately changed once a participant is added or deleted.
3. Assuming that a participant takes part in a conference with the expiration time w, after the expiration time w, he does not have the ability to decrypt the data with his old conference keys for any of the remaining $(t-w)$ periods.

From the above properties, our system is more flexible and practical since it takes into account that a person may be in a session for only a period of time. For example, consider the application of key legal authorities, such as, some CIA (Central Intelligence Agency) wants to read messages and then send the messages to a particular user on a certain date. If a re-keying protocol(updated daily) with time-limited w is used, the appropriate conference key for up to w desired days can be given to the CIA without fear that this will enable the

CIA to read messages for other expired days. Moreover, in our method, one can broadcast data so that only authorized participants with proper keys can decrypt the data to obtain useful information. Broadcasting data can save quite a lot of bandwidth over the point-to-point transmission. Hence, it is more suitable for today's computer environment.

Our proposal is organized as follows: In Section 2, we introduce the design principles of our scheme and then propose our conference key distribution system with re-keying protocol. The security and performance of the scheme is discussed in Section 3. Finally, some conclusions are given in Section 4.

2   The Proposed Scheme

Our protocol uses the time-constrained to update or re-key a common conference key in a conference periodically. The time during the conference is divided into t periods, numbered $1, 2, \cdots, t$. For simplicity, we let t be an integer, i.e., the system ends at time t. This maximum number of (expired) time period t should not be considered as a limitation of the system. For example, if each time period represents a month, then $t = 12$ denotes roughly one year. Let the set $U = \{U_1, U_2, \cdots, U_n\}$ be the initial participant set. The idea of our design is to decompose the secret key function $f(z)$ into n sub-functions $f_i(z)$ for any period z, where $1 \leq i \leq n$. Each participant U_i of U securely handles one function $f_i(z)$, independently. The common conference key in the period of z is $f(z) = \sum_{(} i = 1)^n f_i(z)$, where $i \leq z \leq t$. Without a chairman or trusted center to distribute the session key, each participant U_i broadcasts some messages so that other legal participants of U can evaluate sub-key $f_i(z)$ in a secure computation for each time period of z and then those legal participants can prove the validity of sub-key $f_i(z)$ without any interactive communication.

Now, we are going to propose a novel conference key distribution system with re-keying protocol. The procedure of the scheme contains four phases: initial computation phase, re-keying algorithm phase, sub-key computation and verification phase, and conference key computation phase. First, the system chooses a large prime number p such that $p - 1$ has a large prime factor q ($q \geq 2^{256}$ and $p \geq 2^{512}$). Let g be a generator with order q in $GF(p)$. Assume that the maximum number of time periods is t, starting at 1. Then, the system publishes p, q, g, and t. Let $U = \{U_1, U_2, \cdots, U_n\}$ be the set consisting of n participants in the conference. Each U_i in U, selects a long-term secret key $x_i \in Z_q$ and computes the corresponding public key $y_i = g^{x_i} \mod p$. Then, we state the details of these phases as follows:

Initial Computation Phase

Each participant U_i of U randomly generates a secret polynomial f_i of degree t, of the form

$$f_i(x) = a_{i,0} + a_{i,1}x + \cdots + a_{i,t}x^t \mod q,$$

for $i = 1, 2, \cdots, n$, where $a_{i,0}, a_{i,1}, \cdots, a_{i,t}$ are secretly random numbers. Then, each U_i broadcasts $c_{i,k} = g^{a_{i,k}} \bmod p$ for $k = 0, 1, \cdots, t$.

Re-keying Algorithm Phase

Each U_i does the following steps to generate the z-th period sub-key:

1. U_i computes a sub-key $f_i(z) \bmod q$ for the period of z, where $1 \leq z \leq t$.
2. According to ElGamal's [4] public key cryptosystem, U_i selects a random number $k_i \in Z_q^*$, and computes $r_i = g^{k_i} \bmod p$. Then, he encrypts $f_i(z)$ to other participants as follows:

$$s_{i,j} = f_i(z) \times y_j^{q-k_i} \bmod p ,$$

   for $j = 1, 2, \cdots, n$, and $j \neq i$.
3. Finally, each U_i broadcasts $(r_i, s_{i,1}, s_{i,2}, \cdots, s_{i,i-1}, s_{i,i+1}, \cdots, s_{i,n})$ to other participants by authorized channels.

   For the security, the random number k_i cannot be reused in different period z.

Sub-key Computation and Verification Phase

¿From the broadcasted $s_{i,j}$, the participant U_j of U uses his secret key x_j to recover any sub-key $f_i(z) \bmod p$ in the period of z for $i = 1, 2, \cdots, n$ and $i \neq j$. To ensure the validity of sub-key $f_i(z)$, U_j checks the following equation:

$$g^{f_i(z)} = \prod_{k=0}^{t} (C_{i,k})^{z^k} \bmod p, \tag{1}$$

where $i = 1, 2, \cdots, n$ and $i \neq j$. If Equation 1 holds, then $f_i(z)$ is an accurate sub-key from user in time period z.

$$g^{f_i(z)} = g^{\sum_{k=0}^{t}(a_{i,k}z^k)} = \prod_{k=0}^{t} (g^{a_{i,k}})^{z^k} = \prod_{k=0}^{t} (C_{i,k})^{z^k} \bmod p,$$

Conference Key Computation Phase

If all secret sub-keys $f_j(z)$s' are verified, then each U_i in U can compute the common conference key $f(z)$ for the period of z as

$$f(z) = \sum_{j=1}^{n} f_j(z) \bmod q, \tag{2}$$

where $1 \leq z \leq t$.

From the above procedures, without a trusted center (or chairperson), the proposed scheme can provide the non-interactive communication verifiable secret sharing for each participant. Therefore, it could reduce a lot of communication costs for each participant to generate the common conference key at each time period. The following theorem shows the correctness of our protocol.

Theorem 1: If all participants in a conference follow the protocol, then they can obtain the common conference key $f(z) = \sum_{j=1}^{n} f_j(z) \ mod \ q$ for each period z, where $1 \leq z \leq t$.

Proof: Since each participant U_i of U randomly generates a secret polynomial f_i of degree t, of the form

$$f_i(x) = a_{i,0} + a_{i,1}x + \cdots + a_{i,t}x^t \ mod \ q,$$

for $i = 1, 2, \cdots, n$, where $a_{i,0}, a_{i,1}, \cdots, a_{i,t}$ are random numbers. Then, each U_i $(i = 1, 2, \cdots, n)$ can compute his sub-key $f_i(z) \ mod \ q$ for each period z, and broadcast $(r_i, s_{i,1}, s_{i,2}, \cdots, s_{i,i-1}, s_{i,i+1}, \cdots, s_{i,n})$ to other participants in a conference. Because $s_{i,j} = f_i(z) \times y_j^{q-k_i} \ mod \ p$ and $y_j^q = (g^{x_j})^q = (g^q)^{x_j} = 1 \ mod \ p$, any participant U_j in U can use his secret key x_j to decrypt all secret sub-keys $f_i(z)$'s for a period of z as follows:

$$\begin{aligned} f_i(z) &= s_{i,j} \times r_i^{x_j} \ mod \ p \\ &= f_i(z) \times y_j^{(q-k_i)} \times r_i^{x_j} \ mod \ p \\ &= f_i(z) \times y_j^q \times y_j^{-k_i} \times (g^{k_i})^{x_j} \ mod \ p \\ &= f_i(z) \ mod \ p \end{aligned}$$

for $i = 1, 2, \cdots, n$ and $i \neq j$. Hence, any participant of U can obtain the common conference key $f(z) = \sum_{j=1}^{n} n f_j(z) \ mod \ q$ for each period of z, where $1 \leq z \leq t$. Hence, we have the theorem.

Furthermore, the proposed scheme can be easily implemented in a dynamic conference distribution scheme because all information items from other participants need not be immediately refreshed once the conference adds or deletes a participant. We define the addition and deletion of participants as follows.

Adding a Participant

Suppose that a new person U_{n+1} joins to the existing participant set $U = \{U_1, U_2, \cdots, U_n\}$ at the time period b, where $1 < b \leq t$. First, U_{n+1} selects a secret key x_{n+1} in Z_q and computes the corresponding public key $y_{n+1} = g^{x_{n+1}} \ mod \ p$. Next, U_{i+1} randomly generates a secret polynomial f_{n+1} of degree t, of the form

$$f_{n+1}(x) = a_{n+1,0} + a_{n+1,1}x + \cdots + a_{n+1,t}x^t \ mod \ q, \tag{3}$$

where $a_{n+1,0}, a_{n+1,1}, \cdots, a_{n+1,t}$ are secretly random numbers. And U_{n+1} broadcasts $C_{n+1,k} = g^{a_{n+1,k}} \ mod \ p$ for $k = 0, 1, \cdots, t$. Then, all other participants' information in the system stays the same. Hence, according to our re-keying algorithm phase, each U_i of $U' = \{U_1, U_2, \cdots, U_n, U_{n+1}\}$ broadcasts $(r_i, s_{i,1}, s_{i,2}, \cdots, s_{i,i-1}, s_{i,i+1}, \cdots, s_{i,n}, s_{i,n+1})$ to other participants so that any participant U_a of U' can recover and verify the validity of all sub-keys $f_j(v)$'s, where $j = 1, 2, \cdots, n, n+1$, then the new common conference key for period of v is $f(v) = \sum_{j=1}^{n+1} f_j(v)$, where $b \leq v \leq t$.

Deleting a Participant

To delete some person U_j in the existing participant set $U = \{U_1, U_2, \cdots, U_n\}$ from d-th period, where $1 < d \leq t$. At the beginning of the period d, the system claims that U_j is deleted from a conference and then discards the secret data x_j and the public parameters y_j and $C_{j,k} = g^{a_{j,k}} \bmod p$ for $k = 0, 1, \cdots, t$. Also, other participants' information in the system is not updated. Hence, according to our re-keying algorithm phase, each U_i broadcasts $(r_i, s_{i,1}, s_{i,2}, \cdots, s_{i,i-1}, s_{i,i+1}, \cdots, s_{i,n})$ to other participants so that any participant U_a $(a \neq j)$ of U can recover and verify the validity of all sub-keys $f_i(u)$'s, where $i = 1, 2, \cdots, n$ and $i \neq j$; then the new common conference key for the period time u is $f(u) = \sum_{i=1, i \neq j}^{n} f_i(u)$, where $d \leq u < t$. In other words, any participant U_i in the new set $U'' = \{U_1, U_2, \cdots, U_{j-1}, U_{j+1}, \cdots, U_n\}$ need not compute cipher $s_{i,j}$ of $f_i(u)$ for U_j from the d-th period.

It is obvious that the proposed scheme can easily add/ delete a participant to/from the existing set U. It is more flexible for some practical applications.

3   Analysis of the Security and Performance

In this section, we discuss the security and the performance of the proposed scheme.

3.1   Security Analysis

The security of our proposed method is founded in the difficulty of the discrete logarithm problem. Hence, based on discrete logarithms, it is very difficult to obtain any participant's secret key x_i from the corresponding public key $y_i = g^{x_i} \bmod p$. Thus, each participant's private key x_i can be kept secret and reused during the span of the system. Similarly, in the initial computation phase, each participant U_i of the set $U = \{U_1, U_2, \cdots, U_n\}$ randomly generates a secret polynomial f_i of degree t, of the form

$$f_i(x) = a_{i,0} + a_{i,1}x + \cdots + a_{i,t}x^t \bmod q, \tag{4}$$

for $i = 1, 2, \cdots, n$, where $a_{i,0}, a_{i,1}, \cdots, a_{i,t}$ are secretly random numbers. Then, U_i broadcasts $C_{i,k} = g^{a_{i,k}} \bmod p$ for $k = 0, 1, \cdots, k$. The security of $a_{i,0}, a_{i,1}, \cdots, a_{i,t}$ $(i = 1, 2, \cdots, n)$, are also based on the discrete logarithm. Therefore, $a_{i,0}, a_{i,1}, \cdots, a_{i,t}$ $(i = 1, 2, \cdots, n)$ can be securely reused during all t periods. Then, the conference key's generation function $f(x) = \sum_{i=1}^{n} f_i(x)$ is a secret polynomial function of degree t which is constructed by all participants.

On the other hand, in the z-th period, we have the common conference key $f(z) = \sum_{i=1}^{n} f_i(z)$, where the sub-key $f_i(z)$ is computed by U_i. As shown in the re-keying algorithm, each U_i uses ElGamal's [4] public key cryptosystem to generate the ciphertext $s_{i,j}$ of $f_i(z)$ for each U_j by computing $s_{i,j} = f_i(z) \times y_j^{q-k_i} \bmod p$, where $j = 1, 2, \cdots, n$ $(j \neq i)$ and y_j is U_j's public key. For the security, the random number k_i cannot be reused in different period z. Only the legal participant U_j with his private key x_j can decrypt the sub-key $f_i(z)$. Since

$C_{i,k} = g^{a_{i,k}} \bmod p$ for $k = 0, 1, \cdots, t$ are public parameters, then any participant can use the following equality to ensure the validity of the sub-key $f_i(z)$ without any interactive communication:

$$g^{f_i(z)} = \prod_{k=0}^{t} (C_{i,k})^{z^k} \bmod p, \tag{5}$$

where $i = 1, 2, \cdots, n$ and $i \neq j$. Applying the above Equation 5 and ElGamal's [4] public key cryptosystem, without U_j's private key x_j, anyone does not have the ability to recover and certify the sub-key $f_i(z)$ for the period z, where $1 \leq z \leq t$. Therefore, the proposed protocol is secure against impersonators. Hence, only legal participants in a conference can obtain the common session key $f(z) = \sum_{i=1}^{n} f_i(z) \bmod q$ for any period of z, where $1 \leq z \leq t$. For the security of the proposed method, we consider some possible attacks.

1. Suppose that one conference key $f(k)$ is compromised at time period k. Without the polynomial $f(x)$, it is very hard to derive even one additional secret common conference key, because our scheme $f(x) = \sum_{i=1}^{n} f_i(x)$ is a secret polynomial function of degree t. This enforces that the attacker needs at least $t+1$ points (common conference keys) of $(1, f(1)), (2, f(2)), \cdots$, and $(t+1, f(t+1))$ to reconstruct the secret polynomial function f. In contrast, if less than $t+1$ secret conference keys are compromised, then the polynomial f for the key-evolving cannot be uniquely determined. The conference key updating function f is a perfect secure in a conference. In our proposal, the total number of periods during the conference is t. Therefore, even if t secret conference keys are compromised, the attacker cannot derive the secret polynomial f. Without the conference key updating function f, one cannot obtain any conference key for all different periods. Therefore, if some conference key $f(k)$ is compromised at time period k, it is very difficult for the attacker to generate other periods of conference key.

2. Suppose that some sub-key $f_i(z)$ is compromised at time period z. Similar to point 1, $f_i(x)$ is a secret polynomial function of degree t, which implies that the attacker needs at least $t + 1$ points to reconstruct the secret polynomial $f_i(x)$. In our scheme, the total number of periods in the conference is t. Therefore, during all t periods, the attacker cannot derive any sub-key generation function $f_i(x)$ in order to obtain other session sub-keys.

In addition, if some participant U_j leaves the participant set $U = \{U_1, U_2, \cdots, U_n\}$ at the beginning of period d, then according to our deletion protocol, only the remaining participants can derive the sub-key to obtain the new common conference key of $f(u) = \sum_{i=1, i \neq j}^{n} f_i(u)$, where $d \leq u \leq t$. In this situation, even if U_j tried to eavesdrop on data transmissions, he should not be able to decrypt any data with his old conference keys for any of the remaining $(t - d)$ periods. Therefore, our scheme is secure even if a participant is deleted from the existing participant set.

3.2   Performances

So far, to the best of our knowledge, all existing conference key distribution schemes need a chairman (trusted center) to distribute the common conference key or several interactive communications are needed to generate the common conference key [1, 2, 3, 5, 6, 7, 8]. Therefore, it will result in a further communication burden and inconvenience. Our proposal does not require a chairman (trusted center) and any interactive protocols among participants to construct the common conference key for each time period. With regard to the performance of our scheme, given the public parameters, for every period of z, any participant U_i in $U = \{U_1, U_2, \cdots, U_n\}$ computes $r_i = g^{k_i} \bmod p$ and then generates ciphertext $s_{i,j}$ of $f_i(z)$ by computing $s_{i,j} = f_i(z) \times y_j^{q-k_i} \bmod p$ for $j = 1, 2, \cdots, n$, and $j \neq i$, where y_i is U_j's public key. Hence, any participant U_i requires n modular exponentiation operations to compute and broadcast ciphertext $s_{i,1}, s_{i,2}, \cdots, s_{i,i-1}, s_{i,i+1}, \cdots, s_{i,n}$ of the sub-key $f_i(z)$ for other participants. Next, any participant U_j ($j \neq i$) in a conference with his secret key x_j takes one modular exponentiation operation to get the sub-key $f_i(z)$ by computing $f_i(z) = s_{i,j} \times r_i^{x_j} \bmod p$ for $i = 1, 2, \cdots, n$, and $i \neq j$. Therefore, each participant of U needs $(n - 1)$ modular exponentiation operations to obtain the common conference key $f(z) = \sum_{i=1, i \neq j}^{n} f_i(z) \bmod q$ for any period of z, where $1 \leq z \leq t$. On the other hand, according to our re-keying algorithm, using the public parameters given by the initial computation phase and Equation 1, only the legal participant can authorize the value $f_i(z)$ by exactly computing from U_i without any interactive communication for $1 \leq z \leq t$. Therefore, it is very convenient for any participant in a conference to verify the validity of those sub-keys during all periods.

Since all public items of other participants in a conference need not be immediately refreshed once a participant is added or deleted, the proposed scheme can be easily implemented in a dynamic conference distribution scheme. However, the above mentioned schemes [1, 2, 3, 5, 6, 7, 8] cannot be easily implemented in a dynamic conference distribution system.

4   Conclusions

In this paper, we presented a novel conference key distribution scheme with re-keying protocol to reduce the potential damages over a public network. The important feature of our scheme is that our conference keys in a conference are totally different for each time period. In our scheme, no chairman (or trusted center) is required, all participants can construct the common conference key without any interactive communication. In addition, the proposed scheme has the following properties.

1. Conference key generation and re-keying (key updating) algorithm are quite simple.
2. It can be easily implemented to a dynamic conference key distribution system because other participants' information items of the system need not be immediately updated once a participant is added or deleted.

3. Assuming that a participant takes part in a conference with the expiration time w. Then, after the expiration time w, he should not be able to decrypt the data with his old conference keys for any of the remaining $(t-w)$ periods.

References

1. Berkovits: How to Broadcast a Secret. Proceedings Advances in Cryptology-Eurocrypt'91, (1991) 535–541
2. Chang, C. C., Wu, T.C., and Chen, C. P.: The Design of a Conference Key Distribution System, Proceedings Advances in Cryptology-Auscrypt'92, (1992) 459–466
3. Hwang, M.S. and Yang, W.P.: Conference Key Distribution Schemes for Secure Digital Mobile Communications, IEEE Journal on Selected Areas in Communications, **13** (1995) 416–420
4. ElGamal, T.: A Public-Key Cryptosystem and a Signature Scheme Based on Discrete Logarithms, IEEE Transactions on Information Theory, **31** (1985) 469–472
5. Ingemarsson, I., Tang, D.T., and Wong, C. K.: A Conference Key Distribution System, IEEE Transactions on Information Theory, **28** (1982) 714-720
6. Steer, D., Strawczynski, L., Diffie, W., and Wiener M.: A Secure Audio Teleconference System, Proceedings Advances in Cryptology-Crypto'88, (1990) 520-528
7. Tseng, Y. M. and Jan, J. K.: A Conference Key Distribution System, Computer Communications **22** (1999) 749–754
8. Tzeng, W. G.: A Secure Fault-Tolerant Conference-Key Agreement Protocol, IEEE Transactions on Computers, **51** (2002) 373–379

Multi-modal Techniques for Identity Theft Prevention[*]

Taekyoung Kwon and Hyeonjoon Moon

Sejong University, Seoul 143-747, Korea
{tkwon, hmoon}@sejong.ac.kr

Abstract. The rapid growth of the Internet has caused a large number of social problems including invasion of privacy and violation of personal identity. Currently, it is an emerging trend to verify personal identity based on hybrid methods (for example, by combining the existing off-line and on-line verification methods) using the Internet in the legacy applications. As a result, many security problems of the Internet is now becoming the practical impacts on our social applications. In this paper, we study multi-modal techniques for preventing identity theft in the social applications from the practical perspectives. A digital signature techniques and multi-modal biometrics are exploited in our scheme without requiring users to hold additional hardware devices.

1   Introduction

The rapid growth of the Internet has caused lots of social problems including invasion of privacy and violation of personal identity. From the perspectives of human society, there are many legacy applications requiring proper means of identifying humans, for example, by what they have (passports, driver's licenses, student identification cards, tickets, etc.), and what they know (answers to several questions). Recently, it is being observed and recognized by communities to add new elements of who they are (biometrics) to the legacy applications, though it costs much to measure biometric samples and to maintain biometric templates securely [2].

Due to the wide deployment of the Internet, it is another trend to verify personal identity based on hybrid methods (by combining the existing off-line and on-line verification methods) using the Internet in the legacy applications. For instance, an inspector verifies personal identity not only by reading the presented identification (ID) document but also by connecting to a server for further validation of the presented data. As a result, many security problems of the Internet is now becoming the practical impacts on our social applications in which identity theft is a critical problem. As for accommodating biometrics in

[*] This research was supported by the MIC (Ministry of Information and Communication), Korea, under the ITRC (Information Technology Research Center) support program supervised by the IITA (Institute of Information Technology Assessment).

S. Shimojo et al. (Eds.): HSI 2005, LNCS 3597, pp. 291–300, 2005.
© Springer-Verlag Berlin Heidelberg 2005

the hybrid method, it is necessary to protect biometric templates and to secure the possible communications arising for verification, requiring specific hardware such as a tamper-resistant smart card.

In this paper, we study multi-modal techniques for preventing identity theft in the social applications from the practical perspectives. We aim to present a low-cost but highly-scalable method that uses multi-modal biometrics based on face and fingerprints without requiring users to hold additional hardware devices. Thus, as we studied in our previous related work, multi-modal biometrics is combined with cryptographic techniques for achieving practicality [5]. This is because biometrics has the potential to strengthen identity protection by reducing the risk of ID fraud, while public key cryptography can be used for verifying a person's identity in a stringent way, for example, in public key infrastructures (PKIs) for legacy applications.

The basic model is obtained from the previous work that was aimed for border control applications. Let κ and ℓ denote security parameters where κ is a general one (say 160 bits) and ℓ is a special one for public keys (say 1024 bits). An ID holder is defined formally as $\mathcal{U} = \{\mathcal{B}, \mathcal{P}\}$ where $\mathcal{B}$ and $\mathcal{P}$ are defined as user's biometrics and possession respectively. As for multi-modal biometrics, $\mathcal{B}$ can be regarded as a set of biometrics, for example, $\mathcal{B} = \{\mathcal{B}_0, \mathcal{B}_1\}$. As for the possession, a 2D bar code symbol can hold up to about 4,300 alphanumeric characters or 3,000 bytes of binary data in a small area [9]. That is, $\mathcal{P}$ can simply be printed on the ID document. We define three kinds of transformations $\mathcal{T}_0 : \mathcal{B}_0 \rightarrow \langle \mathcal{B}_{\mathcal{T}_0}, \mathcal{P}_{\mathcal{T}_0} \rangle$ for feature representation $\mathcal{B}_{\mathcal{T}_0}$ and eigenvector $\mathcal{P}_{\mathcal{T}_0}$, $\mathcal{T}_1 : \langle \mathcal{G}_\Sigma(1^\ell), \mathcal{G}_R(1^\kappa), \mathcal{B}_1 \rangle \rightarrow \langle \mathcal{B}_{\mathcal{T}}, \mathcal{P}_{\mathcal{T}} \rangle$ where $\mathcal{G}_\Sigma$ is a probabilistic algorithm returning a public-private key pair from input 1^ℓ, and $\mathcal{G}_R$ is a probabilistic algorithm returning a random integer from input 1^κ, and $\mathcal{T}_2 : \langle \mathcal{B}_1, \mathcal{B}_{\mathcal{T}}, \mathcal{P}_{\mathcal{T}} \rangle \rightarrow \mathcal{G}_\Sigma$. For prevention of identity theft, the authentication procedure is composed of two phases where phase 1 is for face recognition and phase 2 is for digital signature manipulation with fingerprints. The inverse transformation is possible for $\mathcal{T}_0$ in phase 1, while it should be computationally infeasible for $\mathcal{T}_1$ and $\mathcal{T}_2$ in phase 2.

The main difference from the previous work is that an advanced method is proposed for face recognition in the way of using Gabor Wavelet Masks (GWM), and 2) the GQ signature scheme is used for easier manipulation of public keys. We exploit GWM since it is difficult to accurately compute the covariance matrix which contains variations among the face images in a number of projection-based face recognition methods such as eigenface based on Principle Component Analysis (PCA) [13] and fisherface based on Linear Discriminant Analysis (LDA), primarily with linear projection [1]. The reason was that the 2D face image information should be transformed into 1D vectors, and the resulting vectors of face images contains the high-dimensional vector space. We also utilize the GQ signature scheme since the public key of the GQ scheme may easily fit into our model, enabling more efficient verification and certification [3]. The new scheme is advanced in terms of recognition performance and computational efficiency which may allow wide acceptance to the legacy social applications.

The rest of this paper is organized as follows. Section 2 and 3 describes our multi-modal scheme while Section 4 concludes this paper.

2   Phase 1: Face Recognition

2.1   Proposed Face Recognition System

For image representation, we conduct the convolution between the gabor wavelet masks and the positioned pixels through downsampling instead of all pixels in an image. The wavelets are widely utilized to analyze the frequency domain properties of an image. Especially, the gabor wavelets are frequently applied for the image analysis due to their biological relevances and computational properties[6]. In gabor wavelets, the masks are similar to the 2D receptive field profiles of the mammalian cortical simple cells, while exhibiting desirable characteristics of spatial locality and orientation selectivity. This information can be localized optimally in both of the space and the frequency domains[6]. The gabor wavelets are basically sinusoids multiplied by the gaussian envelope. Thus, if an image is convolved with the gabor wavelets, the frequency information near the center of the gaussian is captured, and the frequency information far away from the center of the gaussian has negligible effects. The gabor wavelets can be defined as follows [6]:

$$\psi_{\mu,\nu}(z) = \frac{\|k_{\mu,\nu}\|^2}{\sigma^2} e^{-\frac{\|k_{\mu,\nu}\|^2 \|z\|^2}{2\sigma^2}} [e^{ik_{\mu,\nu}z} - e^{-\frac{\sigma^2}{2}}],$$

where μ and ν specify the orientation and the scale of the gabor masks respectively, and $z = (x, y)$. Also, $\| \cdot \|$ denotes the norm operator, and the wave vector $k_{\mu,\nu}$ is defined as follows:

$$k_{\mu,\nu} = k_\nu e^{i\phi_\mu},$$

where $k_\nu = k_{max}/f^\nu$ and $\phi_\mu = \pi\mu/8$. Here, k_{max} is the maximum frequency, and f is the spacing factor between masks in the frequency domain. The gabor wavelet masks in the equation above are all self-similar since they can be generated from one mask(filter), the mother wavelet, by scaling and rotation via the wave vector. Each mask is the product of a gaussian envelope and a complex plane wave, while the first term in the bracket in the gabor wavelet equation determines the oscillatory part of the mask and the second term compensates for the DC value. The effect of the DC term gets negligible when the parameter σ, which determines the ratio of the mask width to wavelength, has sufficiently large values. We use gabor wavelet masks of five scales($\nu \in \{0, 1, 2, 3, 4\}$) and eight orientations($\mu \in \{0, 1, 2, 3, 4, 5, 6, 7\}$) to represent an image, with the following parameters: $\sigma = 2\pi$, $k_{max} = 3\pi/4$, $f = \sqrt{2}$. The gabor wavelet representation of the image is the convolution of the image with a family of gabor wavelet masks. Let $I(x, y)$ be the gray level distribution of the image, the convolution of image I and a gabor mask $\psi_{\mu,\nu}$ is defined as follows: $O_{\mu,\nu}(z) = I(z) * \psi_{\mu,\nu}(z)$. Because the computation of convolution for all pixels in the image usually takes many times, it is necessary to select a small part of the image through downsampling. P pixels are equidistantly positioned within the prominent image region and computes the convolution in those.

The 2DPCA is introduced to generate a projection space while extracting the projected feature of each image on the space. 2DPCA is based on the 2D image

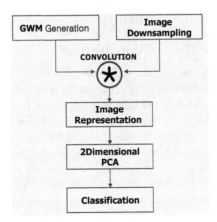

Fig. 1. A flow chart of our new face recognition method

matrices rather than the 1D vectors. Therefore, the image matrix needs not to be transformed prior to feature extraction. Instead, an image covariance matrix is constructed directly using the original 2D image matrices, and its eigenvectors are derived for image feature extraction[14]. Let $G_i(i = 1, 2, \cdots, M)$ denote a P × N gabor-represented image matrix, where P is the number of sampling pixels and N is the number of gabor wavelet masks. Then, the covariance matrix is defined as

$$C = \frac{1}{M} \sum_{j=1}^{M} (G_j - \bar{G})^T (G_j - \bar{G}),$$

where the gabor-represented average of all sample images is denoted by $\bar{G}$. It is easy to verify that C is an N × N nonnegative definite matrix from its definition. To optimally extract the features we adopt the following criterion[14].

$$J(X) = X^T C X,$$

Then, optimal projection axes are selected by maximizing this criterion.

$$X_1, \cdots, X_d = arg\ maxJ(X),$$

where X is a unitary column vector.

$$< X_i, X_j > = \delta_{ij}(i, j = 1, \cdots, d),$$

where δ is a Kronecker's delta function. In fact, the optimal projection axes, $X_1, \cdots, X_d$, are the orthonormal eigenvectors of the covariance matrix C, corresponding to the first d largest eigenvalues. Finally, a N × d feature matrix of a gabor-represented face image is obtained by projecting it onto the optimized projection axes.

$$Y_{i,j} = G_i X_j,$$

where $i = 1, 2, \cdots, M$ and $j = 1, 2, \cdots, d$. Figure 1 depicts the flow of performing our recognition method.

Table 1. Comparison of the best recognition rate and computation time for feature extraction of 2DPCA, GWM+PCA and GWM+2DPCA

Distance	Rank	2DPCA	GWM + PCA	GWM + 2DPCA
COV	R1	63.25(64× 6)	81.00(120)	88.00(40×28)
	R3	78.75(64×19)	88.25(80)	95.75(40×32)
	R5	80.75(64×19)	90.25(160)	97.25(40×36)
L1	R1	63.75(64× 6)	85.00(80)	86.50(40×12)
	R3	76.75(64× 6)	93.00(80)	94.00(40×12)
	R5	80.00(64× 6)	93.75(80)	95.50(40×12)
L2	R1	64.00(64× 6)	85.25(240)	85.25(40×12)
	R3	79.00(64×19)	93.25(200)	93.25(40×20)
	R5	80.75(64× 6)	94.00(200)	94.25(40×32)
CPU Time(sec)		21.6	146.8	14.4

2.2 Experimental Results

The proposed algorithm is evaluated with the 2DPCA and the GWM+PCA based on the XM2VTS face database[8] for face recognition accuracy. The XM2VTS database contains images taken from 295 individuals, each person has four frontal face images taken in four different sessions. The images in the database are taken with a tolerance for a little variation of pose and expression. In our experiment, four face images of randomly selected 100 persons are used for both training and testing (total 400 images). In the preprocessing step, each image has been transformed into resolution 64×64 with 256 gray scales. We measure the percentage of the correct answer in top N match(N = 1, 3, 5) out of 400 images with three nearest neighbor classifiers including covariance(COV), cityblock distance(L1) and euclidean distance(L2) to measure the similarity between two images [11]. Table 1 indicates the experimental results to examine the best recognition rate and the computation time for feature extraction of the 2DPCA, the GWM+PCA, and the GWM+2DPCA. The values in parentheses denotes the dimension of the extracted feature for the best recognition rate. The experimental results shows that the GWM+2DPCA outperforms the other methods in best recognition rate, except for using the L2 distance measure. Also, the 2DPCA shows some advantages in feature extraction against the PCA in computational efficiency. Figure 2 shows the recognition accuracy of the GWM+2DPCA with three distance measures under variations of principal component vectors, where the top graph is recognition result in top 5 match(R5) and bottom in top 1 match(R1).

2.3 Discussion

We presented a novel face recognition algorithm by combining the gabor wavelet masks(GWM) and the 2DPCA. We use the GWM to represent an image in the

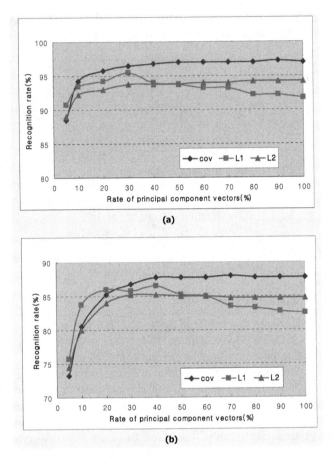

Fig. 2. Face recognition rate of the GWM+2DPCA with three distance measures under variations of the rate of principal component vectors

frequency domain with convolution using downsampled pixel information, then the 2DPCA is applied for forming a face space and extracting the feature vector of the gabor-represented images. Our experiment validated that the proposed method is superior to the 2DPCA or the GWM+PCA in recognition accuracy, and it is also more efficient for feature extraction in computation time. Our future research is geared to combining the proposed algorithm using the nonlinear projection with the kernel functions.

Our experimental results has a number of implications for legacy applications, for instance, border control applications. First, face recognition system should include a range of images in terms of quality. For example, when measuring the concord between algorithm and human performance, the results should be based on experiments on multiple probe categories. Second, the fine details of algorithm implements can have significant impact on results and conclusion. Our face recognition system can be easily extended for many applications since the majority of the algorithms in the literature are view-based and have the same basic architecture.

3   Phase 2: Digital Signature Manipulation with Fingerprints

3.1   Assumption

Let $\Sigma = (\mathcal{G}_\Sigma(1^\ell), \mathcal{S}, \mathcal{V})$ define a digital signature scheme where $\mathcal{G}_\Sigma$ is a probabilistic algorithm returning a public-private key pair from input 1^ℓ, and $\mathcal{S}$ and $\mathcal{V}$ are respectively signing and verifying algorithms, which run in polynomial time. In our scheme, we suppose to use a simple hash-and-sign GQ primitive in a probabilistic manner (with κ_Σ-bit random numbers). The original public-private keys are respectively $\langle e, J_A, N \rangle$ and $\langle a, N \rangle$ where N is the product of two distinct large primes p and q, $\gcd(J_A, N) = 1$ for an integer J_A, $1 < J_A < n$, $\gcd(e, \phi(N)) = 1$ for the Euler totient function $\phi(N) = (p-1)(q-1)$, and a satisfies $J_A a^e \equiv 1 (\bmod\ n)$ [3, 10]. In the GQ scheme, a is a solution to the simultaneous congruences $a \equiv a_1 (\bmod\ n)$ and $a \equiv a_2 (\bmod\ n)$ where $a_1 = (J_A^{-1})^{d_1}$ mod p, $a_2 = (J_A^{-1})^{d_2}$ mod q, $d_1 = e^{-1}$ mod $(p-1)$, and $d_2 = e^{-1}$ mod $(q-1)$. The public key is postulated to be certified by the CA but not in the original form (see Section 3.2). We assume $\mathcal{S}$ returns signature on a message m; $\langle s, l \rangle$ where $s \leftarrow ka^l$ mod N, $l \leftarrow H(m, r)$, and $k \leftarrow_R \{0, 1\}^{\kappa_\Sigma}$. In the previous work, a drawback of exploiting RSA was the huge size of the key. When we apply GQ signature to our scheme, it becomes easier to manipulate the public key.

As for acquiring fingerprint images, the mechanism of correlation is the basis for it [12]. Let $f(x)$ denote a two-dimensional input image array and $F(u)$ its corresponding Fourier Transform (FT) mate, where x denotes the space domain and u the spatial frequency domain. Then correlation is normally used to provide a single scalar value which indicates the degree of similarity between one image, $f_1(x)$, obtained during verification and another obtained during enrollment, $f_0(x)$, that is represented by the filter function, $H(u)$, derived from a set of $T(\geq 1)$ training images $\langle f_0^1(x), f_0^2(x), ..., f_0^T(x) \rangle$. The correlation function is formally defined as

$$c(x) = \int_{-\infty}^{\infty} f_1(v) f_0^*(x+v) dv$$

where $*$ implies the complex conjugate. In practice, it is obtained by computing the inverse Fourier Transform (FT^{-1}) such that $c(x) = \mathrm{FT}^{-1}\{F_1(u)F_0^*(u)\}$, where $F_0^*(u)$ is represented by $H(u)$ that must be the biometric template tolerant to distortion in correlation-based biometric systems [12]. Let $A_0(u)$ be an average of $F^t(x)$'s for $0 \leq t \leq T$. The stored filter function is defined as

$$H_s(u) = e^{-i\varphi_{A_0}(u)} e^{i\varphi_R(u)}$$

where the phase of the complex conjugate of the training set images, $e^{-i\varphi_{A_0}(u)}$, and the random phase-only function, $e^{i\varphi_R(u)}$, are only multiplied. Note that e is different from the exponent e of GQ. The magnitude terms of the optimal filter can be calculated on-the-fly during either enrollment or verification and are denoted by $|\cdot|$.

3.2   Key Generation and Signature Generation

$\mathcal{G}_\Sigma(1^\ell)$ outputs a GQ public-private key pair, $\langle e, J_A, N\rangle$ and $\langle a, N\rangle$. We assume that the exponent e is chosen from a reasonable space, say in κ-bit length. As for the base J_A, we postulate that the information about a user can be represented in a binary form, such as name, address, driver's license number, etc.

In our previous work, we set the public exponent to be huge, for example, about $\log k + \ell$ bits for $e_2 = ee_1^{-1} \bmod \phi(N) + k\phi(N)$, while the hidden exponent is small, for example, only 128 bits [5]. Our concern was only to protect all bits of e_1. In the GQ case, by fixing e to 128 bits in length, we can obtain easily the hidden exponent without any expensive manipulation. As a result, the main difference from the ordinary GQ signature is that the public exponent e is discarded from public and thus the CA may certify $\langle J_A, N\rangle$ (with e being proved), instead of $\langle e, J_A, N\rangle$. Thus, e can be regarded as a secret value with sufficient length for on-line verification.

A series of input images $\langle f_0^1(x), f_0^2(x), ..., f_0^T(x)\rangle$ are given as $\mathcal{B}_1$ and combined with a random phase array to create two output arrays, $H_s(u)$ and $c_0(x)$, where $H_s(u) = e^{-i\varphi_{A_0}(u)}e^{i\varphi_R(u)}$ and $c_0(x) = \mathrm{FT}^{-1}\{A_0(u) \cdot |H_0(u)| \cdot H_s(u)\}$ [12].

Given the hidden key e, the central $\frac{t}{2} \times \frac{t}{2}$ portion of $c_0(x)$ must be extracted and binarized for marority-encoding e. A complex element $a + bi$ at position (x, y) of the $\frac{t}{2} \times \frac{t}{2}$ portion of $c_0(x)$ will be fragmented in the way that a will appear at (x, y) and b at $(x + \frac{t}{2}, y)$ in the $t \times \frac{t}{2}$ binarized template [12]. Now the binarized template, bt, contains $\frac{t^2}{2}$ real values that can be binarized with respect to 0.0, i.e., set as 1 if they are equal to or greater than 0.0, and otherwise 0. From bt, we can compose a lookup table, L, which may encode e in the way that a number of locations whose element values are equal to each bit of e are stored in each corresponding column.

Finally the user's possession $\mathcal{P}(=\langle\mathcal{B}_{T_0}, \mathcal{B}_T, \mathcal{P}_T\rangle)$ is defined as $\mathcal{B}_T = \{H_s(u), L\}$ and $\mathcal{P}_T = \{J_A, N\}$, while $\mathcal{B}_{T_0}$ was obtained in Phase 1. $\mathcal{P}$ is encoded and printed by an arbitrary 2D bar code on the user's ID. A digital signature on the ID holder's information including $\mathcal{P}$ is generated by using $\langle a, N\rangle$. Given the information m, $\mathcal{S}$ chooses a random integer k and raises it to the power of e. Then $\mathcal{S}$ computes $l = h(m, r)$ and $s = ka^l \bmod N$ for obtaining the corresponding signature $S = \langle s, l\rangle$. The signature S is also printed on the ID in barcodes. Note that $\mathcal{P}_T(= \{J_A, N\})$ can be certified by authority in PKIs, so that the inspectors could verify the key integrity without solely depending on paper tamper-proofing techniques in ID documents.

3.3   Signature Verification

An ID holder $\mathcal{U}$ provides a series of fingerprint images $\langle f_1^1(x), f_1^2(x), ..., f_1^T(x)\rangle$ as input $\mathcal{B}_1$ along with $\langle\mathcal{B}_{T_0}, \mathcal{B}_T, \mathcal{P}_T\rangle$, say $\langle H_s(u), L, J_A, N\rangle$, in 2D bar codes. We assume $\langle J_A, N \rangle$ is provided with a certificate and verified in this step. We also postulate that $\mathcal{B}_{\mathcal{T}_0}$ is already verified by an inspecting officer under the comparison of photo id in the ID.

A series of input images are combined with $H_s(u)$ to create a new output array, $c_1(x)$ where $c_0(x) = \mathrm{FT}^{-1}\{A_1(u) \cdot |H_1(u)| \cdot H_s(u)\}$.

Given the lookup table L, the central $\frac{t}{2} \times \frac{t}{2}$ portion of $c_1(x)$ must be extracted and binarized for majority-decoding e. A method to obtain the new binarized template, bt', is exactly the same to that of key generation process. From bt' and L, we can compose a new table L' which may majority-decodes e in the way that a majority bit in each column is derived to each location in e.

Given the signature $S = \langle s, l \rangle$ from the ID, $\mathcal{V}$ computes $u = s^e J_A^l \bmod N$ and $l' = h(m, u)$. Compared with our previous work on RSA [5], the verification process becomes much more efficient. Subsequently $\mathcal{V}$ compares l and l' for verifying the validity of signature.

3.4   Discussion

As for the security of GQ, the exponent e should sufficiently be large to preclude the possibility of forgery based on the birthday paradox. Since we have set e having 128 bits in length, our scheme is free from such an attack. The value e is secure without any tamper-resistant device. It is only recovered by live biometrics and 2D bar codes. The main difference from the ordinary GQ signature is that the public exponent e is actually hidden while J_A and N are only certified and publicized. Note that the public exponent is manipulated carefully in linking biometric information.

In our system, the size of J_A was assumed about ℓ bits. So the liveness check for $\mathcal{B}$ is additionally necessary while its minimized template can be stored in $\mathcal{P}$, say exactly $\mathcal{P}_{\mathcal{T}}$, under the easy consideration of the hill-climbing attack. Note that an ID holder possess $\mathcal{P}$. When we consider the number of the most expensive modular N multiplications [7], our GQ signature verification using the repeated square-and-multiply algorithm will take $\kappa + \ell$ modular squarings and expected $\frac{\kappa + \ell}{2}$ modular multiplications. Note that if the size of parameter κ increases, the verification process could benefit from the simultaneous multiple exponentiation method and further improve the computation costs since the simultaneous method costs only about 25% more than a single exponentiation when we consider a left-to-right binary exponentiation [7].

4   Conclusion

In this paper, we studied a low-cost but highly-scalable method that uses multi-modal biometrics based on face and fingerprints, and public key cryptography for social applications requiring stringent identity verification. In our scheme, the biometric templates and key derivation values are printed in the form of 2D bar codes on the ID document without requiring tamper-resistant hardware in the user side. Thus, it might be easy to apply our scheme to the existing social applications in the way that the identity theft is highly prevented. The scheme proposed in this paper is based on our previous related work [5] but is advanced in terms of recognition performance and computational efficiency which may allow wide acceptance to the legacy social applications.

References

1. P. Belhumueur, J. Hespanha and D. Krieman, "Eigenfaces vs. Fisherfaces: Recognition using class specific linear projection," IEEE Transactions on Pattern Analysis and Machine Intelligence, pp.711-720, 1997.
2. Daon Inc., "Biometric Authentication & Digital Signatures for the Pharmaceutical Industry," White paper available at http://www.daon.com/downloads/publications/esignature.pdf
3. L. Guillou and J. Quisquater, "A practical zero-knowledge protocol fiited to security microprocessor minimizing both transmission and memory," Advances in Cryptology-EUROCRYPT '88, LNCS 330, pp.123-128, 1988.
4. T. Kwon, "Practical digital signature generation using biometrics," Proceedings of ICCSA 2004, Lecture Notes in Computer Science, Springer-Verlag, 2004.
5. T. Kwon and H. Moon, "Multi-Modal Biometrics with PKI Technologies for Border Control Applications," Proceedings of IEEE ISI 2005, Lecture Notes in Computer Science, Springer-Verlag, 2005.
6. C. Liu and H. Wechsler, "Gabor Feature Based Classification Using the Enhanced Fisher Linear Discriminant Model for Face Recognition," IEEE Transactions on Image Processing, pp. 467-476, 2002.
7. A. Menezes, P. van Oorschot, and S. Vanstone, *Handbook of Applied Cryptography*, CRC Press, pp.287-291, pp.312-315, 1997.
8. K. Messer, J. Matas, J. Kittler, J. Luettin, and G. Maitre, "XM2VTSDB: The Extended M2VTS Database," Proc. of International Conference on Audio- and Video-Based Person Authentication, pp. 72-77, 1999.
9. R. Palmer, "The Bar Code Book," *Helmers Publishing*, Peterborough, N.H., 3rd Ed., 1995.
10. R. Rivest, A. Shamir, and L. Adleman, "A method for obtaining digital signatures and public-key cryptosystems," *Communications of the ACM*, vol.21, pp.120-126, 1978.
11. P. Phillips, H. Moon, S. Rizvi, and P. Rauss, "The FERET Evaluation Methodology for Face-Recognition Algorithms", IEEE Transactions on Pattern Analysis and Machine Intelligence, pp. 1090-1104, 2000.
12. C. Soutar, D. Roberge, A. Stoianov, R. Golroy, and B. Vijaya Kumar, "Biometric Encryption," ICSA Guide to Cryptography, McGraw-Hill, 1999, also available at http://www.bioscrypt.com/assets/Biometric_Encryption.pdf
13. M. Turk and A. Pentland, "Eigenfaces for recognition," Journal of Cognitive Neuroscience, vol. 3, No. 1, pp. 71-86, 1991.
14. J. Yang, D. Zhang, A. Frangi and J. Yang, "Two-Dimensional PCA: A New Approach to Appearance-Based Face Representation and Recognition," IEEE Transactions on Pattern Analysis and Machine Intelligence, pp. 131-137, 2004.

Vector Graphics Application Using Self-networking and Replaceable Structure in Wireless Handset

Gu-Min Jeong[1], Seung-Won Na[2], Doo-Hee Jung[3], Hyun-Sik Ahn[1],
and Min-Soo Ryu[4]

[1] Dept. of Electrical Engineering, Kookmin University, Korea
{gm1004, ahs}@kookmin.ac.kr
[2] Terminal Development Team, Platform R&D Center, SK Telecom, Korea
nasw@sktelecom.com
[3] Dept. of Electrical and Electronics Engineering, Korea
doohee@kpu.ac.kr
[4] College of Information and Communications, Hanyang University, Korea
msryu@rtcc.hanyang.ac.kr

Abstract. In this paper, self-networking and replaceable structure in vector graphics contents are presented for wireless internet service. The wireless networks over 2G or 3G are limited in the sense of the speed and the cost. Considering these characteristics of wireless network, self-networking method and replaceable structure in downloaded contents are introduced in order to save the amount of data and provide variations for contents. During the display of contents, a certain data for the contents is downloaded from the server and it is managed appropriately for the operation of the contents. The downloaded materials are reflected to the original contents using replaceable structure. Also, the downloading and modification are independent of the play. In this implementation, the data consists of control data for control and resource data for image, sound or text. Comparing to the conventional methods which download the whole data, the amount of the transmitted data is very small since only the difference is downloaded. Also, during the play of the contents, the changes are adopted immediately. The throughput analysis of the proposed structure is given based on the markov process. The whole functions are implemented in wireless handset and the various applications are discussed.

1   Introduction

According to the development of the network and communication technology, various data services including multimedia are being provided for users. Multimedia becomes a killer application of a data service. The development of wireless network and wireless handset makes it possible to implement many kinds of multimedia solutions in handset.

Recently, many multimedia contents have been commercialized such as image, video, 3D graphics, vector graphics and sound. Due to some restrictions of

S. Shimojo et al. (Eds.): HSI 2005, LNCS 3597, pp. 301–310, 2005.
© Springer-Verlag Berlin Heidelberg 2005

wireless network and handset such as memory limitation, low CPU processing power and narrow network bandwidth, it is very difficult to implement multimedia services. The efforts to reduce the contents size, effective networking without redundant data and fast player in handset are required for wireless internet service.

Considering these characteristics, vector image graphics is thought to be suitable for wireless network and handset. Contents size can be made smaller than raster graphics. In addition, it can be implemented regardless of the LCD size in handset. Also, by use of user interaction, several services can be provided. Nowadays, a few vector graphics technologies are developed for wireless internet such as VIS(Vector Image Service) [1][2], Flash [3]–[6] and SVG(Scalable Vector Graphics) [7][8]. Using these technologies, users can enjoy wallpaper service, game service, map service, and so on. VIS [1][2] is a wireless multimedia solution developed by NeoMtel, Korea. Comparing to Flash, VIS has smaller memory usage, faster decoding speed and smaller program size.

The materials in multimedia contents cannot be changed once they are made. Though there are user interactions, only the scenarios, image and sound which are already included in the contents, can be played. For the effective use of the contents and wireless network, self-networking functions and replaceable structure are required. Combining with the portability and mobility of wireless handset, various applications can be developed by use of self-networking functions. In fact, Flash also can import external SWF files. However, in Flash, the files which can be imported in it are only SWF files. Comparing to Flash, in VIS, various data can be downloaded from the server such as text string, image, sound, VIS and action script. The range of application is wide for wireless handset.

In this paper, self-networking and replaceable structure for downloaded contents are introduced for wireless internet. Self-networking schemes and replaceable structures in contents are proposed and implemented to wireless internet services. The throughput analysis of the proposed structure is given based on the markov process. The gain of the proposed method is analyzed using markov model. Also, the applications using the proposed methods in wireless handset are presented.

The remainder of this paper is organized as follows. In Section 2, the structure of VIS player is introduced. In Section 3, the self-networking and replaceable structure of VIS and its implementation are discussed. In Section 4, the throughput analysis of the proposed method is given. In Section 5, various applications using the proposed structures are presented and the conclusion follows in Section 6.

2   Structure of VIS Player

VIS(vector image solution) is a vector graphic solution for wireless handset developed by NeoMtel cooperation and is on service in Korean market. It is optimized for constraints in current mobile handsets such as processing power and

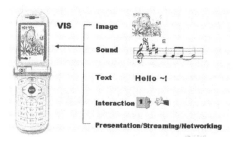

Fig. 1. Components of VIS player

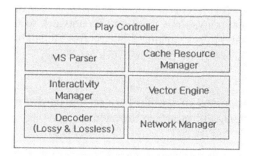

Fig. 2. Structure of VIS player

memory usage by removing relatively impractical components of SVG and adopting additional useful parts for commercial service.

In VIS player, there are raster graphics engine, vector graphics engine, action script for interaction, sound/midi interfaces and self-networking functions. Fig. 1 shows the components of VIS which can be provided for the contents.

Since VIS supports action script, it is possible to play interactive contents, like Flash contents in PC environment, on mobile handset. Moreover, it can be integrated with the previous program of mobile handset without deteriorating stability of the program. Hence, it is possible to support interactive wallpaper service, which responses on key input directly in idle mode of mobile handset.

The structure of VIS player is shown in Fig. 2. Brief functional descriptions of each module are as follows.

- VIS Parser: is an API set for parsing command from VIS file contents. VIS uses command set based on bit-fields to reduce size of repetitive commands and vector type data.
- Cache and Resource Manager: enables rich content to be played in poor resource environment. It keeps frequently used and high cost resource to reduce stream input/output cost and processing cost. This manages resource status dynamically by using memory allocation capability of system.
- Interactivity Manager: supports various event based interactivity, such as action script, flow control, sound control, vibration control, hyperlink, graphi-

cal button operation, etc. It enables rich contents like simple games, graphical clock, graphical battery monitors.

- Vector Engine: is a drawing library for vector graphics which is capable of handling bezier curves, bezier fill, morphing, lines, shapes, gradient color effects, alpha transparency, etc. It is optimized for fast drawing process.
- Decoder (Lossy and Lossless): decodes compressed data of raster graphic image in various compression technique such as Huffman, PNG, JPEG, etc. For present mobile handsets, raster graphic images can be more effectively used due to small size of LCD display.
- Player Controller: shows VIS contents with player skin in player mode where VIS contents are played for preview before it is selected as wallpaper in idle mode.
- Network Manager: relays data from mobile network to Cache and Resource Manager. It is integrated various adaptor functions that is using network operation and makes data from network as if there were from local flash memory.

VIS modules are ported in mobile handset on hardware interface layer by using adaptor functions and interface functions.

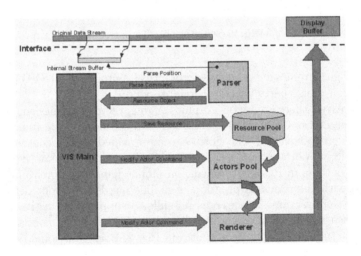

Fig. 3. Structure of vector graphics engine

Especially, the vector graphics engine part has the structures of Fig. 3. The processing algorithms for vector graphics engine is as follows.

- The memory of handset is limited. For the effective processing, predefined size of data is read from the input stream.
- The read data is parsed. After parsing, the position of data is recorded.
- The parsed data is saved in resource pool.

— If there is a modify or actors command to display the resource data, the data
  is transferred to actors pool.
— The data is rendered for the display buffer.

It takes much time in wireless handset to execute the vector graphics engine.
It is possible to prevent other tasks while running the vector graphics engine. In
order not to affect other tasks, after a certain amount of time, the possession of
CPU is transferred to handset program.

3   Self-networking and Replaceable Structure in VIS

3.1   Introduction of Self-networking and Replaceable Structure

The conventional multimedia contents cannot be changed or modified once they
are made, without downloading new contents. But The self-networking and replaceable structure functions can give many characteristics. The user can download only the changed part of the contents and can save the cost. Combining with
the RTOS in handset, various data can be downloaded and many applications
can be developed.

In self-networking, some data is transmitted using networking functions in
contents from the server. The data is adopted to the play of the contents appropriately using replaceable structure. In the implementation of VIS, the structures
which enable to communicate with external server and can modify the contents
and scenario are designed and implemented.

For example, let us think the avatar service. In conventional methods, even
if one wants to change only the part of face, a new contents with different face
should be made separately and it should be transmitted to the handset. Though
the changed part in face is very small, the whole file should be downloaded.
Also, after transmission, prior file which is playing must be stopped and the
transmitted file is played. Comparing to this case, when using the self-networking
functions, only the changed part is transmitted. Also, the changes in file are done
in playing the contents. These characteristics can make various applications in
wireless handset.

In fact, Flash also can import external SWF files using the script function
loadmovie(). However, in Flash, the files which can be imported in it are only
SWF files. Comparing to Flash, in VIS, various data can be downloaded from
the server such as text string, image, sound, VIS and action script. The range
of application is wide for wireless handset.

The data can be transmitted using PUSH, using downloading from the server
or using SMS. The wireless handset has the characteristics of portability and
mobility which make it possible to send the data anytime and anywhere.

3.2   Implementation of Replaceable Structure in VIS

In VIS, the replaceable structure is provided to change the components in the
contents. The following components can be imported to VIS contents:

1. Text string
2. Image
3. Sound
4. VIS contents
5. Action script

Fig. 4 shows the concept of replaceable structure. As in Fig. 4, new components are imported in the contents and the previous components are deleted.

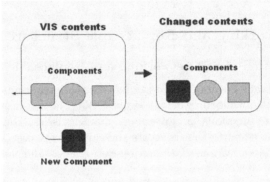

Fig. 4. Replaceable structure of VIS

The characteristics of replaceable structure in VIS is as follows:

1. The same type components can be changed. That is, the sound components in VIS can be changed with sound components.
2. To change the component, the import functions do not use the filename directly but just use the component information.
3. Regarding the limited memory in wireless handset, the maximum data size which can be changed is fixed. Before uploading the contents or changing components to the server, they should be verified from the authoring tool.
4. The history of changing is not managed. After changing the previous data is removed.

3.3   Implementation of Self-networking in VIS

It is good for wireless network services, if the following characteristics are satisfied for the self-networking:

1. Network functions should be provided in contents itself.
2. It is possible to connect to the server and download some data in contents.
3. Not only the play data such as image, sound and text, but also the control data for the play control of contents should be downloaded.
4. The downloaded data can be included in the contents and the contents can be changed using downloaded data.
5. Networking functions can be controlled by the user interactions in contents.
6. The designer of VIS contents can handle the network functions in contents.

Considering these characteristics, VIS self-networking functions are implemented. While VIS file is played, some data is downloaded from the server and it affects the play of VIS contents. In this implementation, the data consist of the control data for the control and the resource data for image, sound, text string, VIS file and action scripts. The amount of transmitted data can be reduced. Also, the downloading and modification in contents are independent of the play and they can operate without stopping the play of contents.

In VIS, to request the data from server and download it, some script functions are called such as **loadVariables()**, **importImage()**, **importSound()** and **importMovie()**. Once the script function runs, the VIS player connects to the server and requests data. In downloading data, the progress of VIS contents is holding and the player should notify the user of the downloading status. After the transmission of data, in the case of failure, the user has a display that notifying failure. In case of success, the operation relating to the data are processed. Usually, the data request is done by VIS player. But in a special case such as **PUSH**, external data is downloaded without the request of VIS player. For example, in broadcasting, transmission of data from web site or data transmission using SMS, the request and download are done by **PUSH**. Also in **PUSH**, the downloaded data are included in VIS files using some appropriate functions. Fig. 5 shows the processes of data transmission of self-networking in VIS.

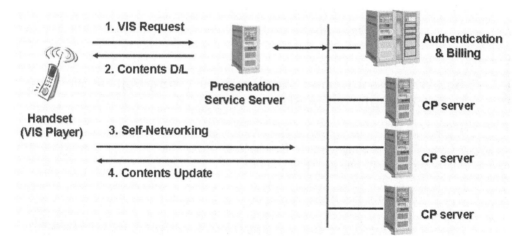

Fig. 5. VIS networking data transmission sequence

The downloaded data can be divided into two parts such as control data and resource data. These data are managed as follows:

- **Control data**
  Using control data, VIS player can change the play of contents. Mainly, the control data changes the value of script variable. Scene variation in the display or value setting of the size and position can be done using these data.

– **Resource data**

In case of resource data, it changes the resource in contents such ad text, sound, image or VIS file. For text, the news or SMS data can be displayed on the screen.

After the downloaded data is applied to the contents, the current state is recorded in the handset. In replaying the contents, the status information is considered and the changes by the network can be adopted.

4 Throughput Analysis of the Proposed Method Based on the Markov Process

In a special case, the self-networking and replaceable structure can be modeled as Markov process. Fig. 6 shows the Markov modeling of the proposed method.

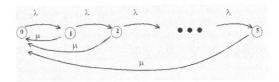

Fig. 6. Markov modeling of the proposed method

5 Wireless Internet Applications Using Self-networking and Replaceable Structure in VIS

Various applications can be developed with self-networking and replaceable structure in VIS combining with the handset and wireless network characteristics. The following applications are the examples.

5.1 Menu in Wireless Handset

The menu in wireless handset can be easily implemented using replaceable structure. Since in the menu VIS components are used, the menu can be composed using various multimedia components and can be easily changed using self-networking and replaceable structure. Also, user-made menu structure can be implemented. Fig. 7 shows the menu component changes in VIS.

5.2 Real-Time News

The news are displayed on the handset in realtime using image, text or sound. Combining with script, the news on economy, sports and others can be selected by the user. Especially, the news flash can be provided using **PUSH** from the server.

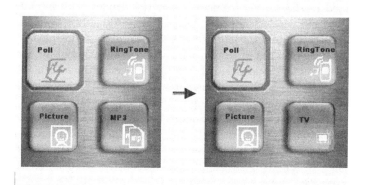

Fig. 7. Menu changes

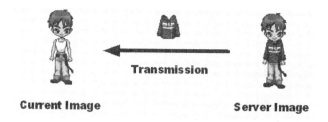

Fig. 8. Avatar images and data transmission

5.3   Mobile Avatar

The clothes, hair style and so on can be downloaded from the server and can be applied to the contents in the handset. Relating to the avatar in website, the variation of it can be adopted to the avatar in handset. Fig. 8 shows the transmission in avatar contents.

5.4   Survey

After making survey contents using VIS, the result from the user input are transferred to the server over wireless network. If one changes the problem of survey, it is possible to get a new result.

5.5   Application of Photos

The user can make his own contents with transmitting his photos. The handset-camera can make the most of the VIS photo contents.

6   Conclusion

In this paper, self-networking and replaceable structure in contents have been described for wireless internet using handset. The conventional multimedia contents are fixed in the sense of scenario and the display. For the effective uses of the contents and wireless network, the self-networking functions are required. When playing the contents, it connects to the server and download some additional data for the changes of contents material or the control for the play. The basic concepts, implementation in VIS and the applications using these methods have been presented. These characteristics can make various applications in wireless handset combining with the portability and mobility.

In this implementation, the transmitted data includes image, sound, text string, VIS file and action script. Using the self-networking and replaceable structure, only the changed part is transmitted. Since the transmitted data is small, it is cost-effective and bandwidth-effective. Also, the changes in contents are adopted at once in playing the contents. The throughput analysis of the proposed method using Markov process has shown that the proposed method is effective in the sense of transferred data in wireless network.

As shown in the example services using VIS self-networking and replaceable structure, various applications can be developed effectively.

Acknowledgments

This work was supported in part by the new faculty research program 2005 of Kookmin University in Korea.

References

1. Neomtel, http://www.neomtel.com
2. Doohee Jung, Gu-Min Jeong and Sung-Kyun Yoon, "Wallpaper interaction in wireless handset using VIS (Vector Image Solution)", to appear in IEICE Transctions on Comminications.
3. Macromedia Cooperation, http://www.macromedia.com
4. Mi-Jeong Kim, Eunkyu Lee, Byoung-Woo Oh, Min-Soo Kim, "A study on geographic data services based on dynamically generated flash in wireless Internet", IEEE Geoscience and Remote Sensing Symposium, Vol. 6, 2003, 3712 - 3714
5. Scott, C.J., "Vector animation: Web-based software training on demand", Aerospace Conference Proceedings, 2000 IEEE , pp. 473-479, 2000.
6. Macromedia Flah File Format SDK, http://www.openswf.org
7. Quint, A., "Scalable vector graphics". IEEE Multimedia, Vol. 10, July-Sept. pp. 99–102, 2003.
8. Scalable Vector Graphics, http://www.w3.org/Graphics/SVG/

Privacy-Aware Location Dependent Services over Wireless Internet with Anycast

Kosuke Tomonaga[1], Masataka Ohta[2], and Keijiro Araki[3]

[1] Graduate School of Information Science and Electrical Engineering, Kyushu University,
6-10-1 Hakozaki, Higashi-ku, Fukuoka 812-8581, Japan
tomonaga@ale.csce.kyushu-u.ac.jp
[2] Graduate School of Information Science and Engineering, Tokyo Institute of Technology,
2-12-1 O-okayama, Meguro-ku, Tokyo 152-8552, Japan
mohta@necom830.hpcl.titech.ac.jp
[3] Department of Computer Science and Communication Engineering, Kyushu University,
6-10-1 Hakozaki, Higashi-ku, Fukuoka 812-8581, Japan
araki@ale.csce.kyushu-u.ac.jp

Abstract. With the spread of mobile communication in recent years, location dependent services become important. Along with it, the privacy protection of mobile subscribers, too, becomes important. This paper describes anycast-based architecture of location dependent services in wide areas with short-range wireless access technologies such as wireless LAN. As an application, it discusses a WWW implementation used in ISP's access network using anycast and mechanisms that subscribers can apply to enforce their privacy policies by themselves before they disclose personal location information to each WWW server out of the access network. A field trial is being performed at MIAKO.net, a public wireless ISP in Kyoto, JAPAN, to provide location dependent tourist information.

1 Introduction

A location dependent service provides mobile subscribers with information like local weather forecast, local traffic reports, yellow pages of local shops, etc., which can vary according to the location of the mobile subscribers.

There are existing location dependent services for cellular phone and Personal Handyphone System (PHS) [1, 2]. Some services provide a gateway server between the telephony network and the Internet, so the mobile phone can get World Wide Web (WWW) contents from the Internet through the gateway server by using its own location information.

However, there is a privacy concern. That is, the location information of each subscriber must not be released to WWW servers without agreement of each, because it indicates where the subscriber is. There are three methods to let subscribers control disclosure of their location information. One method requires each subscriber to set their privacy policy into their cellular phone. The other method requires each subscriber to answer confirmation messages from the gateway server. The third method is to let subscribers' ISPs indirectly control the disclosure. As the third method does not

S. Shimojo et al. (Eds.): HSI 2005, LNCS 3597, pp. 311-321, 2005 follow the end-to-end principle and can not realize dynamic detailed configuration, we adapt the first or the second method in this paper.

This paper describes anycast-based architecture of location dependent services in wide area wireless environment with short-range access technologies such as PHS or wireless LAN. IP anycast [3] is a mechanism to share an address by multiple servers and to deliver an IP packet with the anycast destination address to the closest (according to the network topology) server among servers sharing the anycast addresses. When network topology and geography are closely related, such as the case with short range access networks of wireless LAN, anycast can be used to access the geographically nearest server.

However, as IP headers have no location information, location information must be maintained by upper layers. As an application protocol, this paper describes a WWW implementation used in ISP's access network using anycast and mechanisms that subscribers can apply to enforce their privacy policies by themselves before they disclose personal location information to each WWW server out of the access network. If an ISP assigns the same anycast address to each wireless base station, mobile clients can get information from the nearest wireless base station using anycast, and the information can vary the wireless base station by the wireless base station. Furthermore, if location information is returned to subscribers using HTTP [4] redirection to an HTTP server, the centralized management by the redirected server can be realized.

This mechanism is being tested at MIAKO.net in Kyoto, JAPAN, to provide location dependent tourist information.

2 Background and Related Work

2.1 Location Dependent Services for Cellular Phone and PHS

There are existing location dependent services for cellular phone and PHS. And some services provide a gateway server between the telephony network and the Internet. Each mobile phone can get WWW contents from the Internet through the gateway server by using its own location information which is determined in two different approaches:

1) The location is determined by the base station of a cell serving the mobile terminal [1].
2) The location is calculated as geographical location information through the Global Positioning System (GPS) [2].

With the first approach, the location service can not handle more precise location information than sizes of the cells. With the second approach, each mobile device needs a large amount of hardware of GPS receiver. In this paper, we realize location dependent services in the Internet by using the first approach.

2.2 Location Dependent Services Using Multicast and GPS

In [5], a method to provide location dependent services using IP multicast is described. According to [5], a mobile client tries to find servers using multicast solicitation which includes the location information obtained from a GPS receiver of the client, and the closest corresponding server is chosen to retrieve contents.

The differences between multicast and anycast are discussed in [3]. The major difference between anycast and multicast is that anycast uses existing unicast addressing and routing mechanisms while multicast requires more sophisticated routing support (See Fig. 1). Another difference between the two approaches is that resource location using multicast typically causes large number of packets generated, because with multicast, ring search, which starts with a small TTL and retries with incremented TTL until a desired server is found, is used with multiple retries, packet for which may delivered to a lot of servers at the last retry.

GPS [6, 7] provides highly accurate location information but it is necessary to attach the GPS receiver to each mobile client and install software to obtain and send the location information to location dependent servers. Furthermore, for public service, all clients and servers must use the same protocol to send and receive the location information but there are no common standards at present.

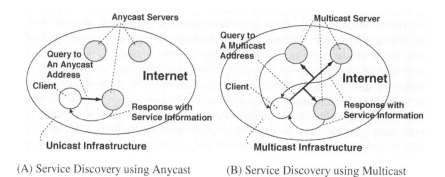

(A) Service Discovery using Anycast   (B) Service Discovery using Multicast

Fig. 1. Comparison of Anycast and Multicast Service Discovery

2.3 Location Dependent Services Using Anycast

IP anycast [3] is a mechanism which provides a stateless best effort delivery of an IP packet to the closest one of a group of servers that shares the same anycast address where 'closest' is defined according to the routing system's measure of distance.

Anycast enables ISP to distribute anycast servers sharing an anycast address and to provide some service to clients from the closest anycast server. This realizes client auto-configuration, automatic discovery of service location, and load distribution between anycast servers.

RFC 1546 [3] proposed the original idea of IP anycast and introduce an example of FTP service. By using anycast, mirrored FTP servers could share a single anycast address and FTP clients could simply use the anycast address to reach the nearest server. On the other hand, RFC 3258 [8] proposed to realize geographic diversity of DNS server placement and reduce the effects of service disruptions due to local problems. In spite of high number of potential applications of anycast, there are not enough practical ones.

Anycast addresses can be assigned from the existing unicast address space. It is possible to use traditional unicast routing protocols such as RIP [9], OSPF [10], BGP [11], or static unicast route configuration to realize anycast routing.

If a mobile ISP using wireless LAN as its access network assigns an anycast address to each wireless base station, mobile clients can get information from the nearest wireless base station using anycast and the information can be specific to the wireless base station. Furthermore if the information is distributed with WWW, centralized management of contents can be realized by using redirection mechanism of HTTP [4] to redirect the original query to a new URL, which is a combination of the original URL and location information to a central server.

A routing table growth is the most serious problem in anycast routing. One anycast address needs one entry in routing tables, because anycast addresses, servers of which are, in general, located at different locations, can not be aggregated. Therefore, advertisement of a lot of anycast addresses between ISPs cause a routing explosion problem on the Internet backbone (Fig. 2). We can see, in Fig 3, that the advertisement inside each ISP prevents the problem at the backbone.

Furthermore, there are some trivial concerns in anycast. For example, if a unicast server replies to an anycast client, packets from server will not be delivered to the client, but to the closest from the server. However anycast is originally proposed for servers and it is not important to consider the problems for anycast clients. On the other hand, an anycast server and a unicast client can not keep session if route changes and the route to the server switches to another anycast server. But, as many applications can detect server change (using, for example, TCP port and sequence numbers) and reestablish another session with the new anycast server that, it is not a problem unless required session length is longer than expected route change intervals.

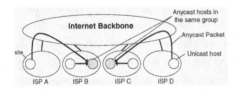

Fig. 2. Anycast over ISP sites

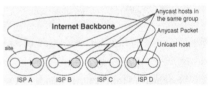

Fig. 3. Anycast in each ISP site

3 Discussion

3.1 Privacy Issues

The location information of each subscriber may be disclosed to his ISP but must not be disclosed to WWW server operated by third party without agreement from the subscriber, because it indicates where the subscriber is. There are three methods to ask subscribers whether they allow disclosure of their location information or not. One method requires each subscriber to set their privacy policy on their mobile device. And the other method requires each subscriber to answer confirmation messages from the gateway server which maintains the location information. The third method is to let subscribers' ISPs control the disclosure. As the third method does not follow the end-to-end principle and can not realize dynamic detailed configuration, we adapt the first or the second method in this paper.

3.2 Transparency of Location Dependent Services to the WWW System

In designing location dependent services, if every process follows the standards of each layer, e.g. IEEE802.11 [12], IP, TCP, and HTTP/1.1, the services are expected to become transparent to WWW software such as browsers, servers, and authoring tools. Therefore we follow the existing standards in this paper.

3.3 Issue of Routing Table Growth of Anycast

Anycast addresses can not be aggregated into one prefix. Therefore advertisement for anycast addresses causes routing table growth even if the anycast is limited inside an ISP. But ISPs can cover the cost of routing table growth if they levy a fixed amount of money per one anycast address.

4 Design of a Location Dependent Services Using Anycast

WWW is the most popular information system on the Internet at present. Many users can make and distribute their own contents easily. In this chapter, we describe a detailed design of privacy-aware location dependent service using WWW and anycast in wireless LAN environments [12].

4.1 Physical and Data-Link Layers

We assume that subscribers of location dependent services are carrying their mobile devices having a wireless LAN interface to be connected to base stations by wireless LAN.

A mobile host connected to a wireless base station might be considered to be connected to a near-by wireless base station because each mobile host is always comparing the signal strength of the physical media and try to stay connected with the wireless base station transmitting the strongest signal, because with weak power of wireless LAN devices, signal can not travel long distance.

The cell size of a wireless base station determines the accuracy of location dependent services. For example, the cell size in general 802.11b [13] environment is approximately from a few ten meters to a few hundred meters.

4.2 Internetworking Layer

We assume that ISP uses traditional unicast routing protocol such as RIP [9], OSPF [10], BGP [11] or static routing configuration in the access network. In this layer, ISP assigns the same anycast address to every wireless base station which ISP wants to provide location dependent services. Therefore, mobile clients can send packets to the closest wireless base station by anycast and the base station is located near the clients.

It is also possible to assign the same anycast address to servers around each wire-less base station. In this case, ISP must prepare one anycast route from the wireless base station to the closest server.

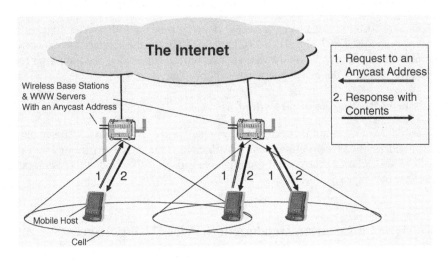

Fig. 4. A Simple Location dependent Service using WWW and Anycast

4.3 Transport and Application Layers

We assume that subscribers wish to use existing software to make, distribute, or browse contents. Therefore standard IP, TCP and HTTP [4] are assumed in internet-working, transport and application layers. As there is no room for standard IP and TCP to carry location information, HTTP is the layer to carry the information.

The simplest location dependent service can be provided, if ISP installs a WWW server on each wireless base station sharing an anycast address. Each WWW server can listen to HTTP contents request messages bound for the anycast address, and respond with its own contents, which depending on the location of the wireless base station (Fig. 4).

In this case, a wireless base station can determine that mobile hosts connected to the station are located in a cell of the station. In this case, the ISP operating the base stations itself operates the servers that the ISP should pay usual attention to operate the base station as servers not to disclose the privacy information to others.

A problem of this approach is that distributed maintenance of the contents on all the servers is burdensome. If the content is large, all the servers must have its own copy of the contents, which is a waste of storage space. Therefore in the next chapter, we will show another method of centralized management of contents on a few web servers.

4.4 Privacy-Aware Integration of Location Dependent Contents

HTTP [4] redirection messages realize centralized management of WWW contents in a flexible way. A WWW server can respond with HTTP redirection message which suggests the client redirect a new URL that corresponds to an old requested URL. If some servers respond with HTTP redirection to a contents server, it means the centralized management of contents is realized because subscribers can maintain their contents on the same contents server (Fig. 5).

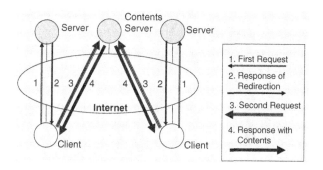

Fig. 5. Centralized Management

The HTTP redirection message also realizes the centralized management of location dependent contents, if location information is embedded in URLs. An example of location information embedded in URLs is:

> http://www.contents-srv.example.com/srv.cgi?lon=130.25.24.
> 506&lat=33.37.07.474

> http://www.contents-srv.example.com/cel-id-hakozaki-shrine /

where the first example embeds location information as latitude and longitude and the second example embeds it as a name of the location. And each URL also includes the hostport part of a location dependent WWW server which contains the every location dependent content of the URL.

With the redirection method, while the wireless base stations as servers are operated by ISPs, redirected servers are operated by, in general, third parties. And the location information of each subscriber must not be released to WWW servers without agreement of each. Therefore we adapt the second method in Chapter 1 that requires each subscriber to answer confirmation messages from the gateway servers.

An anycast server on/around wireless base station responds with the redirection message. And every mobile host gets the redirection message from the anycast server on/around the closest wireless base station. If a mobile host accepts the suggestion of a redirection message and accesses to the URL in the message, they can get the contents from the location dependent WWW server. But if not, they never send any information such as their location information to the WWW server (Fig. 6).

In this case, each subscriber or mobile client can determine whether their location information should be disclosed to each third-party WWW location dependent server or not because they control whether each HTTP redirection message should be accepted or not. Subscribers can, for example, configure their mobile clients a list of servers that they consider safe to be used for HTTP redirections.

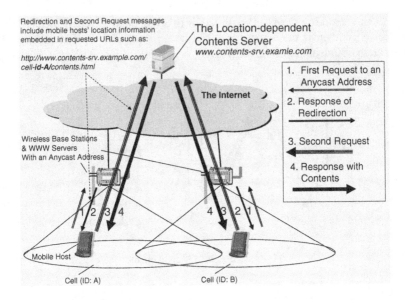

Fig. 6. Centralized Management of a Location dependent Service using Anycast

5 Implementation

We develop a small WWW server to realize our design. In this section, we provide a brief description of our implementation.

The platform of our implementation is ROOT INC's RGW2400 series [14]. RGW is a wireless router based on NetBSD and it is easy for BSD users to program the RGWs. We wrote approximately 1,000 source code lines to develop the server.

Our small WWW server adds at least one anycast address to a link local interface of RGW, and listens to the interface for HTTP request from clients. If the server received a HTTP request, it responds with a HTTP redirect message that includes the hostport part of location dependent WWW server and the location information of RGW.

6 Field Trial

We introduce an example of location dependent service using our implementation.

MIAKO.NET (Mobile Internet Access in KyotO) [15] is a public wireless Internet service in Kyoto Prefecture, JAPAN. It has already set up more than 200 access points in Kyoto and some of them are in outdoors, for example at the roof of a building, at the middle of a telegraph pole, covers streets and squares, etc.

MIAKO.NET provides a location dependent service using anycast in Muromachi area in Kyoto (Fig. 7). The service "GION BAYASHI MEGURI" automatically guide a visitor to a web page that provides the sounds of the nearest parade float of GION MATSURI without specifying any location of the subscriber.

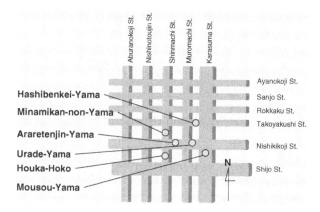

Fig. 7. Service Area around Muromachi and the location of the parade floats (circled)

7 Evaluation

7.1 Privacy Issues

The location dependent service using anycast has two cases to distribute the contents. The first case shows that wireless base stations can identify which mobile hosts are connected to them and distribute content, which depends on locations of base stations, to the host. In this case, ISPs, which are operating the wireless base stations, should pay attention to the privacy policy of subscribers' location information and must keep it as a secret. On the other hand, the second case shows that each anycast server on/around every wireless base station can determine the place of mobile clients and distribute the HTTP redirection messages to the clients. In this case, each mobile host can determine whether their location information can be disclosed or not to servers operated by, in general, third parties indicated by every HTTP redirection message because they make decision about accepting each message. However each mobile host must have a function to make user decide about the accepting. Therefore we adapt the first method in Chapter 1 that each subscriber to set their privacy policy into their mobile hosts. Thus, it can be said that subscribers has full control over disclosure of their location.

7.2 Transparency of Location Dependent Services to WWW Users

The location dependent services using anycast are transparent to WWW servers and authoring tools, because all the components in our design conform to standard IEEE802.11, IP, and HTTP/1.1. Therefore it is not necessary to modify the existing servers and authoring tools. But it is necessary to add code to the HTTP redirection function of every WWW client to ask subscribers whether they accept the redirection messages or not.

7.3 Stability and Robustness of Location Dependent Services

When the number of subscribers increases and a central server is overloaded, multiple central servers may be used. Each anycast server can redirect requests to a different central server and distribute the load of central servers.

7.4 IP Tunneling Problem of Location Dependent Services Using Anycast

If reverse tunneling [16] is used to tunnel packets from a mobile host to its home agent, location dependent services using anycast does not work correctly for the mobile host because encapsulated IP anycast packets are delivered to the closest anycast server at the other side of tunnel, that is, at home agents, location of which is static and has nothing to do with location of mobile hosts.

There are two solutions to the reverse tunneling problem in anycast. One solution is not to use reverse tunneling. Another solution is that wireless base stations which provide location dependent services strip all the encapsulated IP packet to itself and receive them directly.

8   Conclusion

This paper shows how to use anycast to realize location dependent WWW service to subscribers transparent to existing software such as IP, TCP, WWW server and authoring tool. It also describes mechanisms that subscribers can apply to enforce their privacy policies by themselves before they disclose personal location information to WWW servers out of the access network. When an ISP assigns the same anycast address to all the wireless base stations, mobile clients can get redirection messages from the closest wireless base station with strongest signal by using anycast and decide to accept or reject the redirected privacy statement of the wireless base station. The described mechanism was efficiently corroborated in the field trial in MIAKO.net.

References

1. WILLCOM, Inc.:http://www.ddipocket.co.jp/p_s/service/location/index.html
2. NTT DoCoMo, Inc.:http://www.dlpservice.jp/index2.php
3. Partridge, C., Mendez, T., and Milliken, W.: Host Anycasting Service. RFC1546 (1993)
4. Fielding, R., Getty, J., Mogul, J., Frystyk, H., Masinter, L., Leach, P., and Berners-Lee, T.: Hypertext transfer Protocol--HTTP/1.1. RFC2616 (1999)
5. Acharya, A., Badrinath, B., Imielinski, T., Navas, J.:A WWW-based Location-dependent Information Service for Mobile Clients. Rutgers University Computer Science (1995)
6. USCG.: GPS SPS Signal Specification, 2nd Edition. http://www.navcen.uscg.gov/pubs/gps/sigspec/default.htm (1995)
7. USCG.: USCG DIFFERENTIAL GPS NAVIGATION SERVICE. http://www.navcen.uscg.gov/pubs/dgps/dgpsdoc.pdf

8. Hardie, T.: Distributing Authoritative Name Servers via Shared Unicast Address. RFC3258 (2002)
9. Malkin, G.: RIP Version 2. RFC2453 (1998)
10. Moy, J.: OSPF Version 2. RFC2328 (1998)
11. Rekhter, Y., Li, T.: A Border Gateway Protocol 4 (BGP-4). RFC1771 (1995)
12. IEEE.: Wireless LAN Medium Access Control (MAC) and Physical Layer (PHY) Specifications. IEEE802.11 (1999)
13. IEEE.: Wireless LAN Medium Access Control(MAC) and Physical Layer(PHY) Specifications: High-Speed Physical Layer Extention in the 2.4 GHz Band. IEEE802.11b (1999)
14. ROOT INC.:http://www.root-hq.com/e/products/RGW2400.html
15. Komura, T., Fujikawa, K., and Okabe, Y.: The MIAKO.NET Public Wireless Internet Service in Kyoto. Proc. of WMASH 2003 (2003)
16. Montenegro, G.: Reverse Tunneling, revised. RFC3024 (2001)

Economically-Motivated Decentralized Control of Eco-Network Computation Platform

Lei Gao[1] and Yongsheng Ding[1,2]

[1] College of Information Sciences and Technology
[2] Digitized Textile and Fashion Technology Engineering Research Center,
of National Education Ministry,
Donghua University, Shanghai 200051, P. R. China
ysding@dhu.edu.cn

Abstract. The complexity of the evolving web requires autonomous and adaptive web applications. To construct a nature-inspired multi-agent system may be an important means of addressing this. However what mechanisms are appropriate for agents to emerge such an applications is still under consideration. This paper considers a credit card mechanism in economic interactions as a decentralized control approach of the eco-network computation platform (a nature-inspired multi-agent system). The simulation results prove that the approach can offer a guarantee for the platform to emerge autonomous and adaptive web applications.

1   Introduction

The evolving web will be more complex for people to use and manage, so autonomous and adaptive web applications are urgently needed. Nature-inspired computing approaches [1] may be an important means of addressing this. They incline to construct an ecosystem-inspired multi-agent system, where agents is simple but their collective behaviors arising from their interactions exceeds the capacities of any individual agent. However what mechanisms are appropriate for a desired web applications emerge from these agents is still under consideration.

Inspired by the strong resemblance between the flexible response to changing circumstances generated by the economic flows and resource dynamics in ecosystems, this paper considers a *credit card* mechanism as a decentralized control of our ecosystem-inspired multi-agent system named eco-network computation platform [2, 3]. A *credit card management service* of the eco-network platform to control eco-resident behaviors is designed. Hence Section 2 proposes the credit card management service. A simulation is conducted in Section 3 to evaluate the control mechanism. Section 4 concludes our research efforts.

2   Credit Card Management Service

2.1   The Eco-Network Architecture

In our previous work [2, 3], we proposed the eco-network architecture and developed a novel eco-network platform, in which a web application can emerge from

S. Shimojo et al. (Eds.): HSI 2005, LNCS 3597, pp. 322–325, 2005.

a collection of *eco-residents* (An eco-resident is term for an autonomous agent in the eco-network architecture) that like the creatures living in a large ecosystem. Each eco-resident can follow a simple set of behavior rules (e.g. migration, reproduction, and death) and implement a functional component related to its web application. From the top down, the layered eco-network architecture includes *Eco-resident Survivable Environment, Eco-network Core Services, Eco-network Low-level Functional Modules,* Java Virtual Machine, and a heterogeneous distributed system established in a network node for deploying wide-area web applications. (1) Eco-network Survivable Environment layer is runtime environment for deploying and executing the eco-residents. (2) The Eco-network Core Service layer provides a set of general-purpose runtime services that are frequently used by eco-residents. They include naming service, resource sensing service, eco-resident migration service, evolution state management service, and security authentication service. (3) In Eco-network Low-level Functional Modules layer, local resource management modules manage resources of networks and systems.

In the Eco-network Core Service layer, we design a credit card management service that draws inspiration from economic interactions.

2.2   Design of the Credit Card Management Service

The maintenance and evolution of the "inside in order" status in an ecosystem must rely on a kind of cycled flow. Choosing the money as the units to form a cycled flow, we can set a credit card to each eco-resident and enable it to be responsible for its performed behaviors. In the eco-network architecture, an eco-resident must store and consume money in its credit card for its livings. The roles of a credit card are shown as follows: (1) An eco-resident expends money for its usage of resources. (2) To gain money from the users, an eco-resident needs to perform a service. (3) An eco-resident that provides a service with high (low) service quality will rewarded (punished) by increasing (decreasing) the money in its credit card. (4) If the money expenditure of an eco-resident is more than its money earning by providing a service, it will finally lack of money and lose the permission to use resources. As thus, it dies from its wasteful performances.

Three components are designed in credit card management service: information center, bargaining bazaar, and market agency. Also, we use Eco-Network Communication Language (ENCL) [4] for implementing communications among eco-residents. (1) Each platform has one information center, which is responsible for the registration, maintaining and management of the credit card table. Credit card table stores the information of the eco-residents that run in the platform. Evolution state management service of eco-network can add and delete the records of the credit card table. (2) Within bargaining bazaar, the service providers and consumers can seek for suitable service partners, negotiate the price and defray the money. It also includes the pricing center and the bargaining tables. Every bargaining table can manage and track the money defrayment information including message ID, service provider ID, service provider address, and negotiated price. The bargaining tables are created based on ENCL messages seized by market agency. When the service ends, these tables will be destroyed. (3) Market agency seizes the interacting messages from every eco-resident and then delivers these messages to bargaining bazaar. Meanwhile, it sends the messages to update the money amount in the credit cards of the eco-residents.

3   Simulation Experiment

To evaluate the credit card management service, we simulate an application named "web page personalized recommendation" and develop a corresponding simulator on the eco-network computation platform. The minimum capabilities such as *resource sensing service, eco-resident migration service, evolution state management serve,* and *credit card management service* are also implemented.

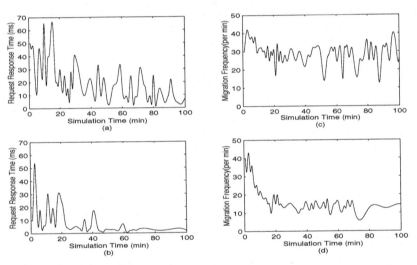

Fig. 1. The request response time and migration frequency of the eco-residents in two experiment settings. (a) The request response time without credit card management service; (b) The request response time with credit card management service; (c) The migration frequency without credit card management service; (d) The migration frequency with credit card management service

The network topology of the simulator has 216 nodes. When the simulator starts, 20 eco-residents and 60 service requesters are produced. Each eco-resident may own one or more web pages for recommendation with different prices and contents. At regular intervals, each requester generates randomly lots of user requests for web pages with different user requirements in different positions of the topology. If the content, response time and quality of personalized recommendation service meet user requirements, the eco-residents participating in serving will receive more money. The credit card management service periodically inquires resource sensing service to check the price of each resource and resource utilization of each eco-resident on the platform, and then according to resource prices, deducts the expense from the credit card of each eco-resident. If there is no money in the credit card of an eco-resident, the credit card management service asks evolution state management serve to destroy the eco-resident.

We conduct a comparison in two experiment settings: with credit card management service and without credit card management service. The eco-residents near the requests have the priorities to serve first. We evaluate the request response time and migration frequency of the eco-residents in two conditions as shown in Fig. 1. We can see from the Fig. 1 (a) and (b), relative to in the setting without credit card management service, the user requests are served more quickly (i.e., the response time is shorter) in the setting with credit card management service. This is due to that the eco-residents are responsible for their behaviors and resource allocation structure obtains optimization within credit card management service. Considering the punishments, some eco-residents will not offer their services. Thus the number of unsuitable service providers decreases and the user requests are served quickly. In (c) and (d), comparing the migration frequency of the eco-residents in two settings, we can see that the excessive migration behaviors decrease while the response time is shorter with credit card management service. So we can conclude that credit card management service can optimize web applications emerged from interactions of the eco-residents.

4   Conclusion

This paper has transplanted some concepts and principles of economic interactions to design a credit card management service as the decentralized control mechanism of the eco-network computation platform. The results of a simulation application show the proposed service can make the eco-residents accountable for their activities. Thus web applications emerged from interactions of the eco-residents can obtain better optimization.

Acknowledgments. The work is partly supported by the National Nature Science Foundation of China (60474037 and 60004006), Program for New Century Excellent Talents in University, and Specialized Research Fund for the Doctoral Program of Higher Education from Educational Committee of China (20030255009).

References

1. Bonabeau, E., dorigo, M., and Theraulaz, G.: Swarm Intelligence: From Natural to Artificial Systems, Santa Fe Institute Studies in the Sciences of Complexity. Oxford University Press (1999)
2. Gao, L., Ding, Y.-S., and Ren, L.-H.: A novel ecological network-based computation platform as grid middleware system. Int. J. Intelligent Systems. **19** (2004) 859–884
3. Zhang, X.-F., Ding, Y.-S., Ren, L.-H., and Gao, L.: Immune emergent computation-based bio-Network architecture and its simulation platform. Infor. Sci. submitted
4. Gao, L., Ding, Y.-S., and Ruan, D.: On communication mechanism of ecological network-based grid architecture for emergent computation. Infor. Sci. submitted

Correlations Between Digital Tools and Humans Cognitive Processes

Lucy García, Miguel Nussbaum, and Joselyn Bolton

Departamento de Ciencia de la Computación, Escuela de Ingeniería,
Pontificia Universidad Católica de Chile,
Vicuña Mackenna 4860, Santiago, Chile
{lcgarcia, mn, jbolton}@ing.puc.cl

Abstract. Chat is one of the Internet's services that have had a particularly strong influence on young people, and its effects on their skills development is worthy of investigation. This study focuses on the possible consequences of the use of Chat on cognitive processes. More specifically, it evaluates the impact of frequent Chat use on the development of memory and on cognitive style. This research, exploratory in nature, began with an instrument for classifying 125 students in 5th to 8th grade at schools in Chile, according to their Chat use. We then applied a memory and attention test based on the Digit Span Subtest of the Wechsler Intelligence Scale for Children, followed by a Group Embedded Figures Test to evaluate cognitive styles. The results show that there are significant differences on both tests between frequent and infrequent users of Chat services.

1 Introduction

In recent years the impact of technological progress has been felt most strongly in the area of information and communication technologies (ICTs). With greatly increased power and lower costs, ICTs have become ubiquitous in business and industry and have also penetrated a high percentage of the world's households, giving rise to the so-called Information Society [2].

Today it is impossible to ignore the changes in people's lives brought about by the Internet and its many tools. The new ways of relating with each other, the breakdown of geographical barriers, and the instantaneity of Internet-based activities are just the most evident examples of this [2], [3]. One aspect of the Internet that has caught the attention of users generally and young people in particular is the various Chat services.[1] A recent study by the Pew Internet and American Life Project [10] found that in the U.S. alone, more than 53 million adults, or 43% of Internet users, use instant messaging (IM) programs. The study also showed that these systems are rapidly penetrating American workplaces, with 21% of users employing them in their jobs, and

---

[1] Synchronous computer-mediated text-based communication, whose main purpose is to allow users to converse over the Internet. The most common examples are Internet Relay Chat (IRC), WebChats and instant messaging, the latter provided by various systems currently on the market.

S. Shimojo et al. (Eds.): HSI 2005, LNCS 3597, pp. 326–335, 2005.
© Springer-Verlag Berlin Heidelberg 2005

some (24% of IM users) report that they use them even more than e-mail. The most interesting discovery, however, was that young people are the biggest users of this tool [10], [20]. Chile is no exception to this trend, as demonstrated by a recent study of the World Internet Project Chile [26] which revealed that Chat services are employed by 33% of the country's Internet users. Among users aged 12 to 20, the proportion who use IM programs simultaneously with other tasks was 47.5%.

This proliferation and intensification of Internet Chat services, especially among the younger sectors of the population, calls for further scientific investigation in order to gain a better understanding of the various phenomena arising from the use of this technology and their eventual impacts, at both the individual and social levels. In the present paper, we will focus on the possible consequences of Chat for cognitive processes.

Chat is of particular interest because of the way it brings together persons in different geographic locations and allows them to interact in synchronous fashion by means of text messages. Thus, participants who do not share a common context, and who are often culturally very distinct, are nevertheless able to communicate, understand each other and establish relationships.

The internalization of ICTs and the way they are used imply new and different forms of thinking or constructing thoughts and result in the incorporation of new information into the daily lives of people, who must adapt to these new elements and structure new processes to suit their needs. More particularly, the use of Chat may influence the mental capabilities of young people in that it facilitates the development of social interaction through language, a characteristic peculiar to human beings, thereby broadening their natural possibilities [23].

Vigotsky's cultural-historical theory of higher mental functions holds that the development of tools and language has enabled rapid cultural growth, resulting in mental processes radically different from those possessed by our ancestors. The theory also maintains that human beings' higher cognitive processes are made possible by the constant interaction with these tools, but this interaction produces cognitive changes only when these tools have been appropriated by their users, not by the mere fact of their occasional use [22].

A number of experimental investigations have unearthed evidence on the effects of ICTs and video game use on the development of certain cognitive skills in human subjects [5], [11]. As regards the influence of Chat on cognitive processes, various studies have reported on the phenomenon of multitasking, in which various tasks are simultaneously executed on or off line. Isaacs et al [8] found that young people who use Chat have more interactions with their peers than those who do not use it, and that the Chat interactions are characterized by shorter conversation sessions, more subject threading and more multitasking activities. Meanwhile, Grinter and Palen [6] point out that frequent users of IM perform other activities on the computer such as schoolwork, Internet navigation and e-mail. Other studies confirm that the multitasking phenomenon is a common activity among Internet users, especially those who use Chat [4], [6], [8], [9], [10], [17].

Access to ICTs is not equal, however, and it is this that gives rise to the Digital Divide, defined by Warschauer [24] as the societal split between those who use these technologies as a routine part of their daily lives and those who do not have access to them, or do have such access but do not use them. Statistics on the phenomenon [21],

[19], [18], [7], [26] show that the cognitive skills discussed by various authors [5], [6], [8], [9], [10], [11], [17], [26], are not being developed in population sectors that do not have access to ICTs. This indicates that there exists a new dimension to the Digital Divide, which we shall call the Cognitive Gap.

In the present study we propose to evaluate whether frequent use of Chat develops working memory by virtue of the continual exercise of this faculty through multitasking activities. Working memory is one of the elements of humans' information storage system and plays a crucial role in cognitive processes. Cognitive tasks involve multiple steps with intermediate results that must be stored temporarily in one's mind if such tasks are to be successfully completed, and it is working memory that fulfills this function [1], [14], [16], and would therefore be strengthened in frequent Chat users.

Moreover, when individuals are interacting during a Chat session they must perceive a series of events that are continually changing because of their patterns of use. Typically, they simultaneously establish multiple interactions, have several windows open and running different programs, and generally fragment their argumentation [28]. However, the perception of the status of the different activities being executed does not occur analogously among all Chat users.

In general there exists among human beings a high degree of diversity in the way they perceive and interpret reality and process information, whose particular characteristics are referred to as cognitive style. Among the various cognitive styles, two of the most recognized and studied are known as field dependence-independence. According to this classification, persons who tend to perceive information analytically without being influenced by its context or medium are categorized as Field Independent (FI). By contrast, those who are classed as Field Dependent (FD) are generally influenced in the manner they perceive by environment or context [27]. In the present work we will attempt to demonstrate that frequent Chat users tend to perceive in analytical fashion due to the fact that they must individually attend to the various tasks and applications they are executing.

The rest of this article is organized as follows: Section 2 sets out the design of the experiment and details the tools that are used, Section 3 presents the results, and Section 4 summarizes the conclusions and suggests possible future lines of research.

2 Research Design

This study proposes the following hypotheses:
  Children who frequently use Chat:

- strengthen their working memory, and
- tend to perceive and organize visual information analytically

2.1 Sample Choice

Because of the exploratory nature of this research, a non-probability sample was chosen. This type of study is characterized by a relatively flexible methodology, which allowed us to focus at this stage of the research on private schools from medium-income families in Santiago, Chile. This context allowed us to choose three schools with students with different levels of access to, and use of, Chat services. The similarity of their socioeconomic and academic[2] characteristics enabled comparisons to be made between groups by controlling for the effects of these variables. The sample consisted of a total of 125 students from 5th to 8th grade (year).

2.2 Design of the Instruments

Sample Classification
An instrument was designed to classify the sample among infrequent, intermediate and frequent Chat users. The questionnaire comprised of closed multiple-choice questions aimed at determining the students' Chat use profile. Questions asked whether Chat was one of their three most frequent activities in their free time, when they began using Chat, how many days a week they used Chat, how long they chatted, how many persons they chatted with at the same time, whether their messages were long or short (the latter typical of users who engage in multitasking), whether they usually engaged in other activities while they chatted, and finally, the number of persons on their contact list. The response to each question was rated on a scale of 0 to 10 points distributed evenly between the different response options, with the lowest score assigned to the option indicating the least use of Chat and the highest score denoting greatest use. The scores for the various questions were averaged, yielding a total score for the individual known as the Chat Use Indicator.

The sample was divided into three groups in accordance with the Chat Use Indicator result to represent the three categories or degrees of interest. Infrequent users were those whose indicator was less than 3.3, intermediate users were those with an indicator falling between 3.3 and 6.6, and frequent users were those who scored between 6.6 and 10. In this study we were primarily interested in the low and high use groups, that is, frequent users of Chat as compared to those who rarely or never use it. The intermediate users were young people whose usage levels did not show a clear pattern, and who were improving their Chat skills but had yet to reach the stage where they could be categorized as frequent users. These users tend to employ Chat on a regular basis for short periods of time, converse with only 1 or 2 persons and do not engage in multitasking.

Memory Test Instrument
The measuring instrument used for testing memory and attention was based on the Digit Span Subtest of the Wechsler Intelligence Scale for Children [25].

To implement the subtest approximately 15 children were chosen at random from each grade (or the entire class where the total was less than 15) to form groups of no more than 30 from two consecutive grades. These students were shown a series of random number sequences, which they were required to observe carefully and then write down on an answer sheet in the exact order they were displayed. Each number was shown for one second, and the quantity of numbers increased for each successive sequence.

The test was divided into two subtests called Digits Forward and Digits Backward, respectively. The Digits Forward subtest consisted of 12 number sequence exercises, the first two containing 3 digits each, the next two 4 digits each, and so on up to the last two sequences each of which contained 8 digits. The Digits Backward subtest was

---

[2] Education Quality Measurement System -SIMCE- 2002 [15].

structured the same way, but in this case the students had to write the sequences on their answer sheets in the reverse order to that in which they were shown.

As regards the scoring criteria, one point was awarded for each exercise if the sequence was correctly rendered by the student, meaning that all the numbers were written down in the exact order required by the subtest. For each participant, a total score on each subtest was calculated as well as a global total.

2.3 Visual Perception Test Instrument

The final measuring instrument used was the Group Embedded Figures Test, or GEFT[3] [27], which determines whether a person's cognitive style is field independent (analytic) or field dependent (global).

In this test, the test subjects are given a booklet showing complex figures that contain other simple figures within them, and must choose the simple figures that match the descriptions given in the instruction sheet, including the indications as to size and orientation. Those who are able to find the simple figures hidden in the complex ones are deemed field independent (FI), meaning that they tend to perceive information analytically. By contrast, those who are field dependent (FD) will generally have difficulty finding the simple figure given that they tend to organize information globally and therefore see the whole clearly while perceiving the elements that comprise it in a more diffuse manner [27]. For purposes of classifying cognitive styles, a score of 11 points or less was considered as FD while a score of 16 or higher was classed as FI [12]. Intermediate scores were taken to indicate persons whose style was not clearly differentiated.

3 Results

During the first semester of 2004, the instruments described above were used at the schools participating in the study with groups of not more than 30 students chosen randomly from among the various grades. The questionnaire was applied first, and the memory and perception tests then given at later dates.

3.1 Sample Classification

The sample classification questionnaire resulted in the categorization of students into groups as shown in Table 1.

Table 1. Sample classification

Type of user	Memory Test Number of users	Perception Test Number of users
Infrequent	40	39
Intermediate	42	42
Frequent	40	43
Sample Total	122	124

---

[3] Version adapted by Marin [13].

Of the 125 children included in the sample, 122 were given the memory test while 124 took the perception test; the small discrepancies in these numbers were due to absentees on the days the tests were held.

3.2 Memory Test Results

Analysis of the results began with the calculation of the descriptive statistics are summarized in Table 2.

Table 2. Summary of statistics for memory test

Type of user	Minimum score	Maximum score	Range	Average score	Variance	Standard deviation
Infrequent	5.0	15.0	10.0	9.13	7.24	2.69
Intermediate	2.0	16.0	14.0	9.09	10.72	3.27
Frequent	5.0	21.0	16.0	11.35	15.05	3.88

The values for Skewness and Kurtosis, shown in Table 3, fell within the expected range (-2 to +2) for a set of data from a normal distribution. The values derived for the Cochran test (0.455947, with a p-value of 0.0776) and the Bartlett test (1.04406, with a p-value of 0.0790878) indicate that the homogeneity of variance assumption is satisfied.

Table 3. Normality analysis for digit test

Type of user	Standard Skewness	Standard Kurtosis
Infrequent	0.497	- 1.206
Intermediate	0.333	- 0.213
Frequent	0.925	- 0.487

The ANOVA test was applied to determine whether there were significant differences between the average scores obtained by frequent, intermediate and infrequent Chat users among the children taking the memory test (dependent variable), using as a classification factor the Chat Use Indicator calculated for each student based on the categories defined in Section 2.2. The F-test value was found to be 6.13 (p value=0.0029) at a significance level of 95%, indicating that there exist significant differences between the memory test scores of the three categories of users.

Multiple comparison tests using the Tukey HSD, Scheffé and Bonferroni methods were then performed, with the results demonstrating at a 95% significance level that intermediate and infrequent Chat users exhibit memory test score averages that are significantly equal (9.13 and 9.09), while being significantly different from that of frequent users (11.35). Note that while this latter group scored the highest average on the test, it also displayed the greatest degree of variability.

3.3 Perception Test Results

The descriptive statistics shown in Table 4 indicate that frequent Chat users had an average score of 16.09 and are therefore field independent, in contrast to infrequent and intermediate users whose style is not clearly differentiated in terms of the classification set out in Section 2.3.

Table 4. Summary of descriptive statistics for perception test

Type of user	Minimum score	Maximum score	Range	Average score	Variance	Standard deviation
Infrequent	4.0	24.0	20.0	13.10	22.41	4.73
Intermediate	1.0	25.0	23.0	14.28	34.11	5.84
Frequent	7.0	25.0	18.0	16.09	18.46	4.29

As regards the assumption of normality of the data, the Skewness and Kurtosis values were found to be in the -2 to +2 range (Table 5), thus confirming that the data are indeed distributed normally. In addition, the Cochran test (0.454886, with a p-value of 0.0777) and the Bartlett test (1.03504, with a p-value of 0.12738) indicate that the homogeneity of variance assumption is satisfied.

Table 5. Normality analysis, perception test

Type of user	Standard Skewness	Standard Kurtosis
Infrequent	1.184	0.229
Intermediate	- 0.581	- 0.518
Frequent	0.639	- 0.415

The ANOVA test was then carried out to determine whether there were significant differences between the average scores obtained by frequent, intermediate and infrequent Chat users among the children taking the perception test. The F-test value was found to be 3.74 (p-value=0.0266) at a significance level of 95%, indicating that there exist significant differences between the perception test scores of the three categories of users.

Multiple comparison tests using the Tukey HSD, Scheffé and Bonferroni methods demonstrated at a 95% significance level that frequent and infrequent Chat users exhibit perception test score averages that are significantly different (13.1 versus 16.1, respectively), while infrequent and intermediate users were shown to have similar averages (13.1 and 14.3, respectively). The averages for intermediate and frequent users were also found to be similar (14.3 and 16.1, respectively).

We can thus conclude that frequent users of Chat are field independent in that they tend to organize perceptual information in an analytic fashion, while non-users and intermediate users fall into a mixed FI-FD category (analytic - global). The scores achieved by infrequent users were clearly closer to the FD (global) than the FI (analytical) category. Moreover, the average score exhibits a rising tendency as one passes from less to more frequent users, and the greatest variability is found in the intermediate user group.

4   Conclusions

This research has shown the relationship between ICT, in particular Chat systems, and the cognitive development of middle-class children at private schools in Santiago, Chile. The results obtained are highly important as they show that young people are developing their mental skills outside the educational institutions using applications with a high social and ludic content. Our research, however, is based on correlations. An experiment as the following one could determine if actually Chat is the key factor for developing memory and spatial abilities. A set of non Chat users is tested on the studied cognitive abilities and then trained and given all possible facilities to use Chat. After some time a post test is applied. If our hypothesis is right, i.e., the use of Chat develops some cognitive abilities, there would be a significant difference between the pre and post test. Additionally we have to study if non chatters have access to internet facilities as do the ones that well performed in the study.

Frequent use of Chat by young people may be developing their memory and attention skills because they are conversing with others over the Internet while at the same time performing other activities both on-line (such as navigating) and off-line (e.g., listening to music). The memory tests we conducted revealed differences between users who make heavy use of Chat (several hours a day, several times a week) and those who use it less frequently, effectively demonstrating that the former are able to remember longer number sequences in direct and reverse order. Heavy Chat users also tend to perceive and organize information in an analytic manner (field independent).

Even our study is still exploratory, our believe is that the existence of differences in access to technology also applies to Chat, and this means that a certain percentage of the population is not obtaining the cognitive benefits of this particular technology. Therefore, we considered that there is a need to study how these technological tools, highly used by young people in a non-school context, can be introduced into the regular school environment so as to prevent the development of a cognitive gap between those who have access to the technology and those who do not. Further research is also needed on the possible consequences of these results for higher cognitive processes such as problem-solving, logical reasoning and, most importantly, learning.

Acknowledgements

This study was partially supported by Fundación País Digital.

References

1. Baddeley, A. D., Hitch, G. J.: Working Memory. In Bower G. A. (ed): Recent Advances in Learning and Motivation, Vol 8. Academic Press, New York (1974)
2. Castells, M.: La Era de la Información: Economía, Sociedad y Cultura. Alianza, Madrid. (2000)

3. Dimaggio, P., Hargittai, E., Russell, W., Robinson J. P.: Social Implications of the Internet. Annual Review of Sociology, N° 27. (2001) 307–336
4. Fernández, F., Goldenberg, S.: WIP Chile: Scanning the Reality of Internet in Chile. Revista Universitaria, N° 84. (2004) 14-16
5. Green, S., Bavelier, D.: Action Video Game Modifies Visual Selective Attention. Nature, N° 423. (2004) 534-537
6. Grinter, R., Palen, L. Instant Messaging in Teen Life. In Conference Proceedings on Computer Supported Cooperative Work - CSCW. Association For Computing Machinery - ACM, New Orleans (2002)
7. International Telecomunication Union: Internet Indicators: Hosts, Users and Number of PCs. Geneva (2004) http://www.Itu.Int/Itu-d/Ict/Statistics/Index.html
8. Isaacs, E., Kamm, C., Schiano, J., Walendowski, A., Whittaker, S.: Characterizing Instant Messaging from Recorded Logs. Conference Proceedings on Human Factors in Computing Systems. Association for Computing Machinery - ACM, Minnesota (2002)
9. Lenhart, A., Rainie, L., Lewis, O.: Teenage Life Online: The Rise of the Instant Message Generation and the Internet's Impact on Friendships And Family Relationships. Pew Internet and American Life Project, Washington (2001) http://www.pewinternet.org/
10. Lenhart, A., Shiu, E.: How Americans Use Instant Messaging. Pew Internet and American Life Project, Washington (2004) http://www.pewinternet.org
11. Li, X., Atkins, M.: Early Childhood Computer Experience and Cognitive and Motor Development. Pediatrics, Vol. 6, N° 113. (2004) 1715–1722
12. Luna, R.: Un Análisis Sobre la Relevancia de las Interacciones entre Estrategias Cognitivas y Modalidades de Procesamiento. Anales de Psicología, Vol. 16, N° 1. (2000) 61-77
13. Marín, R.: Un Estudio Acerca de la Dimensión Estilo Cognitivo Dependencia-Independencia de Campo en Escolares Básicos de la Región del Bio-Bio Chile. M. Sc. Thesis, Escuela de Educación, Universidad Católica de Chile, Santiago (1988)
14. Meyer, D., Rubistein, J., Evans, J.: Executive Control of Cognitive Processes in Task Switching. Journal of Experimental Psychology: Human Perception and Performance, Vol. 27, N° 4. (2001) 763-797
15. Ministerio de Educación: Sistema de Medición de la Calidad de Educación 2002 4° Básico. Editor, Santiago (2003) http://www.simce.cl
16. Miyake, A., Sha, P.: Models of Working Memory: Mechanisms of Active Maintenance and Executive Control. Cambridge University Press, Cambridge (1999)
17. Nardi, B., Whittaker, S., Bradner, E.: Interaction and Outeraction: Instant Messaging in Action. Conference Proceedings on Computer Supported Cooperative Work- CSCW. Association for Computing Machinery - ACM, Philadelphia (2000)
18. Nilesen Net Ratings: Internet Audience Measurement Service. (2000) http://www.Nielsen-Netratings.com
19. Nua Internet Surveys: How Many on Line? (2004) http://www.nua.ie/surveys
20. Nie, N., Simpser, A., Stepanikova, I., Zheng L.: Ten Years After The Birth of the Internet, How Do Americans Use the Internet in Their Daily Lives? Stanford Center for the Quantitative Study of Society, Stanford (2004) http://www.stanford.edu/group/siqss
21. Organisation for Economic Co-operation and Development – OECD: Understanding the Digital Divide. Editor, París (2001)
22. Valsiner, J., Van Der Veer, R.: The Social Mind: Construction of the Idea. Cambridge University Press, Cambridge (2000)
23. Vygotsky, L.: Mind In Society: The Development of Higher Psychological Processes. Harvard University Press, Cambridge (1978)

24. Warschauer, M.: Technology and Social Inclusion: Rethinking the Digital Divide. Massachussets Institute of Technology, Massachusetts (2003)
25. Weschler, D.: Wechsler Intelligence Scale for Children – Revised. Psychological Corporation, San Antonio (1981)
26. World Internet Project Chile: Síntesis de Resultados Wip Chile 2004. Instituto de Estudios Mediales UC, Santiago (2004) http://www.wipchile.cl
27. Witkin, H., Goodenough, D.: Cognitive Styles: Essence and Origins Field Dependence and Field Independence. New York International University Press, New York (1981)
28. Yus, F.: Ciberpragmática: El Uso del Lenguaje en Internet. Ariel, Barcelona (2001)

Detecting Adult Images Using Seven MPEG-7 Visual Descriptors*

Wonil Kim[1], Seong Joon Yoo[1], Jin-sung Kim[2], Taek Yong Nam[3], and
Kyoungro Yoon[4],**

[1] College of Electronics and Information Engineering,
Sejong University, Seoul, Korea
{wikim, sjyoo}@sejong.ac.kr
[2] Electronics Engineering and Computer Science Department,
University of Michigan, Ann Arbor, MI, USA
jinskim@umich.edu
[3] Electronics and Telecommunications Research Institute,
Daejeon, Korea
tynam@etri.re.kr
[4] College of Information and Telecommunications,
Konkuk University, Seoul, Korea
yoonk@konkuk.ac.kr

Abstract. In this paper we introduce an effective method of the adult image classification via MPEG-7 descriptors. The proposed system uses MPEG-7 descriptors as the main feature of the adult image classification systems. The simulation shows that the proposed image classification system performs the 5 class classification task with success rate of above 70%.

1 Introduction

As the Internet is prevalent everywhere in our life, now we access the mass amount of digital multimedia with the finger tips of our hand. Moreover, with the reduction of the cost in mass storage devices, digital multimedia data is exponentially increased in daily life. The dramatic increment of multimedia data causes unexpected deliveries of unwanted contents to the Internet users. Interlaced among millions of Web sites, there are over 500,000 web sites that are related to pornography and other issues that are as harmful as poison to the our children [1-3].

The main purpose of this paper is to devise a system that rates the images according to the harmfulness to the underage minors. We first analyze several MPEG-7 descriptors and create a prototype that extracts image features from adult image data using the selected descriptors, after which we classify given images using these descriptors through the image classification technique.

---

* This research is supported by Electronics and Telecommunications Research Institute (Project No. 0801-2004-0025)

** Author for correspondence: +82-2-450-4129.

S. Shimojo et al. (Eds.): HSI 2005, LNCS 3597, pp. 336–339, 2005.

2 The Proposed Model Using MPEG-7 Visual Descriptors

In this paper, the MPEG-7 descriptors are applied for feature extraction [4]. The visual part of MPEG-7 includes the color descriptors, the shape descriptors, the texture descriptors, and the motion descriptors. In the step of the feature extraction, the proposed system concentrates on finding descriptors to be used for adult image classification, rather than simply extracting feature values of descriptors. We employed descriptors from three categories, i.e. color, texture, and shape, for image classification.

The color descriptors are one of the most important visual features of images. The dominant color descriptor retrieves the image contents through limited number of prevailing colors in the whole image or in an arbitrary area of the image. The scalable color descriptor represents the Haar-Transformed color histogram based on the HSV color space. The color layout descriptor minutely details the distribution of color space layout in the whole or in an arbitrary area of image data.

The texture descriptors can effectively match image or video data by describing the structural pattern of image or video data. Texture means the pattern of structure, direction, and roughness of an image. The homogeneous texture descriptor is much effective for the similarity-based matching by accurately representing statistical characteristics of texture images. The edge histogram descriptor is well used for retrieving images with the similar meaning, based on the edge information of images.

The shape descriptors can be used to match similar images or similar objects based on the shape of objects in images. The region-based shape descriptor describes various shapes; simple shapes such as rectangles and circles and complex shapes such as donuts and symbols. The contour-based shape descriptor describes outer contour of an object contained in an image or regions of video images for closed 2D objects.

The proposed system extracts seven visual descriptors from MPEG-7 for each image; Dominant Color, Color Structure, Color Layout, Edge Histogram, Homogeneous Texture, Region Shape, and Contour Shape descriptors. In the training stage, the feature information extracted from each visual descriptor of the training images is stored in the Image Feature Information database. This information is used to classify the test images into one of the 5 classes, which are swim suit images (S), topless images (T), nude images (N), sex images (X), and normal images (I), by matching the feature information and the class information that is stored in the in the Image Feature Information database.

The process of the image classification can be described as follows in detail. In the initial step, the system creates the list of training images and testing images by writing a parameter file. In the next step, the system executes the feature information generation module for the training images. In the last step, the system classifies the test images using the k-nearest neighbor classification method.

3 Simulation and Results

Table 1 shows the result of the image classification using MPEG-7 visual descriptors. In this table, class in the second column represents the label of the class category, and

Table 1. Success Rates of Adult Image Classification Experiments

Selected descriptor	Resulting class	Classes of Query Image				
		S	T	N	X	I
Color Layout	S	**42.941177**	18.82353	22.941177	10.0	5.294118
	T	31.176472	**34.705883**	14.705883	10.0	9.411765
	N	11.176471	8.82353	**65.29412**	9.411765	5.294118
	X	20.0	9.411765	15.294118	**53.529415**	1.7647059
	I	4.117647	5.8823533	5.294118	3.5294118	**81.176476**
Color Structure	S	**51.17647**	17.058825	10.588236	18.82353	2.3529413
	T	27.64706	**51.17647**	5.294118	11.764707	4.117647
	N	8.82353	5.8823533	**81.76471**	2.3529413	1.1764706
	X	7.0588236	3.52941118	5.294118	**84.11765**	0.0
	I	4.117647	5.8823533	8.235294	0.5882353	**81.176476**
Edge Histogram	S	**43.529415**	21.176472	13.529412	12.3529415	9.411765
	T	27.64706	**41.17647**	16.470589	4.117647	10.588236
	N	11.176471	10.0	**68.82353**	4.117647	5.8823533
	X	25.294119	8.82353	10.588236	**52.352943**	2.9411767
	I	5.294118	4.7058825	4.117647	0.5882353	**85.29412**
Homogeneous Texture	S	**31.176472**	20.588236	9.411765	20.0	18.82353
	T	22.941177	**32.352943**	15.882354	12.3529415	16.470589
	N	14.117647	10.588236	**54.11765**	8.82353	12.3529415
	X	21.176472	19.411766	8.82353	**40.588238**	10.0
	I	8.235294	9.411765	11.176471	11.764707	**59.411766**
Region Shape	S	**27.64706**	16.470589	15.294118	19.411766	21.176472
	T	24.705883	**27.64706**	13.529412	11.764707	22.352942
	N	8.82353	12.941177	**46.47059**	11.176471	20.588236
	X	25.882355	18.82353	12.941177	**38.823532**	3.5294118
	I	11.176471	7.647059	15.294118	11.176471	**54.705883**
Dominant Color	S	**42.352943**	15.294118	8.82353	30.000002	3.5294118
	T	30.000002	**36.47059**	5.294118	18.82353	9.411765
	N	10.588236	8.235294	**70.0**	8.235294	2.9411767
	X	10.588236	5.294118	3.5294118	**80.0**	0.5882353
	I	7.647059	11.176471	4.117647	5.8823533	**71.176476**
Contour Shape	S	**70.0**	8.235294	4.7058825	15.882354	1.1764706
	T	74.11765	**7.647059**	1.7647059	14.705883	1.7647059
	N	82.94118	5.294118	**4.7058825**	5.8823533	1.1764706
	X	47.64706	5.294118	2.3529413	**44.11765**	0.5882353
	I	80.0	1.1764706	1.1764706	7.0588236	**10.588236**

the class labels of the first row represents the class of the query images; S: swimming suit, T: topless, N: nude, X: sex, I: normal. For this experiment, 1702 images from each class are used as experimental image set. Among 1702 images, 90% (1531 images) are used as training images and 10% (171 images) are used as test images.

The success rate of the classification with respect to descriptor type is in the order of Color Descriptor, Texture Descriptor, and Shape Descriptor. The overall success rate of the Color Structure descriptor is the highest, mainly due to the high dimensionality of the feature information (e.g. the dimension of the Color Structure descriptor is 256). The success rate of Dominant Color and Color Layout is relatively high for the important classes as well. Hence, we can conclude that the color information plays a much important role in the adult image classification. The rate of Shape Descriptor is relatively low, compared to that of Color descriptors. Especially, the performance of the Contour Shape descriptor is very low. Thus, the feature information of color is very important since adult images have a lot of information of skin color while the shape information relatively does not play an important role in the image classification of adult images. In fact, deciding whether an image is nude or sexual acts is very difficult task. However, the experimental results are very promising since the success rate of the classification is relatively high except for some classes of images. It is very important to select descriptors in consideration of the characteristics of images of the target class, since the structure of the feature information and the extraction method for each descriptor is different.

4 Conclusion

The proposed system uses MPEG-7 descriptors as the main features of the adult image classification systems. According to the simulation results, the proposed image classification system performs the 5 class classification task with success rate of above 70%. It shows that the MPEG-7 descriptors can be effectively used as features of the adult images classification process and the proposed framework can be effectively used as the kernel of web contents rating systems.

References

1. Arentz, W. A., Olstad, B.: Classifying offensive sites based on image contents. In Computer Vision and Image Understanding, Vol. 94, 293-310 (2004)
2. Jung, Y., Hwang, E., Kim, W.: Sports Image Classifier based on Bayesian Classification. In Lecture Note in Artificial Intelligence, Vol. 3040, 546-555, Springer, New York (2004)
3. Yoo, S.-J.: Intelligent multimedia information retrieval for identifying and rating adult images. In Lecture Note in Computer Science, Vol. 3213, 165-170, Springer, New York (2004)
4. Manjunath, B.S., Salembier, P., Sikora, T. (eds.): Introduction to MPEG-7 Multimedia Content Description Interface, John Wiley & Sons, West Sussex, England (2002)

Multi-proxy Signatures Based on Diffie-Hellman Problems Allowing Repeated Delegations*

So-Young Park and Sang-Ho Lee

Dept. of Computer Science and Engineering, Ewha Womans University,
11-1 Daehyun-Dong, Seodaemoon-Ku, Seoul, Korea
soyoung@ewhain.net, shlee@ewha.ac.kr

Abstract. Because the Internet is vast and insecure, strong cryptographic protocols are required to support secure communication. In this
paper, we propose an efficient way to perform secure delegations in a
hierarchical group. We propose a practical multi-proxy signature scheme
applicable to hierarchial organization using the Diffie-Hellman problem
and secret sharing without secure channels. In addition, we improve the
proposed scheme to a dynamic one allowing repeated delegations.

1 Introduction

In many Internet based e-commerce systems, digital signatures can be used as
the basic cryptographic technique for authentications. Proxy signatures[6] allowing signature authority delegation also can be used for purposes of personal
delegations or efficient system operation. In this paper, we consider an efficient
way to perform secure delegations in hierarchical organization such as public
key infrastructure (PKI). In many PKIs, there is the PAA (Policy Approval
Authority) at the highest level, and the PCAs (Policy Certification Authority)
are at a lower level, and the CAs (Certificate Authority) and RAs (Registration
Authority) are at the lowest level. The higher authorities certify the lower authorities. The PCAs delegate the responsibilities to certify users' public keys to
the CAs, and the CAs delegate the responsibilities to register the users to the
RAs. A multi-proxy signature generated by the CAs or the RAs represents a
certification path implicitly from the highest authority to the lowest authorities
and represents a cross-certification among the CAs or the RAs. Our goal is to
propose a more practical multi-proxy signature scheme to apply in situations
such as this. The multi-proxy signature scheme was first proposed in [3] and
several multi-proxy signature schemes were proposed in [4][5][9]. However, Lal
et al.'s scheme[4] suffers from the weakness that the original signer can forge
the proxy signer's partial signature. And, Lin et al's scheme[5] and Xue et al's
scheme[9] assume a secure network channel. In this paper, we propose a new
multi-proxy signature scheme and extend it to a multi-proxy signature scheme

* This work was supported by the Brain Korea 21 Project in 2004.

S. Shimojo et al. (Eds.): HSI 2005, LNCS 3597, pp. 340–344, 2005.

allowing repeated delegations for a hierarchical group. Using the Diffie-Hellman key exchange protocol[2] and secret sharing[1], the original signer can delegate her signature authority to plural proxy signers without secret channels. In addition, the designated proxy signer can delegate her signature authority to other proxy singers so that the proxy signers group can be constructed dynamically.

2   An Implementation of Multi-proxy Signatures

We describe our multi-proxy signatures. Let p, q be two large primes where $|p| \geq 512$ bits and $q|(p-1)$. $g \in Z_p^*$ is a generator of order q. We assume that there are n signers denoted as $P = \{P_1, P_2, \ldots, P_n\}$, and that every signer has her private-public key pair (xp_i, yp_i) where xp_i is randomly selected in Z_p^* and $yp_i = g^{xp_i} \bmod p$. We assume that P_i wants to delegate her signature authority to t_i ($= 0$ or ≥ 2) proxy signers denoted as $S_i = \{c_{i1}, \ldots, c_{it_i}\}$. For a given message M, all proxy signers in S_i can generate collectively a multi-proxy signature σ for (M, S_i). We assume that the network is insecure so that adversary F can gain any information from the network.

1. **Delegation Ticket Generation:** P_i performs the following steps to delegate her signature authority to her proxy signers. P_i
   (a) selects t_i random numbers such that $rs_{ij} \in Z_q^*$ and generates delegation ticket shares $dt_{ij} = (yc_{ij})^{rs_{ij}} \bmod p$ for proxy c_{ij}, where $j = 1, \ldots, t_i$ and yc_{ij} is the public key of c_{ij};
   (b) sets her delegation ticket $dt_i = \sum_{j=1}^{t_i} dt_{ij} \bmod q$ and computes $DT_i = g^{dt_i} \bmod p$, and then publishes DT_i with a digital signature of P_i;
   (c) generates $k_j = H(dt_{ij}, S_i) \cdot xp_i + rs_{ij} \bmod q$ and $RS_j = g^{rs_{ij}} \bmod p$;
   (d) broadcasts $< k_j, RS_j, S_i >$ to all proxy signers c_{ij} in S_i for $j = 1, \ldots, t_i$.
2. **Multi-proxy Signature Generation:** Each proxy signer c_{ij} creates her partial proxy signature σ_{ij} as follows: A proxy c_{ij}
   (a) generates the delegation ticket share $dt_{ij} = (RS_j)^{xc_{ij}} = g^{rs_{ij} \cdot xc_{ij}} \bmod p$;
   (b) If $g^{k_j} \equiv (yp_i)^{H(dt_{ij}, S_i)} \cdot RS_j \bmod p$ holds, then generates σ_{ij};
      i. selects $a_j \in Z_q$, and computes $l_j = a_j + dt_{ij} \bmod q$, $pa_j = g^{a_j} \bmod p$ and $pr_j = g^{dt_{ij}} \bmod p$;
      ii. broadcasts pa_j, pr_j to proxy signers in S_i and then computes $PA = \prod_{j=1}^{t_i} pa_j \bmod p$ and $PR = \prod_{j=1}^{t_i} pr_j \bmod p$;
      iii. sets $e = H(PA, PR, M, S_i)$ and computes $ps_j = e \cdot xc_{ij} + l_j \bmod q$, then $\sigma_{ij} = < pa_j, pr_j, ps_j >$.
   The final multi-proxy signature is $\sigma = < PA, PR, PS >$ where $PS = \sum_{j=1}^{t_i} ps_j \bmod q$.
3. **Multi-proxy Signature Verification:** An arbitrary verifier can verity the validity of $\sigma = < PA, PR, PS >$ using each proxy signer's public key and the original signer's DT_i. The verifier first verifies the signature of DT_i and then verifies the multi-proxy signature by checking that $PR \equiv DT_i \bmod p$ and $g^{PS} \equiv (yc_{i1} \cdot yc_{i2} \cdots yc_{it_i})^e \cdot PA \cdot PR \bmod p$ hold.

Table 1. Comparison of Computational Complexity

Phase	Lin et al's Scheme[5]	Xue et al's Scheme[9]	Our Scheme
Delegation	$5nT_{exp} + (6n-1)T_{mul} + nT_{add}$	$4nT_{exp} + (3n-1)T_{mul} + nT_{add}$	$(5n+2)T_{exp} + (2n+1)T_{mul} + (3n+1)T_{add}$
Signature Generation	$(n^2+6n)T_{exp} + (n^2+6n)T_{mul} + (3n-1)T_{add}$	$(n^2+4n)T_{exp} + (n^2+3n)T_{mul} + (3n-1)T_{add}$	$(2n)T_{exp} + (2n^2-n)T_{mul} + (2n+1)T_{add}$
Signature Verification	$3T_{exp} + 3T_{mul}$	$3T_{exp} + 4T_{mul}$	$4T_{exp} + (n+2)T_{mul}$
Total	$(n^2+11n+3)T_{exp} + (n^2+12n+2)T_{mul} + (4n-1)T_{add}$	$(n^2+8n+3)T_{exp} + (n^2+6n+3)T_{mul} + (4n-1)T_{add}$	$(7n+6)T_{exp} + (2n^2+2n+3)T_{mul} + (5n+2)T_{add}$

We compare the performance of our scheme with Lin et al's scheme[5] and Xue et al's scheme[9] that are recently proposed, in Table 1. We use three notations (time for modular computations) such that T_{exp} (exponentiation), T_{mul} (multiplication) and T_{add} (addition). We reduced T_{exp} in multi-proxy signature generation phase, in total, the computational overhead of our scheme outperforms that of other schemes.

The security of our scheme is based on the difficulty of the discrete logarithm problem (DLP) in a finite field for a large prime. In the delegation phase, P_i's dt_i is shared between the P_i and c_{ij} by secret sharing and the Diffie-Hellman key exchange protocol. So, it is not feasible for unauthorized proxy signers without delegation ticket shares to generate valid delegation ticket shares, by the Diffie-Hellman assumption and the security of secret sharing. In multi-proxy signature generation phase, each c_{ij} creates σ_{ij} based on the Schnorr signature scheme[8]. So, our scheme is a kind of Schnorr signature-based multisignature scheme. In ASM[7], Micali el al. proved that a Schnorr signature-based multisignature is secure against an adaptive chosen message attack under the DLP assumptions. Therefore it is not feasible for adversaries to forge the multi-proxy signature.

3   Multi-proxy Signatures Allowing Repeated Delegations

Now we discuss how the previous scheme can be improved to become a dynamic one allowing repeated delegations. We assume that P is a hierarchical group that can be represented as a tree with a degree greater than 2 in which each node represents a participant P_i. And each node can delegate its signature authority to its child nodes in the hierarchy. For P_i's proxy group S_i, we suppose that c_{ij} cannot directly perform as a proxy, and let $P_j = c_{ij}$. Then, P_j can delegate her partial proxy signature authority to her child nodes denoted as $c_{j1}, \ldots, c_{jt_j}$ as follows:

1. **Renew the Subgroup Information:** P_j must refresh subgroup information. P_j makes $S_j = \{c_{i1}, c_{i2}, \ldots, c_{ij-1}, c_{ij+1}, \ldots, c_{it_i}, c_{j1}, \ldots, c_{jt_j}\}$ and broadcasts it with her signature to all other existing proxy signers.

2. **Delegation Ticket Generation:** P_j's delegation ticket share generation protocol for her new proxy signers is identical to that described in Section 2 except that P_j's delegation ticket denoted as dt_j is the same as the value of dt_{ij} that P_i generated for P_j, and that P_j creates an additional public delegation ticket share $pdt_j = dt_j - \sum_{l=1}^{t_j} dt_{jl} \bmod q$. P_j generates the public delegation information $DT_j = g^{dt_j} \bmod p$ and publishes the pair $< DT_j, pdt_j >$ signed by her.

3. **Multi-proxy Signature Generation:** The protocol for c_k in S_j to create $\sigma_k = < pa_k, pr_k, ps_k >$ is identical to that described in Section 2 except that $PA = \prod_{k \in S_j} pa_k \bmod p$ and $PR = (\prod_{k \in S_j} pr_k) \cdot g^{pdt_j} \bmod p$. Then, the final multi-proxy signature is $< PA, PR, PS >$ such that $PS = (\sum_{k \in S_j} ps_k) + pdt_j \bmod q$. The signature verification is identical to the basic scheme.

Finally, P_i's proxy signers except P_j, and P_j's proxy signers can generate a proxy signature on behalf of P_i, and this repeated delegation can be continued to participants at the lowest level in the hierarchy.

4   Conclusion

In this paper, we proposed a new multi-proxy signature scheme. By applying the Diffie-Hellman key exchange protocol and secret sharing to our scheme, the original signer and the proxy signers can generate a multi-proxy signature more efficiently through open network channels. More importantly, we extended the conventional scheme to a multi-proxy signature allowing repeated delegation for a tree-structured hierarchical group. However, accomplishing repeated delegation without requiring additional information is a subject for further research.

References

1. Y. Desmedt, "Threshold Cryptography," European Trans. on Telecommunications and Related Technologies, vol. 5, no. 4, pp. 35-43, 1994.
2. W. Diffie and M. E. Hellman, "New Directions in Cryptography," IEEE Trans. on Information Theory, vol. IT-22, no. 6, pp. 644-654, 1976.
3. S. Hwang and C. Shi, "A Simple Multi-proxy Signature Scheme," Proceeding of the Tenth National Conference on Information Security, Hualien, Taiwan, pp. 134-138, 2000.
4. S. Lal and A. Awasthi, "A New Multi-proxy Signature Scheme for Partial Delegation with Warrant," http://www.gfcr.org/ecryp/old/multi.pdf.
5. C. Lin, T. Wu and J. Hwang, "Multi-proxy Signature Schemes for Partial Delegation with Cheater Identification," Proceeding of IWAP '02, 2002.
6. M. Mambo, K. Usuda and E. Okamoto, "Proxy Signature: Delegation of the Power to Sign Message," IEICE Trans. on Fundamentals, vol. E79-A, no. 9, pp. 1338-1353, 1996.
7. S. Micali, K. Ohta and L. Reyzin, "Accountable-Subgroup Multisignatures," Proceeding of ACM Conference on Computer and Communications Security, pp. 245-254, 2001.

8. C. P. Schnorr, "Efficient Signature Generation for Smart Cards," Advances in Cryptology - CRYPTO '89, pp. 239-252, 1990.
9. Q. Xue and Z. Cao, "Improved of Multi-proxy Signature Scheme," Proceeding of International Symposium on Communications and Information Technologies (ISCIT), pp. 450-455, 2004.

Internet Collaboration: A Promise for Technology Transferring to Developing Countries

Duminda Nishantha[1], Yukuo Hayashida[1], Takeshi Katsuki[2], Masaaki Goto[2], Koichiro Ihara[2], and Jayantha Weerasinghe[3]

[1] Department of Information Science, Saga University, Japan
[2] Department of Oral and Maxillofacial Surgery, Saga University, Japan
[3] Department of Oral Surgery, University of Peradeniya, Sri Lanka
{duminda, yukuo}@fu.is.saga-u.ac.jp,
{gotohm, ihara}@cc.saga-u.ac.jp, juw@pdn.ac.lk

Abstract. Internet-based collaboration opens a vast stream of opportunities for developing countries in acquiring international assistance. In this paper, we identify technology transferring from developed countries to developing countries as a potential form of international assistance that can be immensely benefited through collaboration over the Internet. We propose strategic means for facilitating internet collaboration in developing countries and present an example to show the Internet potential in medical technology transferring.

1 Introduction

International cooperation is important and essential for the development of any country. Various global and regional organizations are providing an immense amount of assistance to developing nations to solve a number of socio-economic problems through provision of food, clothing, materials, expert services and many others. Some international cooperative organizations (e.g. JICA) believe that technology transferring can make a sustainable socio-economic development in most of the developing countries. In this paper, we propose Internet-based collaboration as a potential means to enhance technology transfer activities in international cooperation, proposing strategies for its deployment over existing infrastructures.

While the Internet potential is substantially broad and complex, in most of the developing countries, the network infrastructure is not yet well established and thus its benefits are limited to a narrow scope. Hence, we believe that international assistance in the form of technology transfer can best exploit these limited internet facilities [1]. Having an understanding on the Internet accessibility, the donor countries can target institutions best suited for reception of technological know-how with anticipated subsequent technology propagation within the country originating from those local institutions. Presumably, at least a small fraction of the work force of these institutions (e.g. surgeons in base hospitals, lecturers in universities, engineers in technical institutions, researchers in agricultural institutions, directors and managers in the commercial sector) are equipped with some prior knowledge on general computer operations , that creates a conducive environment for realizing Internet collaboration.

S. Shimojo et al. (Eds.): HSI 2005, LNCS 3597, pp. 345–348, 2005.
© Springer-Verlag Berlin Heidelberg 2005

2   Technology Transferring Through Internet Collaboration

Frequent expert-trainee interaction and accessibility to each other when required is a prime necessity for the success and sustainability of the technology transfer process. Internet Collaboration can immensely benefit the above interaction in many ways. The experts who visit recipient countries or the trainees who leave for foreign training centers could get accustomed to the social environment, resources available and nature of the course, before leaving the home country. When the experts or the trainees return to their home countries after completing the service/training, the experts can monitor the progress of the technology transfer activity, evaluate the performance of trainees and attend to forthcoming problems through the Internet. The trainees in recipient countries can present their performance to the experts through PowerPoint presentations, video recording of their performance or showing the real output. The experts on the other hand can arrange Internet training sessions in a regular basis to the trainee groups through similar methods. Moreover, Internet collaboration can be exploited in exogenous situation such as heavy infections, and other hazardous environments where foreign experts may reluctant to undergo direct exposure.

To realize internet collaboration in developing countries overcoming the infrastructural limitations, we propose following strategies.

- **Appropriate handling of multimedia contents:** In order to conduct multimedia communication among geographically dispersed locations, the Internet channels should meet the minimum specifications. Bandwidth and delay requirement for transmission of textual messages is generally affordable over all Internet channels except for disconnections. Minimum bandwidth requirement for an interactive audio communication facility with satisfactory voice quality (e.g. 8-bit resolution mono-GSM encoded) is around 13kbps, and could be realized through most of the Internet channels. Video communication on the other hand, consumes a larger portion of the bandwidth depending on smoothness and quality of the video stream. We have identified motion JPEG (M-JPEG) streaming technology as having sufficient flexibility [2] to exploit this smoothness-quality trade-off to suit narrow band to wide band network channels while preserving acceptable image-quality. According to our own telemedicine experience [3], real-time high-quality patient face images can be accommodated through channel bandwidths as low as 40kbps.
- **Integration of synchronous and asynchronous collaboration:** Integration of the synchronous and asynchronous collaboration procedures enhances the efficiency in two aspects: firstly, the collaborators are allowed to participate in progressive sequence of remote discussions both synchronously and asynchronously, maximizing human and resource utilization. Secondly, collaboration contents could be stored in a persistent database (using mirrored servers) to maximize latency and bandwidth utilization. The authors believe that asynchronous data posting to local servers and subsequent global synchronization is the only effective solution available to overcome bandwidth scarcity in developing countries.
- **Mutual integration of multiple collaborative programs:** The idea is simply that two collaborative projects could be combined to maximize resource utilization. This can be considered as using the output from one project to support another project and/or resource sharing. For example, a software development and medical collaboration can be combined so that the software development team provides software and technical expertise to the local telemedicine team. A donor country

transferring technical know-how to multiple countries in parallel rather than a single country is another example that mutually shares resources effectively.

– **International support for infrastructure development:** Infrastructural provisioning to realize internet communication may be viewed as costly, tedious, or irrelevant exercise by the international organizations that consider localized goals from technology transfer programs. However there are several issues that can be attended without requiring much investment and effort, but has a large impact in realization of Internet collaboration in developing countries. (1) Provisioning of required equipment and software such as computers, video devices, and collaboration software etc. (either as donations or on lending basis) furnishes the basic setup for Internet collaboration. (2) The required technical support must be provided to both collaborating parties through dispatching experts or directing the support of capable local institutions. (3) The network infrastructure itself may require slight modifications to create a viable environment to conduct Internet collaboration.

3   Practical Realization -A Pilot Project

The authors have been involved in designing a group collaboration system [3] for supporting telemedicine in the field of oral & maxillofacial surgery, conducted among

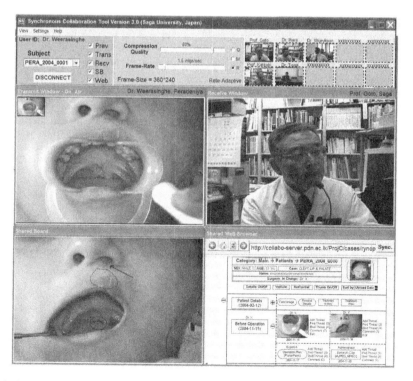

Fig. 1. GUI snapshot of the synchronous collaboration tool. A Japanese medical expert evaluates a maxillofacial case handled by a Sri Lankan medical surgeon. Few other participants from different countries participate this discussion (see top right panel)

4 Conclusions

In this paper, we identified the technology transfer activities as the best point of deploying the Internet in cooperate interactions between developing and developed countries. Our telemedicine exercise among Japan, Sri Lanka and few other countries in Asia was presented to show a glimpse of internet potential.

Acknowledgements

The authors would like to thank Mr. Ranjith Aberathne and Dr. Parakrama Wijekoon of University of Peradenya; and Dr. Masahito Shigematsu of Saga University for their contribution in technical assistance and holding of collaboration sessions. Authors would also like to take this opportunity to express gratitude to the President of Saga University for offering research grants and resources to conduct this project.

References

[1] Nishantha, D.: Internet-based Communication for Transferring Technology to Developing Countries. International Cooperation Research – Research Contest for University Students, Vol. 6. Japan International Cooperation Agency, Japan (2003).

[2] Nishantha, D., Hayashida, Y., and Hayashi T.: Application Level Rate Enhancement of Motion-JPEG Transmission for Medical Collaboration Systems. Proc. of the 24th IEEE International Conference on Distributed Computing Systems Workshops, IEEE Computer Society (2004) 64-69

[3] Nishantha, D., Hayashida, Y., Hayashi, T., Katsuki, T., Goto, M., Ihara, K., Amaratunga, N., Weerasinghe, J., and Tokura, N.: Multimedia Medical Collaboration over the Internet between Sri Lanka and Japan. The Journal of Information and Systems in Education, Vol. 1. Japanese Society for Information and Systems in Education, Japan (2002) 98-108

[4] Home page of the telemedicine project at Saga University. http://turkey.fu.is.saga-u.ac.jp/education/project/Collabo1.html

A Method to Monitor a BBS Using Feature Extraction of Text Data

Yu Ichifuji[1], Susumu Konno[2], and Hideaki Sone[2]

[1] Graduate School of Information Sciences, Tohoku University
[2] Information Synergy Center,Tohoku University

Abstract. Electronic bulletin board (BBS) has a problem which is action to obstruct communications (the authors use "obstruction on bulletin board"). The authors introduced system that aids an operator to find such obstruction based on feature extraction of words which causes harmful psychological effects on readers. We propose a new evaluation method using "Ruination Figure" which is calculated by feature extraction. This index is displayed in two ways of stock chart for BBS operator to see trend of the index and find harmful obstruction in the BBS.

1 Introduction

In recent years, the BBS came into wide use. Anyone can exchange information using text for anonymity in BBS. Now, it occurs harmful problems there. It is necessary for operator to deal with such problems.

There are some services that aid operators to monitor the BBS for corporate services [1, 2]. These services need a lot of people in monitoring the BBS.

Several studies have been made on BBS [3, 4, 5]. Heat-up in BBS is discussed to analyze in relationship with reply-rate of communication [4, 5], and technique for its detection is not reported.

The purpose of this paper is to propose a method to monitor a BBS. The method focuses attention on that "obstruction on bulletin board" is judged by readers and that users communicate using characters. To monitor a BBS, we will introduce the new index "Ruination Figure".

2 Proposal of New Index "Ruination Figure"

2.1 Monitor Object

There are two patterns of obstruction by "obstruction on bulletin board". One is that operator can discover such statements easily. The other is not discovered easily. There are three examples for the latter.

- Large number of people (two members or more) blaming each other
- Continuousness of writings that is hated by other members
- Provocative sentences that causes unpleasant writings

S. Shimojo et al. (Eds.): HSI 2005, LNCS 3597, pp. 349–352, 2005.

In this paper, we suggest a new evaluation index "Ruination Figure" of BBS to help operators to find above three obstructions. This shows how rough each statement is, and is calculated from the words and number of responses.

2.2   The Calculation of "Ruination Figure"

We define "Positive words $[pw]$", "Positive word weight $[pww]$", "Negative words $[nw]$" and "Negative word weight $[nww]$". pw is a word set whose elements give readers a good feeling. pww is a weight of each element of pw, and positive. So, nw is a word set whose elements give readers a bad feeling. Then, nww is a weight of each element of nw, and negative. pw and nw are classified by the meanings which each word has.

We define "Concord Number $[cn]$" and "Opinion Score $[Os]$". cn shows the number of times that pw or nw corresponds. The number of times that a statement matched pw is expressed as cn_{pw}. In the same way, the number of times that nw matches is expressed as cn_{nw}. Os is the score which is calculated from pww, nww, cn_{pw} and cn_{nw}. Os is calculate as follows.

$$Os = pww * cn_{pw} + nww * cn_{nw} \qquad (1)$$

We define "Comment Chain Score $[ccs]$" to consider chains of the argument to give additional point to an opinion leader who is followed by many responses, and it is defined using the number of responses (Res) [4, 5].

$$ccs = log_n Res \ \ (Os \geq 0)$$
$$ccs = -log_n Res \ \ (Os < 0) \qquad (2)$$

The base n is variable to accentuate change of "Ruination Figure".

Statement Score $[Ss]$ for each message is sum of Os and ccs, $Ss(t) = Os(t) + ccs(t)$, where t is the number of a message. A statement with positive Ss gives pleasantness, and negative Ss means unpleasantness.

"Ruination Figure $[RF]$" is sum of Ss from the first to the statement; $RF(t) = \sum_1^t Ss_i$.

3   How to Evaluate "Ruination Figure"

The authors propose two ways to evaluate the trend of "Ruination Figure" to be used by BBS operators. One is use of Candlestick Charting which is a drawing used in stock market [6].

There are two advantages of the Candlestick Charting. One is to show a change in some data on an item. The other is to guess easily whether the present state is settled or not.

A candle stick shows a change in the price of the fixed period, one can know the opening price, high price, low price and closing price.

The other way to evaluate RF proposed by the authors is use of RSI(Relative Strength Index) which shows the rising rate of price [6].

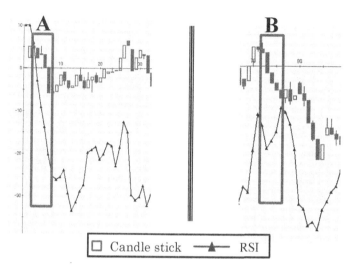

Fig. 1. How to compare candle stick charting with RSI

To use the Candlestick Charting and RSI to monitor a BBS, RF for each statement is used instead of stock price. Figure 1 shows two cases of suspected event. In the part "A", both of Candlestick Charting and RSI fall, and so the operator should consider it is ruining part. In the part "B", Candlestick Charting falls while RSI rises, so it should not be considered as a ruining part.

4   Example of Analysis

4.1   Evaluation of BBS

The result of proposed method is evaluated as comparison with an objective detection of ruining part. A set of thousand messages in a BBS board has been processed by the method and given to six students. Six male students in their twenties and of at least three year internet experience completed the questionaire from.

4.2   Effectiveness of "Ruination Figure"

In experiment, we use 308 negative words and 121 positive words. Figure 2 shows the output of our proposed technique. Each ruining part of the BBS is enclosed with a square.

The result of the proposed method gives fairly good agreement with the subjective inspection. The part from 800 to 840 shows a false alert. It was due to critical statements, so it can not be considered as "obstruction on bulletin board".

In the same way, we did the experiment to nineteen BBS using same pw and nw. Each BBS had different theme (for example, about PC, car, and so on) and content. As the result, 81% of ruined part deteceted by subjective method.

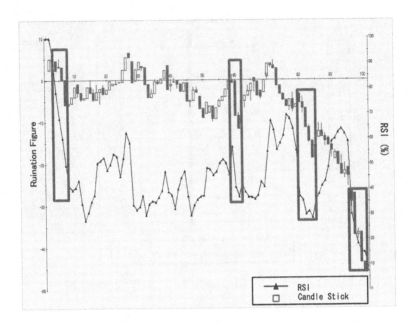

Fig. 2. The result of the experiment by the proposal method

5   Conclusion

In this paper, we focused on words used in the BBS that harms readers psychologically. We calculated a new index "Ruination Figure" based on words and responses to know how the BBS is ruined. We could aid operator to detect ruined part of BBS using proposed method.

References

1. PITCREW CO., L.:   Pitcrew co., ltd (in japanese) (2002) http://www.pit-crew.co.jp/.
2. Corporation, N.J.: Netview 2.0 (in japanese) (2004) http://www.naver.co.jp/.
3. Matsumura, N., Miura, A., Shibanai, Y., Ohsawa, Y., Ishizuka, M.: The dynamism of 2channel (in japanese). IPSJ Journal (Japan) **45** (2004) 1053–1061
4. Matsumura, N., Ohsawa, Y., Ishizuka, M.:   Profiling participants in online-community based on influence diffusion model (in japanese). Transactions of the Japanese Society for Artificial Indtelligence (Japan) **18** (2003) 165–172
5. Matsumura, N., Ohsawa, Y., Ishizuka, M.: Influence diffusion model in text-based communication (in japanese). Transactions of the Japanese Society for Artificial Indtelligence (Japan) **17** (2002) 259–267
6. Yasunobu, C., Maruoka, T.: A fuzzy reasoning method for chart technical analysis in financial trading (in japanese). IPSJ Journal (Japan) **33** (1992) 122–129

Efficient Iris-Region Normalization for a Video Surveillance System

Jin Ok Kim[1], Bong Jo Joung[2], Chin Hyun Chung[2], and Jun Hwang[3]

[1] Faculty of Multimedia, Daegu Haany University,
290, Yugok-dong, Gyeongsan-si, Gyeongsangbuk-do, 712-715, Korea
bit@dhu.ac.kr
[2] Department of Information and Control Engineering, Kwangwoon University,
447-1, Wolgye-dong, Nowon-gu, Seoul, 139-701, Korea
chung@kw.ac.kr
[3] Division of Information and Communication Eng., Seoul Women's University,
126, Kongnung2-dong, Nowon-gu, Seoul, 139-774, Korea
hjun@swu.ac.kr

Abstract. An efficient approach for iris recognition is presented in this paper. An efficient iris region normalization consists of a doubly polar coordinate and noise region exclude. And then a Haar wavelet transform is used to extract features from iris region of normalized. From this evaluation, we obtain iris code of small size and very high recognition rate. This effort is intended to enable a human authentication in small embedded systems, such as an integrated circuit card.

1 Introduction

Biometrics is known as a way of using physiological or behavioral characteristics as measuring means. Some physiological or behavioral characteristics are so unique to each individual that they can be used to prove the person's identity through automated system.

Recently, Daugman [1][2] developed the feature extraction based on 2D Gabor filter. He obtained 2048 bits iris coding by coarsely quantizing the phase information according to complex-valued coefficients of 1024 wavelets, chose a separate point between same match and different match. His research work has been the mathematic basis of most commercial iris recognition systems. But, the system of Daugman concentrated on ensuring that repeated image captures produced irises on the same location within the image, had the same resolution, and were glare-free under fixed illumination. These constraints may restrict to apply it in practical experiences. Wildes [3] proposed a prototype system based on automated iris recognition, which registered iris image to a stored model, filtered with four resolution levels and exploited spatial correlations and Fisher liner discrimination for pattern matching. This system is very computationally demanding. Boles[4] implemented a feature extraction algorithm via zero-crossing representation of the dyadic wavelet transform. It is tolerant to illumination variation, but only feature extraction and matching algorithm are considered.

S. Shimojo et al. (Eds.): HSI 2005, LNCS 3597, pp. 353–356, 2005.

In this paper, we propose an iris region to be normalized and haar wavelet transform using to extract features from iris region.

2   Iris Feature Extraction by Haar Wavelet Transform

In this paper, a wavelet transform is used to extract features from iris region[5][6][7]. Any particular local features of a signal can be identified from the scale and position of the wavelets in which it is decomposed[8]. Wavelets are a powerful tool for presenting local features of a signal. When the size and shape

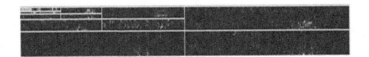

(a) Subband form of wavelet transform

(b) Subband image of wavelet transform

Fig. 1. Iris subband image and form

of a wavelet are exactly the same as a section of the signal, the wavelet transform gives a maximum absolute value, a property which can be used to detect transients in a signal. Thus the wavelet transform can be regarded as a procedure for comparing the similarity of the signal and the chosen wavelet. Fig. 1(a) Here, H and L mean the high-pass filter and the low-pass filter, respectively, and HH indicates that the high-pass filter is applied to the signals of both axes[9].

3   Experiment Results

For this experiment, we use 7 data per person from 20 persons. In order to determine a threshold separating False Reject Rate(FRR) and False Accept

Rate(FAR), we using a Hamming distance. Fig. 2 shows the distribution of Hamming distances computed between 1211 pairs of different images of the different iris. In the figure, x-axis and y-axis indicate the multiply HD by 100 and the count of date.

It can be seen in Fig. 3, that Equal Error Rate(EER), the cross point between the FAR and the FRR curves, achieves a 0%. But what is more important, obtained both the range of cross point and a null FAR for very low rates of False Rejection, which means this system is optimal for high security environments. When we use the threshold of 32, we can get the Recognition rate(RR) of about 99.8%.

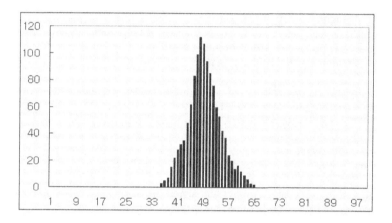

Fig. 2. Hamming Distances for Imposters

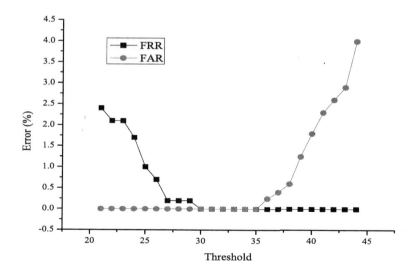

Fig. 3. Result in verification with Hamming distance

4   Conclusion

In this paper, an efficient method for personal identification and verification by means of human iris patterns is presented. An iris region is proposed to be normalized and haar wavelet transform is used to extract features from the iris region. With these methods, we obtain iris feature vectors of 58 bits. The iris feature vectors of 58 bits show that we could present an iris pattern without any negative influence and maintain an high rates of recognition.

References

1. John G. Daugman, "High confidence visual recognition of persons by a test of statistical independence," *IEEE Trans. Pattern Analysis and Machine Intelligence*, vol. 15, no. 11, pp. 1148–1161, November 1993.
2. John G. Daugman, "Recognizing persons by their iris patterns," *Cambridge University*, 1997.
3. R. P. Wildes, "Iris recognition: An emerging biometric technology," *Proceedings of the IEEE*, vol. 85, no. 9, pp. 1348–1363, 1997.
4. W. W. Boles and B. Boashash, "A human identification technique using images of the iris and wavelet transform," *IEEE Trans. on Signal Processing*, vol. 46, no. 4, pp. 1185–1188, 1998.
5. Randy K. Young, "Wavelet and signal processing," *Kluwer Academic Publisher*, 1992.
6. O. Rioul and M. Vetterli, "Wavelet and signal processing," *IEEE Signal Processing Magazine*, pp. 14–38, October 1981.
7. Gilbert Strang and Truong Nguyen, "Wavelet and filter banks," *Wesley-Cambridge Press*, 1996.
8. R. C. Gonzalez and R. E. Woods, "Digital image processing second edition," *Addison Wesley*, 2002.
9. Shinyoung Lim, Kwanyong Lee, Okhwan Byeon, and Taiyun Kim, "Efficient iris recognition through improvement of feature vector and classifier," *ETRI Journal*, vol. 23, no. 2, June 2001.

A Design of Presentation System for Interactive Multimedia Contents Based on Event-Driven Processing Model

Kyu-Nam Lee[1], Jong-Un Yang[2], Hyun-Tae Kim[2], In-Ho Ra[2], Hyung-Jin Kim[3,*],
Young-Ho Nam[4,*], and Sang-Hyun Bae[5,*]

[1] Digital Contents Cooperative Research Center, Dongshin University, Naju, Korea
knlee@dsu.ac.kr
[2] School of Electronic & Information Engineering, Kunsan National University,
Gunsan, Korea
{bedroses, camelk, ihra}@kunsan.ac.kr
[3] Department of Information & Communication Engineering, Iksan National College,
Iksan, Korea
hjkim@iksan.ac.kr
[4] Department of Computer Education, Gyeongsang National University, Jinju, Korea
yhnam@gsnu.ac.kr
[5] Department of Computer Science & Statistics, Chosun University, Gwangju, Korea
shbae@chosun.ac.kr

Abstract. In this paper, we propose a system for multimedia presentation with user's participation based on events to play-out multimedia contents consisting of various heterogeneous media objects through a network. We define various types of events and propose methods for handling them with Event Constructor, Event Scheduler and Event Queue Manager. In addition, Network Manager and QoS Manager are proposed to manage network delays and to maintain the required QoS of an interactive multimedia presentation. With the proposed presentation system, a user can make a multimedia content with user's participation based on a user-defined scenario, and give a synchronous presentation through a presentation manager handling the events with priority. Finally, we implement it in Windows XP environment using Visual C++ 6.0 programming platform, and show an example of multimedia content and its presentation.

1 Multimedia Presentation

A multimedia content is composed of several types of media with temporal and spatial information. For multimedia presentation, there are essential requirements for a composite multimedia content [2]. For the proper presentation of a multimedia content, it should be presented to a user according to the pre-defined specification without processing overhead. Therefore, it is important for the multimedia

---

* This work was supported by Digital Contents Cooperative Research Center, Korea and Corresponding Authors.

S. Shimojo et al. (Eds.): HSI 2005, LNCS 3597, pp. 357–360, 2005.

presentation to consider, not only exact scenario specification, but also proper use of computer system resources in the course of processing a multimedia content. Figure 1 shows the typical processing flow of a multimedia presentation with scenario and presentation phase.

For the multimedia authoring and presentation, many researchers have studied on methods for scenario specification [2], [6], presentation scheduling [4], [5], QoS control, real-time disk scheduling, network specification [3], delay-sensitive data transfer [3], and so on.

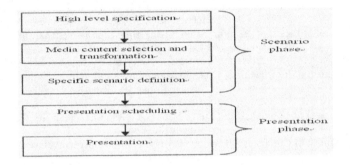

Fig. 1. Processing flow of multimedia presentation

In this paper, we design a presentation system for multimedia contents based on event-driven processing model to satisfy the required QoS by controlling and maintaining events effectively. The rest of this paper is as follows: In section 2, we define an event which provides communication interface among threads and processing modules. In section 3, we describe operational methods of the proposed "Presentation Manager" designed for controlling events so as to perform synchronous multimedia presentation. We show an implemented case of the model for multimedia presentation with the proposed event-driven system. Finally, we conclude the paper with a summary of the points raised throughout this work.

2   Event

It is well known that in order to provide a satisfactory result in multimedia presentation, we must consider diverse factors affecting the quality of services in the course of presentation such as user participation, processing delay, network delay, and resource management. Especially, these factors should be systematically analyzed and completely controlled for an efficient multimedia presentation.

This paper is a study on the design issues of a system model for multimedia presentation, and on the controlling method of events for performing synthetic and dynamic playing-out of a multimedia content. We address diverse factors as considered during a multimedia presentation and propose a presentation model based on events for dealing with these factors synthetically by creating, changing, and discarding them.

2.1 Event Classification

There are some unpredictable interrupting factors in the course of multimedia presentations such as user participation, network state changes, and system resource deficiency [1]. To keep satisfactory quality of service in performing presentations, we define some factors that should be considered in the process of presentations, and propose a method to deal with factors as events. There are five major classes of events, and these are presented in Table 1.

Table 1. Event classification

Class	Function	Time points of issuing
User Event	controls user participation in a presentation	start, suspend, resume, stop, forward, and backward
Presentation Scheduler Event	processes the schedule with a user defined scenario	start, stop of a media or effect, data receiving/sending, buffering control
Network Manager Event	controls network status changes	Network status changes, data receiving or sending
QoS Manager Event	dynamically controls unexpected harmful factors affecting QoS	environment setting, schedule advancing, exception handling
Media Event	processes media or effect threads	creating, suspending, resuming, termination of a thread

2.2 Event Structure

An Event can originate from various sources, and once it is issued then it must be informed to and processed by the presentation scheduler mentioned later. For this purpose, we design the data structure for an event as follows:

Event _content : indicates an event type occurred

Event_target media or thread : it represents information on the target media or thread to be processed. An event is analyzed by the "Presentation Manager", and passed to the dedicated thread with this event.

Event_occurrence time : it represents the occurring time of an event, and it is used for processing duplicate occurrences of an identical event and for handling event priority.

3 Presentation Manager and Implementation

In this paper, we design a "Presentation Manager" by which event based presentation of a multimedia content is performed in a synchronous manner. Figure 2 shows the overall structure of the proposed "Presentation Manager".

"Presentation Manager" sends an event happened at a time point to "Event Queue Manager" and the event will be processed by "QoS Manager". The main operational functionality of the "Presentation Manager" is to absorb the problem caused by irregular and dynamic happening of synchronous elements, and it is designed to handle various synchronizing information synthetically. In addition, it is oriented to support a real-time interactive processing way to enhance the performance of a multimedia presentation.

The proposed system for event-driven multimedia presentation is implemented on Windows XP. Figure 3 shows a screen-capture of an example of running program.

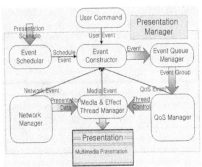

Fig. 2. Overall structure of the Presentation Manager

Fig. 3. An implementation example

4 Conclusions

In this paper, we propose a design model for performing effective multimedia presentation based on an event-driven processing method. We define various types of events generated during a presentation, and give a system model for multimedia presentation with Event Constructor, Event Scheduler, Network Manager, QoS Manager, and Event Queue Manager. We implemented the proposed system model on Windows XP environment using Visual C++ 6.0 programming platform. For future work, we will enhance the proposed system model to support real-time synchronous multimedia presentation through a shared network with different network delays.

References

1. M. Bordegoni, G. F., S. F., M. Maybury, T. R., S. R., P. T., M. W.: A Standard Reference Model for Intelligent Multimedia Presentation Systems, Computer Standards and Interfaces(1997), 18. 477- 496
2. M. Jourdan,N.L.,C.R.,L.S.,L.T.:Madeus, An Authoring Environment for Interactive Multimedia Documents, Proceeding of ACM Multimedia '98, Bristol UK (1998)
3. Staehli, J. Walpole, D. Maier. "A Quality-of-service Specification for Multimedia Presentations. ACM Multimedia Systems," 3:236-263, November 1995.
4. S. Wirag: Adaptive Scheduling of Multimedia Documents, Fakultätsbericht 1997/12, Universität Stuttgart(7. 1997)
5. T. Wahl, S. Wirag, K. Rothermel: TIEMPO: Temporal Modeling and Authoring of Interactive Multimedia, In Proc. of IEEE 2nd Intl. Conference on Multimedia Computing and Systems, Washington DC (5. 1995), 274-277,
6. Y. Theodoridis, M. V., T. S.: Spatio-Temporal Indexing for Large Multimedia Applications, In Proceedings of the 3rd IEEE Conference on Multimedia Computing and Systems (1996)

Searching Color Images by Emotional Concepts

Sungyong Hong[1], Chulbum Ahn[1], Yunmook Nah[1], and Lynn Choi[2]

[1] Department of Electronics and Computer Engineering, Dankook University,
San 8, Hannam-dong, Yongsan-gu, Seoul 140-714, Korea
{syhong, ahn555, ymnah}@dku.edu
[2] Department of Electronics and Computer Engineering, Korea University,
1, 5-ga, Anam-dong, Sungbuk-gu, Seoul 136-701, Korea
lchoi@korea.ac.kr

Abstract. Most of the content-based image retrieval systems focus on similarity-based retrieval of images by utilizing color, shape and texture features. For color-based image retrieval, the average color or color-histograms of images are widely used as feature vectors. In this paper, we propose a new searching scheme, called Fuzzy Membership Value-Indexing, to guarantee higher retrieval quality. This scheme allows us to retrieve images based on high-level emotional concepts, such as 'cool', 'soft', 'strong,' etc. Each image is automatically classified into predefined emotional categories, by analyzing its color values in HSI color space and assigning appropriate fuzzy membership values. Our experimental results show that the proposed technique can reflect user's searching intention more accurately.

1 Introduction

As a multimedia data type and a kind of visual media, color images can deliver information very efficiently. Many previous researches have exploited how to search color images effectively [1,2,3,4,5]. Current systems can extract feature vectors and search images based on these features. But they do not utilize semantics of or sensation on color images that are implied by images themselves.

In this paper, a new indexing scheme, called FMV indexing (Fuzzy Membership Value-indexing), is proposed to guarantee higher searching quality. By following this scheme, images can be searched by emotional concepts, which are derived from color values in HSI (Hue, Saturation, Intensity) color space. Emotional concepts, which are kind of semantic interpretation on color images felt by human, are automatically extracted and represented as FMV-indexes within image databases. Using these FMV-indexes, the proposed system can support image searching by emotional concepts. For example, the emotion-based queries, such as "find cool images" and "find lovely images," can be directly supported based on the semantic features derived from color information of images.

We propose an algorithm to generate FMV-indexes from color information in HSI color space. We also show how these FMV-indexes can be used for grouping and searching images by emotional concepts.

S. Shimojo et al. (Eds.): HSI 2005, LNCS 3597, pp. 361–365, 2005.

2 FMV-Indexing for Color Image Retrieval

When human perceives color of images, he/she normally does it by using hue as a whole. Hue distinguishes what is red from what is blue. Hue is a feeling about color, accepted by human eyes, that is usually spread over color spectrum. In HSI color model, hue is described by using degrees from 0° to 360°. Saturation represents how much white color is contained. Figure 1 shows the overall process of FMV-index based color image retrieval. At first, the RGB histograms are extracted from color images and then converted into HSI values. FMV-indexes are produced from them and stored in emotional categories table. To search an image by emotional concepts, FMV-indexes are utilized.

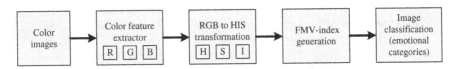

Fig. 1. Procedure for FMV-indexing and classification

FMV-index represents conceptual distance between emotional terms as fuzzy membership values. Emotional terms, which are felt by human, after looking at color images, are very diverse and ambiguous. However, some distinctive colors are clearly and definitely related with emotional terms. In case of 'red,' we can feel 'warm' or 'active.' Similarly, 'yellow' can give us feeling, such as 'cute' or 'pretty.' On the contrary, 'blue' gives 'cool' or 'clean' feeling and 'green' gives 'natural' or 'rural' feeling.

Some emotional terms can be used for grouping similar colors altogether. For example, 'pink' and 'red' belong to the same color family and both are related with the emotional term 'romantic.' The conceptual distance between colors and emotional terms can be measured by the formula $\mu_F(c) = \max(\min(\mu_{ai}(c), \mu_F(ai)))$ for all $c \in U$.

Here, F represents the related emotional term with the color c with the probability α. For instance, let's assume that fuzzy sets of emotional terms for the color 'pink' and 'red' are $pink$ = {(0.9, active), (0.7, strong), (0.9, romantic), (0.9, beautiful), (0.9, pretty)}, red = {(0.95, active), (0.9, strong), (0.7, romantic), (0.75, beautiful), (0.7, pretty)}, respectively, and a fuzzy set of colors for the emotional term 'dynamic' is $dynamic$ = {(0.98, red), (0.98, pink), (0.8, orange), (0.5, green), (0.1, blue), (0.9, yellow)}. Then, the membership value for the emotional term 'active' to 'dynamic' can be calculated like this.

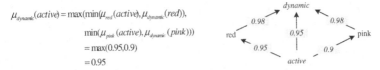

$$\mu_{dynamic}(active) = \max(\min(\mu_{red}(active), \mu_{dynamic}(red)),$$
$$\min(\mu_{pink}(active), \mu_{dynamic}(pink)))$$
$$= \max(0.95, 0.9)$$
$$= 0.95$$

Therefore, the relationship probability, where the emotional term 'active' can be included in the term 'dynamic,' reaches to 0.95.

Figure 2 shows the cone-structure for FMV-indexes. We divide color into 12 basic colors, such as red(0°), orange(30°), yellow(60°), spring(90°), green(120°), teal(150°), cyan(180°), azure(210°), blue(240°), violet(270°), magenta(300°) and pink(330°). In case of red color, it has a value range 0<= r <=15 and 345<= r <=360.

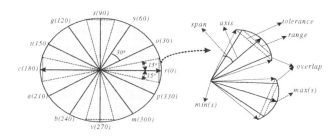

Fig. 2. Cone structure for FMV-indexing

Figure 3 shows an algorithm that produces FMV-indexes. For each color image, FMV indexes are produced and its emotional category is determined. Each emotional category is related with some entries of emotional term thesaurus to support emotional adjectives in image searching process.

```
Algorithm Generate_fmv_index(int num, int row_count, float s, float s_value, float
h_value, float fmv_index)
begin
    num <-- 1;                              // number of images
    row_count <-- select_from_imagetable    // record count
    min(s)<-- 0; max(s) <-- 255 // define saturation min value and max value
    while (num < row_count + 1) do
        h_value <-- select_from_imagetable(num)
        if (h_value == each class(0~360)) then
            s_value <-- select_from_imagetable(num)
            fmv_index <-- (( s_value - min(s))/(max(s) - min(s)))
            update_imagetable(fmv_index, num); num <-- num + 1
        else
            update_imagetable(0, num); num <-- num + 1
        endif
    end
end
```

Fig. 3. FMV-index generation algorithm by H and S

For a given query, e.g., "find cool images," emotional adjectives are scanned first. If there are no proper adjectives, most similar word is used as emotional adjective. That emotional adjective is used to compute fuzzy membership, which is then used to search FMV-indexes in emotional categories table.

3 Experiments

A computer with Intel Pentium-4 1.80GHz and 512MB main memory is used to construct our prototype system for image searching by emotional concepts. Test programs are developed by C++ and Delphi. Randomly selected 1011 images, including scenery, animal, and flower images, are used in experiments. Figure 4 compares the recall and retrieval speed of the FMV-indexing, HSI average histogram, and RGB average histogram-based method.

4 Conclusion

In this paper, the FMV-indexing method is proposed to allow image searching by emotional concepts. We developed an algorithm to automatically generate FMV-indexes. The proposed scheme does support semantic-based retrieval that depends upon human sense (e.g., "cool" images) or emotion (e.g., "soft" images), as well as traditional color-based retrieval. Emotional concepts and images are classified into 12 emotional categories and each category is related with emotional adjectives. Our experiments show the proposed technique can reflect user's searching intention more accurately.

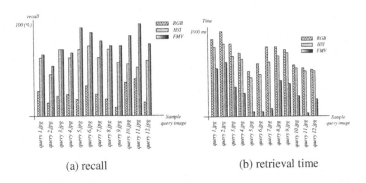

(a) recall   (b) retrieval time

Fig. 4. Performance comparison of RGB, HIS, and FMV-index

There should be further researches on how to finely categorize color information to further improve the searching efficiency. To obtain much higher searching quality, researches on how to adopt other image features, such as shape and texture, within the FMV-indexing, are also required.

Acknowledgements

This work was supported by grant No. R01-2003-000-10133-0 from the Basic Research Program of the Korea Science & Engineering Foundation.

References

1. Stricker, M. and Orengo, M.: Similarity of color images. Proc. SPIE on Storage and Retrieval for Image and Video Databases, Vol. 2420. San Jose, USA (February, 1995) 381-392
2. Swain, M.J. and Ballard, S.H.: Color Indexing. Int. J. Computer Vision, 7(1). (1991) 11-32

3. Rickman, R. and Stonham, J.: Content-based image retrieval using color tuple histograms. Proc. SPIE, 2670. (1996) 2-7
4. Smith, J. and Chang, S.-F.: Tools and techniques for color image retrieval. Proc. SPIE, 2670. (1996) 1630-1639
5. Niblack, W., Barber, R., et al.: The QBIC Project : Querying images by content using color, texture, and shape. Proc. SPIE. (February 1993) 173-187

Author Index

Lecture Notes in Computer Science

For information about Vols. 1–3498

please contact your bookseller or Springer